Applied Spirituality and Sustainable Development Policy

Applied Spirituality and Sustainable Development Policy

EDITED BY

NARESH SINGH

O.P. Jindal Global University, India

AND

DIVYA BHATNAGAR

Shiv Nadar University, India

emerald PUBLISHING

United Kingdom – North America – Japan – India – Malaysia – China

Emerald Publishing Limited
Emerald Publishing, Floor 5, Northspring, 21-23 Wellington Street, Leeds LS1 4DL

First edition 2024

British Library Cataloguing in Publication Data
A catalogue record for this book is available from the British Library

ISBN: 978-1-83753-381-7 (Print)
ISBN: 978-1-83753-380-0 (Online)
ISBN: 978-1-83753-382-4 (Epub)

Printed and bound by CPI Group (UK) Ltd, Croydon, CR0 4YY

INVESTOR IN PEOPLE

To future generations who might live in self-realization and joy on a flourishing planet (Naresh).

To my parents and my brother (Divya).

Contents

List of Figures and Tables *ix*

About the Editors *xi*

About the Contributors *xiii*

Acknowledgements *xvii*

Chapter 1 Introduction and Overview *1*
Naresh Singh and Divya Bhatnagar

Chapter 2 Policy and Practice Informed by the Ancient Science of Spirituality *11*
Mihir Shah

Chapter 3 Politics of Being: Harnessing Spirituality and Science for a New Development Paradigm *41*
Thomas Legrand

Chapter 4 Buddhist and Taoist Systems Thinking: Perennial Wisdom Applications and Implications to Sustainable Transformation *71*
Josep M. Coll

Chapter 5 New Paradigm Politics and Governance for a Planetary Civilization *89*
Anneloes Smitsman

Chapter 6 Spiritual Leadership for Sustainable Development Policy *117*
Naresh Singh

Chapter 7 Law and Applied Spirituality *133*
K. Parameswaran

Chapter 8 A Holistic View to Approach Sustainable Development: Spiritual Roots and Evidence From Quantum Physics *149*
Divya Bhatnagar and Sudip Patra

Chapter 9 Spirituality, Wisdom and Quantum Theory: Wisdom Has a Measurement Problem Too *167*
David Rooney

Chapter 10 Public Policy for Sustainable Development: A Gandhian Paradigm *181*
Pooja Sharma

Chapter 11 An Exploration of the Nonmaterial Dimension as the *Sine Qua Non* of 'Sustainable Development' *201*
Vern Neufeld Redekop

Chapter 12 Applied Spirituality and Mediation: Overcoming Challenges of Sustainability Using Inter-Relational Settlement Model *223*
K. Parameswaran

Chapter 13 Compassionate Policies to Relieve Systemic Suffering: *Visions, Obstacles, Strategies, Actions* *241*
Robertson Work

Index *265*

List of Figures and Tables

Chapter 3

Fig. 3.1.	Life Satisfaction by Economic Development.	47
Fig. 3.2.	Institutions and Individuals in the Politics of Being.	51
Fig. 3.3.	The Inner Path to Sustainability, a Theory of Change.	52

Chapter 4

Fig. 4.1.	The T-Qualia Model.	82
Fig. 4.2.	Yin-Yang Creative Tension.	84
Fig. 4.3.	Elements-Based Behaviour of the Five Corporate Stars.	85
Fig. 4.4.	The Zen Business Model.	86

Chapter 5

Fig. 5.1.	Our Living Systems Protocols.	95
Fig. 5.2.	The Actualization Process.	99
Fig. 5.3.	Seven Systemic Thrivability Barriers.	104

Chapter 8

Fig. 8.1.	Holistic Model.	152

Chapter 11

Fig. 11.1.	Author's Adaptation of the Quadrant Model.	203

Chapter 12

Fig. 12.1. Values Needed to Resolve the Challenges of Sustainability Through Conflict Settlement. 236

Chapter 13

Table 13.1. Based on the Four-Quadrant Integral Framework of Ken Wilber from his book *The Integral Vision*, 2007. 251

About the Editors

Dr Naresh Singh is a Professor and Executive Dean at the Jindal School of Government and Public Policy, where he is also Director of the Centre of Complexity Economics, Applied Spirituality and Public Policy (CEASP) and Co-Director of the Centre for Legal Empowerment of the Poor (CLEP). He is a visiting Professor, University of Ottawa, School of International Development and Global Studies. His current research focuses on insights for sustainable development public policy from systems thinking, consciousness studies and inner knowing.

He has served in several high-profile international positions such as

- Executive Director of the Global Commission on Legal Empowerment of the poor hosted by UNDP and co-chaired by Madeleine Albright and Hernando de Soto;
- Director General in the Policy Branch of the Canadian International Development Agency;
- Principal Adviser on Poverty and Sustainable Livelihoods at UNDP New York.

He has been an adviser to organizations such as the United Nations Development Programme (UNDP), the Food and Agriculture Organization (FAO), the Commonwealth Secretariat and the International Labour Organization (ILO). Professor Singh is recognized globally for his work on sustainable livelihoods. He has a transdisciplinary PhD in Environmental Sciences, has been a visiting Professor at several Universities in the US and Canada, including Boston, Harvard, Waterloo and McGill.

Divya Bhatnagar is an Assistant Professor at the School of Humanities and Social Sciences, Shiv Nadar University, India. She completed her master's degree in public policy from the University of Chicago, with an academic focus on international development. Divya works on education, childhood, sustainable development, and public policy including Indian education policies. She is interested in understanding early-life influences that shape our experiences, factors that affect mental well-being in adolescence, and characteristics of the right kind of education. Divya has previously worked on education, children's rights, and child poverty at UNICEF, New York Headquarters. Before venturing into public policy, she worked in the field of Astrophysics at the University of Victoria, Canada.

About the Contributors

Dr Josep M. Coll is a professor of Strategy, Sustainability and Innovation at EADA Business School, visiting professor at Yonsei University in South Korea, and research associate at Maastricht School of Management. He works as an independent consultant for a wide range of private and public organizations, such as the European Commission and the United Nations. In the United Nations system, he co-led the first corporate developmental evaluation and adaptive management movement in UNFPA. As an initiate in Taoist metaphysics and Zen practitioner, he applies East Asian perennial philosophies into practical systems approaches and methods for regeneration. He regularly speaks internationally on systems leadership and sustainable transformation and coaches organizations, managers and entrepreneurs in transitioning to the new sustainable, regenerative and inclusive business paradigm. *He is the author of several books on sustainability including 'Buddhist and Taoist Systems Thinking' (Routledge), 'Zen Business' (Profit editorial), Wise Cities (Cidob), and co-author of the book Economía de la Felicidad (The Economy of Happiness, Plataforma editorial).*

Thomas Legrand holds a PhD in Economics. Thomas Legrand is the author of 'Politics of Being. Wisdom and Science for a New Development Paradigm' (Ocean of Wisdom Press, 2022). He is the lead Technical Advisor of the UNDP-convened Conscious Food Systems Alliance. He lives next to Plum Village, the monastery of Zen master Thich Nhat Hanh, in the Southwest of France.

Dr K. Parameswaran is a Professor of Law and former Dean of Academics at Gujarat National Law University, India. He holds Bachelor's Degrees in Law, Administration, Masters' in International and Constitutional Law and PhD in International Law. He pioneered a law-subject 'Law, Religion, Spirituality and Justice' for legal research and profession. He teaches and conducts training programs on spirituality, higher values and ethics for law-teachers, PhD scholars, FDPs, students, advocates, judicial officers and professional corporates regularly. He brings spiritual and peace values in legal education and research, writes regularly on contemporary issues keeping Sri Aurobindo's integral consciousness-knowledge for individual and collective developments. He is associated with various law schools in the United States for higher research. He is also a Master Trainer in NLP, proficient in CBT and Integrated Clinical Hypnotherapy.

Dr Sudip Patra (PhD, University of Glasgow, Scotland) is an Associate Professor and Founding Member of CEASP, JSGP. Sudip is also Research Fellow at the Laszlo institute of new paradigm research, Italy. Sudip's research works lie in quantum-like framework in decision science, complexity economics and quantum foundations or philosophy of science broadly.

Vern Neufeld Redekop is a Professor Emeritus of Conflict Studies, Saint Paul University. Vern does research in deep-rooted conflict, reconciliation, spirituality, emergent creativity, integrative peace building and community dialogue. He is the former President of the Canadian Institute for Conflict Resolution and the author of *From Violence to Blessing: How an Understanding of Deep-Rooted Conflict Can Open Paths to Reconciliation* (2002) and co-editor, with Gloria Neufeld Redekop, of *Awakening* (2020) and *Transforming* (2021), both on Spirituality, Emergent Creativity and Reconciliation.

Dr David Rooney is a Professor of Management and Organisational Studies, Department of Marketing and Management, Faculty of Business and Economics, Macquarie University. His research focuses on understanding the role of wisdom and knowledge in the economy, work and leadership. He has published a number of books including *Public Policy in Knowledge-Based Economies, the Handbook on the Knowledge Economy* (Vols 1 & 2), *Knowledge Policy* and *Wisdom and Management in the Knowledge Economy*.

Dr Mihir Shah is a Distinguished Professor and Chair, Rural Management Programme at School of Humanities and Social Sciences (SHSS), Shiv Nadar University. From 2009 to 2014, Dr Mihir Shah was Member of the Planning Commission, Government of India, holding the portfolios of Water Resources, Rural Development and Panchayati Raj. Dr Shah graduated in Economics from St Stephen's College, Delhi University (where he won the prestigious KC Nag Economics Prize) and did his postgraduation from the Delhi School of Economics (where he was Merit Scholar) in the 1970s, before going on to complete a much-acclaimed doctoral dissertation at the Centre for Development Studies, Kerala.

Dr Pooja Sharma is an Associate Professor, Department of Economics, Daulat Ram College, University of Delhi. An alumnus of Miranda House, University of Delhi; she completed her Master's in Economics from Delhi School of Economics, MPhil and PhD from Jawaharlal Nehru University (JNU) and PhD fellow at the University of Agder (Norway). As an avid Gandhian, her contribution varies in the field of Energy security, Energy transition, Renewable energy, Human Capital and Gandhian perspective on energy transition. She is also engaged in CEC UGC live lecture series on Environmental Economics, Climate change and Sustainability. She has published papers in reputed journals. She has contributed two books on Gandhian thoughts, 'Through the Lens of Mahatma: Journey of a Migrant' and 'Living in Truth: The Gandhian Paradigm'.

Dr Anneloes Smitsman (PhD, LLM), is a futurist, systems scientist, award-winning pioneer in human development and systems change, and award-winning bestselling author. She is the Founder and CEO of EARTHwise Centre, architect of the EARTHwise Constitution for a Planetary Civilization, and a Strategic Steward of Hypha and SEEDS. Her programs, practices and strategies are sought after around the world for actualizing our future human potential, and catalyzing the next steps in human consciousness and systemic design for thrivability. She is the co-author of the award-winning bestsellers of *The Future Humans Trilogy* with Dr Jean Houston. She was awarded the Visioneers Lifetime Achievement Award as a Visionary Leader in May 2022, and was crowned overall African winner in the category 'Human Development' of the 2022 Africa's Most Respected CEOs Awards by The Business Executive in collaboration with the Economic Development Board Mauritius. She is also a winner of the BIZZ 2022 Business Excellence Award by WORLDCOB. She holds a Master's degree in Law and Judicial Political Sciences from Leiden University, the Netherlands, and received a degree of Doctor from the Maastricht Sustainability Institute at the School of Business and Economics, Maastricht University, the Netherlands. Her PhD dissertation, Into the Heart of Systems Change, is being implemented worldwide for systemic transformation in economics, education, politics and governance through her proposed Transition Plan for a Thrivable Civilization.

Robertson Work is an ecosystems/justice activist and non-fiction author. He has worked for over 50 years in over 50 countries as United Nations Development Programme (UNDP) principal policy advisor for decentralized governance; New York University (NYU) Wagner Graduate School of Public Service adjunct Professor for innovative leadership of sustainable development; and Executive Director of the Institute of Cultural Affairs (ICA) in four countries conducting organizational, community and leadership development initiatives. He has published five books, including *A Compassionate Civilization* and *Society, Spirit, Self*, and contributed to 11 others. Work has practiced engaged Buddhism for the past 36 years. His graduate studies were at Indiana University and Chicago Theological Seminary with undergraduate studies at Oklahoma State University.

Acknowledgements

We acknowledge the support and encouragement of a wide circle of friends and colleagues from our Centre for Complexity Economics, Applied Spirituality and Public Policy, our students in the course of the same name whose needs for diverse relevant readings in one place provided the main incentive for this work. As editors we acknowledge the congenial, friendly and professional engagement with the chapter authors throughout the writing and editing process. We are indebted to Dr Nick Lee of the Jindal School of Liberal Arts and Humanities who independently read most of the chapters and provided invaluable feedback.

Chapter 1

Introduction and Overview

Naresh Singh and Divya Bhatnagar

> As Men's Prayers are a Disease of the Will, so are their Creeds a Disease of the Intellect. – Ralph Waldo Emerson[1]

> The intuitive mind is a sacred gift and the rational mind is a faithful servant. We have created a society that honors the servant and has forgotten the gift. Attributed to Einstein[2]

We cite these quotations at the outset of this introduction as they provide the right tone for what we set out to do. The book draws deeply from spirituality as a universal human experience and understanding, a secular spirituality, and not from religious creeds or doctrines. The policy thinking moves beyond the traditional linear reductionist and deterministic world view to a more systems approach which includes human intuition and inner knowing.

Humanity is currently plagued with several well documented global-level crises such as climate change, rising air pollution, decreasing forest cover, massive species extinction, challenges of migration and displacement, poverty and inequality, gender inequality, and overall poor health and wellbeing. These problems have been exacerbated by the COVID-19 pandemic which revealed severe fault lines in the current public policies and in the economic and social systems we have in place. For the last two centuries, since the first industrial revolution, our development model equated happiness with material prosperity and economic 'growth'. It measures progress in terms of gross domestic product (GDP) and to some extent in terms of human development dimensions. Public policies are also designed, implemented and evaluated based on this model in all sectors including health, education, economics and sustainability. However, this development model fails to seriously consider the social and environmental dimensions of sustainable development. By constantly emphasizing this old paradigm of growth, we as a society have created complex policy problems for

[1]Emerson, R.W. Self-Reliance.1841.
[2]Although widely attributed to Einstein, internet sources the original source is Bob Samples (1976) in Metaphoric Mind: A celebration of Creative Consciousness.

Applied Spirituality and Sustainable Development Policy, 1–9

doi:10.1108/978-1-83753-380-020231001

which we cannot easily find solution. It is time for a change. A change that is urgent and revolutionary and not only at an individual level but at a cultural level. A change that is sustainable and all-inclusive. A change that needs to come from inside and out and that which supports the wellbeing of oneself, others and the planet.

The global challenges are well defined in terms of the 17 sustainable development goals (SDGs).[3] Perhaps the most immediate crisis is that of social, economic and ecological impacts of climate change. The UN Framework on Climate Change (1992), Paris Agreement on Climate Change (2015) and various reports of the Inter-Governmental Panel on Climate Change (IPCC) have all warned of the crisis.[4,5] It is incredulous that scientists and world leaders recognized this crisis more than 30 years ago, and we are still not on track to keep global warming below 1.5 degree Celsius which is likely to spare us from devastating effects on human civilization as know it. We seem to be sleep walking towards a cliff without being able to wake up in time. While it is true that we have made significant technological progress in areas such as clean and renewable energies, our addiction, indeed reliance on fossil fuel-based capitalism as the main way to support our societies, shows little signs of letting up. Even the singular achievement of global acceptance of the SDGs falls short of what is needed; anchored as the goals are in more material consumption. The 2021 documentary film 'Breaking Boundaries' provides a vivid description of our continuing failures to stop the violation of the planet's vitals systems.[6] We seem to know what to do, we have produced a global consensus on what is to be done and committed to action plans and budgets to do so and yet we are failing. Our economics, technologies, sustainable development policies are important and have the potential to help, but they are clearly not enough. We need a radical rethink of what is missing.

While policymakers and practitioners spend much effort working on the symptoms of these problems and at best their immediate causes which can buy time, we need to go deeper to understand the root causes of the civilizational challenges we face. The root cause of almost all of the global challenges we are encountering is but one: our disconnection from ourselves and each other and our (humanity's) false sense of separation from nature. We have consistently failed to address perhaps the most important part of the solution: the inner core of who we truly are, our absolute consciousness. We wish to take a scientific and pragmatic approach to address the topics of spirituality and our oneness with all beings on Earth including nature. This inner dimension – of self-awareness and mindfulness – is, we believe, the first step towards humanity's quest to shift our civilization to a more sustainable trajectory. Recognizing our true and higher self can bring about massive changes and heal us and our planet from our self-inflicted wounds. Self-awareness will make us more collaborative and conscious on our journey together to a better future – a healthy planet, better health and wellbeing, decent

---

[3]https://sdgs.un.org/goals
[4]https://unfccc.int/
[5]https://unfccc.int/process-and-meetings/the-paris-agreement
[6]https://www.ipcc.ch/

standard of living, equality, social justice, better conflict resolution and a paradigm of politics based on our conscious self. By appreciating and developing our inner self we can expect to leave our future generations with a better world to live in as well. If most of humanity were able to reach this kind of understanding and realization, we have little doubt our main problems will be removed much faster. But we are not optimistic dreamers or naïve romantics. Neither are we spiritual teachers. We are public policy scholars and we wish to interrogate the nexus between this inner understanding of human nature, the almost universal human experience of something greater than body and mind and policy, politics, law, etc., as anchored in sustainable development policy.

The book therefore addresses what is perhaps the most important missing dimension in humanity's continued failure to shift our civilization to a sustainable trajectory – that of the inner core of who we truly are, our spiritual nature. The focus is on human understanding and experience beyond the phenomena of the senses and the physical material world but asks what will be required to reflect this experience and understanding in the way sustainable development policy is designed, implemented and evaluated. While such an assessment will reveal the changes we need to make as individuals, it will go beyond that to assess the policy framework that is required to level the playing field and shift our core value system for large-scale national and planetary change. As Rabbi Lerner asked in his book *Revolutionary Love*: what would public policies in the USA look like if their objective was greater love and harmony in the society? Or, as we ask if the public policy process in India were to reflect the understanding of the shared cosmic consciousness of all its citizens, what would the policies look like and how would they be implemented and evaluated.[7] Would these policies be supportive of poverty eradication, human freedoms and flourishing, healthy social and ecological systems, social justice and inclusion? Would India move in the direction to become the global leader it needs to be in bridging the gap between its rich spiritual legacy and a planet in crisis?

Applied spirituality is based on what we consider as secular spirituality seen as a universal human experience and not on doctrines or dogma of a given organized religion. However, happily, the concepts of secular spirituality are consistent with the core mystical teachings of all the world's major religions (Christianity, Islam, Hinduism, (plus other religions of India), Buddhism, Daoism, etc.). Our approach is to explore reawakening our sacred gift (our spirituality) while working with our faithful servant (rationality). The secular spirituality principles which underpin the ideas in the book are derived from our review of pertinent texts of the world's major religions as well as current scientific research and built on areas of strong evidential convergence. Contemporary science sources include quantum field theory, quantum social science, complexity theory and cognitive neuroscience. The conclusions of importance to us for sustainable development policy are: (a) the unity or oneness of the underlying fundamental consciousness that living things share, (b) the ephemeral nature of duality and the underlying non-duality

[7]Lerner, M. (2022). *Revolutionary love*. University of California Press.

which constitute a oneness, (c) the illusion of separation of humans from each other and from nature and (d) the imaginary nature of the ego as the source of fear, insecurity and feelings of inadequacy that lead to greed, over consumption and default public policy which prioritizes GDP per capita growth above all else. Such growth is unfortunately driven by fossil fuel consumption and a capitalistic mode of production and distribution, which in turn leads to concentration of wealth in the hands of few resulting in a global situation in which 20% of the world's population consumes 80% of the world's resources and contribute 80% of the world's waste.

The wisdom traditions of the world whose insights support the conclusions on the nature of reality and human spirituality include (a) Christianity as described by John of the Cross, Meister Eckhart, Thomas Keating, Thomas Merton, the Desert Fathers among others; (b) the mystical side of Islam – Sufism as described by Rumi, Ibn Arabi and many other Sufi mystics; (c) Hinduism mainly from Advaita Vedanta as described in the Upanishads, the sutras of Patanjali, the Ashtavakra Gita, the Bhagwad Gita and teachers like Ramana Maharshi, Nisargadatta Maharaj and Rupert Spira among others.[8–13] The convergence of the insights from all these sources as complemented by those from Buddhism and Daoism provides compelling evidence. The western scientific evidence and conclusions from scientists such as David Bohm on quantum physics, explicate and implicate order; Menas Kafatos on quantum physics and Kashmiri Shaivism; Stuart Kaufmann on complexity theory; Raima Larter on complexity and spirituality; Danah Zohar on Spiritual Intelligence and Quantum Society and cognitive neuroscientist Donald Hoffman in the Case Against Realty, the psychiatrist Iain McGilchrist among many others can no longer be ignored.[14–19]

Yet as Chris Lucas put it 'In our supposedly material world, the cultivation of spiritual excellence is often regarded as at best irrelevant or at worst a psychotic delusion. Complexity Science however can throw a very different light on this subject, revealing spiritual development to be not only advantageous, but perhaps

---

[8]See for example: Paths to transcendence: According to Shankara, Ibn Arabi and Meister Eckhart.

[9]See for example: Dark night of the soul.

[10]See for example: Complete Mystical Works of Meister Eckhart: https://www.pdfdrive.com/the-complete-mystical-works-of-meister-eckhart-e162766430.html.

[11]See for example: Open Heart Open Mind (2006).

[12]See for example The Wisdom of the Desert and the Seven Story Mountain.

[13]See numerous works: www.Rumi.org.uk.

[14]Theise, N. D., & Kafatos, M. (2016). Fundamental awareness: A framework for integrating science, philosophy and metaphysics. *Communicative and Integrative Biology*. https://doi.org/10.1080/19420889.2016.1155010.

[15]Kauffman, S. (2008). *Reinventing the sacred.*

[16]Larter, R. (2021). *Spiritual insights from the new science. Complex systems and life.*

[17]Zohar, D. (2001). *Spiritual intelligence: The ultimate intelligence.* Bloomsbury.

[18]Hoffman, D. (2019). *The case against reality. Why evolution hid the truth from our eyes.* Norton.

[19]McGilchrist, I. (2019). *The master and his emissary.* Yale University Press.

the most valuable asset currently available to the human race'.[20] As we continue to fall short of the requirements for keeping anthropogenic induced global temperature rise below 1.5°C compared to preindustrial levels, should we not explore everything in our arsenal? Is it not in our enlightened self-interest to revisit long held assumptions such as our essential separation from nature and from each other, that human nature is essentially greedy and that we will always seek to acquire much more than we need for a life worth living? A brief root cause analysis of climate change dilemma will show why we need to dig deeper than we have been doing so far to make greater progress at a faster rate.

Growth at any cost is the high priest of progress in our current civilizational ethic. Over exploitation for over consumption based on corporate and individual greed work hand in hand to make change intransigent. This challenge is so fundamental to what we have come to accept as the good life that we put all our efforts elsewhere tinkering at the edges with all kinds of brilliant technological and economic innovations which merely add up to re-arranging the chairs on the deck. We have come to accept that it is human nature to be greedy and hence overconsumption will always be with us and that capitalism is the most efficient way to continue to satisfy our natural urge to over consume. On the other hand, if we wake up and see that we are not merely our bodies with only material needs, that there is something else to us, a new possibility arises. This insight is of course not new, and it has always been with us but then we lost it as the left hemisphere of the brain with its grabbing, individualistic, reductionist and deterministic characteristics became dominant in western civilization and is now mimicked by all. The bottom line of this argument simply put is that deep reflection on our own nature quickly reveals that we are inherently spiritual, that we share a common consciousness, that our sense of separation from each other and from nature is false, that our sense of insecurity and inadequacy which we try correct with the constant acquisition of material things is the result of imaginary ego mistaken as our selves.

Traditionally, spirituality is considered as a personal private matter and that continues to be true. But our world and public policy priorities badly need to reflect a novel set of values and what better than our own innermost values and realizations. Many wicked policy problems including the SDGs will not otherwise benefit from the revolutionary transformations necessary for their achievement. The challenge to be addressed of course is can this be done and if so how. This is new territory for public policy and so the agenda must be pursued in an open-minded manner, with respect for a diversity of views and weaving different perspectives together in a common search for a radically new approach to public policy for sustainable development.

We aim to bring about a new development model that is not just based on narrow definitions of GDP and economic growth, rather a model that includes the overall development of the economic, social, environmental and inner dimensions of all individuals and the planet. This book is expected to have a readership

[20] Lucas, C. (1999). Dynamical Psychology Journal.

among sustainable development practitioners and researchers, post-graduate students, faculty, policymakers and politicians searching for deeper methods and frameworks for sustainable development. In addition, it is likely that there will be a significant readership among engaged lay readers. The objective is to put forth an interdisciplinary perspective and address topics in spirituality, consciousness studies, public policy, law, gender, Indic and Buddhist philosophy, Gandhian thinking and inter-link quantum physics with consciousness models. The book brings the cross-cutting knowledge from the expertise of professionals from fields of Public Policy, Economics, Law, Philosophy, Environmental Science and Physics. The goal is to rejuvenate how we think about development, nurture appreciation and development of our true nature, and bring about changes at the policy level for all-inclusive growth and sustainable development.

In summary readers can expect to

- be able to get to the root causes of social, ecological and economic problems and formulate solutions that go way beyond addressing symptoms of these problems as is current practice.
- have a sound appreciation of their own spiritual nature and a better grasp of the nature of reality.
- have an advanced capacity to question the basic assumptions people live by and conceptualize an alternative future of humanity.
- be able to advise how an understanding of secular spirituality can foster the transition to overcome the social fragmentation and exclusion, the separateness among people and between people and nature.
- help corporations engage the stakeholders in their corporate ecosystem and advance beyond corporate social responsibility to enlightened business practice in sync with their emerging clientele.
- have greater capacity to support social movements and other people-based actions to foster transitions in governments and their policies that are more respectful of people and the planet while supporting prosperity and resilience.

To help the reader navigate the chapters and meet their interests effectively we set out below a brief synopsis of each chapter.

The book starts with the chapter 'Policy and Practice Informed by the Ancient Science of Spirituality' by Mihir Shah. In this chapter, he proposes that our policies and practices ought to be informed by the Ancient Science of Spirituality for not just sustainable development, but also to build a society based on the principles of liberty, equality and fraternity and, ultimately, for human survival. A distinctive feature of this science of spirituality is that the learning process and the knowledge gained from it are deeply experiential in nature, which infuses the spiritual journey with joy, adventure, discovery and innovation. This is also a reason to hold spirituality to an even higher standard of rigour and verifiability and to reject or accept a practice based on its helpfulness in moving ahead in the spiritual journey.

Next, 'Politics of Being: Harnessing Spirituality and Science for a New Development Paradigm' by Thomas Legrand presents a spiritual or wisdom-based approach to development. It proposes that societies explicitly make the fulfilment ('being') of all its members – humans and non-humans – their main goal, which should guide the development and implementation of public policies. It stands in opposition to the current development paradigm focused on economic growth (or 'having') which is rooted in values of individualism, materialism, reductionism, anthropocentrism. By nourishing our relational nature and cultivating spiritual values and qualities - such as love, peace, happiness, life, mindfulness – the politics of being can address the root causes of the meta crisis the world is facing, reconciling human flourishing with sustainability and supporting the cultural evolution that is needed.

In the fourth chapter, Josep M. Coll in 'Buddhist and Taoist Systems Thinking: Perennial Wisdom Applications and Implications to Sustainable Transformation' reiterates a well-known characteristic of the current anthropogenic world – that it exploits natural and human resources for financial profit and our all-pervasive reductionist thinking compartmentalizes knowledge and sees nature as a machine. However, this proposition has failed as we hurtle towards self-destruction. This is because, unlike our current socioeconomic system, nature works as a system based on the principles of interdependence and interconnectivity. Systems thinking focuses on interrelationships, perspectives and boundaries to understand how systems behave. Buddhist and Taoist systems thinking offer a way to develop the embodied mind and connect with reality. Therefore, the aim of this chapter is to bridge the consciousness gap by exploring the meaning and application of Buddhist and Taoist systems thinking to regenerate systemic leadership, design, development and sustainable transformation.

Anneloes Smitsman's chapter titled 'New Paradigm Politics and Governance for a Planetary Civilization' prepares us for an emerging new era of transformational shifts in politics and governance, and therefore fundamental shifts in human consciousness. This new paradigm is designed for regeneration and thrivability by applying the evolutionary dynamics of living systems. It focuses on the underlying drivers of sustainable development and demands a shift from politics of power to participatory and decentralized governance and decision-making models. In a sense, this chapter goes much further than describing new political models and governance systems, it is a call for us to become the future humans of a thrivable world, a species that has become planetary conscious.

The challenges of sustainable development policy require leadership at all levels of society - not only public-office holders but about those who participate in public debate and action. 'Spiritual Leadership for Sustainable Development Policy' by Naresh Singh, the sixth chapter, explores the concept of spirituality and its potential to provide moral and practical guidance for leaders of public policy to achieve sustainable development goals. The chapter focuses on how spirituality can stimulate integrity, motivation and most importantly, resilience as core characteristics in various relevant leadership styles. Leadership is complex since it involves policy inconsistencies that are interconnected, various objectives, varied publics and a large range of stakeholders that leaders should learn to deal with.

The VUCA context (volatile, uncertain, complex and ambiguous) is essential to be considered for leadership skills to deal with complex challenges of sustainable development.

Next, we explore 'Law and Applied Spirituality' in which K. Parameswaran discusses how legal systems aim to regulate social behaviour for the collective peace and harmonious development of society. He claims that the elements of justice, equality, liberty, fraternity, dignity, integrity and unity, guaranteed by legal systems come from an integration of external and internal human behaviour on social, political and economic matters. Spiritual experiences of freedom and consciousness-awareness have the potential to solve human crises by promoting synchronization in individual and collective lives of citizens. Sustainable development requires harmonizing economic growth, social inclusion and environmental protection through qualities of self-restraint, intergenerational equity, inclusivity and harmonization. The chapter offers us how spirituality can be integrated into legal discipline, academia and research for a more harmonious and sustainable world.

The idea of sustainable development is inherently interdisciplinary and holistic in nature and this change in view is possibly the missing key for progress towards achieving the SDGs set by the United Nations in 2015. Divya Bhatnagar and Sudip Patra in their chapter 'A Holistic View to Approach Sustainable Development: Spiritual Roots and Evidence from Quantum Physics' take a deep dive in the history and details of two seemingly different but conjoined disciplines of science and spirituality to understand what it may teach us about the concept of holism. They find ideas precisely similar to the notion of holism across time, space, culture and thinkers – ranging from mathematics, philosophy, sociology, medicine, education, religion and quantum physics to finding its roots in ancient Indian Vedic tradition and later usage in Greek and Roman cultures and more recently in the formulation of SDGs. This chapter, therefore, conveys the profundity of the most fundamental spiritual tenet – that of the unity and interconnectedness of all the universe – or in one-word holism – and its applications to approach sustainable development.

Next, David Rooney's chapter 'Spirituality, Wisdom and Quantum Theory: Wisdom Has a Measurement Problem Too' calls on us to reflect on the significance of wisdom in approaching sustainability. He highlights the contextual nature of wisdom and the role that spirituality and subjectivity (including inter-subjectivity) play in being wise. Therefore, to begin the quest of becoming better at modelling this, Rooney ponders on the (im)measurability of wisdom from the perspective of quantum-like social science and quantum theory. Thereby, the chapter throws open the doors to further research in modelling wisdom in the context of sustainable development and creating new opportunities for a better future.

Pooja Sharma in her chapter 'Public Policy for Sustainable Development: A Gandhian Perspective' explores insights and ideas from Gandhi's life that can act as catalysts to public policies and governance for sustainable development. New models of policy formulation and governance may take consultations from Gandhian philosophy of Trusteeship, Economy of Permanence, Sarvodaya, and

Satyagraha, based on spiritual inquiry and ethical value judgement. These ideas advocate for decentralization, self-sufficiency, and self-reliance in governance and economics, for example Nayi Talim education model involves austerity, body labour, and self-supporting schools with training in crafts. Sharma claims that application of Gandhian philosophy will foster empathy, self-transformation, non-violence, and ethical responsibility in socio-economic and political systems, as well as environmental and ecological sustainability.

Vern Neufeld Redekop posits a critical yet often neglected aspect of sustainable development in his chapter 'An Exploration of the Nonmaterial Dimension as the Sine Qua Non of "Sustainable Development"'. The nonmaterial dimension of development includes aspects such as consciousness, values, ethics, spirituality, cultural memes, language, and customs, which are interconnected with how development action is taken and its sustainability. Redekop argues that spirituality, which is one of the nonmaterial dimensions of reality, has immense potential to shape and guide development in a more sustainable and holistic way. Generative dialogues and the embodiment of nonmaterial visions, norms and values can enable individuals and societies to tap into their deep emotional systems, tacit knowledge, and spiritual sensitivity. This will permit us to identify and promote memes that are good for both humanity and the biosphere, thus bringing us closer to achieving sustainability.

In 'Applied Spirituality and Mediation: Overcoming Challenges of Sustainability using Inter-relational Settlement Model', K. Parameswaran highlights the need for a mediator to embody the interconnected skills and values of objective awareness, stillness with sensory concentration, empathy, and pragmatic sensibility, to help resolve conflicts related to sustainability. These skills are manifestations of the inward dimension of our spiritual core. A successful mediator requires the ability to connect both the inner and outer dimensions to find a harmonious and sustainable settlement. In a way, this chapter puts a spotlight on the importance of spiritual exploration and integral knowledge in understanding and addressing sustainability challenges.

'Compassionate Policies to Relieve Systemic Suffering: Visions, Obstacles, Strategies, Actions' by Robertson Work is a thought-provoking chapter serving as a wake-up call that will take readers through several guided reflection points and vivid visualization process in an attempt to transition us all to a more sustainable living. Work advocates his inner desire of a societal transformation towards a new civilization that is based on compassion, sustainability, equality, justice, participation, tolerance and peace. He outlines a compassionate policy framework that is necessary for ecological regeneration and human wellbeing.

Chapter 2

Policy and Practice Informed by the Ancient Science of Spirituality[1]

Mihir Shah

Abstract

Today, as we hurtle towards imminent planetary destruction in the age of the Anthropocene, we believe it may be instructive to try and understand if the ancient science of spirituality can prove useful in humankind's ability to change course, even at this late hour. We argue that such a paradigm shift is critically essential for human survival and that without the inner transformation proposed by this science, it may prove impossible to build a society based on the principles of liberty, equality and fraternity. This chapter draws from foundational texts and authoritative sources across multiple religious traditions, based upon which it outlines a brief sketch of the ancient science of spirituality. We begin with an account of the differentia specifica of this science, where we delve into what kind of science this is. Since it is centrally concerned with inner transformation, we briefly outline the theory of change embedded in this science and the kind of rejuvenation it enables, which makes it possible for us to clearly perceive the key elements and the structure of reality. We then spell out the impact this has on the nature of human action, continually teasing out implications for policy and practice in our time. We provide a few concrete illustrations of the same. Inter alia, we also show how many of these insights can be found even within modern scientific and philosophical traditions, thereby indicating possibilities of convergence and synthesis between ancient and modern science, following thereby the guidance of genuine spirituality.

[1]I wish to thank Sanchita Bakshi, Vivek Banerji, Divya Bhatnagar, Vinay Dabral, Ajay Dandekar, Bhargabi Das, Arshima Dost, Piyuli Ghosh, Sushma Iyengar, Jinendra Jain, Mayank Jain, Oran Jain, Rahul Jain, Shobhit Jain, Sowmya Kidambi, Ashwini Kulkarni, Himanshu Kulkarni, Neelashi Mangal, Vipul Mudgal, Vanita Mukherji, Seema Purushothaman, Sriram Ramaswamy, Cherian Samuel, Arvind Sardana, Naresh Singh, Rohini Singh, R Subrahmanyam, Sandali Thakur and SM Vijayanand for their invaluable comments and inputs into the making of this chapter.

Applied Spirituality and Sustainable Development Policy, 11–40

doi:10.1108/978-1-83753-380-020231002

Keywords: Structure of reality; dialogue; inter-connectedness; freedom; love-power-justice

Introduction

Today, as we hurtle towards imminent planetary destruction in the age of the Anthropocene, it may be instructive to try and understand if the ancient science of spirituality can prove useful in humankind's ability to change course, even at this late hour. I would argue that such a paradigm shift is critically essential for human survival and concur with Ambedkar that without the inner transformation proposed by this science, it may prove impossible to build a society based on the principles of liberty, equality and fraternity (Ambedkar, 1956).

This chapter draws from foundational texts and authoritative sources across multiple religious traditions, based upon which I outline a brief sketch of the ancient science of spirituality.[2] In so doing, I am inspired by the words of Swami Vivekananda in his lecture on *The Way to the Realisation of a Universal Religion* at the Universalist Church, Pasadena, California on the 28th of January 1900:

> I accept all religions. I shall go to the mosque of the Mohammedan; I shall enter the Christian's church and kneel before the crucifix; I shall enter the Buddhistic temple, where I shall take refuge in Buddha and in his Law. I shall go into the forest and sit down in meditation with the Hindu. Not only shall I do all these, but I shall keep my heart open for all that may come in the future. Is God's book finished? Or is it still a continuous revelation going on? It is a marvellous book – these spiritual revelations of the world. The Bible, the Vedas, the Koran and all other sacred books are but so many pages, and an infinite number of pages remain yet to be unfolded. I would leave my heart open for all of them.

The chapter is structured as follows:

a. a brief outline of the *differentia specifica* of the ancient science of spirituality, where we delve into what kind of science this is;
b. the theory of change embedded in this science;
c. the kind of inner transformation it enables, which makes it possible for us to clearly perceive
d. the key elements and the structure of reality;
e. the impact this has on the nature of human action, continually teasing out implications for policy and practice in our time,
f. finally, providing a few concrete illustrations of the same.

Inter alia, we also show how many of these insights can be found even within modern scientific and philosophical traditions, thereby indicating possibilities of

[2] Of course, given the limitations of my own vast ignorance, I end up citing more from those traditions with which I have greater, even if still extremely limited, familiarity.

convergence and synthesis between ancient and modern science, following thereby the guidance of genuine spirituality!

Spirituality: What Kind of a Science Is It?

Spirituality is based on repeated and creative experimentation carried out over thousands of years by pioneers across spiritual traditions. The aim of spirituality is to provide a pathway towards personal transformation that helps build inner strength of a kind that enables seekers to negotiate what the Bhagavad Gita (8.15) has called this 'abode of transience and sorrow' (*dukhaalayam ashaashvatam*) or what the Buddha in the *Lokavipatti Sutta* describes as the vicissitudes (or winds) of life: 'loss and gain, disrepute and fame, praise and blame, pleasure and pain' (Ṭhānissaro Bhikkhu, 1997), opening up the possibility of enduring joy.

In a word, the science of spirituality seems to say: 'It is the programming in your body that is ultimately responsible for the suffering you are currently undergoing. Without changing the programming, this suffering will not be able to find a lasting solution. We can propose a number of ways to do this re-progamming, which you could experiment with and this could potentially open up the pathway to boundless joy'. There is a rich diversity of such practices across multiple spiritual traditions, ranging from meditation, breathing techniques, mantras, rituals, prayers and *koan* study to martial arts etc.[3–5] Each tradition invites us to experiment with prescribed practices, and then through our own experience of the effectiveness of those practices in

---

[3]Many of the foundational texts of the science (across traditions) were, in the first place, *Śruti*, or heard revelations. 'Śruti is the process of the sound becoming the word... The Vedas as texts may be old collections of words, but the knowledge arising from sound contained in them is eternal. The source of the word is sound, which is ever-present and available... The purpose of sādhanā is to move from word to sound, where we may gain access to eternal knowledge'. (Chinnaiyan, 2022, p. 53). Aurobindo explains the power of the sound of the mantra: 'The Rig Veda rises out of the ancient Dawn with the sound of a thousand-voiced hymn lifted from the soul of man to an all-creative Truth and an all-illumining Light... the word is a living thing, a thing of power, creative, formative... as living or even a more living force than its idea; sound determines sense' (Aurobindo, 1995). As Om Swami says: 'The energy of the mantras is aimed at calling upon the universal energy, a way of drawing its attention towards us. Mantra yoga is a path to strengthen your bond with the universal energy around you, so you may realize your own potential' (Swami, 2017, p. 8). I have some personal experience of this through my daily sadhana of the *Lalita Sahasranama*, the thousand names of the Supreme Goddess. 'The Word was regarded as a symbol of the Godhead, or more exactly as revealing the divine presence within the cosmos, as the force that creates, maintains, and upholds the universe... the Word is an energy, that may be tapped and used by anyone who is able to penetrate its secret nature and mysteries' (Padoux, 1990, pp. x–xi).

[4]See Sutherland (2022) for an account of the powerful transformative impact of *koan* study.

[5]Peter Ralston (2010) brings out the power of this path based on his own long years of experience in Judo, Jujitsu, Karate, Kempo, Ch'uan Fa and Northern Sil Lum Kung Fu. His interest in the 'internal' martial arts led him to study T'ai Chi Ch'uan, Hsing I Ch'uan and Pa Kua Chang.

the attainment of our goals of inner transformation and building inner strength, we can decide whether to accept or reject the practices. Thus, this knowledge is replicable, verifiable and falsifiable.[6] As Vivekananda says,

> Our business is to verify, not to swallow. Religion, like other sciences, requires you to gather facts, to see for yourself, and this is possible when you go beyond the knowledge which lies in the region of the five senses. Religious truths need verification by everyone.
>
> (Vivekananda, 2007, Vol. 6, p. 133)

The only requirement, of course, is that we remain open to the possibility of discovering the truth on this path and that we don't reject it without even giving it a try. For we must always acknowledge that the intransigence of atheism can be as virulent as the obduracy of religious fanaticism!

Some distinctive features of this science deserve requisite emphasis. First, both the learning process and the knowledge it generates are deeply experiential in nature: 'all the religions of the world have been built upon that one universal and adamantine foundation of all our knowledge – direct experience'. (Vivekananda, 2007, Vol. 1, p. 126)

Second, it rejects the paradigm of linear unidirectional causality, which has tended to dominate a lot of Western thought ever since the Greeks. With its emphasis on a web of mutual causal interaction, spirituality is much closer to General Systems Theory, as both reject the reductionism of positivist science and view any system as far greater than the sum of its parts.[7]

Consequentially, in spiritual science, we also find the breaking down of the Cartesian subject-object duality:

> Vedic Science reveals that complete knowledge can only be gained on the level of consciousness through direct subjective experience. The field of pure consciousness can be known only by itself, by consciousness aware of its own unified nature. Modern science by its very emphasis on the object has excluded from its investigation the subject – the knower – and the process of knowing.
>
> (Wallace, 2016b, pp. 15–16)

In spirituality, however, there is one more rider – the experimenter must herself be transformed (and seen to be so), only then is the experiment truly meaningful. The experiment is of the nature of a *sādhanā*, a repeated practice performed with observation and reflection, study and investigation, with a goal of inner

---

[6]Falsifying becomes even more important here because the spiritual traditions, precisely owing to their huge potential power, have spawned many fakes and pretenders, who have greatly damaged their credibility!

[7]A remarkable work showing the similarities between General Systems Theory and Buddhism is Macy (1991).

realization and transformation. Thus, because its claim is both deeper and more expansive, spirituality must be held to an even higher standard of rigour and verifiability.[8]

A key concept within Western philosophy that closely approximates what is being posited here is Herder's *Bildung*, which Gadamer has described as 'perhaps the greatest idea of the eighteenth century' (Gadamer, 1989, p. 8).[9] According to Gadamer:

> Bildung evokes the ancient mystical tradition according to which man carries in his soul the image of God, after whom he is fashioned, and which man must cultivate in him ... because the result of Bildung is not achieved in the manner of a technical construction, but grows out of an inner process of formation and cultivation, and therefore constantly remains in a state of continual Bildung. (*op. cit.*, p. 10)[10]

The breakdown of the subject-object duality is most evident in the ancient science of *Śrīvidyā,* which is premised on the unity of the macrocosm (*brahmāṇḍa*) and the microcosm (*piṇḍāṇḍa*) and which posits the end of suffering and attainment of freedom (*svātantrya*) on the realization of this unity (Chinnaiyan, 2022).[11,12]

As a science, spirituality is always deeply engaged with moral and ethical issues and derives such morality from the very nature and structure of reality enunciated by it. By contrast, conventional religious morality, as also secular ethics, have been imposed on generations of children, filling them with needless guilt, stress and confusion. Contrary to popular belief and common religious practice, the

---

[8]Over the past few decades, a lot of work has gone into making the ancient science and its impacts, comprehensible and commensurable, in terms of modern science. Mention may be made here only of Wallace (2016b), Dalai Lama et al. (1991) and Benson (1984).

[9]For an appreciation of the work of Herder, see Forster (2022), who describes Herder (1744–1803) as 'a philosopher of the first importance' and recounts his wide-ranging influence on Hegel, Schleiermacher, Nietzsche, Dilthey, Mill and Goethe.

[10]Gadamer's own goal in his magisterial work *Truth and Method* (which is often described as one of two or three key philosophical texts of the 20th century) was to understand 'what happens to us over and above our wanting and doing' (op. cit., p. 26).

[11]*Śrīvidyā* is the ancient science centred on the supreme creative force *Lalitā Mahātripurasundarī* and has been described as 'the path that brings us to the realization of *Śrī*, the all-pervading principle at the heart of reality... a path to *nirvāṇa* or liberation' (Chinnaiyan, 2022, p. 55). Chinnaiyan traces the roots of *Śrīvidyā* to the Vedas but also to pre-Vedic tribal traditions.

[12]This brings to mind Tu Weiming's 'anthropocosmic vision', which understands 'human beings and the cosmos as a single, organismic whole. The goal of human life is to harmonize oneself with heaven and earth and to return to the transcendent source of both humans and the world' (Chittick, 2007, p. 109). As David George Haskell (2012) has said: 'The search for the universal within the infinitesimally small is a quiet theme playing through most cultures' (p. xii).

spiritual traditions do not postulate an abstract personal morality or societal ethics, independent of the structure of reality. Rather, the ancient science of spirituality is a universal invitation to joy, with spiritual morality and ethics drawing their tenets from a knowledge of the world, which is profoundly experiential. And it is a spirit of adventure, discovery and innovation that marks the spiritual journey. Sadly, the history of organized religion shows that it has largely lost track of this true spirit. As Aurobindo describes it, society has historically used religion to

> ...give an august, awful and would-be eternal sanction to its mass of customs and institutions; it made of them a veil of mystery against human questioning and a shield of darkness against the *innovator*. So far as it saw in religion a means of human salvation and perfection, it laid hands upon it at once to mechanise it, to catch the human soul and bind it on the wheels of a socio-religious machinery, to impose on it, in the place of *spiritual freedom*, an imperious yoke and an iron prison. It saddled upon the religious life of man, a Church, a priesthood and a mass of ceremonies and set over it a pack of watchdogs under the name of creeds and dogmas, dogmas which one had to accept and obey under pain of condemnation to eternal hell by an eternal judge beyond... This false socialisation of religion has been always the chief cause of its failure to regenerate mankind.
>
> (Aurobindo, 1991, p. 225, emphasis added)

On the other hand, the spiritual core of religion seeks to do exactly the opposite:

> Neither in the individual nor in the society will it seek to imprison, wall in, repress, impoverish, but to let in the widest air and the highest light. A large liberty will be the law of a spiritual society and the increase of freedom a sign of the growth of human society towards the possibility of true spiritualization. (*op. cit.*, p. 228)

It is this kind of science of spirituality that we seek to explicate and endorse in this chapter.

The Theory of Change

Since this is a science of transformation, it is important to understand its theory of change. For that we need to first describe the state upon which this transformative power is to be worked. We explore what the science tells us about why we are unable to see the structure of reality clearly and why we need to undergo prescribed spiritual practices, so that we can overcome suffering and unfreedom. We begin with *duḥkha*, the First Noble Truth of the Buddha, which arises from our pre-programmed responses to the transience and finitude of all things in the world. The Buddha's goal is for us to be able to see clearly the nature of *duḥkha*, from where it arises and how we can overcome it. The Buddha traces the origin of *duḥkha* to *trishna,* an unquenchable thirst, so that the more we have of something, the more we want to have the more of it. Once we are on that treadmill, there is no getting off it, leading not only to individual suffering but today bringing us to the verge of planetary extinction.

Next, we deploy the spiritual resources of the science of Kashmir Shaivism, which describes three kinds of *malas* or dirt, which become a veil, impairing clarity of vision and obscuring the true nature of reality that, in turn, results in different kinds of suffering[13]:

- *Āṇava mala*: the fundamental, all-pervasive feeling of lack, which could be called an atomistic sense of inadequacy (the word *āṇava* being derived from *anu* or atom/infinitesimal), as it stems from our feeling of being always incomplete or unfulfilled (*apūrṇatā).* In the words of a great scholar of Kashmir Shaivism:

  > Though you feel incomplete, knowing that there is some lack in you, yet you do not know what this lack really is. You want to hold everything, and yet no matter what you hold, you do not fill your sense of lacking, your gap.
  >
  > (Lakshmanjoo, 2015)

- *Māyīya mala*: closely related to the *āṇava mala* is the *māyīya mala*, which is the sense of alienation we feel, the separation we experience from others, leading to a perception of comparative inadequacy, resentment, jealousy and other forms of suffering, creating an inability to share the joys and sorrows of others as our own, thereby multiplying this sense of separation and the suffering it induces
- *Kārma mala*: and because of this sense of separation, arises the *kārma mala*, the sense of overbearing agency, the feeling that we are the doers and determiners of the outcomes of our actions to which we get so attached that all our happiness becomes governed by our success or failure. We have an imperious sense of determining agency in all that we do. That arrogance confines us in a prison of our own expectations, anxieties and disappointments. Since we cannot be fundamentally certain about the outcomes of our actions, about the fulfilment of our desires, this uncertainty fills us with fear and trepidation about the future; and a sense of frustration and anger through failure to attain our goals.

What we need to note carefully is that while finitude and transience are the basic conditions of our existence, what produces suffering is the nature of the relationship we build with them. So, we need to decide: do we understand and accept that this limitedness and transience is the very nature of reality? Or do we resist and resent, crave and cling, get obsessed with this sense of lack, building frustration and suffering all the way?

---

[13]A most accessible description is to be found in Chinnaiyan (2020).

Seeing the nature of reality with open and clear eyes helps us understand that *duḥkha* arises only if we see separation everywhere and bolster the separate, 'false self' within us.[14] We then realise that neither can nor should we depend on the essentially transient external factors for providing us enduring joy, which is already present within us, if only we could come out of the delusion created by the *malas*. As we explain below, this opens up endless human possibilities of joy and freedom, peace and harmony, understanding inter-connectedness, living within planetary boundaries, with respect for all of creation, living or non-living, from the smallest speck to the largest entity.

Thus, what the science of spirituality enables for us, instead of resentment towards the undeniable facts of existence, is the capacity to leverage them, to effect change, rooted in inner poise. The spiritual traditions propose a series of practices, which show a possible way forward that we can experiment with, through our own life experience. The claim is that these practices lead to the formation of novel neuro-hormonal pathways, which completely alter the pattern of our responses to the ups and downs of life, which are no longer able to overpower us or keep us in their grip (Chinnaiyan, 2022).

The Transformed State of Being

Thus, what the spiritual practices produce within us is a completely new software, a code that effects a total transformation in the way we respond to the vicissitudes of life, as we are now more and more free from the grip of our pre-programmed reflexes.[15] A range of fundamental religious texts describe the qualities of this transformed state.

The *Yogasūtras* of Patanjali and the *Brahmaviharas* of the Buddha provide us four inter-related threads or keys (*sūtras*) for living in this world, in harmony with its natural rhythm: *maîtri/mettā* (goodwill towards all), *karuṇā* (feeling the sorrow of others as one's own), *muditā* (feeling the joy of others as one's own) and *upeksha/upekkhā* (equanimity in the face of the vicissitudes of life).[16,17] Something strikingly similar is also to be found in the *Tattvārtha Sūtra*, one of the earliest, canonical texts of Jainism, the only one regarded as authoritative by both the *Digambara* and *Śvētāmbar*a sects. *Sūtra* 11 in Chapter 7 of the *Tattvārtha Sūtra* speaks of *maitri, pramoda, karunya and madhyastha*:

---

[14]A powerful exposition of the distinction between the 'true self' and the 'false self' is by the Franciscan friar Richard Rohr in his talk 'Contemplative Prayer' https://www.youtube.com/watch?v=geXe_zXE3PQ. Of course, a distinction between the 'lower self' and 'higher self' is to be found as early as in the Bhagavad Gita (Chapter 6, Verses 5–6: 'the higher Self alone is one's friend, the lower self itself one's enemy').

[15]The best parallel in Western philosophy is the work of the Stoics. For a wonderful new exposition, see Farnsworth (2018). The key difference, of course, is that, in our view, the transformation is more sustained and sustainable when the devices to attain this state are spiritual, rather than primarily intellectual, as in the case of the Stoics.

[16]*Yogastūras of* Patanjali Chapter 1, Verse 33 (Beloved, 2007).

[17]Ṭhānissaro Bhikkhu (2022, pp. 67–69).

> Benevolence towards all living beings, joy at the sight of the virtuous, compassion and sympathy for the afflicted, and tolerance towards the insolent and ill-behaved.
>
> (Jain, 2011)

This state of being is also described through the Islamic term *sakina* (or 'the peace of reassurance', mentioned in 6 verses of the Holy Quran).[18] Explaining the significance of the holy month of Ramadan, the great Islamic scholar Hamza Yusuf speaks of *sakina*, an indwelling presence that provides stillness, peace, balance, composure and equipoise, the blessing of God that enables restraint in the face of provocation. Despite the massive aggravations and violence of life today, this *sakina* gives us the capacity to respond with restraint, compassion and mindfulness, to move beyond pre-programmed patterns of behaviour, to liberate ourselves from the rule of the reflexes, to walk gently on this earth.[19]

The Irish poet and exponent of Celtic Christianity, John O'Donohue gives beautiful expression to what we are trying to say here:

> There is a quiet light that shines in every heart. It is what illuminates our minds to see beauty, our desire to seek possibility and our hearts to love life. This shy inner light is what enables us to recognize and receive our very presence here as blessing... In the parched deserts of post-modernity, a blessing can be like the discovering of a fresh well.
>
> (O'Donohue, 2007)

The Vedic Rishis of ancient India describe this process as one that brings us in contact with Being, the unmanifested Reality of all that exists. The nature of Being is *sat-chit-ananda* (true-bliss-consciousness).[20] This does not require abandoning the world; rather, it calls for a new way of living within it. In this transformed state of consciousness, we are clearly and directly able to see the structure of reality for what it truly is. And as we do so, the nature of our actions is transformed. When we experience this joy, abundance and oneness, the absence of something does not become a source of suffering because we do not respond to it with frustration, resentment and rage. Indeed, we work more energetically, with

---

[18]'The sakinah seems to be related to the Hebrew Shekhinah, the term for God's presence in the world' (Armstrong, 1992, p. 224).

[19]'... with the dignity of a lion', as Hamza Yusuf (2011) puts it in *Ramadan Advice, Fasting & Taqwa* (https://www.youtube.com/watch?v=y5s-VKHqrHo).

[20]'Seyyed Hossein Nasr has remarked that we can see an equivalent of this Sanskrit expression in the three Arabic words *wujūd–wijdān–wajd*, 'being–consciousness–ecstasy' (Chittick, 2007, p. 140). And as Helwa says: 'Islam is the path of showing you how to become who you already are ... The Qur'a says that God has planted within all humankind a seed of innate goodness, known in Arabic as the *fitra*. This primordial nature of goodness, placed in our hearts, inclines us toward actions that are righteous, beautiful, and in perfect alignment with the Divine' (Helwa, 2020).

greater wisdom and equipoise, to overcome the absence but our joy is no longer dependent on the success or failure of this endeavour. Thus, when we speak of the experience of abundance, this is not an argument for keeping things exactly as they are, it does not mean turning a blind eye to the injustices and wrongdoings of our time. Quite the contrary, in fact! What this experience of inner joy and abundance does is to imbue us with the necessary strength and resilience to work for change in a sustained and sustainable manner, whether at a personal or societal level, understanding all along that the two must go together.

It cannot be denied that mainstream religious discourse, across traditions, has throughout history, tended to propose an acceptance of the status quo or has been conveniently interpreted as saying so, by the powers that be, in order to buttress their authority. The degeneration of religious traditions, which has happened to each one of them without exception, has very much to do with the unholy alliance that has emerged historically between institutionalised religion and the structures of power in society. This is truly ironic because the founders of these religious traditions were all social revolutionaries of their day, advocating the overthrow of oppressive systems of power. The Franciscan friar Richard Rohr (2018) explains this paradox:

> As long as Jesus' followers were on the bottom and the edge of empire, as long as they shared the rejected and betrayed status of Jesus, they could grasp his teaching more readily. . . In 313, Constantine legalized Christianity. It became the official religion of the Roman Empire in 380. After this structural change, Christianity increasingly accepted, and even defended, the dominant social order. The church slowly lost its free and alternative vantage point. . . When the Christian church became the established religion of the empire, it started reading the Gospel from the position of maintaining power and social order instead of experiencing the profound power of powerlessness that Jesus revealed.

Something very similar can be traced in the history of all major religions. The challenge, then, is to acknowledge with clear and open sight exactly what went wrong with religion, but recognize and recover what is invaluable in each of these spiritual traditions.

Structure of Reality and Its Key Constituent Elements

We now summarise a few of the key constituent elements of the structure of reality as described by the spiritual traditions. A clear recognition of these changes our entire relationship with the world and with the sources of suffering within us.

Omnipresence of the Divine

Multiple spiritual traditions describe the presence of divinity in all of existence. As an illustration, we cite two verses from the *Bhagavad Gita* here[21]:

> Everything in this universe is pervaded by my unmanifest form. I encompass all beings but they do not fully contain me. (9.4)
>
> I am the one residing in the heart of every being. I am the beginning, the middle and the very end of all beings. (10.20)

Islam too recognizes that

> . . .divine beauty is imbedded in every atom of existence. . . When we combine outer practice (*islam*) and inner faith (*iman*) with the awareness of God's omnipresence, we enter into the mysterious realm of *ihsan*.
>
> (Helwa, 2020)

That the Divine is in everyone provides the most profound basis, the ultimate ground for adoption of policies of non-discrimination and non-exploitation and the equal rights of all of creation. There cannot be any justification for discrimination and unequal treatment on grounds of caste, race, community, religion, gender, sexual orientation, region, language etc. As Aurobindo says,

> . . .each man contains in himself the whole divine potentiality and therefore the Shudra cannot be rigidly confined within his Shudrahood, nor the Brahmin in his Brahminhood.
>
> (Aurobindo, 1991, p. 127)

Once we see everything as sacred, our entire relationship with them is profoundly transformed. The human, material and natural world are not then seen as mere instruments for exploitation but as invaluable in themselves. As Eisenstein says, the sacred has two aspects:

> . . .uniqueness and relatedness. A sacred object or being is one that is special, unique, one of a kind. It is therefore infinitely precious; it is irreplaceable . . . the sacred is also the gateway to the underlying unity of all things.
>
> (Eisenstein, 2021, pp. 15–17)

This completely changes the way we conceive our relationship with and our policies and practices in the world. We no longer seek domination and control but try to achieve harmony and balance in what we do.

---

[21]All translations of verses of the Gita in this chapter are from Shah (1991a).

Inter-connectedness of All Existence

As Richard Rohr says:

> ...we are already connected to everything – inherently, objectively, metaphysically, ontologically, and theologically. This gives us a foundation for understanding the sacredness of everything and our connection with everything.
>
> (Rohr, 2017)

The spiritual tradition of the Buddha proposes a vision of a deeply inter-connected cosmos, where 'you are, therefore, I am'. Buddhism teaches that all life is inter-related:

> All things, mutually supportive and related, form a living cosmos, a single living whole. By engaging ourselves with others, our identity is developed, established and enhanced.[22]

Recognising this, enables us to overcome the sense of separation (*māyīya mala*). We then understand that it is impossible to build our own happiness on the unhappiness of others. We also see that by ourselves we are incomplete and we need others and partnerships with them to bring true joy into this world. This helps us overcome the overbearing sense of agency (*kārma mala*), since we realise that the outcomes of our actions are necessarily subject to countless indeterminate factors way beyond our control.

This is the Buddhist teaching of *Pratitya Samutpada*.[23] In the words of the Vietnamese Buddhist monk Thích Nhất Hạnh:

> ...this is sometimes called the teaching of cause and effect, but that can be misleading, because we usually think of cause and effect as separate entities, with cause always preceding effect, and one cause leading to one effect. According to the teaching of Interdependent Co-Arising, cause and effect co-arise (*samutpada*) and everything is a result of multiple causes and conditions... For a table to exist, we need wood, a carpenter, time, skillfulness, and many other causes. And each of these causes needs other causes to be. The wood needs the forest, the sunshine, the rain, and so on. The carpenter needs

[22]www.sgi.org/about-us/buddhism-in-daily-life/interconnectedness.html.

[23]'The word *pratitya* has three different meanings – meeting, relying and depending – but all three, in terms of their basic import, mean dependence. *Samutpada* means arising. Hence, the meaning of *pratitya samutpada* is that which arises in dependence upon conditions'. In the Theravada-tradition, *Pratitya samutpada* implies that 'several causes give rise to several results: a single cause does not give rise to either a single result or several results; nor do several causes give rise to just one result; but rather several causes give rise to several results' (Dalai Lama, 1992).

> his parents, breakfast, fresh air, and so on. And each of those things, in turn, has to be brought about by other causes and conditions. If we continue to look in this way, we'll see that nothing has been left out. Everything in the cosmos has come together to bring us this table. Looking deeply at the sunshine, the leaves of the tree, and the clouds, we can see the table. The one can be seen in the all, and the all can be seen in the one. One cause is never enough to bring about an effect. A cause must, at the same time, be an effect, and every effect must also be the cause of something else. Cause and effect inter-are.
>
> (Thich Nhat Hanh, 1999)

Restraint as a Condition for Freedom

Recognition of inter-dependence and divinity in all, also signals to us the paradoxical relationship between restraint and freedom. Especially in a society with multiple axes of power, around which severely exploitative relationships are formed, only restraints on the freedom of those in power can guarantee the freedom of the oppressed. Thus, the freedom of men, the rich, the 'upper' castes/races and those in the mainstream, needs to be kept in check, if we are to ensure the well-being of women, the poor and the marginalized, based on caste, creed, race or ethnicity. Programmes and policies for land reform, redistributive taxation and affirmative action, laws against sexual harassment etc. are all examples of this. Perhaps the most important example of restraint in public policy is the Indian Constitution itself, which restrains acts of Parliament that militate against the basic structure of the Constitution, thus firmly circumscribing a possible 'tyranny of the majority'.

Restraint or *maryaada* is a key spiritual precept. It is so fundamental that one could say without restraint, life itself would become impossible. We can already see this in the imminent destruction of the planet, thanks to the unsustainable use of water and energy, fuelled by endless consumerist greed. But, of course, we must hasten to add, that as with many other religious precepts, restraint has historically been invoked, invariably by those already in the seat of power, in order to perpetuate the subjugation of the oppressed. Thus, great care (restraint!) needs to be exercised in the advocacy of restraint as a spiritual principle. We can specify four inter-related meanings of *maryaada*:

(1) giving up what is not strictly necessary; needs some restraint and some giving up, certainly;
(2) responding to external stimuli not in a pre-programmed tit-for-tat manner but with mastery and restraint, which develops in us through regular spiritual practice;
(3) restraint in the way we consume natural resources; and
(4) respectfulness towards (non-violation of) the Other.

Implications for the Nature of Our Action and Its Goals

A series of verses in the third chapter of the *Bhagavad Gita* (3.14–3.16) brings out not only the profound inter-connectedness of all existence but also the implications of this understanding for the nature of our action and its goals. 'In these verses the Vedic conception of sacrifice is set in the larger context of interdependence of beings in the cosmos'. (Radhakrishanan, 2011, p. 112). As the Gita states in verse 3.16,

> He, who does not, in this world, act in alignment with this cyclical flow of interdependence, delighting only in selfish pleasure, lives in vain.
>
> (Shah, 1991a)

The Gita can be seen as an exposition of *karma yoga*, of how to act in this world so that our actions do not become a source of sorrow and unfreedom. Indeed as verse 3.9 says:

> All actions other than those done in a spirit of giving, end up becoming a source of unfreedom in this world. Therefore, O Arjuna, act in this way, for the sake of giving, with equanimity, without desperation or anxiety about outcomes.
>
> (Shah, 1991a)

The cosmic order is a wheel, a cycle whose dynamic equilibrium must be sustained. Through the imaging of sacrifice, we are called upon to do all our work, small or big, dedicated to the preservation of this 'moral ecology', in gratitude towards all that lives (Shah, 1991b).[24] Moral ecology comprehends all

---

[24]The recent term 'ecopsychology' appears to me to capture some of what I mean here by moral ecology: 'Ever since the Enlightenment, technological civilization has assumed a clear divide between the presumably "exterior" world of material nature and the presumably "interior" world of the mind and emotions… it has taken a tremendous toll – on ourselves, on our relationships and on the animate earth around us. Nevertheless, the bifurcation persists: the science of ecology studies the external realm of earthly interactions, while psychology ponders and ministers to the internal realm of our mental life. As its name implies, ecopsychology (or ecological psychology) neatly explodes this age-old divide between mind and matter, between the psyche "in here" and nature "out there." Ecopsychology suggests that the psyche cannot really be understood as a distinct dimension isolated from the sensuous world that materially enfolds us, and indeed that earthly nature can no longer be genuinely understood as a conglomeration of objects and objective processes independent of subjectivity and sentience' (David Abram in his Foreword to Fisher, 2013).

the smaller notions of social and ecological balance put forward from time to time and also provides them with an altogether more profound ethical foundation.[25] Without which, they risk running aground somewhere, at some point or the other – as the repeated historical experience of social reform, religious and revolutionary movements shows.

Thus, it is suggested that neither joy nor freedom can be attained without recognising the fundamental inter-connectedness that characterises 'the rhythm of being' (Panikkar, 2013).[26] Hence, the Sufis urge us to move towards *fanā*, the annihilation of the ego, as an essential step on the spiritual path. Understanding the inter-dependent nature of the world, we develop an attitude of humility and an acknowledgement of the need to build genuine, mutually respectful dialogue, based on deep listening, across multiple forms of diversity, in a true spirit of partnership. Whatever solutions we propose will be much more powerful and effective, if they are arrived at through a robust process of this kind.[27]

The Gita concludes with a description of the highest goal of action by exhorting us to work for *lokasamgraham* (verses 3.20 and 3.25), the holding together of the peoples of the world, to create harmony among all beings, to preserve the moral ecology of the universe, in recognition of the inter-dependence described earlier.

> While the unwise act from attachment to their work, the learned, following the example of Janaka and other wise men, act without attachment and set their sights only on the nurturing of *lokasamgraham*.
>
> (Shah, 1991a)

Something very similar is affirmed in Islam:

> The sign of true *iman* is that it affects how you interact with the entirety of creation, not just the Creator. The best of people are those that bring the most benefit to the rest of humankind.
>
> (Helwa, 2020)

---

[25]Because it arises from a much deeper understanding of the structure of reality itself, and a comprehensive appreciation of the multiple kinds of inter-dependence that characterise the world we live in. It is, thereby, not some externally imposed morality but one which flows organically from the nature of reality.

[26]Recent advances in neurobiology have revealed that 'societies in which most individuals behave unselfishly will last longer and better than societies in which too few people show reciprocal altruism' (Pfaff, 2007, pp. 16–17).

[27]This has been the experience of the three decades of work my colleagues and I have done as part of Samaj Pragati Sahayog, in the remote tribal areas of central India, patiently building dialogue across sharp, at times, violent differences that would, from time to time, threaten to explode beyond repair. Each time we learnt, each instance taught us the art of building bridges where breakdowns seemed irremediable (see sampajpragtisahayog.org).

Policy and Practice Informed by the Ancient Science of Spirituality: Some Illustrations

Having very briefly outlined key features of the ancient science of spirituality and hinted at its multiple implications for action, it is time now to provide concrete illustrations of how policy and practice in various spheres could greatly benefit from the insights of this science.

Transforming the Very Process of Policymaking[28]

If finitude is a fundamental aspect of our existence on earth, if our knowledge of the world is bound to be both limited and uncertain, we need to ensure that the process of policymaking adequately reflects and acknowledges this reality. We get a remarkable restatement of finitude from none other than the greatest economist of the 20th century:

> ...our knowledge of the future is fluctuating, vague and uncertain.... By 'uncertain' knowledge, I do not mean merely to distinguish what is known for certain, from what is only probable. The game of roulette is not subject, in this sense, to uncertainty. Or, again, the expectation of life is only slightly uncertain. Even the weather is only moderately uncertain. The sense in which I am using the term is that in which the prospect of a European war is uncertain or the price of copper and the rate of interest twenty years hence. About these matters there is no scientific basis on which to form any calculable probability whatever. We simply do not know.
>
> (Keynes, 1937)

Responding to this uncertainty, John Maynard Keynes laid the foundations of the modern welfare state whose interventions he saw as correcting the fallibility of the market mechanism. Arguing from the opposite end of the ideological spectrum but agreeing with Keynes fundamentally on the nature of knowledge was Friedrich von Hayek. Hayek questions the very possibility of rational calculation by central planners, pointing to complex multi-variable and non-linear phenomena involved in understanding an economy. Of course, the irony is that Hayek had a touching faith in the power of unrestrained markets, assigning them near omniscience, quite ignoring his own insights into the nature of knowledge and also dismissing the fundamental revolution in Economics inaugurated by the work of Keynes.

---

[28]The approach towards policymaking described in this section was somewhat approximated in the process adopted while developing the proposals for water, rural development and decentralized governance in India's 12th Five Year Plan (2012), as also in the formulation of India's new National Water Policy (2020), both of which I had the privilege to helm.

Perhaps the economist who captures most beautifully the insights of both Keynes and Hayek is the relatively unsung G.L.S. Shackle. In a much more radical position, he questions both Hayek's naiveté about markets and Keynes' simplistic optimism about state intervention. Shackle introduces the notion of 'inceptive choice', where the person who chooses cannot

> ... foreknow what the sequel of his present choice will be, for if his own choices are inceptive, if his own choices are non-implicit, in some degree, in their antecedents, so are the choices of others and so are all the choices-to-come of himself as well as others.
>
> (Shackle, 1975, p. 23)

Since 'the ultimate permissive condition of knowledge is the repetition of recognisable configurations' (Shackle, 1972, p. 6), this limits the possibilities of knowing the courses of action that will be chosen in future. Shackle criticises his teacher Hayek for not fully acknowledging the implications of the decision-maker's 'unknowledge' for the possibilities of self-regulation in a market economy.

Shackle's work takes Economics into novel territory such as the role of imagination to assess the plausibility of alternative outcomes while taking economic decisions. But the very freedom that is the basis for imagination makes perfect knowledge an impossibility. Shackle, therefore, posits a fundamental hiatus between freedom and knowledge, as also between time and reason. In an incredibly insightful, less than 3-page long, Chapter 2 (titled *Time, Novelty, Geometry*) in his 1972 work *Epistemics and Economics,* Shackle writes:

> Time is a denial of the omnipotence of reason. Time divides the entirety of things into that part about which we can reason and that part about which we cannot. Yet the part about which we cannot reason has a bearing on the meaning of the part that is amenable to reason. The analyst is obliged to practice, in effect, a denial of the nature of time. For he can reason only about that which is *in effect* complete; and in a world where there is time, nothing is ever complete.
>
> (Shackle, 1972, p. 27)

As Shackle has shown there are a range of phenomena for which no 'pre-image' exists in our minds. We have no previous observations on the basis of which probability distributions can be constructed since the phenomena we are dealing with are unprecedented. (Shackle, 1972, p. 18).[29]

---

[29]This leads Shackle to advocate an exciting diachronic approach for unraveling the 'broad current of self-determining, or organically evolving history' (Pfaff, 2007).

It is quite evident how some of these great minds of the 20th century clearly share the insights of spiritual science. We now tease out the implications of this recognition for the very process of policymaking.[30]

Rejection of Fundamentalism

Such an understanding of the very nature of knowledge clearly implies a rejection of any kind of fundamentalism. The spiritual path demands humility, the non-presumption of the arrogance of complete knowledge or certainty, the aspiration for which leads to a suppression of dissent, enquiry and the sense of wonder and mystery, which has to be the beginning of all science and all policy.

Valorisation of Nimble-Footedness

Policymaking, therefore, requires an openness to mid-course correction as new knowledge is acquired and fresh experience is gained over time. This means an abandonment of the heavy-handed inflexibility and dogmatism, which characterises so many of our development interventions.

The Criticality of Dialogue

An acknowledgement of our own finitude opens up the possibility that we also look elsewhere, to other sources for support in our quest for knowledge. This necessitates deep listening and the building of common ground across differences, respecting a diversity of approaches and standpoints. It calls for an attempt to learn from the context where change is being attempted – an open and rich dialogue, a true engagement, which is both transparent and participatory, and thereby also more accountable and open to mid-course correction. This also facilitates the building of social trust, which is a powerful and indispensable resource in situations of uncertainty (Luhmann, 1979). Dialogue is a corrective to the stridency of both the bottom-up activist and the top-down planner. Neither by itself is appropriate or adequate. What matters, what enlightens, is deep dialogue, an engagement from which something quite unanticipatable, something novel, emerges and guides action.

[30]I explored these questions in some detail in Shah (2010). Since then, there has been a veritable explosion of work on the issue. A truly remarkable work is Martínez et al. (2021): 'Starting from the premise that clarity and fixity as ideals of modernity prevent us from approaching that which cannot be easily captured and framed into scientific boundaries, the book argues for remaining on the boundary between the known and the unknown' (op. cit., blurb). The book provides deep insight into 'a form of knowledge that is interwoven with unknowns'. (op. cit., p. 165). In her latest work, the essayist Emily Ogden (2022) celebrates the joys and wisdom of "unknowing." And asks us to cultivate 'a capacity to hold the position of not knowing yet – possibly of not knowing ever'. She suggests that 'this zone of the in-between, where we lack both total ignorance and absolute knowledge, has its own virtues: flexibility, humility, wonder, playfulness' (Domestico, 2022).

Inside-Outside

As Richard Rohr argues, transformational change comes only from those who 'live on the edge of the inside', which is when 'you have learned the rules well enough to know how to break the rules properly, which is not really to break them at all, but to find their true purpose: "not to abolish the law but to complete it" as Jesus would say' (Matthew 5:17).[31] Thus, we are not content to be mere critics from the outside but strive to be those who can bring about real change through constructive, critical engagement with those in power:

> Not an outsider throwing rocks, nor a comfortable insider who defends the status quo, but one who lives precariously with two perspectives held tightly together – the faithful insider and the critical outsider at the same time. Not ensconced safely inside, but not so far outside as to lose compassion or understanding.
>
> (Matthew 5:17)

'A Fusion of Horizons'

As the Brazilian anthropologist Eduardo Viveiros de Castro (2003) explains,

> The real problem lies in knowing which are the possible relations between our descriptive practices and those employed by other peoples. There are undoubtedly many possible relations; but only one impossible relation: the absence of a relation.
>
> (de Castro, 2003, p. 11)

In Gadamer's words, understanding is always a 'fusion of horizons':

> What do we mean by 'placing ourselves' in a situation? Certainly not just disregarding ourselves. This is necessary, of course, in that we must imagine the other situation. But into this other situation we must also bring ourselves. This always involves the attainment of a higher universality that overcomes not only our own particularity but also that of the other. To acquire a horizon means that one learns to look beyond what is close at hand, not in order to look away from it, but to see it better within a larger whole and in truer proportion. Understanding is always a fusion of horizons which we imagine to exist by themselves.
>
> (Gadamer, 1960, pp. 271–273)

Our knowledge thereby loses the dogmatism of its own voice by acknowledging the need to listen to and understand the knowledge produced by the other,

---

[31]https://cac.org/about/the-eight-core-principles/.

whose situation we may be trying to transform. These are situations and contexts with a dynamic of their own. The impact of what we do is mediated through the ongoing dynamic of the context where our initiative rolls out. We need to study and understand this dynamic.[32]

Finally, we must recognise that policymaking is invariably located in contexts of deep inequalities and discrimination, some historically inherited, others created anew, whether based on gender, caste, ethnicity, race, community or class. A recognition of divinity in all creation would be the best guarantee that policy-making and practice happens without the discrimination and exploitation, which has marked human history. We could then avoid situations where millions across the globe sleep hungry every night even as granaries the world-over, overflow with grain. Or the terrible tragedy of thousands of African children dying of sleeping sickness every year, only because they cannot afford to buy medication developed by pharma companies working solely to maximise their own profits.

A key insight of Keynes' work was that the interests of the capitalist class are intimately bound up with those of the workers. Hence, when there is widespread unemployment, a government would be well-advised to create purchasing power in the hands of the workers so that they would have the capacity to buy what the capitalists produce, enabling them to earn profits and carry on the process of capitalist accumulation, thereby generating more employment, and so on, in a virtuous cycle of inter-dependence. Today, no less than the very bastion of free market fundamentalism, the International Monetary Fund, argues that the sharp increase in inequality in recent decades has played a key role in slowing down the rate of growth of the economy (Dabla-Norris et al., 2015).

Thus, the inter-dependence emphasised by the ancient science of spirituality can be seen wherever we turn – nature, economy and society. Many African nations, therefore, espouse a commitment to *Ubuntu* as a governing principle:

> In South Africa, *Ubuntu* is our way of making sense of the world. The word literally means 'humanity'. It is the philosophy and belief that a person is only a person through other people. Our humanity is bound up in one another, and any tear in the fabric of connection between us must be repaired for us all to be made whole. This interconnectedness is the very root of who we are.
>
> (Tutu & Tutu, 2014)

[32]Much of the devastation wrought by colonial settlers in their assignation with the aboriginal/indigenous people across the globe had to do with the presumption of *terra nullius* ('land belonging to no one' or 'empty land'). Many of the mistakes planners in emerging economies continue to make with indigenous communities even today have a similar origin.

Water Policy in India[33]

There is nothing perhaps that illustrates the perils of ignoring inter-connectedness and diversity than the water cycle. Sadly, water policies and programmes all over the world, throughout the 20th century, were formulated ignoring the profound inter-connectedness of different elements of the water cycle.

India is the largest consumer of groundwater in the world. Today we face a water crisis, almost entirely engendered by the way we have gone about managing, or rather mismanaging, our groundwater. Groundwater is a shared, common pool resource. It is found in underground reservoirs called aquifers. These aquifers do not recognise legal boundaries of land ownership. Thus, the water in an aquifer belongs to and can be accessed by all those who have land over it. It needs, therefore, to be shared and managed collectively. If I over-extract groundwater below my land, I directly impact the access to this groundwater for those who share the aquifer with me. Unfortunately, both our legal and economic system are designed to incentivise atomistic over-exploitation of groundwater to such an extent that a more powerful extractor can eliminate access for others to even their water for life, ultimately leading to the resource itself being been destroyed, both through a decline in levels, as also in its quality. This is a direct consequence of not recognising the inter-connectedness and diversity that characterises groundwater.

We have paid an even worse price for ignoring the inter-connectedness of groundwater with surface water. As a result, India's peninsular rivers have begun to dry up. It has not been acknowledged that the flow of water in these rivers after the monsoon comes from groundwater. Once we over-extract groundwater, we dry up this vital source of water for peninsular rivers. Something similar happens when we destroy underground springs, which feed Himalayan rivers.

Even more potentially catastrophic is the plan to link India's Himalayan rivers with Peninsular rivers for inter-basin transfer of water, estimated to cost Rs. 11 lakh crore. Not only does this plan have unimaginable ecological and energy costs, the scheme could have a disastrous impact on the very integrity of the monsoon cycle. The presence of a low salinity layer of water with low density is a reason for maintenance of high sea-surface temperatures in the Bay of Bengal, which contributes to low-pressure areas and the intensification of monsoon activity. Rainfall over much of the sub-continent is controlled by this layer of low salinity water, which arises because the fresh water of India's rivers flows into the sea. A disruption in these flows, and as a result, in this low salinity layer, could have serious long-term consequences for climate and rainfall in the subcontinent, endangering the livelihoods of a vast population. Once again not recognising how each element in the monsoon cycle is deeply inter-connected with the other, could be a disastrous mistake.

Such projects, part of the overall depredation of the planet, help us understand the profound wisdom of Jesus in the *Sermon on the Mount*, when he says 'the

[33]This section very briefly summarises the many paradigmatic changes needed in water policy. See Shah (2013) for full details.

meek shall inherit the earth', to which I add 'they are the only ones fit to do so, for the arrogant shall destroy it'! As Pope Francis recently said:

> ...we are building a tower of human arrogance with bricks of power, bricks of economy. And to build that, so many people work like slaves. And if a slave falls, nothing happens. But we've taken an extra step. If Nature falls, nothing happens. The economic arrogance, the arrogance of the power of a few people, that use everything, that use people, that use Nature, that use everything and destroy it.
>
> (Brown, 2022)

An Agro-Ecological Direction for Farm Policy

A recent overview of global food systems rightly points to the 'paradox of productivity':

> ...as the efficiency of production has increased, the efficiency of the food system as a whole – in terms of delivering nutritious food, sustainably and with little waste – has declined.
>
> (Bailey, 2019)

Benton and Bailey, therefore, urge policymakers to move from the traditional preoccupation with Total Factor Productivity towards Total System Productivity (TSP):

> A food system with high TSP would be sufficiently productive (to meet human nutritional needs) whilst imposing few costs on the environment and society (so being sustainable), and highly efficient at all stages of the food chain so as to minimize waste.
>
> (Bailey, 2019)

In the light of this understanding, attempts are being made all over the world to foster an eco-system approach, with higher sustainability and resilience, lower costs of production, as also economy in water use. Broadly, these alternatives to chemical farming come under the rubric of agro-ecology (see Shah, 2022 for fuller details).

Essentially, this is an attempt to redefine our relationship with Nature, where we seek to weave our interventions into the contours of Nature, rather than seeking mastery over it. Here again, we follow Jesus, in an attitude of humility and wonder, becoming genuine students of Nature, marvelling at and leveraging its power, to solve the problems of humanity. COVID-19 has reminded everyone, like never before, of how circumscribed the economy necessarily is by the nature of the larger eco-system governing it. As the imprint of humans on the planet grows heavier in the epoch of the Anthropocene, a decisive shift in our relationship with Nature becomes imperative. The pandemic is clearly a result of non-recognition of the value of the smallest to the largest creation of the Divine. It is not merely a matter of realising the constraints within which we operate but of re-envisioning the response: moving from a paradigm of linear mechanics to thinking in terms of complex dynamics. We need, more and more, to learn to deal with the unforeseen and the inherently unpredictable. The pandemic forces everyone to acknowledge that this is now imperative, not just for greater prosperity but for the very survival of human life on Earth.

Sadly, however, even in farming we have attempted complete control over Nature, rather than seeking to align with it, even while harnessing its power. The dominance of chemical farming has had very serious but not fully understood consequences. According to Kate Brown, MIT Professor of Science, Technology and Society:

> Within the uniform predictability of modern agriculture, the unpredictable emerges.... Two-thirds of cancers have their origins in environmental toxins, accounting for millions of annual fatalities ... we inhabit not the Earth but the atmosphere, a sea of life; as swimmers in this sea, we cannot be biologically isolated ... Biologists have begun questioning the idea that each tree is an 'individual' – it might be more accurately understood as a node in a network of underworld exchanges between fungi, roots, bacteria, lichen, insects, and other plants. The network is so intricate that it's difficult to say where one organism ends and the other begins.[34]

More specifically, it is clear that

> There is a large list of deadly pathogens that emerged due to the ways in which we practice agriculture, among which are: H5N1-Asian Avian Influenza, H5N2, multiple Swine Flu variants (H1N1, H1N2), Ebola, Campylobacter, Nipah virus, Q fever, hepatitis E, Salmonella enteritidis, foot-and-mouth disease, and a variety of influenzas.
>
> (Altieri & Nicholls, 2020)[35]

This necessitates a paradigm shift in our structures of thought and action, to grasp complex adaptive systems (where the complexity of the behaviour of the whole system cannot be completely grasped by an understanding of its individual

---

[34]https://councilontheuncertainhumanfuture.org/the-pandemic-is-not-a-natural-disaster/

[35]The pandemic has also thrown sharp light on the perils of the current paradigm of industrial livestock production, something that is beyond the scope of the present paper but merits equal if not even greater attention (Wallace, 2016a).

parts), of which farming is a very important example. This is nothing, if not a reiteration of the ancient science of spirituality.

Mental Health: A Global Challenge

How serious a challenge mental health has become globally becomes evident from even a cursory glance at the World Health Organization's *Comprehensive Mental Health Action Plan 2013–2030*. The increased stresses and strains of a fiercely competitive economy and society are especially taking their toll on young people in the 21st century. While allopathic medicine and western psychiatry and psychotherapy struggle to find a meaningful response to this emergent crisis, the ancient spiritual traditions provide a new ray of hope, as they begin to be adopted by mental health providers across the world.[36] While detailed examination of these possibilities is beyond the scope of this chapter, it would be a serious omission if we did not take cognizance of the powerful possibilities opened up by work in this direction. Special mention must be made here of the pioneering work of Stephen and Ondrea Levine (1982), which draws upon multiple spiritual traditions, Theravada Buddhism, Native American, Sufism and mystical trends within Christianity.[37] Over 34 years, Stephen and Ondrea counselled concentration camp survivors and their children, Vietnam War veterans, as well as victims of sexual abuse. Yoga and meditation are now more and more widely used in the treatment of mental health issues, where the idea is to address deeper neuroses, rather than merely provide opioid care, which has itself become a crisis blowing out of hand in the West.[38,39]

Transformative Politics

Meaningful politics in an unjust society comprises any endeavour to alter the balance of power in favour of the deprived and oppressed. How radical such an attempt is, turns on how far-reaching a challenge is mounted to these structures of power, how comprehensive, how universal and how enduring is the vision of transformation embedded in this politics. The word radical derives from the Latin *radix*, meaning root. Thus, a truly radical politics must go to the very root of the problem. It must seek a transformation that is much more fundamental than the one sought by what one may call the more sectarian movements, each undoubtedly invaluable in themselves, but finally limited to a specific structure of power, whether based on gender, class, caste, race, region or community. For ultimately what matters is whether we get to experience freedom at the deepest

[36]Ahmad Ghaderi, Seyed Mahmoud Tabatabaei, Saharnaz Nedjat, Mohsen Javadi and Bagher Larijani (2018): 'Explanatory definition of the concept of spiritual health: A qualitative study in Iran', *Journal of Medical Ethics and History of Medicine*, April.

[37]Stephen and Ondrea Levine (1982). *Who Dies?: An Investigation of Conscious Living and Conscious Dying*, Gateway Books.

[38]https://www.nccih.nih.gov/news/press-releases/more-adults-and-children-are-using-yoga-and-meditation

[39]https://www.who.int/news-room/fact-sheets/detail/opioid-overdose

level. Or do we continue to remain caught in the endless cycle of desire, fulfilment and lack – that becomes an eternal source of bondage and unfreedom, even enslavement, more overpowering than any external servitude?

This demands re-imagining the relationship between the personal and the political. While political movements for social change have tended to neglect the personal, the religious traditions have, in the main, neglected attention to the social sphere. Indeed, they have often been used by the powers-that-be to buttress structures of power in society. Both need to change: the political movements need to understand the inextricable inter-connections between the personal and political sphere, acknowledging that without a radical transformation of basic human aspirations, a just and sustainable social order cannot be created.[40] Likewise, religious traditions must see how oppressive social and economic structures are a formidable obstacle to the divinization of life on earth.[41] A bridge needs to be built between the two sides, a bridge that is longer, deeper and stronger than anything seen thus far.[42]

A long and unbroken chain of spiritual political activists, including Gandhi and Ambedkar (see Shah, 2019), have embodied this kind of politics in our time. This pantheon of great thinker-activists centred their politics and attempts at social transformation, around a spiritual understanding of the world. They brought to bear reconstructed spiritual resources to address what they saw as the key challenges of their own time and context. These include Gustavo Gutierrez (1973), who saw the Theology of Liberation as

> . . .an attempt at reflection, based on the gospel and the experiences of men and women committed to the process of liberation in the oppressed and exploited land of Latin America. This is the goal of the so-called theology of liberation.

As also Paulo Freire (1970), who in his path-breaking *Pedagogy of the Oppressed* argues:

> In order for this struggle to have meaning, the oppressed must not, in seeking to regain their humanity, become in turn oppressors of the oppressors, but rather restorers of the humanity of both. This,

---

[40]In his work on St. Francis of Assisi, Bruce Epperly (2021) speaks of a kind of a 'mystical activism' where we 'are called to be mystics of the here and now to bring beauty and healing to the world' (p. 12).

[41]Buddha considered politics and economics important . . . because they constitute external environments that can facilitate or impede an individual's pursuit of happiness defined as spiritual advancement and achievement of wisdom about the true nature of oneself' (Long, 2020, p. 34).

[42]Safety in the external world is necessary if we are to seek and find safety in the inner world. Inner prosperity is a far-fetched dream if the majority of our time and energy is consumed in meeting our daily needs. . . we need to use the forces of inner protection and prosperity to further enrich our life in the external world' (Tigunait, 2020, p. 9).

> then, is the great humanistic and historical task of the oppressed: to liberate themselves and their oppressors as well. (pp. 44, 49)

Careful attention needs to be paid here to Martin Luther King who formulated brilliantly the relationship between love, power and justice. King questions the legacy of viewing love and power as polar opposites, where love appears as a rescinding of power, and power as a rejection of love. King (1967) argues that 'power without love is reckless and abusive, and love without power is sentimental and anaemic'. And this new understanding of power helps King positively formulate the unbreakable bond between love, power and justice: 'power at its best is love implementing the demands of justice, and justice at its best is power correcting everything that stands against love'.[43]

The Christian Buddhist feminist bell hooks explains the turn towards the spiritual in her own political struggles (from Malcolm to King, so to speak):

> I experienced renewed spiritual awakening, an ever growing awareness of the transformative power of love... When I travelled the nation asking folk what enabled them to be courageous in struggling for freedom – whether working to end domination of race, gender, sexuality, class, or religion – the response was love.
>
> (hooks, 2013)

Elaborating on her political stance, she says:

> If I were really asked to define myself, I wouldn't start with race; I wouldn't start with blackness; I wouldn't start with gender; I wouldn't start with feminism. I would start with stripping down to what fundamentally informs my life, which is that I'm a seeker on the path. Where I stand spiritually is, steadfastly, on a path

---

[43]One of the foremost King scholars of our time is the Harvard don Brandon Terry who has initiated a serious re-reading of King, similar to my re-interpretation of Ambedkar's politics, which gives a central place to his spirituality (Shah, 2019). In an essay in a recent volume on King co-edited by Terry (Shelby & Terry, 2018), Martha Nussbaum tackles the very important question of the emotional states most suited for political action. As Nussbaum (2018) says, for King, retribution is an unacceptable response to oppression. Without extinguishing anger, the process of self-purification remains incomplete for a social activist working for change. The ethic of love, with its rejection of anger, is a sign of moral strength, courage and dignity, not an indicator of weakness, passivity or servility, as commonly assumed. It would appear to me that Judith Butler in her remarkable work *The Force of Nonviolence* misunderstands the nature of equanimity, equating it with a kind of disinterested passivity. As Nussbaum makes clear and as we do in this chapter, it is anything but that. But then Butler is perfectly on point when she argues for the need to craft and cultivate rage in a way that exposes and counters violence without itself being violent, what the Buddha would have termed 'banking the fire' (Brazier, 2002).

> about love. If love is really the active practice – Buddhist, Christian, or Islamic mysticism – it requires the notion of being a lover, of being in love with the universe.
>
> (Tworkov, 1992)

Conclusion

Humanity faces a basic question: can a world based on liberty, equality and fraternity be founded within a capitalist framework, which while bringing much prosperity, has also generated vast inequality, much needless deprivation and brought the planet close to destruction? And if we are seeking for alternatives to capitalism, can these be built merely on programmes for social and political change, without transforming individual aspirations? I would go as far as to say that till fundamental human objectives are not transformed, it will remain impossible for humanity to look beyond capitalism. After all, capitalism has proved to be the most efficient economic machine to deliver goals based on human acquisitiveness, unbridled competitiveness and greed. But if these fundamental aspirations of people are not altered, if they continue to seek endless joy in external sources, then their suffering and that of the planet cannot be ended. My aim in this chapter has been to remind ourselves of what we need to urgently learn from the ancient science of spirituality, especially about the relationships humans must have with each other, as also with all other creatures on the planet, and the planet itself.

The champions of technology, the free market and the totalitarian state, each peddled their own fundamentalisms throughout the 20th century. Instead of the Shangri-La they promised, each one of them, in their own ways, have pushed the planet perilously close to annihilation. Our challenge is not to allow ourselves to be overwhelmed by the undeniable darknesses of our time but to seize the light that still shines within us. The ancient science of spirituality offers an alternative path of humility, restraint, freedom, creativity and joy. Humanity, in stewardship of the Earth, would do well to heed this counsel – before it is too late!

References

Altieri, M. A., & Nicholls, C. I. (2020). Agroecology and the reconstruction of a post-COVID-19 agriculture. *Journal of Peasant Studies*, *47*(5).

Ambedkar, B. R. (1956). *Buddha or Karl Marx* (1st ed.). Createspace Independent Publishing.

Armstrong, K. (1992). *Muhammad: A biography of the Prophet*. Victor Gollancz Ltd.

Aurobindo, S. (1991). *The human cycle*. Sri Aurobindo Ashram Publications.

Aurobindo, S. (1995). *Secret of the Veda* (Kindle Edition). Lotus Press.

Bailey, T. G., & Benton, R. (2019). The paradox of productivity: Agricultural productivity promotes food system inefficiency. *Global Sustainability*, *2*. https://doi.org/10.1017/sus.2019.3

Beloved, M. (2007). *Yoga Sutras of Patanjali*. Michael Beloved.

Benson, H. (1984). *Beyond the relaxation response*. Berkley Books.

Bhikkhu, Ṭ. (1997). *Lokavipatti Sutta: The failings of the world.* https://www.dhammatalks.org/suttas/AN/AN8_6.html

Bhikkhu, Ṭ. (2022). *Sublime determinations: A retreat on the Brahmavihāras.* Ṭhānissaro Bhikkhu.

Brazier, D. (2002). *The feeling Buddha: A Buddhist psychology of character, adversity and passion.* St. Martin's Griffin.

Brown, N. (2022). *The letter: Laudato Si film: The Pope, the environmental crisis, and frontline leaders.*

Chinnaiyan, K. (2020). *Glorious Alchemy: Living the Lalitā Sahasranāma.* New Sarum Press.

Chinnaiyan, K. (2022). *Fractals of reality: Living the Śrīcakra.* Sfaim Press.

Chittick, W. C. (2007). *Science of the cosmos, science of the soul: The pertinence of Islamic cosmology in the modern world.* Oneworld.

Dabla-Norris, E., Kochhar, M. K., Suphaphiphat, M. N., Ricka, M. F., & Tsounta, M. E. (2015). *Causes and consequences of income inequality: A global perspective.* International Monetary Fund.

Domestico, A. (2022, July 5). Eight books in which ignorance is the point. *The Atlantic.*

Eduardo Batalha Viveiros de Castro. (2003). *After-dinner speech given at Anthropology and Science, the 5th Decennial Conference of the Association of Social Anthropologists of the UK and Commonwealth, 2003.* Department of Social Anthropology, University of Manchester, Manchester.

Eisenstein, C. (2021). *Sacred economics.* North Atlantic Books.

Epperly, B. (2021). *Walking with Francis of Assisi: From privilege to activism.* Franciscan Media.

Farnsworth, W. (2018). *The practicing stoic.* Godine.

Fisher, A. (2013). *Radical ecopsychology – Psychology in the service of life.* State University of New York Press.

Forster, M. N. (2022). *Herder's philosophy.* Oxford University Press.

Freire, P. (1970). *Pedagogy of the oppressed.* Continuum.

Gadamer, H.-G. (1989). *Truth and method.* Bloomsbury.

George Haskell, D. (2012). *The forest unseen.* Penguin Publishing Group.

Gutierrez, G. (1973). *A theology of liberation – History, politics, and salvation.* Orbis Books.

hooks, b. (2013). *Writing beyond race: Living theory and practice.* Routledge.

Hanh, T. N. (1999). *The heart of the Buddha's teaching.* Three River Press.

Helwa, A. (2020). *Secrets of divine love. A spiritual journey into the heart of Islam.* Naulit Publishing House.

Jain, V. K. (2011). *Acharya Umaswami's Tattvarthasutra.* Vikalp Printers.

Keynes, J. M. (1937, February). The general theory of employment, *Quarterly Journal of Economics.*

King, M. L. (1967/1986). Where do we go from here? In J. M. Washington (Ed.), *A Testament of Hope: The essential writings of Martin Luther King, Jr.* Harper & Row.

Lakshmanjoo, S. (2015). *Kashmir Shaivism: The secret supreme.* Universal Shaiva Fellowship.

Lama, D. (1992). The meaning of life. Translated and edited by Jeffrey Hopkins. Wisdom Publications.

Lama, D., Benson, H., Thurman, R. A. F., Gardner, H. E., Goleman, D., & Participants in The Harvard Mind Science Symposium. (1991). *MindScience: An East West Dialogue. Proceedings of a symposium sponsored by the Mind/Body Medical Institute of Harvard Medical School & New England Deaconess Hospital, and Tibet House*. Wisdom Publications.

Long, W. J. (2020). *Tantric State – A Buddhist approach to development and democracy in Bhutan* (Kindle Edition). Oxford University Press.

Luhmann, N. (1979). *Trust and power*. John Wiley.

Macy, J. (1991). *Mutual causality in Buddhism and general systems theory*. SUNY Press.

Martínez, F., Di Puppo, L., & Frederiksen, M. D. (2021). *Peripheral methodologies: Unlearning, not-knowing and ethnographic limits*. Routledge.

Nussbaum, M. C. (2018). From anger to love: Self-purification and political resistance. In T. Shelby & B. M. Terry (Eds.), *To shape a new world*. Harvard University Press.

O'Donohue, J. (2007). *Benedictus: A book of blessings*. Transworld.

Ogden, E. (2022). *On not knowing: How to love and other essays*. University of Chicago Press.

Padoux, A. (1990). *Vāc: The concept of the word in selected Hindu Tantras*. SUNY Press.

Panikkar, R. (2013). *The rhythm of being: The Gifford lectures*. Orbis Books.

Pfaff, D. W. (2007). *The neuroscience of fair play – Why we (usually) follow the golden rule*. Dana Press.

Radhakrishnan, S. (2011). *The Bhagavadgita*. HarperCollins.

Ralston, P. (2010). *The book of not knowing: Exploring the True nature of self, mind, and consciousness*. North Atlantic Books.

Rohr, R. (2017, June 19). Remain in love. *Richard Rohr's Daily Meditations*.

Rohr, R. (2018, September 3). Early Christianity A changing religion. *Richard Rohr's Daily Meditations*.

Shackle, G. L. S. (1972). *Epistemics and economics*. Cambridge University Press.

Shackle, G. L. S. (1975). *Time and choice*. Oxford University Press.

Shah, M. (1991a). *The Bhagavadgita*. Translated into Hindi and English), unpublished manuscript.

Shah, M. (1991b). *The Bhagavadgita: A commentary*. Unpublished manuscript.

Shah, M. (2010). The power of uncertainty: Reflections on the nature of transformational initiatives. *Economic and Political Weekly*.

Shah, M. (2013). Water: Towards a paradigm shift in the 12th plan. *Economic and Political Weekly*.

Shah, M. (2019). *Political radicalism of Ambedkar's spirituality*. The India Forum.

Shah, M. (2022, January). Dismantling barriers to upscaling agro-ecological farming in India. *ecology, Economy and society*.

Shelby, T., & Terry, B. M. (Eds.). (2018). *To Shape a new world – Essays on the political philosophy of Martin Luther King, Jr*. Harvard University Press.

Sutherland, J. (2022). *Through forests of every color—Awakening with Koans*. Shambhala.

Swami, O. (2017). *The Ancient science of Mantras, Black Lotus* (Kindle Edition).

Tigunait, R. (2020). *Sri Sukta*. Himalayan Institute.

Tutu, D., & Tutu, M. A. (2014). *The book of forgiving: The fourfold path for healing ourselves and our world.* Harper Collins.
Tworkov, H. (1992). *Agent of change: An interview with bell hooks.* Tricycle.
Vivekananda, S. (2007). *The complete works of Swami Vivekananda* (Mayavati Memorial Edition. 9 vols). Advaita Ashrama.
Wallace, R. (2016a). *Big farms make big flu: Dispatches on influenza, agribusiness and the nature of science.* Monthly Review Press.
Wallace, R. K. (2016b). *The neurophysiology of enlightenment* (Kindle Edition). Dharma Publications.
Yusuf, H. (2011). *Ramadan advice, fasting & Taqwa.* https://www.youtube.com/watch?v=y5s-VKHqrHo

Chapter 3

Politics of Being: Harnessing Spirituality and Science for a New Development Paradigm

Thomas Legrand

Abstract

This chapter presents a spiritual or wisdom-based approach to development, its rationale, conceptualization, methods and examples of applications. The politics of being proposes that societies explicitly make the fulfillment ('being') of all its members – humans and non-humans – their main goal, which should guide the development and implementation of public policies. It stands in opposition to the current development paradigm focused on economic growth or 'having', and rooted in a set of modern western values – individualism, materialism, reductionism, anthropocentrism, etc. By nourishing our relational nature, the politics of being can address the root causes of the meta crisis the world is facing, reconciling human flourishing with sustainability and supporting the cultural evolution that is needed. It proposes a dialogue between wisdom and science, the two main areas of knowledge, to guide its design and implementation. It conceptualizes 'being' as the actualization of our truest 'being' and our highest 'being'. This means that societies should provide the right conditions for their human members to express themselves and fulfil their healthy aspirations, as well as to develop human virtues and qualities. Wisdom traditions and spiritual teachings offer relevant insights into the nature of human fulfilment and the process of spiritual evolution that can be applied to societies. They emphasize the cultivation of spiritual values and qualities such as love, peace, happiness, life, mindfulness, mystery and the understanding of interconnectedness. In recent decades, these qualities have become areas of scientific research and been at the core of social change and development initiatives. Together they can serve as the foundations of the politics of being and allow to identify actionable public policy agendas in many sectors mainly based on existing examples.

Applied Spirituality and Sustainable Development Policy, 41–69

doi:10.1108/978-1-83753-380-020231003

Keywords: Spirituality; wisdom; sustainable development; evolution; culture; institutions; development paradigm; public policies

Introduction[1]

This chapter proposes a spiritual or wisdom-based development paradigm termed 'politics of being', in which societies pursue 'being' – instead of 'having' or economic growth, – as their main collective goal. To help frame this new field of research and action, the chapter presents its rationale, conceptualization, methods – in particular how to bring wisdom traditions and science together into a fruitful dialogue – and examples of applications in many sectors. It also identifies the different scientific and social fields where the seeds of this new paradigm can be found and shows how the politics of being can provide an integrative framework in which all relevant claims and initiatives can fit together. After presenting the need for a cultural evolution and a new development paradigm in the first section, we will introduce the 'politics of being' concept next and followed by how spiritual values can serve as its foundations, before highlighting concrete, actionable public policies agenda that can embody and advance this new vision for our societies.

The Need for a Cultural Evolution

An Evolutionary Civilizational Crisis

With the COVID-19 pandemics and the war in Ukraine, it has become clear to many that our world has entered a stage of systemic crisis and disruption. Our crises are not only economic or related to public health; they are also environmental, social, political, food-related, energetic, demographic, ethical, cognitive, etc. This meta-crisis points to an overall obsolescence of our current model of development focused on economic growth.

This model is itself embedded in a specific cultural programme: the modern paradigm and its set of values – materialism, reductionism, individualism, humanism, anthropocentrism, scientism, etc. Together these values shape a worldview and cultural narrative that Charles Eisenstein (2013) calls the 'story of separation', in which human beings see themselves as separate from each other and nature. This cultural programme, which originated in the west, has spread throughout the world, first through colonization, and then through globalization. Though it has brought in the past benefits to societies (e.g. economic and technological development, human rights, etc.), it is becoming more and more maladjusted to the present world's conditions and its destructive effects have become unsustainable.

While this worldview reflects scientific understandings of reality that often date back to the 19th century, the evolution of science and cultures are now allowing a

[1]The content of this chapter is derived and adapted from Legrand (2022).

new story to emerge, that Eisenstein calls the 'story of interbeing', which highlights our fundamental interdependence with one another and the natural world. This change in narrative has been called different things. For instance, MIT professor Otto Scharmer describes this as moving from an ego-system focused entirely on oneself to an ecosystem awareness that emphasizes the well-being of the whole (2016).

This vision allows us to characterize the civilizational crisis our societies are facing as an evolutionary crisis, which impels humanity's cultural evolution from the narrative of separation to that of interbeing, for the sake of its own survival and flourishing.

This crisis results from an imbalance between humankind's material and technological power and the relative underdevelopment of the consciousness, wisdom and ethics we need to manage this power and the increasing complexity it has brought to our world. Humanity has seen its power multiply, to the point that many scientists consider that human beings have become the dominant influence on climate and the environment, characterizing a new geological epoch called 'anthropocene'. But our development path has not allowed the kind of human growth necessary to build a wiser society that makes good use of this power.

On the contrary, modern values and our current model of development keep fostering a certain inner underdevelopment, as illustrated by a global mental health crisis (Marcus et al., 2012), a sharp decline in interpersonal trust in some rich countries (Algan et al., 2019; General Social Survey data, 2022), the ethical failure of our societies (Rahn & Transue, 1998; Sachs, 2012), and our inability to understand reality systemically (Morin, 2008).[2] Meanwhile, our technological power keeps expanding rapidly, particularly with the development of artificial intelligence, biological engineering and our capacity, in the near future, to drastically transform human beings.

Our technology, if used wisely and ethically, could solve most of our problems. However, its current misuse may provoke the collapse of our civilization, whether through climate chaos, the sixth mass extinction of global biodiversity or a nuclear war.

The Cultural or Collective Inner Transition

While it has long remained the major blind spot of global sustainability efforts, cultural or inner individual change is increasingly recognized as a fundamental dimension of sustainability and our response to many challenges the world is facing.

The 2020 Human Development report, published by the United Nations Development Program (UNDP), affirms that 'nothing short of a wholesale shift in mindsets [. . .] is needed to navigate the brave new world of the Anthropocene' (Conceição, 2020).[3] Likewise, the 2022 IPCC assessment reports on climate

---

[2]https://ourworldindata.org/trust, Accessed on 6 October, 2022.
[3]Conceição (2020, p. 412).

change mitigation and adaptation (IPCC 2022a, 2022b) also highlight the role of inner transition and the transformation of our beliefs and values as a lever for accelerating sustainable development. It builds on a growing body of scientific literature demonstrating the relationship between inner and outer transformation, and the importance of integrating inner dimensions into sustainability efforts (Wamsler et al., 2021) and social transformation.

While this literature often builds on knowledge and theories from different disciplines and fields of research, Donella Meadow's iceberg model from systems thinking is a common reference. The iceberg models recognize that our world's reality (events) is the visible manifestation of underlying patterns, structures and mindsets. The deepest part of the iceberg such as mental models or mindsets are the most powerful leverage points for systems transformations, though also the most difficult to activate (Meadows, 1999).

Concrete initiatives emphasizing the importance of inner transitions for sustainability, such as the Inner development Goals or the UNDP-convened Conscious Food Systems Alliance have also emerged in recent years.[4,5]

Wisdom Traditions and Humanity's Spiritual Evolution

Representatives of wisdom traditions have asserted the need to address the human, ethical or inner dimension of this civilizational crisis. They were proactive in drafting the Earth Charter (2000) – 'a declaration of fundamental ethical principles for building a just, sustainable, and peaceful global society in the 21st century', initiated by the United Nations.[6] This document emphasizes the spiritual nature of this required cultural evolution by calling for 'a change of mind and heart', which reflects the general position of many spiritual leaders.

The fourteenth Dalai Lama believes that 'the fundamental problem [. . .] is that at every level we are giving too much attention to the external, material aspects of life, while neglecting moral ethics and inner values.'[7] 'So long as people give priority to material values, then injustice, corruption, inequity, intolerance, and greed – all the outward manifestation of neglect of inner values – will persist'.[8] The Indian spiritual and humanitarian leader Amma also agreed: 'In short, today we search externally for the causes and solutions to all the problems of the world.[9] In our haste, we forget the greatest truth of all that the source of all problems is to be found within the human mind. We forget that the world will become good only if the mind of the individual becomes good. So, along with an understanding of the outer world, it is essential that we also come to know the inner world'.[10] Pope Francis has expressed this in his encyclical letter on care for our common home,

---

[4]https://www.innerdevelopmentgoals.org/
[5]https://consciousfoodsystems.org/
[6]https://earthcharter.org/about-us/faqs/#ec1, Accessed on 22 July 2020.
[7]His Holiness the Dalai Lama (2013, p. X).
[8]His Holiness the Dalai Lama (2013, p. XIII).
[9]http://amma.org/, Accessed on 22 July 2020.
[10]Amma (2004).

Laudato Si, which has played an important role in reframing the ecological crisis: 'The external deserts in the world are growing, because the internal deserts have become so vast'.[11]

Many prominent spiritual teachers of recent times have also emphasized the need and possibility of a spiritual transformation of humankind in the near future. Pioneers include the founder of the Bahá'í faith Baha'u'llah (1817–1892), Hindu spiritual teacher Sri Aurobindo (1872–1950) or Jesuit priest Pierre Teilhard de Chardin (1881–1955). This vision is becoming increasingly widespread among spiritual communities and contemporary spiritual teachers (e.g. Zen master Thich Nhat Hanh (1926–2022), Eckhart Tolle (born in 1948), or Hindu guru Said Baba (1926–2011)), who are increasingly getting organized in support of 'conscious evolution' (see for example the evolutionary leaders network).[12]

The belief in humankind's spiritual evolution is inherent to many spiritual traditions, for example those believing in reincarnation and the existence of the divine within living beings, that we can, life after life, learn to manifest more fully. These include many traditional cultures and religions, such as Buddhism, Jainism and Hinduism. Many interpretations of the latter seem to agree that we are moving out of the 'kali yuga', the 'age of quarrel and strife'. The faith in the upcoming unification and progress of humanity is also present in numerous indigenous prophecies. The indigenous people's track at the 2018 Parliament of the World's Religions was titled: 'The Spiritual Evolution of Humanity & Healing Our Mother Earth'. Most religions also have an eschatological dimension: they are concerned with the destiny of humanity, which, after many crises, is said to be radiant in the end. This is illustrated in Christian concepts such as the 'kingdom of God' – which is generally considered to be the central theme of Jesus's teaching, and, according to some interpretations, means the earthly fulfilment of God's will – or the 'new Earth'.

An Ongoing Transformation

We can see several signs that this spiritual transformation is not only possible, but ongoing. Scientific development has considerably extended our knowledge and power not only over nature but also over our very human condition and now describes a vision on the world that is much more compatible with core spiritual teachings. Together with science, globalization and the development of information and communication technologies, especially the internet (also known as 'humanity's brain'), are evolutionary forces in themselves, which have deepened our sense of interconnectedness. Humankind is experiencing an unprecedented process of information exchange and synthesis through which it can either get lost or get to know itself, reflect on its history and consciously choose what direction

[11]Holy Father Francis (2015). The quote is taken from Benedict XVI (Homily for the Solemn Inauguration of the Petrine Ministry, April 24, 2005).
[12]https://www.evolutionaryleaders.net/, Accessed on 20 October 2022.

to evolve in. These are important conditions for a collective spiritual transformation.

According to Ronald Inglehart (2018), the most recognized political scientist studying the evolution of values on a global level, in 'developed countries', the unprecedented prosperity and security of the post-war era has already brought about a great cultural change. With most of the new generations taking survival for granted, these societies have seen a shift from materialist to post-materialist values – which was part of an even broader shift from survival to self-expression values. Consequently, 'spiritual concerns, broadly defined, are becoming more widespread in post-industrial societies', (p. 75) while religiosity declines. Indeed, this deep cultural shift moves from prioritizing economic and physical safety, as well as conformity to group norms, towards increasing emphasis on individual freedom and autonomy, openness to new ideas, tolerance and empathy for out-groups (including LGBTQ+ and foreigners), gender equality, participation in decision-making, environmental protection, secularization, etc.

Inglehart shows that values mainly change through intergenerational population replacements as one's basic values largely reflect the conditions that prevailed during a person's pre-adulthood. This cultural change is considered the main driver of long-term institutional changes, which tend to occur quickly only when the cultural change has reached a critical mass and is then diffused in society through media and education. That is why while our underlying values have been changing for 50 years, societal changes are relatively recent. However, a recent decline in economic and existential security, associated with rising inequalities and immigration, is causing a cultural backlash and the return of survival values – heavy emphasis on group solidarity, rejection of outsiders, rigid adherence to cultural norms and obedience to strong leaders – among those who hold traditional cultural values and fear losing the world as they know it. This has invigorated xenophobic, populist and authoritarian political movements and is, according to Inglehart, the main cause for the rise of far-right populism.

While self-expression values as identified by Inglehart are tinged with a strong focus on individuality and do not necessarily correspond to the cultivation of our higher selves, they may represent one step in that direction, as part of an even broader trend towards the actualization of our true selves (see our definition of 'being' below). The spiritual dimension of the ongoing cultural change has been highlighted by sociologist Paul Ray and psychologist Sherry Ruth Anderson (2000). Studying the evolution of social values, they have named the growing sociological group at the forefront of current progressive cultural change 'the cultural creatives'. Among them, they distinguished a core group of more educated, socially committed and influential people who share a strong focus on spirituality. This led to them to identify an 'emerging planetary wisdom culture'.

If we are serious about addressing the current challenges, we need to recognize that our politics should turn inward and address this question of a cultural shift, and more precisely, of a shift in consciousness. This should not be opposed to the many other policy reforms we urgently need, which are in some cases well-known but often not implemented. In many cases, it should rather be seen as complementary, two sides of the same coin, with inner change enabling outer change and outer change embodying and facilitating this shift in consciousness.

The Politics of Being as a New Development Paradigm

In Search of a New Development Paradigm

The civilization crisis we face calls for a new development paradigm. This is widely recognized and was at the core of the UN debate on the post-2015 global development agenda when then-UN Secretary-General Ban Ki-moon said, 'The old model is broken. We need to create a new one'.[13]

Not only is our development model unsustainable, but it increasingly appears that material development is not the main avenue for societal happiness, in particular for high-income countries. If economic development can strongly increase life satisfaction in its early stages, once a certain level of material prosperity is reached, its correlation to life satisfaction plateaus (see Fig. 3.1). The same is true for the relationship between economic development and life

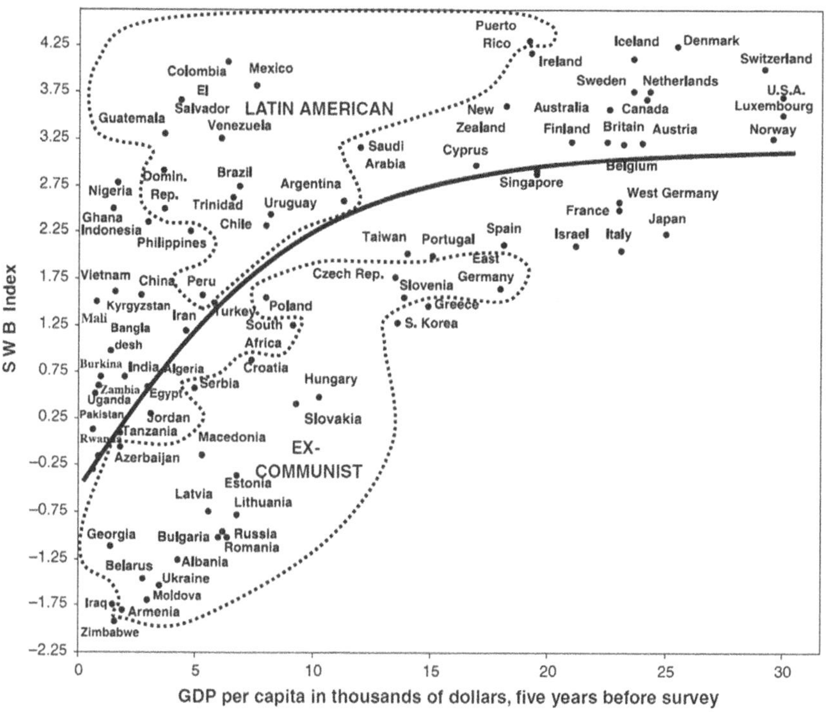

Fig. 3.1. Life Satisfaction by Economic Development. *Source:* Inglehart (2018, p. 148).

[13]https://www.un.org/en/development/desa/news/financing/new-paradigmjob-creation.html, Accessed on 7 October 2022.

expectancy (Wilkinson & Pickett, 2010 based on data from UNDP, 2006). In fact, the latter has started to diminish in the United States before the COVID-19 pandemics (Arias et al., 2022).

Economic growth and its main metric – Gross Domestic Product – have long been criticized and alternative visions and measures of development have been proposed. In particular, these include human development (UNDP, 1990) and sustainable development (World Commission on Environment and Development, 1987).[14,15] Cultural development has also been emphasized not only as the fourth pillar of sustainable development but it most fundamental dimension according to indigenous peoples, and many scholars have affirmed that true human development is cultural in nature (Schafer, 2022).[16] More recently, as part of the discussion on the post-2015 global development agenda, the Kingdom of Bhutan proposed 'happiness' as a new development paradigm (NDP Steering Committee and Secretariat, 2013).

The Earth Charter (2000) and its visionary approach to the new millennium offers a simple yet profound perspective on what this new development paradigm in essence should be. It affirms that 'when basic needs have been met, human development is primarily about being more, not having more'. This focus on 'being' gets to the heart of the matter and offers a vision that can potentially encompass alternative visions for a more integral, human, qualitative and sustainable development. This sentence has been integrated in the interreligious statement at the Rio +20 Conference, which claims that 'to make development truly sustainable, our economic, scientific, and technological accomplishments should assist the processes of individual and collective, psychological, and spiritual development. We must reorient our economic bottom line to support this full human development if we wish to live in a flourishing Earth community' (Jacob Soetendorp Institute for Human Values, p. 1).

---

[14]For more updated information, see https://hdr.undp.org/about/human-development, Accessed on 7 October 2022. According to the Human Development Report website from UNDP, Development is 'about giving people more freedom to live lives they value'. The Human Development Index is a 'crude measure' of human development based on life expectancy (health), years of schooling (education) and income per capita (standard of living).

[15]In 1987, the World Commission on Environment and Development defined sustainable development as 'development that meets the needs of the present generation without compromising the ability of future generations to meet their own needs'. Sustainable development is often associated to three pillars: economic development, social development and environmental protection. The sustainable development goals (SDGs) adopted in 2015 put sustainable development at the centre of the development agenda.

[16]Political declaration of Indigenous people at the Rio+20 International Conference on Self-determination and Sustainable Development. https://www.forestpeoples.org/sites/default/files/publication/2012/06/final-political-declaration-adopted-rio20-international-conference-indigenous-peoples-self-determina.pdf, Accessed on 8 October 2022.

The Politics of Being

The Earth Charter suggests that the focus on 'being more' would apply only for countries or people that have their 'basic needs [...] met'. At first sight, this seems congruent with the diminishing returns of economic growth in terms of life satisfaction and life expectancy (see above). It is also consistent with some psychological analyses such as the Pyramid of Maslow and its hierarchies of needs (assuming that basic needs have to be met before one can pursue 'growth' or 'being' needs), or sociological analyses such as the work of Inglehart's and the transition observed in rich countries from materialism to post materialism and more fundamentally from survival to self-expression values.

However, there are also good reasons to argue that human development is always about 'being more'. First, while 'having more' might get more attention from those whose basic needs have not been met, it still needs to be considered as a means (among others) for 'being more' rather than an end in itself. Secondly, studies have shown that people can simultaneously be motivated by different needs, without necessarily having their basic needs met (Tay & Diener, 2011), something even Maslow himself recognized (1987). Moreover, the paradigm of economic growth is rooted in western modernity and its strong materialistic values. Many low-income countries and communities – examples include Bhutan, Bolivia and Ecuador, as well as many indigenous people (see section 'The Politics of Being as a New Development Paradigm') – may be more naturally inclined than western countries towards development paradigms reflecting a 'being' focus, that are closer to their own cultural values. Failing to recognize these 'being' aspirations before basic needs have been met (assuming they probably never were from modern standards) seems like a highly condescending, dehumanizing and erroneous vision. Finally, the focus on 'being more' at the collective or individual level can also be the key to fulfil basic needs. Investing in personal development at scale, in particular for poor people, can have an important positive impact on the development of poor countries, as shown by the example of Nordic European countries and their 'popular enlightenment' ('folk-bildung') education policies in the 19th century (Andersen & Björkman, 2017). Furthermore, 'being more' may also be the key to build more solidary and equitable societies as pointed out by Indian spiritual and humanitarian leader Amma: 'In today's world, people experience two types of poverty: the poverty caused by lack of food, clothing and shelter, and the poverty caused by lack of love and compassion. Of these two, the second type needs to be considered first – because, if we have love and compassion in our hearts, then we will wholeheartedly serve those who suffer from lack of food, clothing and shelter'.[17]

The politics of being is the new development paradigm emphasizing 'being more'. It applies to all 'beings' – not only humans – recognizing their fundamental rights to be. 'Being' here means the fulfilment or realization of our full potential

---

[17]https://www.facebook.com/MataAmritanandamayi/photos/in-todays-world-people-experience-two-types-of-poverty-the-poverty-caused-by-lac/10155064627348302/, Accessed on 8 October 2022.

(an obvious and widely accepted definition of human development), which, I propose, can be defined as our highest and truest being, in all its dimensions. Our highest being refers to the development of inner values, virtues, or qualities while our truest being relates to the process of becoming who we really are. They both converge in the manifestation of our true interbeing nature (see below). The emphasis on highest and truest being complete, balance and ultimately meet each other. Focussing only on our highest being is neither healthy nor sustainable. Self-improvement comes with many pitfalls (e.g., ego strengthening, disconnection from oneself, masking deeper problems, etc.). At the social level, the exclusive focus on righteousness can foster a hypocritical morality when it fails to recognize that it is fine to make mistakes, which are necessary parts of any evolutive process. People at all developmental stages should feel respected and supported in their journey. This focus could also slip into legitimizing new forms of social control. The social credit system in China offers us a glimpse of such risk. It assesses the trustworthiness of individuals, companies and government entities, and, based on their scores, offers rewards and punishments. Reciprocally, when the subjective quest to become who we are does not lead us to objectively develop the best in ourselves, as is often the case in individualistic societies, it is a vain attempt and comes with many social ills.

This definition of 'being' makes it similar to other terms such as spiritual or inner development, human flourishing (Keyes, 2005, 2007), eudaimonia (Huta, 2013), or to some extent, self-actualization (Maslow, 1987). A truly human development is not merely focused on the external material dimension but recognizes the primacy of the inner dimension, all the dimensions of being, as well as our relational nature. Thus, being is about realizing one's unique potential through physical, emotional, psychological, mental, ethical and aesthetic development in relation to self, others and the environment.[18] The politics of being recognizes that life is a spiritual journey and aims at aligning our institutions with our true reason for being here on Earth: becoming who we are, the best and most complete version of ourselves.

This definition of 'being' poses the question of our true nature. First, it has been recently discovered that mystics from all sorts of spiritual traditions attest to the same experience of our true nature – that of being one with everything that is, – which can be called for example oneness, unity consciousness or interbeing (Teasdale, 1999). This recognition of our deep interconnectedness at the level of our being echoes the recent emphasis in human science on our 'relational' nature (Walsh et al., 2021). We are made of relationships: from birth, we develop our identities and potential through relationships, and we live our lives and flourish within relationships.

Secondly, the question is about the goodness or meanness of human nature. On the one hand, spiritual teachings usually emphasize the fundamental goodness of our spiritual nature. On the other hand, as human beings living in a historical

[18]Paraphrasing to some extent the definition of well-being proposed by O'Toole and Kropf (2012, p. 75).

reality, we have the potential for goodness and meanness. Our culture and social institutions play an important role in helping us manifest one or the other. For example, the dominant paradigm of retributive justice builds upon and strengthen our instinct for retaliation, while the practice of restorative justice allows all those involved to cultivate human values and qualities such as understanding, deep listening, compassion, healing, inclusivity, courage and responsibility.

While philosophers, from Aristotle to Confucius, have stressed the importance of the state and society to foster human virtues and qualities, the current domination of the story of 'separation' have on the contrary led to the institutional cultivation of greed, competition and selfishness, strengthening the root causes of our very problems. As one social psychologist (Miller, 1999) put it: 'the image of humans as self-interested leads to the creation of social institutions (e.g., workplaces, schools, governments) in that image, which, in turn, transforms that image into reality'. The result is that we as a society believe we are much less altruistic than is true (Crompton et al., 2016; Harwood Group, 1995).

This led American political economist Elinor Ostrom (2009) – arguably the most influential scholar in institutional analysis – to affirm that: 'designing institutions to force (or nudge) entirely self-interested individuals to achieve better outcomes has been the major goal posited by policy analysts for governments to accomplish for much of the past half century. Extensive empirical research leads me to argue that instead, a core goal of public policy should be to facilitate the development of institutions that bring out the best in humans'.

Institutions are often defined as 'rules of the game' shaping human interactions (North, 1990) and include laws, policies, organizations, social norms, etc.

The politics of being holds that all our institutions should be designed in a way that favours the daily experience, practice and nourishment of the greatest qualities in everyone – our intrinsic motivation and capacity for cooperation, altruism, care, understanding and creativity, etc. Virtues are developed with practice, as sages from Buddha to Aristotle have long taught. Together, this kind of human development can lead to the required wisdom to refine, adapt and wisely implement our institutions, in order to create a virtuous circle (see Fig. 3.2).

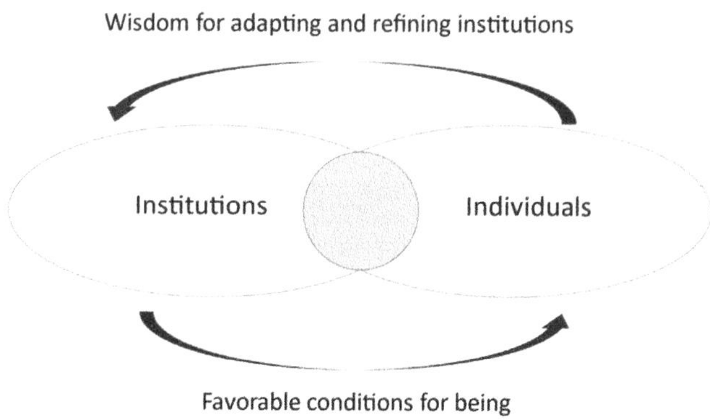

Fig. 3.2. Institutions and Individuals in the Politics of Being.

Spiritual teachings tell us that we cannot separate means from their goals. 'There is no way to happiness; happiness is the way', the Buddha once supposedly said. 'Being' is not something that can be produced mechanically by our institutions but those can invite everyone to cultivate their human qualities, while respecting their freedom.

A Theory of Change

How would a politics of being support the transformation of societies towards sustainability? Fig. 3.3 presents a theory of change for how inner development can support sustainability and collective flourishing.

First, is the recognition that the sustainability crisis is a human, relational crisis (Leichenko & O'Brien, 2020; Vásquez-Fernández & Ahenakew, 2020; Walsh et al., 2021; Wamsler et al., 2021), rooted in the story of separation. Our social and environmental crises arise from our disconnection with others and nature, which is itself linked to the disconnection with ourselves. Our current model of development, focused on economic growth, fosters and feeds on this disconnection through consumerism, greed and the focus on 'having', workaholism and the primacy of doing. It not only fuels excessive materialism, which has been shown to be associated with ill-being (Kasser, 2002); more generally, it impels people to prioritize what self-determination theory calls extrinsic goals (money, fame, image, conformity, etc.), on which our model of development relies for its continuation, over intrinsic goals (autonomy, social relationships, personal growth, mental health, physical fitness, etc.).[19] The former are those through which we search for others' positive evaluation, while the latter 'are inherently

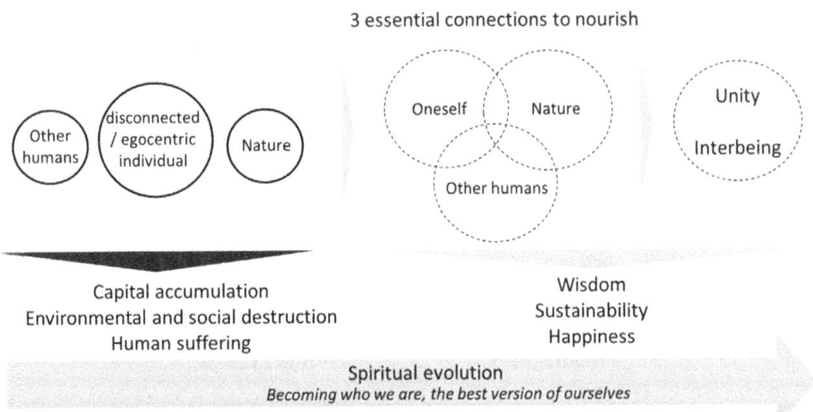

Fig. 3.3. The Inner Path to Sustainability, a Theory of Change.

[19]https://selfdeterminationtheory.org/theory/, Accessed on 10 October 2022.

satisfying to pursue because they are likely to satisfy innate psychological needs' (Schmuck et al., 2000, p. 226). Prioritizing extrinsic goals not only reflects a sense of insecurity about oneself (Kasser et al., 1995) but leads to a lower level of subjective well-being and to suffering 'disproportionately from a host of maladies including anxiety, depression, physical symptoms, unpleasant emotions, drug abuse, alcohol abuse, behavioural disorders, lower levels of self-actualization, less vitality, less life satisfaction and fewer pleasant emotion' (Ahuvia & Izberk-Bilgin, 2013, p. 490). The scientific literature also shows that those who pursue extrinsic goals tend to have attitudes and behaviours towards others and the environment that are more harmful (Thompson et al., 2013).

Second, a close link can be established between our connection with others, nature and oneself on the one hand, and our well-being on the other. The quality of relationships, in particular with a partner and family, is generally recognized as the most important factor for individual happiness (Demir, 2013; Waldinger, 2016). At a collective level research also highlight the social (cf. social capital, Sachs, 2015; Helliwell et al., 2017, 2019) and cultural (Ye et al., 2015) foundations of happiness, well above economic factors. Moreover, science is documenting the important psychological well-being, cognitive and physiological benefits of interacting with nature (Keniger et al., 2013), and how it strengthens our pro-environmental attitudes and behaviours (Nisbet et al., 2009). Research also highlights the social health benefits of urban nature.[20] As for the importance of the connection with oneself, research has indicated the importance of prioritizing intrinsic goals for our happiness (Ahuvia & Izberk-Bilgin, 2013). More fundamentally, premodern philosophical and spiritual traditions all over the world for centuries have emphasized that happiness fundamentally depends on us, and our attitudes towards life rather than our life conditions. In that perspective, the concept of eudaimonia – sometimes translated as 'flourishing', or equivalent to 'being' – which goes back to Aristotle, emphasizes the cultivation of moral virtues and human capacities (Huta, 2013).[21,22] Eudaimonic life pursuit has been shown to be a central determinant of our individual well-being (Peterson et al., 2005; Vella-Brodrick et al., 2009). Eudaimonic well-being has also been identified in turn as a driver of pro-social and pro-environmental attitudes and behaviours (Ahuvia & Izberk-Bilgin, 2013; Brown et al., 2005; Huta, 2016).

To summarize, science shows that what we call 'being' or eudaimonia can reconcile human thriving with sustainability through increased prosociality. The human capacities and virtues associated with 'being' can be cultivated, including through educational programmes and spiritual practices such as meditation (Baer, 2015; Bristow et al., 2020; De Vibe et al., 2012; Keng et al., 2011).

---

[20]https://depts.washington.edu/hhwb/

[21]Although 'flourishing' includes also positive emotions often associated to 'hedonia' to which 'eudaimonia' has been often opposed to.

[22]Huta (2013, p. 201) defines eudaimonia 'roughly speaking' as including 'states and/or pursuits associated with using and developing the best in oneself, in accordance with one's true self and one's deeper principles'.

While in the 'having' paradigm, environmental and social limits can be considered as hindrances to economic growth in the short term; in the 'being' paradigm, our connection with others and nature are on the contrary the foundations for human flourishing. This is recognized in alternative development paradigms rooted in indigenous or traditional worldviews such as Bhutan's Gross National Happiness or the buen vivir/vivir bien Andean political philosophy (Gudynas & Acosta, 2011; NDP Steering Committee and Secretariat, 2013; Solon, 2008).

The spiritual understanding or our true interbeing nature (Teasdale, 1999) allows us to comprehend why the spiritual development process of 'being more' naturally lead people to an increased sense of connectedness (or oneness at a very advanced stage) with all that is, from which stems prosociality and service. By becoming who we are, we also tend to express the best human qualities, associated with our relational nature.

Spiritual Values as the Foundations of the Politics of Being

The seeds of the politics of being can be found in new fields of scientific research, as well as social change and political initiatives rooted in some specific values, which lie at the core of spiritual teachings. They constitute different communities, organized to promote these values as new lenses through which to look at our current challenges – each contributing their part to the new story of interbeing – or new paradigms to transform our societies.

Understanding of Our Interconnectedness

New ways of thinking are needed to overcome the reductionistic mindset that characterized modern science and help navigate a more and more interconnected and complex world. Over the last decades, systemic thinking (Meadows, 2008) has emerged as a critical alternative to address many of our current challenges in an integrated manner, moving beyond sectoral and disciplinary silos, as well as direct linear causality. As mentioned above, the iceberg model emphasizes mental models or paradigms – or participants' ways of being (Scharmer, 2016) – as the most powerful leverage points for systems' transformations (Meadows, 1999). Changing the goal of the systems and relationships among actors are also highlighted as particularly important for systems change in that perspective.

Complexity theory arose from the recognition of the fundamental complexity of natural and human systems, and the inherent uncertainty and nonlinearity associated with it. Its ambition is to evolve our very concept of science, its methodology, epistemology and ontology (Morin, 2008). Developmental psychology tends to consider the complexity of our meaning-making the main measure of a person's developmental stage (Commons et al., 1998; Kegan, 1982; Wilber, 2001).

Integral theory intends to develop a comprehensive view of our reality through its division in four 'quadrants', corresponding to the interior and the exterior of the individual and the collective reality, as well as the consideration of different stages of personal, behavioural, cultural and social development (Wilber, 2001). It has led to the development of new approaches in many sectors including integral politics, health, education, business etc. (Wilber, 2001).

These new ways of thinking, based on the recognition of our interconnectedness, echo traditional wisdom (Meadows, 2008) and in particular spiritual traditions emphasizing the need to overcome dualistic thinking, such as Buddhism (e.g. the concept of right view) or Taoism (e.g. the yin-yang philosophy) (Legrand, 2022).

Life

Another influential value is that of life, and the recognition that we as human beings are not separate but part of nature (Descola 2014; De Waal, 2016) – a living system: the Earth and even the Cosmos, – and, as such, we should organize our societies according to and in harmony with natural principles and laws. Those have been the subject of contemplation of virtually all wisdom traditions – in particular indigenous cultures – and are considered to reflect a cosmic sacred order whose names – Tao, Dharma, Maat, etc. – often translate to (right) 'path' or 'way', as well as 'justice'. These principles and laws include reciprocity, mutuality, balance, self-organization, circularity, localism, unity in diversity, etc.

The environmental crisis calls for aligning all our social institutions and systems with ecological principles. Indeed, as illustrated by the development of biomimetics (Benyus, 2002), nature is increasingly a source of inspiration and innovation – not only for the development of new technologies but also for redesigning our economic (e.g. circular economy), agricultural (e.g. agroecology), organizational (Laloux, 2014), or urban systems. This is at heart of new political visions and movements such as China's commitment to become an ecological civilization (Xi Jinping, 2017) and the buen vivir/vivir bien movement in South America.

Happiness

As mentioned above, the development of happiness science (historically linked to positive psychology) is going hand in hand with a growing influence in policy-making (O'Donnel, 2013) and development efforts.[23] Beyond the example of Gross National Happiness in Bhutan, the governments of New Zealand (which adopted in 2019 its first 'well-being budget'), Scotland, Iceland, Wales and Finland for example have also officially committed to building wellbeing economies.[24] This interest is due to the recognition that happiness is a natural end to pursue for societies, and that it can be a key lever for sustainability (see above), as well as being associated with many positive effects on health, social functioning

---

[23]See for example https://worldhappiness.report/, Accessed on 13 October 2022.

[24]https://weall.org/wego, Accessed on 13 October 2022.

and work performance (Government Office for Science, 2008). This can explain why the wellbeing paradigm is becoming influential in many sectors through concepts such as positive education, positive health, positive organizations or positive leadership (David et al., 2013).

Love

Happiness's best friend is love, the most positive emotion: it is the state of mind that most activates areas in the brain associated with positive emotions, contributing greatly to our well-being, health and development (Fredrickson, 2013). Scientific studies show that parental love is the key source of all human development: physiological, emotional, psychological, cognitive and behavioural (Khaleque, 2018). It is the foundation for secure attachment, the basis of our empathic and relational capacities that are indispensable for our happiness and our social functioning (Davis, 2017).

As mentioned above, science is now challenging the story of separation and the vision of selfish human beings to offer a new agenda for societies – cultivating empathy, – around which a new field of scientific research is developing (Seppälä et al., 2017). Educational and meditation-based programmes, such as the Compassion Cultivation Training (CCT), have been proven effective in cultivating compassion, empathy and cooperation (Goldin & Jazaieri, 2017). New social change initiatives rooted in this vision are emerging such as the Charter for compassion, which supports hundreds of initiatives committed to help their local and national communities grow compassionate and better address social and environmental issues.[25]

Peace

The development of peace studies since the creation of the first academic department of peace research in 1959 has led us to increasingly understand peace not only as the absence of overt violent conflicts – 'negative peace' – but rather also as collaborative and supportive relationships between groups or nations – 'positive peace' (Galtung, 2017). It has turned the lens from outward physical violence towards more inward structural violence, defined by Johan Galtung as the systematic ways in which a regime prevents individuals from achieving their full potential, such as through institutionalized racism or sexism.

This has led the United Nations to promote the concept of a culture of peace, which emphasizes ending all forms of oppression – political, social, economic and cultural – and the peaceful settlement of conflicts.[26] A culture of peace is similar to what Eisler and Fry (2019) calls a 'culture of partnership' (as opposed to 'cultures of domination'), which prioritizes feminine values of care, equity, collaboration and non-violence. Examples of cultures of partnership include modern Nordic

[25]https://charterforcompassion.org/, Accessed on 13 October 2022.

[26]Resolutions 52/15, 53/243 and 53/25 of the UN General Assembly.

countries, as well as traditional societies in different parts of the world. These cultures hold a unique potential to support human flourishing and sustainability, in particular through gender, economic and racial equity, as well as by freeing children from violence (Eisler & Fry, 2019; Wilkinson & Pickett, 2010).

Mindfulness

Science has recently evidenced a wide range of potential health, wellbeing, socio-emotional and cognitive benefits associated with the practice of mindfulness – the non-judgemental awareness or presence to what is happening inside and outside of us – meditation (Baer, 2015; Bristow et al., 2020; De Vibe et al., 2012; Keng et al., 2011). In a stressed-out multi-tasking culture, where a multitude of messages are constantly competing for our attention, secular mindfulness is increasingly considered a major resource that is being harnessed in many sectors including business, education, health, justice, etc. This has led the British Mindfulness All-Party Parliamentary Group (MAPPG) to publish a report titled 'Mindful Nation UK' (Mindfulness Initiative, 2015), highlighting why and how public policies in these four sectors could harness the potential of mindfulness, in particular to deal with the mental health crisis and its huge costs for the country.

Mystery

Modern science has the potential to deeply transform our worldviews and consciousness, as more and more it tells the story of an energetic, vibrant and maybe even conscious reality, made of parallel universes. As new instruments will continue to push the limits of scientific observations towards more and more subtle aspects of reality, and our societies grow spiritually, we will become more inclined to look deeply, at the collective level, into the many mysterious aspects of the reality that connects us to the spiritual dimensions of our lives – from new forms of energy to subtle bodies, spirits, or psychic powers. Many puzzling phenomena that could easily be scientifically verified or denied have not received enough attention from the scientific community, often because of a lack of interest or distrust, or simply out of professional disincentives shaped by the current scientific paradigm. A politics of being would make this a priority for our societies and would better take into account the subtle and vibrational nature of reality in its public policies, in particular for example in the field of human health, landscape management (and the associated traditional ecological knowledge) and agriculture.

A Vision of the Good Society

These values arguably constitute some of the highest human ideals and qualities, and reflect a perfection or absolute that is beyond them. Recognizing that their cultivation is the way to the good society is not new, this has been the dominant view in western philosophy since Plato, who emphasized truth, goodness and beauty. Known as the transcendentals, these values have been considered properties of being, and the Catechism of the Catholic Church considered them to 'reflect the infinite perfection of God'.[27] They are also fundamental foundations of the Politics of Being and characterize cultural and spiritual evaluation. This list of values is not exhaustive and also includes freedom, a central aspect of progress or even the nature of human development according to Sen (1999), which was also regarded by German philosopher Hegel (1770–1831) as the essential quality of mind or spirit whose realization history is moving towards.

At a collective level, the focus on 'being' emphasizes the cultural nature of development, as the cultivation of these highest human values. In fact, these are implicitly acknowledged by most countries as our North stars as they constitute the lexical field of most national mottos.

An Agenda for Action

The scientific literature and social change initiatives associated with these values allow us to identify concrete public policies with existing examples of applications that constitute an actionable agenda for the politics of being. This policy agenda represents a 'second-stage' investments in human development, emphasizing its inner dimension, replacing or complementing more traditional policies. These investments can be direct – through education, mental health and childhood well-being policies – or indirect – addressing concrete social needs through institutions that cultivate human qualities, as in the case of restorative justice. We present some of these as examples, without pretending to be exhaustive.

Early Childhood and Family

As mentioned above, childhood wellbeing and parental love is decisive in building not only our capacity to flourish, but also to contribute positively to our communities. Thus, investing in childhood well-being can generate very positive returns for society (Kirby, 2017; Lynch & Vaghul, 2015). These investments can include developmental screening and guaranteed access to quality nutrition, education, health care, social protection and trauma prevention and healing for all children. Parental leaves policies and parenting programmes can also be priorities for public action.

Education

Rather than filling brains with knowledge, educational systems should be redesigned to support 'being', which would better prepare pupils to succeed in the 21st century. Many well-tested educational approaches can support this including personalized educational curricula, topic-based teaching (instead of structuring

[27]In paragraph 41 in part one, section 1, chapter 1. IV. https://www.vatican.va/archive/ENG0015/_INDEX.HTM, Accessed on 14 October 2022.

curriculum by disciplines) positive education and socio-emotional learning (Boniwell, 2013), character and values education (Berkowitz, 2011), cooperative learning (Johnson et al., 2008). The Finish educational systems, often highlighted as a successful example, integrate most of these approaches (Korpela, 2017). In fact, while it is traditionally feared that the focus on individual characters and personal skills could supplant the time needed to learn content, studies show that, on the contrary, these approaches can generate benefits in terms of well-being and character, while improving academic achievement. Improving children's personal capacities just helps them learn better.

Work and Organizations

Evidence is growing that values-driven organizations (Cameron et al., 2004, Sisodia et al., 2007), as well as more decentralized and adaptable organizations based on trust, empowerment and the development of human socio-emotional capacities – sometimes called 'Teal organizations' (Laloux, 2014) or 'liberated companies' (Carney & Getz, 2016) – may be particularly suited to thrive in complex and uncertain environments. Enabling legal frameworks could support and incentivize these companies by recognizing their specific organizational and managerial practices and the objective of ensuring employees' flourishing as part of their specific purpose, which can also include other social and environmental benefits. A universal basic income or a minimum guaranteed income can also enable people to engage in a wider range of self-fulfiling and socially useful activities, transforming our relationships to work for good while decreasing inequalities.[28]

Health

The World Health Organization (1948) definition of health as 'a state of complete mental, social and physical well-being, not merely the absence of disease or infirmity' should inform the redesign of our healthcare systems and public health policies. A new paradigm for health is needed from one based on sickness, whose increasing costs for an ageing population appears unsustainable (World Economic Forum, 2019), to one centred on prevention and well-being, in which individuals are more responsible for taking care of themselves.

Mental health is a major determinant of people's well-being (Layard et al., 2013) and is closely associated with the definition of human flourishing (Keyes, 2005). It also significantly influences our physical health (Vitteta et al., 2005). Part of this influence is indirect through our lifestyles (physical activity, food, sleep, drug, alcohol, tobacco consumption, stress, etc.), the main cause of chronic diseases, which now represent 75% of global healthcare expenses (World Economic Forum, 2019). Despite the fact that mental health is a major public health

---

[28]https://basicincome.org/basic-income/and https://basicincome.stanford.edu/, Accessed on 15 October 2022.

problem (Vigo et al., 2016) with huge costs for societies (OECD, 2012) and that effective treatments exist (Layard et al., 2013), access to treatments is very low: in rich countries, less than a third of people who suffer from mental illness receive treatment and care (Layard et al., 2013). Mental health should be made a public health priority as part of a new integrative medicine paradigm that considers all the dimensions (physical, emotional, mental, spiritual) and the determinants (social, environmental) of health, and integrates conventional medicine with complementary therapies.[29]

Food and Agriculture

A study has shown that a 'planetary health diet' could support both human and planetary health, and identified public policies to support its adoption (EAT-Lancet Commission study 2019). The way we eat is fundamental not only for our physical health but also for our mental health (Jacka et al., 2013), which in turn can affect our food behaviours (Torres & Nowson, 2007). Thus, the promotion of a 'planetary health diet' should go along with access to mindfulness-based interventions that have been proven effective in promoting healthy eating and treating eating disorders (Beshara et al., 2013).

The ongoing paradigmatic change in agriculture goes from industrial agriculture and the dysfunctionalities of a growth-based model relying on external inputs to small-scale, multifunctional agro-ecological farming systems working with nature and embodying some of the highest human values presented in section 2. Public policies to support the transition to agroecology have been identified and include shifting public support and procurement, as well as research and education (International Panel of Experts on Sustainable Food Systems, 2016).

Nature

The required paradigm shift in the way we consider and relate to our planet - as a sacred living entity, of which we are part – is best embodied at the policy level by recognizing the rights of nature, which is already occurring in many countries (Chapron et al., 2019). Recognizing the rights of nature questions our unlimited right to exploit the Earth and helps us seek a balance between the rights of people, corporations and nature. It invites our legal systems to probe: what do we really need as human beings to thrive? The acknowledgement of nature as a subject of rights could go along with the legal recognition of severe environmental destruction as a crime, as well as ensuring the custody of sacred sites by indigenous people.

---

[29]https://integrat.ivemedicine.arizona.edu/about/definition.html, Accessed on 15 October 2022.

Justice

As mentioned above, the politics of being includes the promotion of restorative justice as an alternative to the current domination of retributive justice. Restorative justice is based on a non-adversarial process involving all stakeholders through dialogue, focused on healing and reintegration. While the retributive justice paradigm is at the root of the current criminal justice system's crisis in many countries (Penal Reform International, 2016), restorative justice displays very high satisfaction rates from victims and offenders, offers a potential to reduce the costs of doing justice and increase the response to crime efficiency and performs at least no worst and probably better than conventional approaches in terms of reoffending (UNODC 2006; Walgrave, 2011). Ultimately restorative justice's effectiveness depends on the quality of these programmes, which heavily rely on human qualities, whose advancement is at the core of the politics of being.

Economy

Our economic systems need to be redesigned to ensure the satisfaction of everyone's basic material needs and support the expression of our full potential – including spiritual, artistic, or cultural content and experiences, as well as care works – within ecological boundaries rather than the interest of a few (Raworth, 2017). All the current economic institutions need to evolve, including:

- Economic globalization to better regulate and limit international trade and capital flows, so as to decrease the international economic competition, which hinders the rise of social and environmental standards, and increase economic resilience.
- Corporate governance to give a competitive edge to organizations supporting the public good, to foster small, cooperative and public companies (Korten, 2016) and to give more voting rights within companies to employees and external stakeholders.
- Intellectual Property Rights to adjust to the new reality of the digital economy and foster an 'open revolution' in which 'all digital information is open, free for everyone to use, build on and share; and where innovators and creators are recognized and rewarded', generating important gains for societies (Pollock, 2018, p. 5).
- Monetary systems to support the public emission of money (Benes & Kumhof, 2012), the adoption of a global currency (United Nations, 2009) and the promotion of local currencies.

Investments into a global green new deal to foster the climate and ecological transition (United Nations Environment Programme, 2019), as well as reducing inequalities – and the important associated social and health problems (Wilkinson & Pickett, 2010), including with a guaranteed minimum income are other important priorities.

Governance

Liberal democracy is increasingly questioned for its current ineffectiveness, particularly its inability to take the long-term and common good into account. This discontent has more to do with the way it does not work in practice, rather than the central principle of self-governance behind it (Inglehart, 2018). Democracy needs to evolve beyond its current form of 'adversary democracy' (Mansbridge, 1980), in which political parties compete for power, spurring polarization and paralysis.

This implies a deepening of democracy through greater citizens participation – through a more direct, deliberative and digital democracy, integrated to representative democracy – a better balance between competence and popular control, as well as a better regulation of social media and the influence of money over politics (Berggruen Institute, 2020). This kind of 'intelligent governance for the XXIst century' (Berggruen & Gardels, 2013) shows a striking parallel with the governance system of the Baha'i faith that have been considered since its origin more than a century ago 'an embryonic model to be adopted voluntarily when the world sees its advantages, acknowledging that it is not simply institutions and procedures, but that it depends on the requisite values, norms and commitments' (Dahl, 2017). In fact, the development of civic virtues and key (inter) being skills, including our capacity to listen, to keep an open mind and discern the truth, to understand each other and solve conflicts in a respectful and peaceful manner, is instrumental to the functioning of such deeper and wiser form of democracy and should be actively promoted through public policies.

Ultimately, the politics of being will have to be enacted in our political Institutions and, in each country, a special council – the 'wisdom council' or 'being council' – would be established to ensure that national efforts are serving this vision and that societies and cultures do evolve towards 'being more'.

Conclusion

Box 3.1 synthesizes 10 core messages associated with the Politics of Being. This concept applies, not only at the individual but at all levels. 'Being more' means for all nations to cultivate the universal values highlighted above, which can provide the ground for world unification and a 'civilization of the universal', in which all nations can contribute their specific 'genius'. Indeed, 'being more' means also for nations to define and pursue its own version of the good life (and not a single common metrics such as Gross Domestic Product) and of the politics of being, which calls for a deep reconnection with themselves. As 'sociocultural change is path dependent and cultural heritages are remarkably enduring' (Inglehart, 2018, p. 11), to evolve, nations need to reexamine their own traditional wisdom – most often rooted in the story of interbeing – and history (often disrupted by colonization). Our collective inner lives should be brought at the centre of public debate, through regular psychological assessment and efforts to heal collective traumas, as a gateway to 'being'.

Box 3.1. Politics of Being: 10 Core Messages.

(1) *We need a collective shift of consciousness, a cultural evolution of a spiritual nature, to address our current challenges.* It is already ongoing, and we are currently facing an evolutive crisis, which requires individuals and societies to look inward and transform.

(2) *As a wisdom-based, science-informed approach, a politics of being can support this evolution.* Its main goal is to support the fulfilment of all beings, that is to say the realization of our truest and highest being. 'Being' is a wiser and more adequate development objective than 'having'; it applies to the whole Earth community.

(3) *Cultivating our fundamental 'interbeing' or relational nature is instrumental to allow us to live in harmony with one another and the Earth community.* Our spiritual nature makes us interconnected at the level of being with everything that is. Only by recognizing their interconnectedness and sustaining the whole can each part thrive.

(4) *Societies progress as they increasingly honour the highest values, qualities and ideals, such as freedom, goodness, beauty, truth, understanding, life, happiness, love, peace, etc.* These are spiritual qualities in the sense that they reflect an awakened human being or divine perfection. Science and practical initiatives shaped around these universal values can help us design a politics of being. Cultural development relates fundamentally to an evolution of our values, which shape our worldviews and institutions.

(5) *The focus on being, the highest values, wisdom and science, provides a simple conceptual framework for a politics of being, which can integrate all relevant claims and initiatives.* As such, it can help unify this vision and strengthen this movement.

(6) *Our institutions should help cultivate human virtues.* They should acknowledge and facilitate the expression of our potential for goodness, cooperation and intrinsic motivation.

(7) *Concrete and actionable policy recommendations supporting this agenda already exist in many sectors.* A politics of being can bring them together and scale them up, articulating them in a coherent and meaningful narrative.

(8) *Spiritual teachings and wisdom traditions, through dialogue among them and with science, have much to bring to inspire, help design and implement a politics of being.* They are our most valuable common heritage, able to offer a profound understanding of human nature, as well as practical knowledge and tools for inner, and ultimately social, development.

(9) *Each nation needs to reconnect to its own soul and wisdom to develop its version of a politics of being* that can support its development and help

(*Continued*)

(*Continued*)

it bring its unique contribution to the world. Unity in diversity is the key to harmonious coexistence of nations in a globalized world.

(10) *Healing trauma is, for individuals and societies, the gateway to being.* It is fundamental in order for new ways of being and living together to be possible, and for the whole Earth community to flourish.

References

Ahuvia, A., & Izberk-Bilgin, E. (2013). Well-being in consumer societies. In S. David, I. Boniwell, & A. C. Ayers (Eds.), *The Oxford handbook of happiness* (pp. 482–498). Oxford University Press.

Algan, Y., Beasley, E., Cohen, D., & Foucault, M. (2019). *Les Origines du Populisme*. Le Seuil.

Andersen, L. R., & Björkman, T. (2017). *The Nordic Secret: A European story of beauty and freedom*. Fri Tanke.

Arias, E., Tejada-Vera, B., Kochanek, K. D., & Ahmad, F. B. (2022). *Provisional life expectancy estimates for 2021*. Vital Statistics Rapid Release; no 23. National Center for Health Statistics.

Baer, R. (2015). Ethics, values, virtues, and character strengths in mindfulness- based interventions: A psychological science perspective. *Mindfulness*, *6*(4), 956–969.

Benes, J., & Kumhof, M. (2012). *The Chicago plan revisited*. International Monetary Fund Working Paper.

Benyus, J. (2002). *Biomimicry: Innovation inspired by nature*. Harper Perennial.

Berggruen Institute. (2020, March 9). *Renewing democracy in the digital age*. Report on the future of democracy.

Berggruen, N., & Gardels, N. (2013). *Intelligent governance for the 21st century: A middle way between west and east*. Polity Press.

Berkowitz, M. (2011). What works in value education. *International Journal of Educational Research*, *50*(3), 153–158.

Beshara, M., Hutchinson, A. D., & Wilson, C. (2013). Does mindfulness matter? Everyday mindfulness, mindful eating and self-reported serving size of energy dense foods among a sample of South Australian adults. *Appetite*, *67*, 25–29.

Boniwell, I. (2013). Introduction to positive education. In S. David, I. Boniwell, & A. C. Ayres (Eds.), *The Oxford handbook of happiness* (pp. 535–539). Oxford University Press.

Bristow, J., Bell, R., & Nixon, D. (2020). *Mindfulness: Developing agency in urgent times*. The Mindfulness Initiative.

Brown, L. S., Warren, K., & Kasser, T. (2005). Are psychological and ecological wellbeing compatible? The role of values, mindfulness, and lifestyle. *Social Indicators Research*, *74*, 349–368.

Cameron, K. S., Bright, D., & Caza, A. (2004). Exploring the relationships between organizational virtuousness and performance. *American Behavioral Scientist*, *47*(6), 766–790.

Carney, B. M., & Getz, I. (2016). *Freedom, Inc: How corporate liberation unleashes employee potential and business performance* (2nd ed.). Somme Valley House.
Center for Disease Control and Prevention. (2012). *Mental health and chronic diseases*. Issue Brief No. 2. 6p.
Chapron, G., Epstein, Y., & López-Bao, J. V. (2019). A rights revolution for nature. *Science, 363*(6434), 1392–1393.
Commons, M. L., Trudeau, E. J., Stein, S. A., Richards, F. A., & Krause, S. R. (1998). Hierarchical complexity of tasks shows the existence of developmental stages. *Developmental Review, 18*(3), 237–278.
Conceição, P. (2020). *The human development report: The next frontier; human development and the Anthropocene*. United Nations Development Programme.
Crompton, T., Sanderson, R., Prentice, M., Weinstein, N., Smith, O., & Kasser, T. (2016). *Perceptions matter: The common cause UK values survey*. Common Cause Foundation.
Dahl, A. (2017). *Governance from a Bahá'í perspective*. Unpublished.
David, S., Boniwell, I., & Ayers, A. C. (Eds.). (2013). *The Oxford handbook of happiness*. Oxford University Press.
Davis, M. H. (2017). Empathy, compassion and social relationships. In E. M. Seppälä, E. Simon-Thomas, S. L. Brown, M. C. Worline, C. Daryl Cameron, & J. R. Doty (Eds.), *The Oxford handbook of compassion science* (pp. 299–315). Oxford University Press.
De Vibe, M., Bjørndall, A., Tipton, E., Hammerstrøm, K., & Kowalski, K. (2012). Mindfulness-based stress reduction (MBSR) for improving health, quality of life and social functioning in adults. *Campbell Systematic Reviews, 2012*(3).
De Waal, F. (2016). *Are we smart enough to know how smart animals are?* W. W. Norton & Company.
Demir, M. (2013). Introduction to relationships and happiness. In S. David, I. Boniwell, & A. C. Ayer (Eds.), *The Oxford handbook of happiness* (pp. 817–820). Oxford University Press.
Descola, P. (2014). *Beyond nature and culture*. University of Chicago Press.
Eisler, R., & Fry, D. P. (2019). *Nurturing our humanity: How domination and partnership shape our brains, lives, and future*. Oxford University Press.
Fredrickson, B. L. (2013). *Love 2.0: Finding happiness and health in moments of connection*. Plume.
Galtung, J. (2017, July 13). Peace: A peace practitioner's guide. *Ideas for Peace*.
Goldin, P., & Jazaieri, H. (2017). The Compassion Cultivation Training (CCT) Program. In E. M. Seppälä, E. Simon-Thomas, S. L. Brown, M. C. Worline, C. Daryl Cameron, & J. R. Doty (Eds.), *The Oxford handbook of compassion science* (pp. 237–245). Oxford University Press.
Government Office for Science. (2008). *Foresight mental capital and wellbeing project*. Final Project Report. The Government Office for Science.
Gudynas, E., & Acosta, A. (2011). La Renovación de la Crítica al Desarrollo y el Buen Vivir Como Alternativa. *Utopía y Praxis Latinoamericana, 16*(53), 71–83.
Harwood Group. (1995). *Yearning for balance views of Americans on consumption, materialism, and the environment*. Merck Family Fund.
Helliwell, J., Huang, H., & Wang, S. (2017). Social foundations of world happiness. In J. Helliwell, R. Layard, & J. Sachs (Eds.), *World Happiness Report 2017* (pp. 8–47). Sustainable Development Solutions Network.

Helliwell, J., Huang, H., & Wang, S. (2019). Changing world happiness. In J. Helliwell, R. Layard, & J. Sachs (Eds.), *World Happiness Report 2019* (pp. 11–46). Sustainable Development Solutions Network.

His Holiness the Dalai Lama. (2013). *Beyond religion: Ethics for a whole world*. Rider.

Holy Father Francis. (2015). *Laudato Si': Encyclical letter of the Holy Father on care for our common home*.

Huta, V. (2013). Eudaimonia. In S. David, I. Boniwell, & A. C. Ayer (Eds.), *The Oxford handbook of happiness* (pp. 201–213). Oxford University Press.

Huta, V. (2016). Eudaimonia versus Hedonia: What's the difference? And is it real? In *International Journal of Special Issue Existential Psychology & Psychotherapy, Proceedings of the 2016 Meaning Conference*. Accessed on August 11, 2020.

Inglehart, R. F. (2018). *Cultural evolution: People's motivations are changing, and reshaping the world*. Cambridge University Press.

International Panel of Experts on Sustainable Food Systems. (2016). From uniformity to diversity. A paradigm shift from industrial agriculture to diversified agroecological systems. Executive summary.

IPCC. (2022a). *Climate Change 2022: Impacts, adaptation, and vulnerability*. Contribution of Working Group II to the Sixth Assessment Report of the Intergovernmental Panel on Climate Change. Cambridge University Press.

IPCC. (2022b). *Climate Change 2022: Mitigation of climate change*. Contribution of Working Group III to the Sixth Assessment Report of the Intergovernmental Panel on Climate Change. Cambridge University Press.

Jacka, F. N., Ystrom, E., Brantsaeter, A. L., Karevold, E., Roth, C., Haugen, M., Meltzer, H. M., Schjolberg, S., & Berk, M. (2013). Maternal and early postnatal nutrition and mental health of offspring by age 5 years: A prospective cohort study. *Journal of the American Academy of Child and Adolescent Psychiatry*, *52*(10), 1038–1047.

Jacob Soetendorp Institute for Human Values. (2012). *Towards RIO + 20 and beyond—A turning point in Earth history*. Interreligious statement to the Rio+20 Conference.

Johnson, D. W., Johnson, R. T., & Johnson Holubec, E. (2008). *Cooperation in the classroom* (7th ed.). Interaction Book Company.

Kasser, T. (2002). *The high price of materialism*. MIT Press.

Kasser, T., Ryan, R. M., Melvin, Z., & Sameroff, A. J. (1995). The relations of maternal and social environments to late adolescents' materialistic and prosocial values. *Developmental Psychology*, *31*(6), 907–914.

Kegan, R. (1982). *The evolving self: Problem and process in human development*. Harvard University Press.

Keng, S.-L., Smoski, M. J., & Robins, C. J. (2011). Effects of mindfulness on psychological health: A review of empirical studies. *Clinical Psychology Review*, *31*(6), 1041–1056.

Keniger, L., Gaston, K. J., Irvine, K. N., & Fuller, R. A. (2013). What are the benefits of interacting with nature? *International Journal of Environmental Research and Public Health*, *10*(3), 913–935.

Keyes, C. L. M. (2005). Mental illness and/or mental health? Investigating axioms of the complete state model of health. *Journal of Consulting and Clinical Psychology*, *73*(3), 539–548.

Keyes, C. L. M. (2007). Promoting and protecting mental health as flourishing. A complementary strategy for improving national mental health. *American Psychologist, 62*(2), 95–108.

Khaleque, A. (2018). Worldwide implications of parental love and lack of love on children's and adults' psychological adjustment and maladjustment: Meta-analytic evidence. *Journal of Mental Disorders and Treatment, 3*(2), 1–2.

Kirby, J. N. (2017). Compassion-focused parenting. In E. M. Seppälä, E. Simon-Thomas, S. L. Brown, M. C. Worline, C. Daryl Cameron, & J. R. Doty (Eds.), *The Oxford handbook of compassion science* (pp. 91–105). Oxford University Press.

Korpela, S. (2017). *Education in Finland: Key to the nation's success.* Ministry for Foreign Affairs.

Korten, D. (2016). *The new economy: A living earth system model.* A report for the Next System Project.

Laloux, F. (2014). *Reinventing organizations: A guide to creating organizations inspired by the next stage of human consciousness.* Nelson Parker.

Layard, R., Chisholm, D., Patel, V., & Saxena, S. (2013). Mental illness and unhappiness. In J. Helliwell, R. Layard, & J. Sachs (Eds.), *World Happiness Report* (pp. 38–53). Sustainable Development Solutions Network.

Legrand, T. (2022). *Politics of being: Wisdom and science for a new development paradigm.* Ocean of Wisdom Press.

Leichenko, R., & O'Brien, K. (2020). *Climate and society: Transforming the future.* John Wiley & Sons.

Lynch, R., & Vaghul, K. (2015). *The benefits and costs of investing in early childhood education.* Washington Center for Equitable Growth.

Mansbridge, J. J. (1980). *Beyond adversary democracy.* The University of Chicago Press.

Marcus, M., Yasamy, M. T., van Ommeren, M., Chisholm, D., & Saxena, S. (2012). *Depression: A global public health concern.* WHO Department of Mental Health and Substance Abuse.

Maslow, A. H. (1987). *Motivation and personality* (3rd ed.). Pearson Education.

Meadows, D. H. (1999). *Leverage points: Places to intervene in a system.* The Sustainability Institute.

Meadows, D. H. (2008). *Thinking in systems: A primer.* Chelsea Green Publishing.

Miller, D. T. (1999). The norm of self-interest. *American Psychologist, 54*(12), 1053–1060.

Mindfulness Initiative. (2015). *Mindful Nation UK.* Report by the Mindfulness All-Party Parliamentary Group (MAPPG).

Morin, E. (2008). *On complexity.* Hampton Press.

NDP Steering Committee and Secretariat. (2013). *Happiness: Towards a new development paradigm* (p. 78). Report of the Kingdom of Bhutan.

Nisbet, E. K., Zelenski, J. M., & Murphy, S. A. (2009). The nature relatedness scale: Linking individuals' connection with nature to environmental concern and behavior. *Environment and Behavior, 41*(5), 715–740.

North, D. (1990). *Institutions, institutional change and economic performance.* Cambridge University Press.

O'Donnel, G. (2013). Using wellbeing as a guide to policy. In J. Helliwell, R. Layard, & J. Sachs (Eds.), *World Happiness Report* (pp. 96–111). Sustainable Development Solutions Network.

OECD. (2012). *Sick on the job? Myths and realities about mental health and work*. Mental Health and Work Series. OECD Publishing.
Ostrom, E. (2009, December 8). Beyond markets and states: Polycentric governance of complex economic systems. *Nobel Prize Lecture*. https://www.nobelprize.org/uploads/2018/06/ostrom_lecture.pdf
O'Toole, L., & Kropf, D. (2012). *Changing paradigms, sharing our hearts, beginning a dialogue*. Learning for Well-being Foundation. Universal Education Foundation.
Penal Reform International. (2016). *Why criminal justice reform is essential to the UN Agenda for Sustainable Development*.
Peterson, C., Park, N., & Seligman, M. P. (2005). Orientations to happiness and life satisfaction: The full life versus the empty life. *Journal of Happiness Studies*, *6*, 25–41.
Pollock, R. (2018). *The Open Revolution. Rewriting the rules of the information age* (N.p). A/E/T Press.
Rahn, W. M., & Transue, J. E. (1998). Social trust and value change: The decline of social capital in American youth, 1976–1995. *Political Psychology*, *19*(3), 545–565.
Raworth, K. (2017). *Doughnut economics: Seven ways to think like a 21st-century economist*. Chelsea Green Publishing.
Sachs, J. (2012). *The price of civilization*. Vintage.
Sachs, J. (2015). Investing in social capital. In J. Helliwell, R. Layard, & J. Sachs (Eds.), *World Happiness Report 2015* (pp. 152–166).
Schafer, P. (2022). *The world as culture*. Rock's Mills Press.
Scharmer, C. O. (2016). *Theory U: Leading from the future as it emerges*. Berrett-Koehler.
Schmuck, P., Kasser, T., & Richard, M. R., (2000). Intrinsic and extrinsic goals. *Social Indicators Research*, *50*(2), 225–241.
Sen, A. (1999). *Development as freedom*. Oxford University Press.
Seppälä, E. M., Simon-Thomas, E., Brown, S. L., Worline, M. C., Cameron, C. D., & Doty, J. R. (Eds.). (2017). *The Oxford handbook of compassion science*. Oxford University Press.
Sisodia, R., Sheth, J. N., & Wolfe, D. B. (2007). *Firms of endearment: How world-class companies profit from passion and purpose*. Financial Times/Prentice Hall.
Solon, P. (2018). *Vivir Bien: Old Cosmovisions and new paradigms*. Great Transition Initiative.
Tay, L., & Diener, E. (2011). Needs and subjective well-being around the world. *Journal of Personality and Social Psychology*, *101*(2), 354–356.
Teasdale, W. (1999). *The mystic heart: Discovering a universal spirituality in the world's religions*. New World Library.
Thompson, S., Marks, N., & Jackson, T. (2013). Well-being and sustainable development. In S. David, I. Boniwell, & A. C. Ayer (Eds.), *The Oxford handbook of happiness* (pp. 498–516). Oxford University Press.
Torres, S. J., & Nowson, C. A. (2007). Relationship between stress, eating behavior, and obesity. *Nutrition*, *23*(11–12), 887–894.
UNDP. (1990). *Human Development Report 1990: Concept and measurement of human development*.
UNDP. (2006). *Human Development Report*. Oxford University Press.

United Nations. (2009). *Report of the Commission of Experts of the President of the United Nations General Assembly on Reforms of the International Monetary and Financial System.*

United Nations Environment Programme. (2019). *Emissions Gap Report 2019.* UNEP.

Vásquez-Fernández, A. M., & Ahenakew pii tai poo taa, C. (2020). Resurgence of relationality: Reflections on decolonizing and indigenizing 'sustainable development'. *Current Opinion in Environmental Sustainability, 43*, 65–70.

Vella-Brodrick, Dianne, A., Park, N., & Peterson, C. (2009). Three ways to be happy: Pleasure, engagement, and meaning—Findings from Australian and US samples. *Social Indicators Research, 90*, 165–179.

Vigo, D., Thornicroft, G., & Atun, R. (2016). Estimating the true global burden of mental illness. *Lancet Psychiatry, 3*(2), 171–178. https://doi.org/10.1016/S2215-0366(15)00505-2

Vitteta, L., Anton, B., Cortizo, F., & Sali, A. (2005). Mind-body medicine: Stress and its impact on overall health and longevity. *Annals of the New York Academy of Sciences, 1057*, 492–505.

Waldinger, R. (2016). What makes a good life? Lessons from the longest study on happiness. Video. https://www.youtube.com/watch?v=8KkKuTCFvzI. Accessed on July 29, 2020.

Walgrave, L. (2011). Investigating the potentials of restorative justice practice. *Washington University Journal of Law & Policy, 36*(1), 91–139.

Walsh, Z., Böhme, J., & Wamsler, C. (2021). Towards a relational paradigm in sustainability research, practice, and education. *Ambio, 50*, 74–84.

Wamsler, C., Osberg, G., Osika, W., Hendersson, H., & Mundaca, L. (2021). Linking internal and external transformation for sustainability and climate action: Towards a new research and policy agenda. *Global Environmental Change, 71*, 102373.

Wilber, K. (2001). *A theory of everything. An integral vision for business, politics, science and spirituality.* Shambhala Publications.

Wilkinson, R. G., & Pickett, K. (2010). *The spirit level—Why equality is better for everyone.* Penguin Books.

World Commission on Environment and Development. (1987). *Our common future.* Oxford University Press.

World Economic Forum. (2019). *Health and healthcare in the fourth industrial revolution.*

World Health Organization. (1948). *Constitution of the world health organization.*

Xi, J. (2017). *Report at 19th CPC National Congress on October 18.* http://www.chinadaily.com.cn/china/19thcpcnationalcongress/2017-11/04/content_34115212.htm. Accessed on October 13, 2022.

Ye, D., Ng, Y.-K., & Lian, Y. (2015). Culture and happiness. *Social Indicators Research, 123*(2), 519–547.

Chapter 4

Buddhist and Taoist Systems Thinking: Perennial Wisdom Applications and Implications to Sustainable Transformation

Josep M. Coll

Abstract

The world needs more Eastern knowledge and, ergo, more consciousness. Humanity will unlikely experience a quantum leap in consciousness if we keep ignoring Eastern and other sources of perennial wisdom in the design and development of our socioeconomic and ecological systems. This chapter aims to bridge the consciousness gap by exploring the meaning and application of Buddhist and Taoist systems thinking to regenerative systemic leadership, design, development and sustainable transformation.

Keywords: Reductionist thinking; east-west knowledge gap; Taoist approach; Buddhist approach; systems leadership

> Addressing the core challenges of our time means to create pathways for transformation. Creating these pathways means to deepen our capacity for systems thinking. And to do that we can return to some of the earliest sources of holistic systems thinking: Taoism and Buddhism. In his fascinating book, Josep M. Coll takes us on a journey from the frontline of transformation for sustainability to the origins of Buddhist and Taoist thought. Highly recommended!
>
> Otto Scharmer, Senior Lecturer, MIT; Founding Chair, Presencing Institute; author, Theory U

Applied Spirituality and Sustainable Development Policy, 71–88

Published under exclusive licence by Emerald Publishing Limited
doi:10.1108/978-1-83753-380-020231004

Introduction: The Path to Consciousness: Bridging the East-West Knowledge Gap

Our current anthropogenic world has been built from the social design of political, economic and educational structures that have led to a socioeconomic system that exploits natural and human resources at the exchange of a financial profit. The knowledge that has provided the input for the design of such structures has been mainly developed from a Western Eurocentric perspective. The foundations of what is known as the modern world were settled in Europe during the scientific revolution that took place in the 16th and 17th centuries. This revolution was characterized by the epistemological and ontological emergence of science as the primary way of knowing, and reason as the primary source of authority and legitimacy.

This paradigm led to extraordinary advancements in the fields of astronomy, physics, chemistry, mathematics, biology and medicine, for instance. Its ideological foundations resulted into an intellectual and philosophical movement called the Enlightenment. This movement spread the benefits of the scientific method and its underlying rationality, empiricism, utility, and reductionism not only in Europe but also at global level.

Reductionist thinking, also known as linear thinking, played a critical role in the development of science as a philosophy and method. The philosophy of science underpinning its method was based on two key assumptions. The first assumption is that we can best explain a phenomenon by breaking it down into its individual parts. This explains the compartmentalization of knowledge into fields and subfields of specialization. It is the sum of its parts that explain the behaviour of any system. The second assumption is that nature is a machine, which shaped a conventional worldview where the Earth serves as a material resource with no intrinsic value, ready to be exploited for satisfying humanity's self-interested utilitarian view of needs.

In this context emerged, also in Europe, the Industrial Revolution in the 18th and 19th centuries. As an outcome of the scientific revolution, Adam Smith and other classical economists built the intellectual foundations of a socioeconomic system ruled by the invisible hand or the unforeseen forces that explain the workings of free market economics. Once a moral philosopher, Smith made the case for a society governed by the individual self-interest of a *homo economicus* that operates in the best final interest of society incentivized by his freedom to produce and consume what is 'socially' necessary in a free market economy.

More than two centuries later, the general proposition that 'self-interest automatically leads to society's wellbeing' has proved instrumentally flawed for two main reasons. The first reason is that self-interest ignores the fundamental universal principle of interdependence. That means that self-interest not always behaves on the best interest of others. For example, someone buying and playing drums at night in an apartment every day may increase this person's utility, but at the expense of the neighbours' wellbeing. Or when the use of intensive agriculture for producing mass food by a corporation is done at the expense of biodiversity loss and soil erosion.

The second reason is that individual self-interest as it is expressed in the market economy cannot capture the multiplicity and diversity of perspectives embedded in social communities of people dealing with social matters of public domain such as justice, equality, environmental degradation or human rights, to name a few. The self-centrism of free market economics leads to have winners and losers of an economic system that lost its foundational social purpose. The negative effects or externalities of free market economics, such as environmental degradation and growing inequalities, are often called market failures. What the invisible hand of the market economy cannot fix, the visible hand of the State then should operate to make it work. The reality though is that the state and the political system in general play a servant role to the economy, and not the other way around. The political system also fails to engage with the multiplicity of social and ecological perspectives that are needed in order to support society's wellbeing.

The East-West Knowledge Gap

Reductionist thinking underpinned the Industrial Revolution and the subsequent economic development that came with it. A major key factor for the massive economic development and progress that was experienced especially since the 20th century and most concretely after the Second World War – the period called the Great Acceleration – was the rise of the global corporation. Corporations are a product of free market economics and the spread of a global economic system characterized by the free flow of financial capital, labour and technology, the three major drivers of growth. An extractive and highly productive industrial economic system led to unprecedented levels of economic growth and social progress at a global scale, as well as to rapid levels of environmental deterioration and growth of inequalities.

Modern corporations focused on maximizing the financial profit for its shareholders, making use of a mechanistic management approach grounded on reductionist thinking. They operated under the 'organization-as-a-machine' metaphor, an approach that was aimed at improving efficiency and productivity in the workplace through a hierarchical structure of power in the organization, specialization of labour and financial incentives to the fulfillment of objectives. This approach, known as scientific management after United States engineer Frederick Taylor's book was published in 1901, set the foundations for classical management theory.

North American universities and business schools became the birthplace of contemporary business and management studies, research and training. Most business and organizational theories, management concepts and leadership paradigms depart from a Western perspective. And most popular management scholars also depart from a Western perspective. This perspective led to shape a commonly accepted worldview that conceives the organization as a machine that thinks linearly about the economic and social roles that corporations play in the communities and ecosystems they operate in, and in the World in general.

The Western-based theories of business, management and economic development were widely adopted at a global scale. Asian managers were either educated in prestigious business schools and universities in the US and Europe or in Asian business schools that were teaching the same Western-based business and management theories and practices taught in the West. Whether in the West or in the East, the single-minded purpose of a corporation was to grow its financial profit through increased efficiency and productivity, even at the cost of environmental degradation and social exploitation.

The Western-based reductionist thinking that has informed the design and development of the current political and socioeconomic system has systematically ignored Eastern and indigenous knowledge that is grounded on a systems view of life that sees nature as a living organism. This systemic failure is what I call the East-West knowledge gap. My proposition is that if we want to design and implement sustainable and regenerative policies we need to raise our level of consciousness, and for doing that, we need to learn from earlier sources of nature-based systems thinking such as Taoism and Buddhism.

The Earliest Systems Thinkers

Taoism is probably the first indigenous philosophy that explicitly articulated – through the recorded development of universal systems theories and principles in the *I Ching* such as the Yin-Yang and the Five Elements – a systems view of life, human beings and the universe grounded on the human-nature interdependence. Alan Watts and Fritjof Capra, renowned authors in bridging East and West, acknowledge the natural philosophy of Taoism. Watts expresses this idea ontologically: 'you are the big bang. You are the original force of the universe manifesting as whoever you are in the moment' (Watts, 2019). From an epistemological point of view, Capra describes Taoism as a natural way or a natural process that connects with 'an ultimate reality which underlies and unifies the multiple things and events we observe' (Capra, 1975).

Taoist researchers developed a pioneering approach to study nature and humans within nature, as humans are nature. This approach was an empirical method based on direct observation, involving the experimental analysis and synthesis of natural dynamics – context, patterns, networks and relationships – observed in the Universe, the Planet and the human being. It is fascinating that this systems approach to the study of life was articulated through the School of Naturalists – also known as the School of Yin and Yang – created by Zou Yan in the 3rd and 4th centuries BC.

Buddhism, like Taoism, is essentially a way of liberation from human suffering. In the context of the Anthropocene, both perennial philosophies offer insights on how we can address the major planetary challenges of our time that are causing environmental and socioeconomic turmoil in our ecosystems and human life. Buddhism developed a complementary methodology to the study of human nature, based on the direct observation of the internal nature of the individual. This method inquires and explores the nature of the human mind from direct experience. The Buddhist assumption is that we are all of divine nature as we are nature, and like Taoists, that we all have the potential to experience enlightenment and union with nature, that direct experience of oneness. Buddhist teachings were articulated through the Dharma Wheel around the 5th century BC – also known as the Noble Eightfold Path–, a systemic approach to practice and raise our level of consciousness.

Complexity Awareness and the Consciousness Path in Our Times

Taoism – through the direct external observation of humans and nature – and Buddhism – through the direct internal exploration of the human mind – form an inner-outer symbiosis that integrate the wisdom that humans need to learn in order to live in harmony. This Eastern-based process of knowing gained a huge interest in the West during the 20th century. In fact, the encounter between Western thinking and ancient Eastern wisdom is often described as one of the more fruitful features of the 20th century (Macy, 1991; Zhu, 2000).

The fascination for Zen, the resulting outcome of this Taoism and Buddhism symbiosis, illustrates how Eastern perennial wisdom is still, in the 21st century, influencing leadership development worldwide. The teaching and practice of mindfulness and meditation, for example, has grown exponentially since the 2000s. Buddhism and Taoism have inspired global leaders in different fields, such as business, politics and culture. This is the case of Jack Ma, founder of Alibaba, Arianna Huffington, founder of The Huffington Post, Steve Jobs, founder of Apple, Christiana Figueres, executive secretary of the United Nations Framework Convention on Climate Change from 2010 to 2016, and singer and songwriters Tina Turner and Leonard Cohen, among many others.

The road less explored, which is the one I'm advocating in this chapter, is the learning and practice of Buddhism and Taoism not only for personal self-development but also for conscious systems leadership. That is to say that the ancient teachings of Buddhism and Taoism, in the context of the Anthropocene, can really help us in finding the pathways needed for changing and transforming the systems we live in. These are the economic, social and ecological systems which structures and dynamics are already constraining the capacity we have, as humanity, to live an inclusive and regenerative life of thriving.

It is in this light that Buddhist and Taoist systems thinking explicitly refer to the application of universal principles and systems methods in finding and designing pathways for systems transformation. This process of transformation is grounded on two fundamental concepts. The first one is the concept of inter-being, coined by Zen master Thich Nhat Hanh. The realization that we are all empty of a separate self means that we are related to everything else and, therefore, we are full of everything. This realization brings two important implications. One, it allows us to recognize and become aware of the complexity of our own being in relation to the other beings. The nature of these relationships explains the behaviour of our systems. Two, it opens doors of infinite possibilities in imagining and creating pathways of transformation.

The second concept that grounds Buddhist and Taoist systems thinking is oneness. The experience of oneness is the epitome of spirituality that helps raise our level of consciousness. It is the direct non-intellectual experience that we humans are nature as one. It is when we feel we are everything, that there is no boundary that separates us from the rest of the world and the universe. This experience is often called mystical and spiritual, and it is independent of cultural and historical contexts (Capra & Luisi, 2014), as it is universal.

The experience of oneness has a critical implication. When we as individuals feel we are nature and that we are the others, we are likely to treat nature, and the others, better. The path to oneness, therefore, is the path to consciousness. It refers to the qualitative process of our conscious experience that allow us to develop the compassion and humility that is required to pre-design the pathways that stem from that level of consciousness. It is in this process that we feel systemically, and then reflect systemically, and then create the policies, strategies, programs, products and services or any kind of intervention aimed at transforming our dysfunctional systems.

A Universal Principles-Based Systems Approach to Liberation From Anthropogenic Challenges

Systems thinking, as a relatively new scientific discipline born in the West in the 20th century, is based on the theory and application of three core concepts: interrelationships, perspectives and boundaries (Cabrera et al., 2021; Williams & Imam, 2007). The underlying idea here is that for understanding how systems behave we need to focus our attention on the interrelationships of mutual causality between the variables or elements that define a system (either physical and intentional), and that by doing so we need to engage with multiple perspectives of the actors that have a stake in the system. As we do so, and as an attempt to reduce or simplify the level of complexity in which most systems operate, we need to critically reflect on the boundaries of that particular system we want to change. That means that we need to make choices by assessing which connections or relationships are more important to us in a specific context and for a specific purpose, so that we focus on finding the solutions, or leverage points in that system we are trying to change.

These systems concepts really represent a blueprint that departs from earlier reductionist or linear thinking, still the prevalent type of thinking in the genesis and functioning dynamics of our systems. As such, systems thinking really focuses the attention on the patterns of connections, the diversity of perspectives and their – limitations to act upon them. However, systems science still fails to incorporate the systems thinker mindset in its theories and practice. The mindset whereby systems thinkers approach the study and application of systems concepts and methods is fundamental in order to deeply feel and sense the interrelationships, listen to the different perspectives, and for acknowledging and expanding the boundaries that hamper our individual and collective action.

In this context, this chapter proposes Buddhist and Taoist systems thinking as a way to start sensing the complex reality of a system, consciously thinking about it and clearly acting upon it. The root of all thinking lays in our feelings. They are 'the missing element in the design and construction of cognitive models for humans systems' decision-making, agency, learning and transformation' (Coll, 2021). Damasio's point to acknowledge feelings into the primary way of knowing (Damasio, 2005) goes in line with Varela's concept of the embodied mind (Varela et al., 1991). This concept was the result of studying the neuroscience of Buddhist practices, and it expands the notion of the mind. In fact, it acknowledges that humans learn through an 'embodied mind', which states that the very structure of reason arises from the human experience sensed through our bodies and brains in an intricate process.

Buddhism and Taoism offer perennial insights and approaches on how to think systemically from an embodied mind. To me, this idea is a breakthrough in our times. Our economic system, that is a product of 'feelings-free rationality', has led to negative externalities in our social and ecological systems in unprecedented speed. Systems thinking approaches that do not integrate feelings into the process of thinking about systems are unlikely to find transformative pathways to solve our systemic challenges.

This inner-outer dimension is the axis from which transformation happens in Buddhist and Taoist terms. The current type of thinking that leads to designing creative policies, strategies and interventions in our systems is predominantly intellectual, classically rational. If we really want to explore interrelationships, perspectives and boundaries, we need to feel them first by developing our latent power of our embodied mind. This is something that we can learn by reconnecting to earliest sources of systems and indigenous thinking, such as Buddhism and Taoism. These philosophies have developed time-tested systems methods to develop the embodied mind such as the Noble Eightfold Path, the Ying-Yang, or the Five Elements, and time-tested techniques such as meditation and mindfulness, Taichi or Qiqong, to name some of the most relevant.

These techniques have something in common. They are effective in developing the embodied mind without directly stimulating our intellectual mind. In fact, these techniques strengthen our ability to have a direct non-intellectual experience that connects as to the absolute or ultimate reality. This type of mystical experience allows us to see clearly about reality, and it places us in the path to enlightenment.

Buddhist and Taoist methods and techniques are grounded on universal principles that are shared between these two philosophies. These universal principles are key to inform the understanding of reality and therefore the development and practice of systems thinking from an integral-based and embodied mind point of view. They are, in synthesis, the principles of interdependence, emptiness, impermanence and *wuwei* or 'natural doing'.

Interdependence

The experience of oneness or the absolute reality – the Tao or the Buddha-nature – is conducive to perceiving the reality as a whole. This perception can only be realized through the awareness of interdependence. This universal principle guides us in how we approach the study of reality. The focus is on realizing about the interconnectedness of all things directly experienced by the individual. The Buddha used the term interdependence to describe the state of profound connectedness, as the nature of human life, and therefore, of reality.

The direct experience of interdependence is associated with the reflective examination of how reality unfolds. We understand reality in terms of cause and effect. In Buddhism it is known with the concept of dependent co-arising or mutual causality. It expressed as 'when there is this, that comes to be; with the arising of this, that arises. When there is not this, that does not come to be; with the cessation of this, that ceases' (Ñāṇamoli & Bodhi, 1995). Mutual causality transcends the idea of linear cause and effect, and it recognizes the circularity between causes and effects, as in causal loops of feedback.

The Taoist approach to understand interdependence is based on the concept of transcending duality between apparently contradictory opposites whose existence depends on each other. There is no sun without moon, no wealth without poverty, no positive without negative and no hot without cold, for example. These interdependencies are well illustrated in the theory of Yin and Yang. This theory, instead of observing succession of unrelated phenomena, places the attention on the alternations of patterns of the same phenomenon. This understanding brings the important insight that contradictions or paradoxes coexist, as we see in our own reality. We therefore do not have to avoid extremes, but harmonizing the different polarities we have in our systems, as they are different and interdependent manifestations of the same phenomenon.

The direct experience and awareness of interdependence has direct implications on how we become aware of the interrelationships between the variables that explain systems behaviour, one of the systems concepts we have analysed. Imagine that as a systems thinker you facilitate a creative design process of a systemic intervention that aims to improve or change the system. Imagine that you start that process with a collective sense of the interdependencies that explain the system and a clear sense on where to intervene in the system. What can you expect to emerge? The collective intelligence may find leverage points that would otherwise not be found with the conventional intellectual mind. In any case, this is an assumption. If we are to truthfully follow Buddhist and Taoist empirical approach, we should try by ourselves and assess whether it works or not as a result of our own experience.

Emptiness

Emptiness is the principle that guides the experience of oneness, and therefore, of the interdependence of reality. In order to understand a system's behaviour by direct experience, we need to behave in a state of emptiness. Emptiness starts with the realization that we are empty of a separate self, so we are full of everything. Without emptiness is difficult to become fully aware of the key variables that influence a system's behaviour and its interrelationships. But the question is: how do we practice emptiness?

This practice does not take place in the intellectual mind. In fact, the practice of emptiness consists in detaching from our intellectual mind, where our ego resides. This process of detachment requires suspending our judgement, and transcending the limitations of our self-identities: our cultural, social and economic circumstances that shaped the way we describe ourselves in relation to the world we live in, and therefore, our systems. Silencing our intellect, for example through meditation, is the Eastern approach to develop our detached embodied mind. This process allows our embodied mind to enter a state of calmness called emptiness, which allows us to see reality clearly, without conditions.

This state of emptiness puts us in a place of enhanced creativity and greater expansion of our sense of inter-being. This is the state described by Zen master Shunryu Suzuki (2009) as the beginner's mind. As he recalls, 'if your mind is empty, it is always ready for anything, it is open to everything. In the beginner's mind there are many possibilities, but in the expert's there are few'. Can you imagine a creative workshop – to design a new policy or solution, for example – where participants contribute from this empty state of mind? The creative process, probably, would not find the usual limitations of ego-narrowness and pre-judgemental assessments on proposed ideas and solutions, and it would focus the attention on envisioning and spotting emerging novelty instead of traditional problem-solving.

Impermanence

One of the most profound Buddhist and Taoist insights is that transformation and change are essential features of nature and the universe, and so that change is a constant in life. Nothing lasts forever and therefore, all is impermanent. Buddhism conceives impermanence as one of the three marks of existence – *anitya* in Sanskrit-, and Taoism embeds impermanence in all its theories, such as in the Taijitu (*hyeon* means in Korean the line of change) and the Five Elements or five transitioning energies that are in constant transformation.

Impermanence means that all phenomena in life will change and will end, at some point. The problem in our current systems is that we are too attached to the material and non-material things that bring us the illusion of happiness. If this is the case, the practice of impermanence hinges upon the practice of detachment, so that we can free ourselves from the desire of permanence and stability. This practice entails becoming aware of the extent to which our frustrations arise as a response to the attachment, and how the realization of impermanence brings us freedom of being, which is reassuring of our own nature. Attachment to current systems dynamics that are benefitting to some beings in detriment to other beings is also a sign of societal frustration and, therefore, social unrest. It may prevent our systems to evolve by perpetuating current dysfunctional systems behaviours.

That may be the case of capitalism and climate change of social inequalities, for instance.

On the other hand, the practice of detachment may also bring frustration if we cannot change the system as expected. When our aspirations of systems transformations are not met, we may incur in frustration and anger, which may cause our creative energy level to shrink. In this situation, we may start blaming others or just get rid of our systems agency, which is also a systemic balancing response of the current reality. If this is the case, the principle of impermanence can also help. It means that all systems are also impermanent, and that sooner or later they are going to change and even end. They are actually in permanent motion, indeed. The point here is whether the pace of natural evolution suits our own pace and expectations.

In any case, the way to react and proact within a system is also part of the system. What if the way we respond to the crisis is part of the crisis? Philosopher and systems thinker Bayo Akomolafe often asks this question. Systems self-regulate in constant evolution, and when we plan to intervene in a system, we are part of that plan. This insight changes the way we relate to systems change, and therefore, the way we think about the system, as well as our role within that system.

Wuwei *or Natural Doing*

The practice of Taoist philosophy requires mastering the subtle art of *wuwei*. *Wuwei* literally translates from Chinese as 'non-action', but the meaning of this principle is not doing nothing but rather doing nothing against the natural flow of things. This is to say that *wuwei* guides our decision-making process by making it spontaneous, without forcing the natural course of things. We could say that this natural or spontaneous doing is about going with the flow. This process requires a deep connection with our intuition, our fundamental inner source of knowledge, as it emerges as we experience events in life.

Deep connection stems from deep listening, which is an empirical method that emerges from direct experience and interaction with natural phenomena. The practice of *wuwei* leads us to sense emerging phenomena, as well as to see ourselves in direct interaction with the phenomena we experience. 'Sensing' requires a certain level of consciousness and direct experience of our own reality. That is why the practice of interdependence, emptiness and impermanence helps develop a conscious path towards the practice of *wuwei*. In other words, the felt knowing of interdependence, emptiness and impermanence of life will help us in making decisions that are spontaneous, natural – the natural doing – and deeply rooted in our intuition.

A similar concept in Buddhism is found in the Middle Way. The Middle Way refers to finding a middle ground between extremes, often opposites, so it is a way to sort the dilemmas or paradoxes of life by focussing on the natural doing that happens in the middle: not forcing things too much by pulling the extremes.

This principle of natural doing is critical for navigating and managing complexity, uncertainty and turbulence by making decisions that feel natural to us, that go with the flow of life in the present moment. Systems thinking, in holistic terms, might include this 'systems sensing' about how we see and perceive the system, and thereby, about how we act naturally upon the system. When working on systems change, might be useful to make sense out of change, and as Alan Watts puts it, 'the only way to make sense out of change is to plunge into it, move with it, and join the dance'.

A Set of Simplex Methods to Address Systemic Challenges

Buddhist and Taoist systems thinking comprise a set of universal principles – interdependence, emptiness, impermanence and natural doing – that guide the application of a set of simplex methods with the aim to address systemic challenges as we are part of the system and sense the need for change. These simplex methods are a result of the reinterpretation of early Buddhist and Taoist systems theories to the 'contemporary' context of the Anthropocene. They are simplex in the sense that they shed clarity on complex challenges and provide guidance to navigate and make decisions to address them.

Renewing and reinterpreting perennial wisdom is an idea that Zen master Thich Nhat Hanh had long advocated. Perennial principles mean that the teachings embedded in these principles are timeless, always relevant to the release of suffering and therefore to the attainment of happiness. And the universality of these principles means that they are useful regardless of cultural and historical contexts, of direct applicability to all. However, the application of principles is in all cases context specific. That is why principles help us navigate complexity. They are not prescriptive by nature, they do not tell us what to do. They are rather descriptive. They help us in becoming aware of the important things in life and they guide our pathway of development that is always dependent on our social, cultural, historical, economic and environmental context.

I have developed and practiced with several methods that are part of Buddhist and Taoist systems thinking based on my own study and experience of Buddhist and Taoist systems approaches, such as T-Qualia, the Yin-Yang Creative Tensions and the Zen Business Model (Coll, 2021). There could be many more. In a way, this chapter is an open invitation to you to reflect upon them and, if you resonate with the idea, to refine and develop your own methods or approaches based on perennial wisdom, being Buddhism, Taoism or other indigenous sources of nature-based knowledge. I deeply believe we need to connect with perennial wisdom to inform the design of systemic interventions to help us address the global challenges of the 21st century.

I use Buddhist and Taoist systems methods to facilitate a process of systemic transformation in organizations. They may be public, or private, profit and non-profit, but in all cases they express a genuine purpose of change and transformation. They are organizations that are becoming aware of their role in the system and therefore, they want to improve the positive impact they have on the system at the economic, social and environmental level. Some of the methods are introduced as follows.

T-Qualia

T-Qualia is a five-phase nature-based empirical model of cognition and learning for systems transformation. I named it T-Qualia for two reasons. First, because 'T' refers to the Tao-like nature of absolute or ultimate reality, and second, because Qualia refers to the qualitative nature of the direct experience that allows us to become aware and therefore more conscious of our own reality and the reality of the systems that explain it. This method is indicated for organizations that want to become more conscious about the challenges they face, about the current reality, and about the potential they have in harnessing the power of collective intelligence of their teams.

The application of T-Qualia in organizations involves the practice of the following five phases as illustrated in Fig. 4.1.

(1) *T-Qualia*: the model starts with the practice of qualitative methods and techniques that help us enter into a state of being where we have a direct experience of reality. These techniques may be a combination of meditation, mindfulness, Taichi, Qiqong, nature walks, and so on. They can be applied,

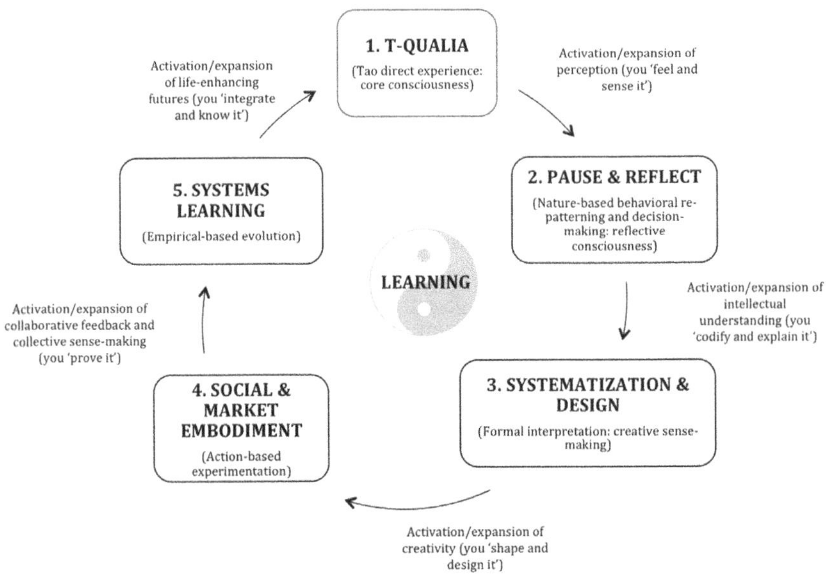

Fig. 4.1. The T-Qualia Model. *Source:* Buddhist and Taoist Systems Thinking (Coll, 2021).

preferably, in team settings, such as in team retreats facilitated by expert practitioners. The objective of this phase is to activate and expand the team members level of perception so that they can feel and sense the reality directly.

(2) *Pause and reflect*: this phase consists of collectively sharing the previous experience and making sense of it at the individual and team level. It allows team members to assess their dominant behaviours and it provides the evidence for re-patterning based on desired new behaviours that align with the insights provided by the direct experience of the T-Qualia phase. The objective of this phase is to activate and expand the intellectual understanding of what just happened.

(3) *Systematization and design*: this phase consists of a formal organizational interpretation of the previous experiences in order to connect the state of consciousness of team members to the design of regenerative interventions – a programme, a policy, a product, a service, an activity or a process – with the purpose of improving their positive contribution and impact to a social or environmental challenge. The objective of this phase is to activate and expand the systemic creativity of the organization in formal design processes.

(4) *Social and market embodiment*: this phase consists of testing the output of the previous phase, be it any sort of solution that aims to change a system. It allows trying the solution out in the market if it is a market-based solution or out in the society if what was developed is a non-market based solution. In any case, the objective of this phase is to receive external feedback on the utility and relevance of the solution so that it can be adjusted, improved and adapted to fulfil with the purpose of the intervention.

(5) *Systems learning*: once the solution is being implemented, this phase consists of a retrospective reflection on what the organization or the team has learnt about the development and implementation of the solution. The objective of this phase is to activate and expand the way organizations learn from experience and reflection upon the experience, so that the process allows to root the learning as feedback for further life-enhancing futures.

Yin-Yang Creative Tensions (YYCT)

This is an inquiry-driven method that allows to identify the main systemic challenges, structural issues, dilemmas or bottlenecks – called tensions – that organizations face in their transition to the new sustainable and regenerative business paradigm. I added Yin and Yang to the term creative tensions, a concept developed by Robert Fritz (1984) and later popularized by Peter Senge (1990). A creative tension emerges when there is a clear articulation between the vision – a desired goal – and the current reality – the uncomfortable way it is. This gap creates a tension that automatically seeks resolution.

The qualification of the creative tension as Yin and Yang indicates that the gap between the current and desired reality is expressed in terms of the two polarities of the phenomenon that is creating the tension. For example, an archetypical creative tension arises when a corporation that is making profits out of non-sustainable practices (i.e. an oil company) wishes to become more sustainable. The purpose of the company creates a tension that manifests through the polarities of profit-making – the Yang polarity – and the sustainability aspiration – the Yin polarity – as illustrated in Fig. 4.2.

Fig. 4.2. Yin-Yang Creative Tension. *Source:* Buddhist and Taoist Systems Thinking (Coll, 2021).

An organization can apply the YYCT by facilitating collective dialogs that explore the tension through the identified Yin and Yang polarities. The discussion focuses on harmonizing the two polarities in order to find pathways that release the creative energy found in the tension. This method is indicated for organizations that want to have meaningful, open and safe conversations about key challenges and issues that are normally not spoken about, and therefore, not addressed in the system. These conversations provide a critical and creative examination of the challenges, which is a precondition for designing solutions that address and overcome those challenges.

The Zen Business Model (ZBM)

The ZBM is a biomimetic systems method to organizational sustainable development and harmony (Coll, 2021, 2022). It is grounded on the Five Elements theory, which describes the systemic dynamics of nature's energy transformations as illustrated as follows: Wood generates Fire, Fire generates Earth, Earth generates Metal, Metal generates Water and Water generates Wood (the creation cycle). Simultaneously, Wood restricts Earth, Earth restricts Water, Water restricts Fire, Fire restricts Metal, and Metal restricts Wood (the restriction or destruction cycle). A natural complex system pursues a natural equilibrium through self-regulation, what in Taoist terms is described as balance and harmony.

By analogy, the ZBM takes these natural systems dynamics to the organizational dynamics of value generation. It departs from the organization-as-a-machine metaphor by assuming that organizations are living systems, whose dynamics depend on the connections and interactions that people have within and outside the organization. These interactions include interrelationships between stakeholders and the environment, including Mother nature as a key stakeholder from which organizations generate value from, and to which organizations should generate value for.

The five elements correspond to the five corporate stars, which are the corporate generating value areas within a given organization. Therefore, Fire correspond to the Human Leadership star, Earth to the Stakeholders star, Metal to the Marketing and Innovation star, Water to the Full Profit star, and Wood to the Brand Impact Recognition star. The properties of the Five Elements are embedded into the behaviour of the five corporate stars, and the organizational dynamics of value generation follow the Five Elements' two cycles of creation and restriction, the so-called value generation and control cycles (Coll, 2021, 2022). Fig. 4.3 describes the elemental-based behaviour of the five corporate stars, and Fig. 4.4 illustrates the ZBM and its dynamics.

The ZBM can be applied for different objectives in an organization, but the overall purpose is to use it as an open methodology to start a transition towards a more inclusive, sustainable and regenerative business organization. Organizations and entrepreneurs may start with a diagnosis of its strengths and weaknesses, assessing the systems dynamics of where are the balance and imbalances in the system according to the value generating and control cycles.

The diagnosis helps to bring the relevant conversations for an organization that aims to increase their positive impact to the economy, the society and the environment. The process can start with inquiring about what is the purpose of

5 Stars	**5E**	**Elements' Behavior**	**5 Corporate Stars**	**Value phase**	**Guiding principle**
Knowledge	Fire	Light. Exploding outward. Diffusion, Prosperity	Human Leadership	Identifying	Purpose
Social Relations	Earth	Balance, Decline, Transition, Transformation	Stakeholders	Co-creating	Collaboration
Expression	Metal	Cutting, reforming, construction, reconstruction, execution. Creativity	Marketing & Innovation	Delivering	Agility
Money	Water	Vitality, pregnancy, life	Full Profit	Sustaining	Abundance
Career	Wood	Sprout, Growth. Expansion	Brand Impact Recognition	Recognizing	Impact

Fig. 4.3. Elements-Based Behaviour of the Five Corporate Stars.
Source: The Zen Business Model (Coll, 2022).

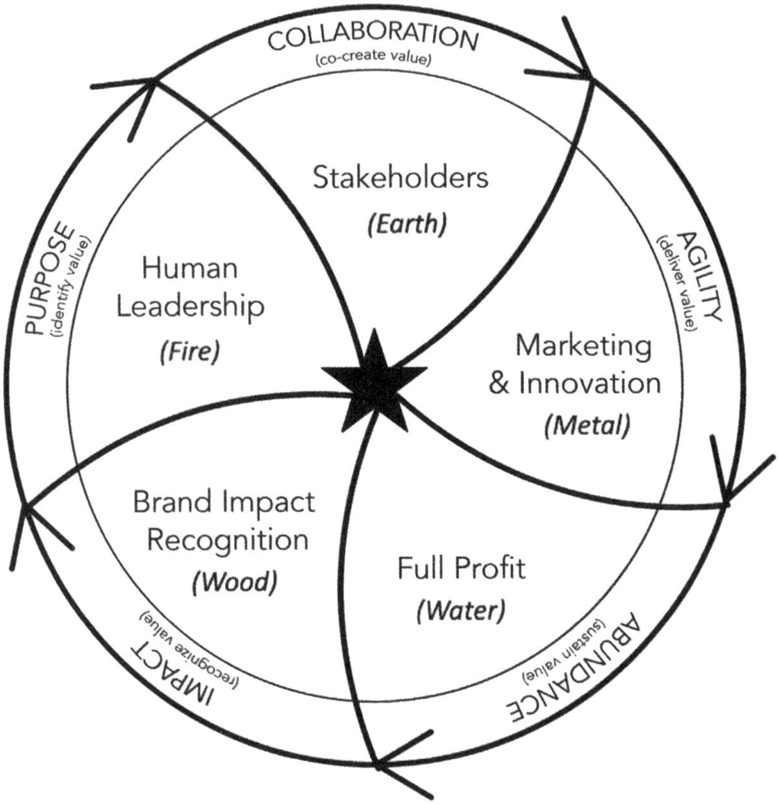

Fig. 4.4. The Zen Business Model. *Source:* Buddhist and Taoist Systems Thinking (Coll, 2021).

the organization and the values that define the DNA of such an organization or group of entrepreneurs (Human Leadership star). Having discovered a genuine purpose and identifying values contribute to engage stakeholders that resonate with the formulated purpose of the organization or the startup (Stakeholders star). Engaging with different stakeholders in co-creating and developing interventions for a regenerative business and economy, such as programs, products or services, leads to launch and deliver value to the market with agility to consumers that are becoming conscious of the Anthropocene and thereby looking for increasingly sustainable solutions (Marketing and Innovation star).

The successful delivery of value to consumers increases the financial sustainability of the organization, which is also a critical value generation area in business sustainability. In this corporate star (Full Profit) the organization develops the tools that allow capturing the value they, including revenue models and accounts of social and environmental costs. Lastly, the organization rigorously evaluate and communicate the impact is has at the social, economic and environmental level, and it learns and explains how it is achieving its purpose, and therefore, recognizing the impact it delivers to society (Brand Impact Recognition star).

In sum, the ZBM may guide the sustainable development of an organization from a systems perspective, including an ever ongoing process of transformation that evolves with the systems evolutions, and with an increasing organizational consciousness that helps the organization continuously inquire about its purpose, its impact and the strategies and actions that lead to have the expected impact to the larger whole.

We Are the Bridge: Concluding Remarks

Anyone wishing to contribute to systemic change is a participator. A participator is more than just a participant or observer. Participators are interactive, action-based participants, as they are aware of the mutual influence they have, as change agents, to the phenomenon they want to change. This is one of the late discoveries of quantum physics that resemble what the earlier Taoist and Buddhist researchers already knew: the participator becomes involved in the system he observes and acts upon, to the extent that he influences the properties of the system. Simultaneously, the system influences the participator as well.

Awareness of our role in the systems we try to change is essential for empowering ourselves in the realm of systems change and transformation. As aware conscious systems thinkers and change agents, we then need the knowledge that can help us in acting upon the system. To this aim, reconnecting with indigenous sources of nature-based wisdom offers us new possibilities to reinterpret and bring universal principles to the design and redesign of our socio-economic and ecological systems in the context of the Anthropocene.

Buddhist and Taoist systems thinking offer a wide array of timeless wisdom that are directly applicable to the challenges of our time. Buddhist and Taoist already knew about the complexity, interdependence and impermanence of all things, and for the need of natural doing and decision-making, accepting things as they are, letting go of the things are no longer useful to us and connecting with our inner and outer power for transformation.

Life brought me to reconnect with these earlier sources of perennial wisdom, and so I started my ongoing learning journey as a Westerner studying Taoist metaphysics and practicing Zen in East Asia while I was working as an international business and organizational management consultant for European organizations in Asia. But that was my journey.

Anyone can reconnect with any perennial philosophy that is grounded on nature-based wisdom, such as indigenous knowledge. We can learn from different sources, as we resonate with them, and combine them as mixed methods in the frame of contingency theory. This theory means that there is no best method, or knowledge, or tool. The optimal pathway is contingent upon the internal and external environment, and therefore, context specific.

Change agents are flexible in choosing methods and designing pathways of transformation that are relevant and useful in a particular context and for the people and systems involved. The critical takeaway here is that it is not the methods that will bring us to the desired transformation, but why, how and for whom we use them. Methods, approaches or tools are not the bridge, we are the bridge.

References

Cabrera, D., Cabrera, L., & Midgley, G. (2021). The four waves of systems thinking. In D. Cabrera, L. Cabrera, & G. Midgley (Eds.). *Routledge handbook of systems thinking*. Routledge.

Capra, F. (1975). *The Tao of physics* (pp. 104). Shambala.

Capra, F., & Luisi, P. L. (2014). *The systems view of life: A unifying vision*. Cambridge University Press.

Coll, J. M. (2021). *Buddhist and Taoist Systems Thinking: The natural path to sustainable transformation*. Routledge.

Coll, J. M. (2022). A biomimetic systems method to organizational sustainable development and harmony: The Zen Business Model. *Systems Research and Behavioral Science*. https://doi.org/10.1002/sres.2916

Damasio, A. (2005). *Descartes' error: Emotion, reason and the human brain*. Penguin Books.

Fritz, R. (1984). *The path of least resistance*. Fawcett.

Macy, J. (1991). *Mutual causality in Buddhism and general systems theory*. State University of New York Press.

Ñāṇamoli, B., & Bodhi, B. (1995). *The middle length discourses of the Buddha, a translation of the Majjhima Nikāya*. Wisdom Publications.

Senge, P. (1990). *The fifth discipline*. Doubleday.

Suzuki, S. (2009). *Zen mind, beginner's mind*. Weatherhill.

Varela, F., Thompson, E., & Rosch, E. (1991). *The embodied mind*. MIT Press.

Watts, A. (2019). *Out of your mind*. Souvenir Press.

Williams, B., & Imam, I. (2007). *Systems concepts in evaluation: An expert antology*. Edge Press.

Zhu, Z. (2000). Dealing with a differentiated whole: The philosophy of the WSR approach. *Systemic Practice and Action Research*, *13*(1), 21–57.

Chapter 5

New Paradigm Politics and Governance for a Planetary Civilization

Anneloes Smitsman

Abstract

The call for a new paradigm in politics and governance has become a planetary imperative. Humanity is at a critical juncture; unless we mature as a species and become net-positive to nature the human experiment may (soon) end. We have become our own biggest threat. This chapter explores the foundations, as well as systemic barriers, for the shift to a new and life-centred paradigm in politics and governance. Offering a systemic exploration of the root causes of our sustainability crises and how to address this, based on the cosmology and evolutionary principles of complex living systems. Applying Living Systems Protocols from the EARTHwise Constitution for a Planetary Civilization, and its framework of five Future Archetypes, for developing our transformative capacities to address the systemic thrivability barriers of mechanistic systems and worldviews. With case-study examples of new paradigm tools, systems and technologies that enable a decentralization of governance and democratization of ownership. As such empowering the systemic conditions and maturation pathways for a thriving planetary civilization. The chapter completes with a brief practice for developing our future human capacities and inner consciousness shifts for a new paradigm in politics and governance.

Keywords: Thrivability; DAOs; EARTHwise Constitution; EARTHwise DAO; new paradigm governance

Introduction

The systemic conditions for life on Earth are radically shifting in ways we are not prepared for. The sustainability crises are part of a larger meta-crisis that can only be resolved by addressing the underlying systems and worldviews of our modern

Applied Spirituality and Sustainable Development Policy, 89–115

Published under exclusive licence by Emerald Publishing Limited
doi:10.1108/978-1-83753-380-020231005

civilizations. Systemic leadership is urgently required to shift trajectories from collapse to regeneration and thriving.

According to the latest research in climate science by McKay et al. (2022), the world is on the brink of five disastrous climate tipping points, while we are heading towards 2–3°C of global warming. In addition, several other tipping points are starting to converge, including those that relate to increasing biodiversity loss, social-economic inequality, political polarization, disruptive technologies and resource scarcity.

Furthermore, policy making for systemic transformation is vastly lagging behind and increasing wealth inequalities reveal even larger leadership gaps (Chancel et al., 2022; The Guardian, 2022). In other words, a new paradigm in politics and governance is urgently required. We are not ready for what we have set in motion. The extractive systems, growth models and worldviews of the Industrial Age are still ruling our societies today. Even though we now know that many of these are unsustainable by design. The old paradigm of institutionalized duality, design for separation, growth without boundaries and freedom without responsibility takes us on the highway to collapse.

The energy and resource transitions to post-carbon, regenerative societies require first and foremost a shift from political party leadership to planetary stewardship. We are part of the Earth, we too are nature. What we do to the Earth we ultimately do to ourselves, and each other. As the world is again in the grip of another arms race, brought on by the Russian invasion of Ukraine, it reveals how far away we are from securing peace on planet Earth. As the juvenile species of Gaia, we are on a track to destroy the planetary conditions of life on Earth, and by doing so cause our own extinction. It is time we mature by learning from the consequences of our actions and apply our collective intelligence in favour of life.

The Rise of New Paradigm Politics and Governance

Democracy as a form of delegated decision-making is about so much more than electing governments and parliaments. New disruptive technologies applied to decentralized organizational structures are making it possible to radically shift how governance is made by people. A new paradigm in politics and governance is decentralizing and democratizing decision-rights, voice, ownership and economic opportunities. Empowering people to govern together in whole new ways and acting collaboratively on agreed priorities to co-create our own economies of scale.

New paradigm politics and governance is part of a larger paradigm shift that is democratizing and decentralizing how we co-create and design our economies and societies. The new regenerative economic models prioritize joint ownership of assets, distributive value and inclusive opportunities. Regenerative growth models replace earlier economic growth models for extractive exponential growth. Regenerative growth results from applying evolutionary design principles that return value to all who have contributed – mimicking the evolutionary patterns of complex living systems.

The larger paradigm shift that is unfolding is also a shift in focus and values – from survivability and competition to regeneration and thrivability (Smitsman, 2021a; Smitsman & Laszlo, 2022). Furthermore, new paradigm politics and governance causes a significant shift from governments to governance, and from constitutions to constitutionalizing a new paradigm ethos of wholeness and unity with life (Smitsman, 2021b). Creating a new paradigm in politics and governance requires that we transcend nationalism and political ideology, and take an active role in the healing and transformation of our divided cultures. Uniting to resolve the greatest challenges of our time.

In contrast, old paradigm politics and governance are characterized by factions, ideologies, competition, domination and constructed identities that divide and alienate. The human trend of institutionalized violence and normalized separation has been going on for thousands of years (if not longer). Old paradigm politics cannot provide the necessary leadership for a thrivable world and future, which requires an ethos of planetary stewardship.

Planetary stewardship is about uniting people and nations in the collective caring for our Earth and future generations. The majority of mainstream political movements remain loyal to the political ideologies out of which they emerged. When political parties started to form hundreds of years ago, there was no sustainability crisis. Resources seemed infinite and the modernization of society (through mechanistic systems) provided many new benefits to larger groups of people. Prioritizing planetary health for human wellbeing was not on the radar, except for indigenous nations that strived to maintain a close relationship with the natural world.

Since the onset of the Industrial Age, humanity has expanded significantly in size, connectivity and complexity. We are now confronted with the planetary consequences of our materialistic worldviews, and challenged to reinvent our technologies and economic models in reciprocity with life. Continuing 'business as usual' is simply not an option. Mainstream political parties are called to transform and make planetary health and security a priority, which requires radical transformation of the ways we utilize, extract and share resources and energy. Many of the vested power brokers of the earlier materialistic paradigm are resisting the required transformations, especially as they continue to make enormous profits. In 2022, the 'big five' oil and gas companies made a combined 'monster profit' of $200 billion – revealing a self-destructive fossil fuel resurgence that shows little hope in driving down emissions (Milman, 2023).

Climate change is now a lived reality for almost everyone on our planet, making it clear that 'business as usual' is the road to increasing suffering, and not the promise for a better life. People are discovering new technologies, platforms and ways for effecting change and making their voices heard for a better world and future.

Civilizational transformation is imperative, and can be accelerated by the use of appropriate disruptive technologies for decentralizing governance and democratizing ownership. Especially when linked to design, tools and capacities for regenerative and distributive economies, regenerative agriculture, bioregionalism, digital cooperatism, sociocracy, decentralized governance organizations, commoning governance, bio-digital innovations, direct and liquid democracy, climate innovation and so forth (Democracy International, 2021; Ecocivilisation, 2022; Great Transition Initiative, 2022; Smitsman & Laszlo, 2022).

Our world is in the midst of a civilizational metamorphosis (Smitsman & Houston, 2021, 2022). The structures of the old caterpillar world are dissolving inside the cocoon, while the new structures and capacities of a butterfly world are starting to emerge in some places. The old forms of democracy are also under pressure to evolve. The systems, tools and structures of an emerging new paradigm politics and governance may not yet be visible (or tangible) for the general public. Especially, while mainstream media is continuing to spotlight the politics of materialism.

What many of the new paradigm innovations have in common is the understanding that governance is not limited to governments. The undercurrents of democracy are alive and shifting. We need to learn how to meet and guide this underbelly of change for becoming the planetary stewards of an emerging planetary civilization. If we fail to do so, it will play into the cards of populist and extremist parties who grow their followers from discontent with mainstream political institutions.

We can now develop collective stewardship capacities for the governance of our commons. We now have the tools and technologies for democratizing and coordinating creativity, capacity development, resource allocation, value distribution and collective decision-making. New digital technologies and decentralized governance tools are making it possible to co-create thriving ecosystems of impact. I will provide some concrete examples in the next sections.

New Paradigm Tools, Systems and Technologies

In July 2021, the Laszlo Institute of New Paradigm Research hosted a Global Symposium on a New Paradigm in Politics, which I co-facilitated together with Alexander Laszlo. We published the main outcomes of the symposium through a book by the same title, *The New Paradigm in Politics*. Ninety-seven percent of the participants shared through a survey that: 'We need effective democracy (participatory decision-making) at various levels of scale – including family, neighbourhood and workplace'. People further clarified how 'effective democracy' requires new tools, methods and technologies that make it easier for people to participate in decision-making and co-steward their resources, opportunities and responsibilities (Smitsman & Laszlo, 2022).

Many of the innovations that are happening in governance take place in the digital landscape of what is referred to as Web3. Whereas, Web2 is the interactive internet that most people are familiar with – dominated by companies that provide services in exchange for our personal data – Web3 is part of a larger movement for decentralizing the web and democratizing corporate control. Web3 applications are made through open source-codes and decentralized digital architecture for peer-to-peer governance, collaboration and decision-making. Web3 technologies enable transparent blockchain based agreements through distributive networks.

Web3 technologies are radically transforming the centralized applications of Web2 through open and transparent blockchain-based 'smart contracts', tokenization of value flows and contributions, and new forms of Decentralized Autonomous Organizations (DAOs) that create their own token economy in collaboration with other DAOs. A DAO is designed to utilize collective intelligence through new types of collaborative structures and tools by using blockchain-based technologies. Enabling transparency, voice, collective sense-making, inclusive decision-making, and collective ownership of value, equity and opportunity through a multi-signature blockchain-based treasury of tokens (Smitsman et al., 2022).

The making of new paradigm politics and governance is happening in the digital corridors of Web3 innovation. By empowering new paradigm movements with these Web3 tools, civilizational transformation can accelerate significantly. The following case-study will illustrate this further.

The EARThwise Constitution for a Planetary Civilization

In 2022, we launched the 'EARTHwise Constitution for a Planetary Civilization' to address the root causes of the sustainability crisis.[1] The constitution opens with 'Our Promise', rather than 'Our Declaration', to affirm how we are the promise of a new beginning (Smitsman, 2022):

> We, as future ancestors of a planetary civilization, commit to co-creating thrivable worlds and futures with the wisdom of living systems, *in partnership with life and our Earth.*

The constitution is open-source and registered under a Creative Commons licence, to make it freely accessible for everyone to work with and adapt to their unique circumstances. The constitution serves as a

- Cosmic Compass and social contract for co-creating our worlds and futures with the wisdom and evolutionary capacities of living systems;
- meta-attractor and evolutionary blueprint for cohering and aligning myriad of movements, projects and initiatives through a common vision and focus.

Whereas constitutions are usually associated with human agreements for the architecture of nation-states (and sometimes companies), the EARTHwise Constitution is based on the architecture of living systems. According to the latest research in quantum information and quantum field theory, as well as

[1]To read the EARTHwise Constitution online, visit: https://www.earthwisecentre.org/constitution.

evolutionary systems sciences, it appears that the informational architecture of the universe is fundamentally unified and nonlocal (Currivan, 2017; Smitsman & Currivan, 2021; Smitsman et al., 2023). This informational architecture can be likened to the 'constitution of our universe'. A constitution of wholeness that makes life possible, and which is in stark contrast to most of our human-made constitutions.

The constitution of the universe fractals out to all scales and levels of existence. Article 3 of the EARTHwise Constitution explains this as follows:

> We acknowledge how our universe exists and evolves as a single unified entity, an undividable wholeness. This evolutionary principle helps us understand life as a unified reality, whereby energy-matter and space-time are complementary informational expressions of consciousness. We acknowledge how our universe evolves coherently and through increasing embodied complexity, making life possible precisely because of the relational dynamics it embodies and fosters. This evolutionary principle shows us how to embody complexity and foster evolutionarily coherence in 'right relationship' with life and each other. ~ Article 3, EARTHwise Constitution

To support people in becoming stewards for a thriving planetary civilization, the EARTHwise Constitution offers 13 Living Systems Protocols, as shown in Fig. 5.1 and explained in detail in the Constitution. Protocols 5 and 10 are specifically relevant for the upshift to new paradigm politics and governance.

Protocol 5 of Article 6: 'Evolve through Conscious Choice and Empowered Participation: Life creates conditions for empowered participation in the co-evolution of our worlds and futures. The universe is a participatory system that evolves as a whole, through the choices we make individually and collectively. Empower conscious choice-making and participation.

- Create opportunities and support for empowered participation in the decisions that impact our lives, worlds and futures.
- Design for equitable distribution of choice and voice in governance and decision-making processes for individuals, communities and ecosystems.
- Apply the power of conscious choice for activating the higher order possibilities of a planetary civilization, and for evolving and transforming human consciousness and the ways we operationalize and apply this'.

Protocol 10 of Article 6, 'Contribute as a Future Ancestor: Act as a future ancestor of the worlds and futures we seek to co-create and experience, based on partnership with life and stewardship for our collective thrivability. Consider and support the wellbeing of current and unborn future generations.

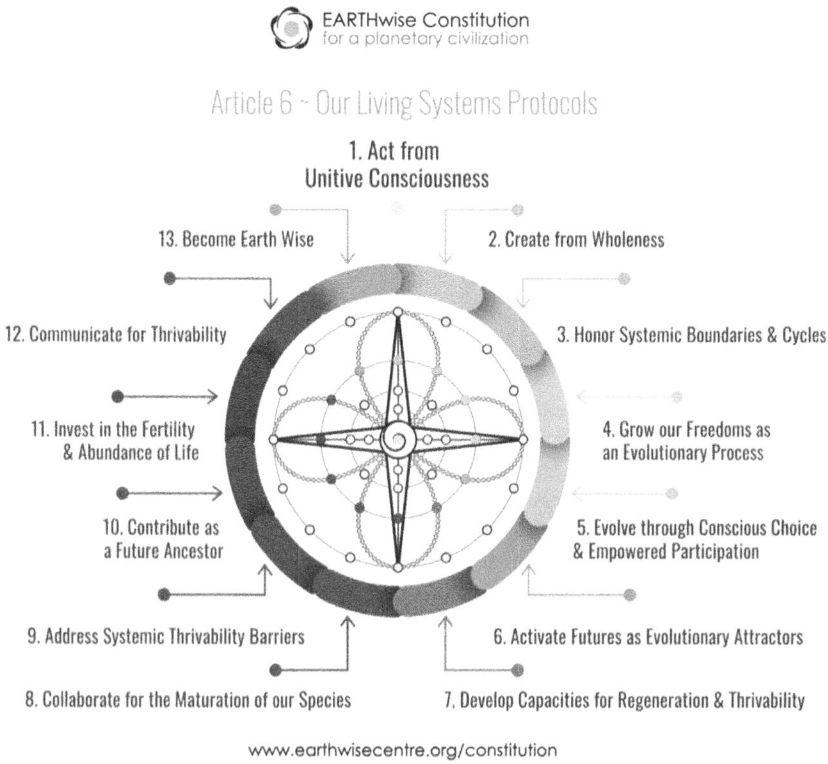

Fig. 5.1. Our Living Systems Protocols.

- Apply a 'community of life' approach through decentralized inclusive governance and regenerative distributive economies that reward co-stewardship and co-ownership of ecological assets, ecosystem services and value.
- Promote systemic resilience, planetary health and quality of life by increasing caring and carrying capacities for regeneration and thrivability, and distributing the value produced by communities to the communities where this belongs.
- Be transformative, act as a future ancestor by honouring the rights and well-being of future generations that require the end of human harm. Actively support the necessary systemic transformations'.

The EARTHwise DAO for Planetary Governance

To operationalize the values, principles, protocols and commitments that are outlined in the EARTHwise Constitution, we are developing the EARTHwise DAO as a prototype for planetary governance and stewardship. The new paradigm tools and technologies mentioned earlier are implemented in the DAO for co-creating tipping point solutions for civilizational transformation in the form of a game.[2]

We are developing this DAO with the help of the Hypha DAO solutions for building a Decentralized Autonomous Organization with a human focus. Using transparent and democratic tools for groups to organize, govern, recognize and coordinate in a decentralized and self-organizing manner. The Hypha DAO tools enhance fast, responsive and inclusive decision-making and collective sense-making for solving complex problems. Contributions are accounted for and rewarded through transparent blockchain treasuries with DAO utility, cash and voice tokens.

The EARTHwise DAO also serves as an online Collaboratory and collective governance system, grounded in real-life activities and regular meetings for our EARTHwise project teams and Partnership Alliance for a Planetary Civilization. It provides tools and incentives for making collaboration easier and more rewarding, and is built from the architecture of the EARTHwise Constitution. We have applied a 'commons approach' in the way we are programming the DAO to enable collective governance of resource allocation, distribution and inclusive decision-making.

Furthermore, the DAO is designed as an ecosystem for accelerating the large-scale civilizational shifts for thrivable worlds and futures, by making it possible to fractally create child DAOs from the EARTHwise DAO architecture, and expand through DAO-2-DAO ecosystem collaboration. EARTHwise DAO includes the following features:

- Community-focused and collectively owned and managed by its members (meaning, everyone who is a token-owner of the DAO).
- To manage funds, the DAO has a built-in transparent treasury, which no single person has the authority to access without the approval of the allocated team.
- Decisions within the DAO are governed inclusively and by a variety of governance styles that can be chosen and adjusted by the DAO members.
- To ensure inclusive participation in decision-making, everyone has a voice in governance and voice tokens.
- Trust arises from the transparency of the DAO's blockchain ledger, which records all governance decisions and financial transactions, and functions as a highly secure and decentralized online spreadsheet stored on distributed servers around the globe. In other words, transparency by 'digital' design.

In order to enhance our governance capacities, we are integrating a unique Artificial Intelligence technology that senses patterns of thoughts and relevance to surface collective intelligence, and enhances decisions with community priorities. It records a tamper proof, auditable trail of proposals, discussions, results, presenting potential new ideas with greatest resonance for benefiting the entire community. To summarize, the EARTHwise DAO serves as follows:

---

[2]For more information, visit: https://www.earthwisecentre.org/game-campaign

- *Prototype for Ecosystemic Governance* – Life-coded design based on the architecture of the EARTHwise Constitution with AI integration. Supports problem solving complex issues and solutions for sustainability, regeneration and thrivability.
- *Creating an Integral Model of the Collective Mind of our DAO* – Our AI integration serves as learning feedback for the development of the collective consciousness of the DAO to eventually become self-aware and coherent, as a collective intelligence and entity.
- *AI-based Community Learning* – The AI platforms will be fed with data from voting, behavioural patterns and decision-making of the EARTHwise community, trained in planetary stewardship for regeneration and thrivability. via our EARTHwise games. The AI outcomes will be fed back to this community to continuously improve our planetary stewardship and evolve our consciousness.
- *AI Data-input for Ecosystemic Governance* – Data-inputs will be guided by the EARTHwise Integral Thrivability Framework, which includes indicators for: ecosystemic thresholds, equitable allocations, planetary boundaries, social ceilings, tipping point potentials, systemic blind spots and systemic thrivability barriers.

There are many more case-studies like this, such as the SEEDS global platform and the SEEDS DAO and Hypha DAO Constitutions (https://hypha.earth/), for which I served as the lead architect, using the same Cosmic Compass Design as I applied for the EARTHwise Constitution (SEEDS, 2021).[3] All this to illustrate that it is now possible to become architects and co-creators of whole new civilizations, and pioneers of the systems and technologies for new paradigm politics and governance. The making of democracy is decentralizing, after hundreds of years of centralized control. However, let us always remember to place life in the centre of our creative process.

New Paradigm Forms of Political Agency

We are each born with the power of agency – that is, the power to act, actualize and effect change. Your power of agency includes your power of choice, inquiry, intention, creativity, communication and action. Political agency does not mean you have to join or form a political party. Political agency can also take the form of catalysing a new paradigm in politics and governance through the ways described in the case-studies earlier. You can even apply your political agency at home, with your own family or community, by democratizing how you make better decisions together.

[3]SEEDS is an acronym for: Sowing Ecological, Equitable and Decentralising Societies, and acts as an online ecosystem for uniting and supporting the regenerative renaissance movements and projects. For more information visit, https://joinseeds.earth/.

You can also practice your political agency in the way you collaborate for civilizational transformation. The many new digital technologies and tools of the web3 world make it possible for people from all over the world to collaborate and coordinate by means of their internet access. To support this we made the EARTHwise Constitution open-source and freely accessible. As such empowering myriad organizations, networks, projects and movements to unite around a common vision and shared agreements for our world and future.

Furthermore, new paradigm movement building requires a 'Unitive Narrative' that is inclusive of diversity and embracing of complexity (SDG Thought Leaders Circle, 2022). By applying our power of agency from new paradigm values – that is, decentralized governance, inclusive decision-making, empowered participation, distributive value flows, and planetary wealth and wellbeing – we can all join the making of new paradigm politics and governance.

Working With New Paradigm Future Archetypes

The political power structures are shifting, which also signals a deeper archetypal shift as we become the catalysts for an emerging new era. Through my PhD research on systems change as an external researcher of the Maastricht Sustainability Institute of Maastricht University (from 2014 to 2019), I explored archetypal patterns that activate during paradigm shifts, and may signal some of the key qualities of the emerging new era. I decided to refer to these archetypal patterns as future archetypes, and noticed how they were already active in the world of today. Especially in how younger generations are catalysing change and responding to challenges.

To support people in working more consciously with these future archetypes for a planetary civilization, I identified five archetypal codes, stages, states, patterns and capacities that mimic a metamorphic transformation (Smitsman, 2019a, 2019b). I named the five future archetypes: The Wholeness Coder, Future Creative, Evolutionary Catalyst, Pattern Weaver and New Paradigm Storyteller.

Over the years I continued to develop this system further, which features in *The Quest of Rose* (Smitsman & Houston, 2021) and the EARTHwise Constitution (Smitsman, 2022). The 5 Future Archetypes are also applied in the design of role assignments and governance responsibilities for the SEEDS, Hypha, EARTHwise and Regen Living DAOs (among others).

Here below is a short description of these five future archetypes from the EARTHwise Constitution, and how they can be applied for supporting the actualization of our future human potential (Smitsman, 2019b). Their application to education, design, governance and economics are described in the EARTHwise Constitution, see Fig. 5.2.

- *The Wholeness Coder* – We activate the future potentials of our evolutionary next steps, as architects, designers and coders for thrivable worlds and futures. We catalyse change at the causal levels by creating the systemic codes, structures, archetypes and algorithms of an emerging planetary civilization.
- *The Future Creative* – We create the openings and pathways for our evolutionary next steps, as futurists, innovators and pioneers for thrivable worlds

Fig. 5.2. The Actualization Process.

and futures. We catalyse change at the imaginal level by exploring and initiating the future possibilities of an emerging planetary civilization.

- *The Evolutionary Catalyst* – We develop our future capacities as transformational catalysts, healers and facilitators. We provide transition support for the death and transformation of what no longer serves and needs to end, while supporting the emergence and birth of the new. We catalyse change at the evolutionary level by embodying the emerging new consciousness and capacities of a planetary civilization.
- *The Pattern Weaver* – We create collaborative capacities, partnerships and communities with the new evolutionary patterns as weavers, connectors and evolutionary builders. We catalyse change integrally by creating the conditions for transformative emergence, and building the communities and root systems of an emerging planetary civilization.
- *The New Paradigm Storyteller* – We inspire and communicate our future human actualization as storytellers, artists and cultural creatives. We fertilize and cohere our world with the new paradigm narratives, and by embodying the evolutionary patterns of thrivable worlds and futures. We catalyse change by creating sensory-rich experiences of our greater future possibilities.

Politics and Governance for Tipping Point Times

As mentioned briefly in the introduction, several catalytic tipping points are starting to converge – climate tipping points, biodiversity tipping points, social tipping points, political tipping points and economic tipping points. The convergence of these tipping points is what is referred to by the term 'meta-crisis'. Social philosopher Daniel Schmachtenberger explains how the meta-crisis is a way of assessing the totality of risks humanity faces and the totality of the problem-space (Schmachtenberger, 2022).

In 2009, sustainability scientist Johan Rockström and his global team developed the Planetary Boundaries (PB) framework, which identifies nine critical processes that regulate the stability and resilience of the Earth System (Stockholm Resilience Centre, 2022). Nine Planetary Boundaries were identified that indicate a safe operating zone within which humanity can continue to develop and thrive for generations to come (Rockström et al., 2009). The latest scientific review of these nine Planetary Boundaries show how five out of these nine critical Earth System boundaries have been crossed (Wang-Erlandsson et al., 2022). Accordingly, we are reaching critical limits of adaptation, for ourselves and many species and ecosystems (IPCC, 2022; Steffen et al., 2018). In other words, politics and governance for tipping point times is imperative.

Tipping points are irreversible nonlinear structural changes that can push a system into unpredictable new trajectories. Tipping points are also defined as the point or threshold at which small changes in a system will trigger a nonlinear change process. This process is driven by structural feedback mechanisms that lead to a qualitatively different, and often irreversible, state of the system as a whole. Birth is also a tipping point, as is death.

Once tipping point dynamics activate, the change that unfolds cannot be controlled or predicted through top-down interventions. Political leaders who seek to exploit the chaos and uncertainty of tipping point times may do so by seducing voters through simplistic narratives of 'us-versus-them' and offering false promises of greatness and security. Leadership and governance is about facilitating the actions and changes for where we need to go, from a future perspective of a thriving world that works for all.

Putting the climate and biodiversity crisis on the political agenda is not sufficient for securing the conditions for a liveable planet. Political leadership for tipping point times requires above all vision, courage and empathy. To lead for what is necessary, and not merely for what is popular and securing a seat in government. The rise of authoritarian politicians, and their populist and extreme-right parties, is a clear sign that political leadership for tipping point times is hugely lacking (Treisman & Guriev, 2022). Tipping point times increase people's sense of uncertainty, danger and hardships, which authoritarian and populist leaders use to provide false security through simplistic narratives, and false promises that hollow our democracies from the inside-out.

Planetary stewardship requires leadership and governance for genuine and inclusive progress and collective wellbeing, by facilitating the required systemic transformations. To do so requires that we learn how to act, relate and evolve *as living* systems. Life is thrivable and regenerative by design. A new paradigm in politics and governance requires transforming the systems and growth models that are unsustainable and harmful to life on Earth. We need leaders and decision-makers who understand the value of life, as well as the price of inaction. Leaders who take responsibility for the wellbeing and rights of future generations, and who can think and act systemically.

The Problem With Mechanistic Systems and Worldviews

Many people feel trapped in societies that have little to do with life – driven by algorithms, models and technologies that are designed for extractive economic growth; not evolutionary growth and planetary wellbeing. The ways we have modernized and developed our societies, although bringing short-term benefits, has also created immense harm and division. This raises the question whether mechanistic models can truly deliver the 'progress' that they were once designed for. Sustainability crises are caused and exacerbated because of the mechanistic worldviews that still dominate today, isolating us from our oneness with the natural world and the universe.

Mechanistic thinking is based on a predominantly materialistic view of life and reality, based on dualistic notions of consciousness and human potential. The mechanistic worldview emerged from a Newtonian scientific worldview that portrayed the universe in a machine-like manner – that is, composed of separate parts and particles that are held together through immutable mechanical laws, creating random events (Smitsman, 2019a; Smitsman et al., 2023). This mechanistic view of life and reality became the foundation for the Scientific Revolution, and later the Industrial Age. Newtonian sciences were particularly suitable for classical economic growth models and equivalent rational-choice based models (Smitsman et al., 2023).

It appears that our belief in human superiority over nature increased as our technological abilities accelerated – creating a sense of control over, rather than alignment with the natural world. The mechanistic worldview also gave rise to mechanistic governance models that divided societies through win-lose competition and the pursuit of power over people. Almost two centuries after Newton, Darwin's theory of 'natural selection' and 'survival of the fittest' provided the economic and political rationalization for an expanding paradigm of domination and exploitation. The doctrine of 'survival of the fittest' further justified the exploitation of perceived weaker and inferior elements, including many indigenous nations.

The theories of Newton and Darwin developed during a Zeitgeist of increasing competition, colonialism and ongoing wars between nations and their empires. With the exception of certain indigenous forms of governance, humanity has a long history of political and economic paradigms of domination.

Since the mid-1920s a new paradigm in science and research has started to emerge – propelled through the rise of quantum physics, and with significant input from fields such as: complexity science, evolutionary biology, biocosmology, quantum physics, quantum information science, nonlinear thermodynamics, cybernetics and evolutionary systems design. Offering a holistic exploration of the nature of reality and the role of consciousness (Cortes & Smolin, 2021; Currivan, 2017, 2022; Penrose, 2017; Hameroff & Penrose, 2014; Kafatos & Nadeau, 2000; Laszlo, 2016, 2018; Smitsman, 2019a; Smitsman & Currivan, 2019, 2021). Furthermore, a growing number of cosmologists hold the view that the universe is not ruled by predetermined or fixed laws, as proclaimed in Newtonian paradigms, but rather by evolving laws (Kauffman, 2019).

This new paradigm scientific worldview reveals a universe that is informationally unified at deeper implicate orders of reality, which inform the evolutionary process of life (Arkani-Hamed, 2017; Bohm, 1980; Currivan, 2017; Smitsman & Currivan, 2021). Although this new paradigm scientific worldview is not yet widely accepted in the mainstream, it does offer essential keys for how to resolve the sustainability crisis. In particular, how to design for regeneration and thrivability by applying the evolutionary dynamics of living systems.

Furthermore, this new paradigm scientific worldview confirms what indigenous people have lived by for thousands of years. Namely, that we are part of an evolving universe through an interdependent web of life, which provides the conditions for maturing and evolving collaboratively and integrally (Capra & Luisi, 2014; Lane, 2019; Smitsman, 2019a).

Governance of Mechanistic Growth Is Unsustainable by Design

Mechanistic economies are designed for profit maximization and unlimited economic growth. The mechanistic growth models of classical economics do not account for the value and loss of natural and social capitals and their ecosystem services (Baue & Thurm, 2020; Smitsman, 2021a). In other words, these are treated as 'externalities' and are not accounted for. Mechanistic growth models are the result of singular goals, dualistic drivers and imposed objectives that decouple human development from the evolutionary process of life. As such, mechanistic growth patterns run contrary to living systems.

On 25 September 2015, 193 countries adopted the United Nations sustainable development goals (SDGs). To achieve the SDGs, it is essential that regenerative growth models are implemented to achieve the transition to inclusive and distributive post-carbon economies. Currently, the majority of mainstream societal systems are still operated by the mechanistic growth models of the Industrial Age, which are degenerative by design. Mechanistic systemic also cause systemic barriers that undermine the necessary transitions and transformations for successful implementation of the SDGs. These systemic barriers are rarely diagnosed by those responsible for the governance of SDG implementation. I will further explain this in the following sections.

The Earth, and her ecosystems, evolved as a result of intricate collaborative strategies, co-creative evolutionary capacities, and networked relationships. Competition within and between species is part of the planetary story, but it is not the dominant pattern (Currivan, 2022; Lent, 2021). Evolution is a complex learning process that emerges from multi-layered feedback loops and informational dynamics that are regulated through systemic boundaries, affordances and future attractors. Evolutionary development creates informational fields of coherence that further regulate the healthy growth and development of entire ecosystems, as well as the individual and collective systems that form part of this (Currivan, 2022; Smitsman, 2019a, 2019b).

Mechanistic growth models miss the complex feedback loops and ecosystemic embedding of living systems. Furthermore, mechanistic leaders do not think in terms of future attractors, and how to create the necessary systemic boundaries for regulating the growth patterns and evolutionary capacities of human societies in partnership with the natural world. As such, the harmful growth patterns of mechanistic governance take place at the expense of essential systemic boundaries and thresholds. Furthermore, mechanistic systems are, by design, predominantly growth oriented – rather than developmental and integral.

In other words, mechanistic systems create systemic thrivability barriers by imposing goals and activities that undermine our self-regulating, adaptive and transformative capacities as living systems. One of the key systemic barriers of mechanistic systems is blocked collaboration and coherence, which further undermines the systemic transformations necessary for resolving the root causes of our worsening sustainability crisis. Furthermore, these systemic thrivability barriers limit our capacities to evolve as a species, by keeping us stuck in the behavioural loops of juvenile species.

Diagnosing 7 Systemic Thrivability Barriers

Through my PhD case-study research I mapped out seven systemic thrivability barriers, as visually displayed and further explained in Fig. 5.3 (Smitsman, 2019a, 2019b):

(1) *Collaboration and coherence are blocked* – Competitive win-lose dynamics, either-or thinking and dualistic choices force a sense of separateness from life and inhibit healthy collaboration. This causes divisions, distrust, conflicts and disunity between people and their communities, and polarizes our diversity.

(2) *Interdependencies are harmed by mechanistic goals* – Economic goals for maximizing extractive growth and development are imposed on, and harming, our interdependencies with life, and the planet's capacity to support populations.

(3) *Reciprocity with living systems is blocked* – By treating life and our planet as mere commodities, mechanistic systems are degenerative and block our reciprocity with living systems and nature. Reciprocity requires internalization of feedback loops that regulate the systemic interdependencies that are safeguarded by systemic boundaries. Without this internationalization, systems will not adapt and regulate their behaviour to changes that could potentially undermine their systemic integrity and health.

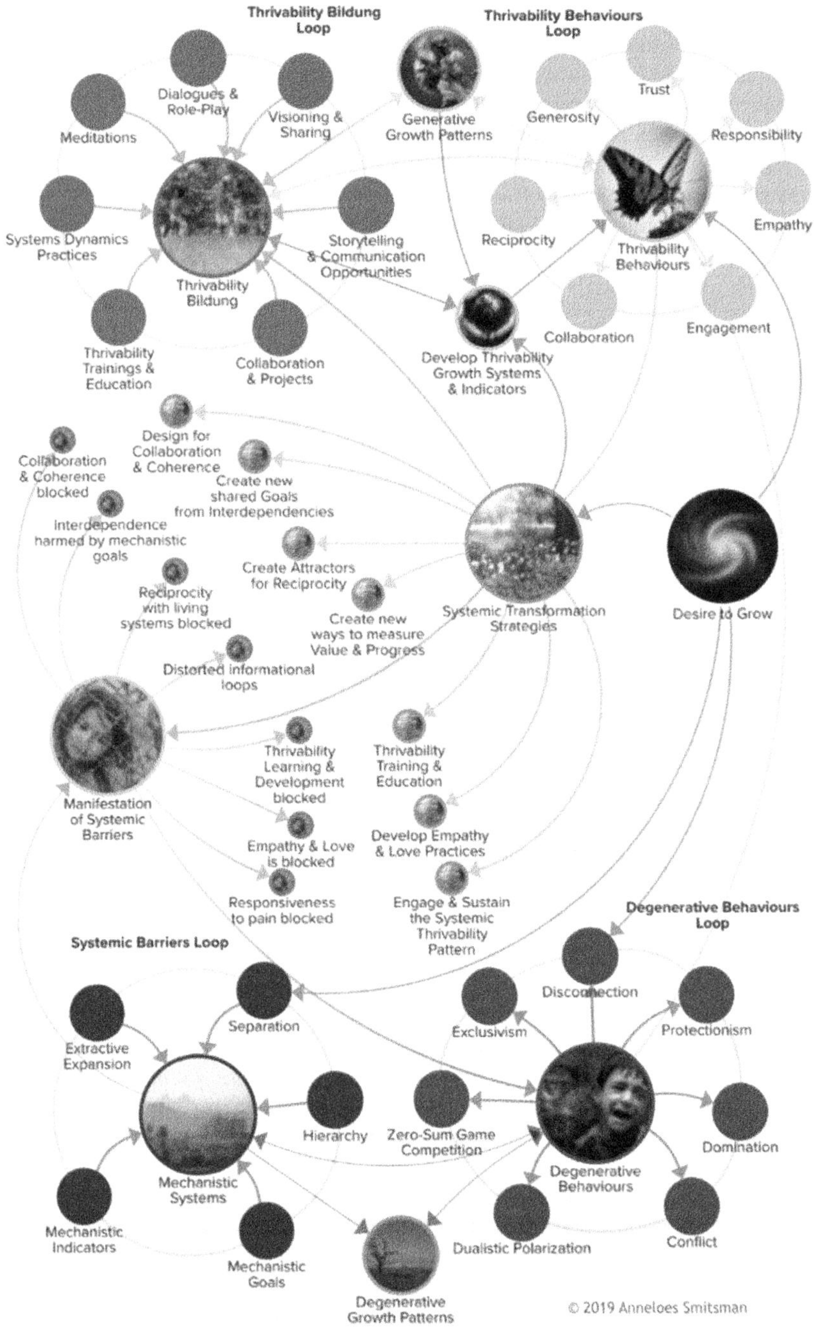

Fig. 5.3. Seven Systemic Thrivability Barriers. *Source:* Overview of Systemic Thrivability Barriers by Smitsman (2019a).

(4) *Distorted informational loops* – By not accounting for the externalities and impacts of mechanistic development and governance, and by not internalizing planetary feedback loops that regulate systemic health conditions, we create illusionary models of progress, growth, and distorted worldviews. A distorted informational loop is one that is not sourced and regulated by the interdependent relationships and value flows of life.
(5) *Thrivability learning and development are blocked* – By creating cultures of competition, division and narrow educational goals, our learning and development capacities for regeneration and thrivability become blocked and are underdeveloped.
(6) *Empathy and love are blocked* – By incentivising domination and duality, and by blocking the development of thrivability consciousness, our capacities for empathy and love become blocked and diminished. Accordingly, people feel isolated, disconnected, disempowered and alone.
(7) *Responsiveness to pain is blocked* – By ignoring essential feedback in the governance and cultures of our human development, and by numbing ourselves to the pain we inflict on our planet and each other, our responsiveness to pain becomes blocked and we fail to learn from the vital signals that pain provides us. When we numb or normalize pain, we fail to learn from the wisdom of pain and the reasons for the hurt. Responsiveness to pain means opening our hearts, developing our empathy and allowing ourselves to receive life's feedback so we may learn and mature in consciousness.

By merely focussing on sustainability targets, rather than the underlying drivers, we become blind to the deeper transformational change process that is necessary. To address our systemic blindspots, it is essential that we make the systemic barriers visible and couple this to policy making, education, governance and institutional design for a thrivable world and future. We cannot resolve our sustainability crisis from the same worldviews and systems that are at the root of the problem. Our sustainability crisis is essentially a systemic barrier issue that reveals a deeper crisis in human consciousness.

Ending the Politics of Dualism and the Dualization of Politics

The electoral systems of democracies tend to be dualistic by design through win-lose mechanisms that mandate the power of governance to a winning majority – whether as a single party, or as a coalition of parties. Although this electoral mechanism for citizen-based decision making may have been conceived to stop the concentration of power by a small minority, it is not able to provide the broader inclusive and collaborative governance capacities for resolving the sustainability crisis.

Sustainability issues extend beyond the nation-state and cannot be reduced to mere party politics. As explained in the previous section, unless we address the deeper underlying drivers of the sustainability crisis, the global crisis conditions will only divide humanity further. Furthermore, vested corporate interests in the political domain make it difficult for genuine political leaders to even get elected. Many upcoming new parties that transcend conventional party politics are blocked from gaining positions of power. It takes tremendous courage, tact, and networking capacities, as well as enormous amounts of funding, to gain sufficient political influence. All the more reason why the new paradigm governance and movement building tools are so important during this tipping point time. Empowering citizens to freely meet and collaborate through their own decentralized governance networks.

To end the politics of dualism, and the dualization of politics, adopting a larger planetary perspective of our world in transformation is essential. The planetary perspective empowers us as citizens of the Earth to ground our actions in dialogue with the places where we live.

As illustrated earlier, new governance ecosystems are developing that empower people to make decisions together and collaborate in whole new ways. We are at the forefront of a major paradigm shift in the making of democracies and governance. Mainstream governments will have to transform their political systems and policy making processes, if they are to secure sufficient engagement from society for the changes ahead. The shift from centrally organized nation-state governance to decentralized self-organizing citizen-led governance is, in my view, part of a larger civilizational shift. A shift that is accelerating because multiple tipping points are starting to converge, at a time when new participatory governance tools are becoming more widely accessible.

Furthermore, a new paradigm in politics and governance can attract people out of the political vacuum of growing distrust. As such, buffering the influence of extremist and populist parties that prey on distrust and uncertainty. During the 2021 Symposium for a New Paradigm in Politics, participants indicated the following requirements for a new paradigm in politics and governance (Smitsman & Laszlo, 2022):

- New paradigm principles of engagement that are based on the fundamental unity of life, and which address the old paradigm engagement of dualistic win-lose competition, domination, control and short-term interests;
- Planetary ethics based on respect for planetary boundaries, systemic thresholds, tipping points, fair allocations and stewardship for an inclusive and thriving world and future.
- Ecological economies, evolutionary constitutions, and planetary governance that empower planetary health and wellbeing, regeneration, planetary security, resilience, thrivability and planetary citizenship.
- Partnerships that include life and our Earth, based on the understanding that the universe is alive, sentient and responsive;
- Giving primacy to the sentience of consciousness in all its forms;
- Developing human capabilities that act in service of life on Earth, and with responsibility for the wellbeing of our planet and future generations, and;
- Acknowledging the primacy of consciousness and sentience of life as the foundation for transforming and redesigning humanity's governmental, economic, legal, political and educational systems.

We have to become the new paradigm people in order to co-create and sustain a new-paradigm world. The shift to becoming planetary conscious is about realizing how we are born as Earth citizens of an ever-evolving planetary civilization. The transition to a planetary civilization cannot be brought about via nation-state thinking.

Education for planetary citizenship should become a central focus for schools, universities and other educational institutions, and as part of education for sustainability and thrivability (Smitsman, 2019a, 2021; Smitsman et al., 2020, 2021). Planetary education is about developing our future creative capacities for a thrivable world and future, which also includes learning how to transform and stop the systems, behaviours and models that are harmful and unsustainable. To summarize, ending the politics of duality and the dualization of politics requires:

- Commitment to collaborate for the issues that require us to stand together in solidarity with the Earth, and for the urgency of this time.
- Willingness to risk losing popularity by understanding what it means to act as a future ancestor for the changes ahead.
- Leading from vision by initiating pathways for resilience and thrivability that empower the necessary economic, governmental, political, cultural and educational transformations for this time.
- Act on the mandate of the Earth and the future generations, instead of campaign managers, voter statistics and short-term profits.
- Courage to stop the manipulation of voters through persistent disinformation and polarizing narratives that divide people for political and economic gain.

Evolutionary Coherence and Planetary Consciousness

The sustainability crisis of the modern world is a major wake-up call for our species. As explained earlier, we have reached a critical stage in our evolutionary development. The choices we now make, and those we fail to make, will determine the quality of life for generations to come. Human societies are divided, polarized and fragmented, while growing more complex. Increasing complexity without deepening evolutionary coherence leads to self-destruction and collapse.

> Evolutionary coherence is a dynamic state of harmonic resonance and spontaneous collaboration between the diverse elements and relationships of complex living systems. A natural state of attunement to the innate wholeness and unity of life.
>
> (Smitsman, 2022)

On the whole, the human world is not evolutionary coherent, which may also explain the increase in violence, suicides, shootings, tensions and (self)destructiveness. We operate like a cancer with dysfunctional growth patterns that exceed natural boundaries and undermine the health of the whole. Yet in the midst of all this (or perhaps because of it) there is a new connective pattern of consciousness that is starting to emerge. Technology can play a transformative role if it amplifies the connective patterns of our evolutionary development. Namely, by making it possible, and easier, for people to co-create and collaborate for the world and future we want to live in. Becoming conscious of ourselves at the planetary level is the only way to evolve to become a maturing and wiser species (Kafatos, 2016; Smitsman, 2022). Planetary consciousness transcends former nationalistic or separatist political identities.

Coherence cannot be enforced through top-down interventions. Furthermore, coherence is different from cohesion. Forests, oceans, wetlands and most of nature's ecosystems are naturally evolutionary coherent. The trees do not require a policy for how to collaborate with the myriad of life-forms that depend on them. They do not have to be told how and when to distribute resources and information through their mycelium networks for the health of the entire ecosystem. Evolutionary coherence is a field dynamic and informational pattern of ecosystems in which organisms spontaneously collaborate, co-create, co-evolve and share resources.

The shift to planetary consciousness is about learning how to become evolutionary coherent with life. When we are in a state of evolutionary coherence there is a natural sense of unity, flow and desire to collaborate and learn together. Evolutionary coherence is the field dynamic and collaborative pattern of planetary consciousness. As one of the youngest members of the planetary family, we are yet to learn this dance. Evolutionary coherence is also the organizational pattern of higher orders of complexity – that is, an integral awareness that transforms dualistic tendencies and separatist thinking.

The sustainability crisis masks a deeper crisis in our collective consciousness. A crisis of meaning, purpose and maturation. A developmental crisis that challenges us to release and transform many of our preconceived ideas and beliefs, as well our addictive patterns and developmental dysfunctions. The shift to planetary consciousness is an evolutionary imperative.

Systemic Boundaries Are Necessary for Maturation and Autonomy

One of the most celebrated beliefs of Western civilizations is the existence of individual freedoms apart from the whole. When this belief gets fuelled by the desire to live without limitations – that is, without boundaries and constraints – the systemic context for maturation and autonomy gets lost.

When your body cannot constrain and regulate your internal temperature you will die. If you never get feedback from people around you and do not listen to the boundaries that tell you to stop, pause, reflect and integrate, you will most likely become an impossible person with little or no maturity. Western liberalism has long promoted a frontier mentality that perceives boundaries and limitations as a weakness to overcome. Believing that human superiority means mastery over the body and physical conditions of life. With little or no awareness of the fundamental role that systemic boundaries serve to regulate the health and learning capacities of systems. Systemic boundaries are how living systems enable autonomy and create conditions for life to thrive, and for consciousness to mature. Without systemic boundaries there would be no autonomy, creativity and evolution.

In other words, the political and economic ideologies of liberalism and neoliberalism do not offer the maturation pathways that our species need for resolving the meta-crisis of our time. Neither do their political polarities, like communism and socialism. Many of the old paradigm ideologies continue to define how political parties, and their policies, are shaped today. As such adding further barriers to the required civilizational transformations.

In case this is not yet clear, a systemic barrier is *not* a systemic boundary. Systemic boundaries serve to regulate the healthy growth and development of living systems, and support maturation. Systemic barriers, however, result from mechanistic growth archetypes that impose goals and activities that undermine our self-regulating, adaptive and transformative capacities as living systems.

A planetary and systemic understanding of our fundamental rights and freedoms is essential for maturing as a species. As well as for learning how to navigate through the storm of systemic collapse, which will put pressure on many of our rights and freedoms. The Zeitgeist of individualism is continuing to blow the sails of people's expectations, and this will make it more difficult for political leaders to explore a careful balancing between ecosystemic priorities and material privileges.

- What is our compass for navigating through this tipping point time?
- What destination, and what kind of civilization, are we setting sail for?

Individual rights and freedoms are essential, however, we cannot achieve this by harming and undermining the ecosystemic conditions and interdependent relationships on which these rights and freedoms depend. What does freedom mean for people who are forced to abandon their islands due to sea level rise, and become climate refugees? What does freedom, and the right to safety, mean in the midst of climate disasters because we failed to limit global warming to 1.5°C degrees? What does freedom, and the right of safety, mean for those who live in war-torn countries because their country's resources became a higher priority than their autonomy and sovereignty?

Freedom requires autonomy, which requires one is able to regulate and adjust their inner and outer activities, and apply their creative power for self-renewal, healing, transformation and development. Autonomy is not about being separate or apart from life or others. Freedom cannot be achieved through dualistic approaches that ignore the larger systemic contexts for our fundamental freedoms. By realizing and respecting how we are part of a finite planet with limited carrying capacities, and interdependent needs and relationships, we will discover the ways to work with (rather than against) life. Furthermore, separating human rights from the rights of nature creates another destructive dualism that further undermines the necessary conditions for our personal and collective thrivability.

Nothing in nature grows exponentially. Everything is embedded within ecosystemic relationships of interdependence, regulated through systemic boundaries that make autonomy possible – and within which the experience of individuated self-aware consciousness can emerge. Getting real about the limits of our destructive growth models, as well as our unrealistic expectations, is a necessary step towards growing up and maturing as a species. If it is freedom we are after, let us with humility and respect care for life and each other as a whole. Only then will we (eventually) mature as a species.

Acknowledging Global Interdependence and Universal Responsibilities

The underlying driver for the modernization of human societies was the premise that this would bring increased freedoms and a better quality of life. The whole purpose of systemic boundaries, however, is not to impose on freedom, but rather to regulate our freedoms through interdependent autonomies so we may grow, develop and evolve as a whole. The Earth Charter provides a useful example of a declaration on global interdependence and universal responsibilities. As such, the Earth Charter offers a much needed planetary context for how to exercise our human rights and freedoms, which is missing from the Universal Declaration of Human Rights (UDHR).

As stated in the Earth Charter, it seeks to inspire, 'in all people a new sense of global interdependence and shared responsibility for the well-being of the whole human family, the greater community of life, and future generations. It is a vision of hope and a call to action', (The Earth Charter, 2020). Moreover, the 16 principles of the Earth Charter lay the groundwork for a 'global movement towards a more just, sustainable and peaceful world'.

Unfortunately, the Earth Charter was never adopted formally by the United Nations, hence its impact is somewhat limited. Acknowledging global interdependence and universal responsibilities are essential for developing our planetary stewardship capacities and becoming planetary conscious. This maturation stage of our evolutionary development is also a rite of passage, which will challenge the very foundations upon which we have been building our societies and lives.

The Inner Shifts for a New Paradigm in Politics

Each of us is endowed with inherent political power – your creative agency to effect change in the world – which has nothing to do with your job, or your position in society. To complete this chapter, I would like to offer the following exercise to support the inner shifts for a new paradigm in politics. You can go through this exercise by envisioning and exploring how you can hold these holistic aspects of politics in your being, and then apply this in your life and work:[4]

(1) *Politics as Consciousness* – Politics is how we express, develop and evolve our consciousness, individually and collectively. *Envision the consciousness of a healthy, whole and enlightened politics. A consciousness that evolves the practice of politics for the maturation of humanity and the collective wellbeing of all life on Earth.*

---

[4]These 13 aspects of politics are adapted from the 16 aspects that feature in, *The New Paradigm in Politics* (Smitsman & Laszlo, 2022).

(2) *Politics as Sentience* – Politics is how we sense, explore and reach out to one another for what is appropriate, relevant and in service of life as a whole. *Our sentience enables our consciousness to grow in self-awareness through embodied feelings, resonance and connection. Sentience also enables us to experience, develop, and give empathy, love, and compassion. Apply your sentience capacities to grow your wisdom and compassion, and express this in how you practice your political agency for our world in transformation.*

(3) *Politics as Unity* – Politics serves to unite us in our diversity, by placing the well-being of life and our planet at the centre of our common priorities and decision-making. *Imagine a world in which politics serves to unite us in our diversity.*

(4) *Politics as Collaboration* – Politics is how we collaborate and work together for the issues, opportunities and tasks that require concerted and coordinated actions, shared visions and common responsibilities. *Develop your collaborative capacities and actions by reaching out to others from a place of common stewardship for our world and future. Enhance your collaboration by nurturing and supporting what makes a thrivable world and future possible.*

(5) *Politics as Community* – Politics serves to bring us together in community with the Earth and each other, to decide, dialogue and envision together how to act on our individual and collective responsibilities, rights and opportunities. *Make the commitment to joyfully contribute to the health and wellbeing of the communities you are part of.*

(6) *Politics as Relationship* – Politics is a relational process that involves feelings, dreams, aspirations, expectations, beliefs and actions. Politics as relationship reminds us how to partner with life and each other for a thriving world and future. *Invest in your relationships and explore partnering life as a future ancestor of a more evolved and caring world.*

(7) *Politics as Choice* – Politics serves to enable, respect and protect our power and right of choice. Politics as choice reminds us of our autonomy and our universal rights and responsibilities. *Explore the choices that make a new paradigm in politics possible, such as decentralizing governance, democratizing ownership, and empowering inclusive participation. As well as choosing love over hatred, forgiveness over revenge, and healing over division. Apply your political agency as your choice for a new paradigm world, as a future ancestor of a thriving planetary civilization.*

(8) *Politics as Creativity* – Politics serves as a possibility-increasing process that creates the conditions for us to thrive and evolve. Politics as creativity empowers, inspires and evokes in us the evolutionary response of the worlds we seek to become. *Explore your political power as creativity by becoming aware of, and shifting, how you respond to challenges and opportunities in support of life.*

(9) *Politics as Learning* – Politics is a continual learning process that challenges us to develop and grow in consciousness. *Reflect on what you are currently learning about yourself and others, and the areas of your consciousness that challenge you to evolve further.*

(10) *Politics as Healing* – Politics is a process through which we can heal the wounds and traumas of division, conflict and disunity. Politics as healing helps us to develop the heart spaces for learning how to trust, let go, surrender, open, renew, and evolve together. *Explore the areas in yourself, and your life and relationships, that require healing support.*
(11) *Politics as Love* – Politics serves to empower and enhance our caring capacities and empathic awareness. Politics as love is how we make it safe, empowering and joyful to 'human well' together. *Envision politics fuelled by the power of love and apply your political agency as a force of love.*
(12) *Politics as Wisdom* – Politics serves to make us wiser people by listening to each other and learning how to steward our Earth in partnership with life. *Commit to growing and cultivating your inner wisdom and sharing this with the world around you.*
(13) *Politics as YOU – Vividly imagine the ways you can be the New Paradigm in Politics.*

Conclusion

A new paradigm in politics and governance is emerging as a decentralized and planetary response for transforming our democracies, governance systems and economies. Empowering people to steward the wellbeing and planetary security of our world and future through collaborative incentives, participatory decision-making, joint ownership of assets, decentralized coordination of resources, distributive value flows and inclusive opportunities. Based on a paradigm shift in values from survivability and competition to regeneration and thrivability. As well as a shift in focus from governments to governance, and from constitutions to constitutionalizing a new paradigm ethos of wholeness and unity with life.

The ultimate vision for a new paradigm in politics and governance goes much further than creating new political models and governance systems for solving the sustainability crises. It's about our maturation as a species by partnering our Earth in the evolutionary process of life and becoming planetary conscious. So that together we may co-create and become the conditions for our collective thrivability, for generations to come.

References

Arkani-Hamed, N. (2017, December 1). *The doom of spacetime – Why it must dissolve into more fundamental structures* [Video]. PSW Science. https://bit.ly/2SbsI5Y

Baue, B., & Thurm, R. (2020). *Sustainable finance blueprint*. r3.0. https://bit.ly/31IMJTJ

Bohm, D. (1980). *Wholeness and the implicate order*. Routledge.

Capra, F., & Luisi, P. L. (2014). *The systems view of life: A unifying vision*. Cambridge University Press.

Chancel, L., Piketty, T., Saez, E., & Zucman, G. (2022). *World inequality report 2022*. World Inequality Lab. https://wir2022.wid.world/

Cortes, M., & Smolin, L. (2021). Physics, time, and qualia. *Journal of Consciousness Studies*, *28*(9–10), 36–51.

Currivan, J. (2017). *The Cosmic Hologram: In-formation at the Center of Creation*. Inner Traditions/Bear & Company.

Currivan, J. (2022). *The story of Gaia: The big breath and the evolutionary journey of our conscious planet*. Inner Traditions/Bear & Company.

Democracy International. (2021). *Annual Report 2011–2021*. Democracy International. https://www.democracy-international.org/

Ecocivilisation. (2022). Home page. https://www.ecocivilisation.eu/en/home/

Great Transition Initiative. (2022). Home page. https://greattransition.org/

Hameroff, S., & Penrose, R. (2014). Consciousness in the universe: A review of the 'Orch OR' theory. *Physics of Life Reviews*, *11*(1), 39–78. https://doi.org/10.1016/j.plrev.2013.08.002

IPCC. (2022). *Climate change 2022: Impacts, adaptation and vulnerability*. IPCC Sixth Assessment Report by Working Group 2. IPCC. https://www.ipcc.ch/report/ar6/wg2

Kafatos, M. C. (2016). *Planetary consciousness and humanity's destiny. Embrace of the Earth*. https://digitalcommons.ciis.edu/embraceoftheearth2016/2

Kafatos, M. C., & Nadeau, R. (2000). *The conscious universe: Parts and wholes in physical reality*. Springer-Verlag.

Kauffman, S. A. (2019). *A world beyond physics: The emergence and evolution of life* (1st ed.). Oxford University Press.

Lane, P. (2019). *Sixteen indigenous guiding principles for co-creating a sustainable, harmonious, prosperous world*. Four Worlds International Institute. https://bit.ly/32b5IV5

Laszlo, E. (Ed.). (2016). *What is reality? The new map of cosmos and consciousness*. SelectBooks, Inc.

Laszlo, A. (2018). Living the new paradigm: Syntony and spark in life, being and becoming. In *The handbook of new paradigm research*. A publication of the Laszlo Institute of New Paradigm Research. Waterfront Press.

Lent, J. (2021). *The web of meaning*. Profile Books Ltd.

McGrath, M. (2021, August 9). *Climate change: IPCC report is 'code red for humanity*. https://www.bbc.com/news/science-environment-58130705

McKay, D. A., Winkelmann, R., Sakschewski, B., Loriani, S., Fetzer, I., Cornell, S. E., Rockström, J., & Lenton, T. M. (2022). Exceeding 1.5°C global warming could trigger multiple climate tipping points. *Science*, *377*(6611).

Milman, O. (2023, February). Monster profits' for energy giants reveal a self-destructive fossil fuel resurgence. *The Guardian Analysis*. https://bit.ly/3xlBVtH

Rockström, J., Steffen, W., Noone, K., Persson, A., Chapin, F. S., Lambin, E. F., Lenton, T. M., Scheffer, M., Folke, C., Schellnhuber, H. J., Nykvist, B., de Wit, C. A., Hughes, T., van der Leeuw, S., Rodhe, H., Sörlin, S., Snyder, P. K., Costanza, R., Svedin, U., … Foley, J. A. (2009). A safe operating space for humanity. *Nature*, *461*, 472–475. https://doi.org/10.1038/461472a

Penrose, R., Hameroff, S., & Kak, S. (Eds.). (2017). *Consciousness and the universe: Quantum physics, evolution, brain & mind*. Cosmology Science Publishers.

Schmachtenberger, D. (2022). The Metacrisis with Daniel Schmachtenberger. Part 1, Green Pill #26. Bankless Shows. https://youtu.be/WVEP0zAK-xQ

SDG Thought Leaders Circle. (2022). Unitive narrative. https://sdgthoughtleaderscircle.org/unitive-new-narrative/

SEEDS. (2021). The official SEEDS constitution. https://bit.ly/3DhWFUi

Smitsman, A. (2019a). *Into the heart of systems change*. Ph.D. Dissertation. International centre for integrated assessment and Sustainable development (ICIS). Maastricht University. https://bit.ly/3EtGV1P

Smitsman, A. (2019b). *Transition Plan for a Thrivable Civilisation*. Medium. https://bit.ly/3RQEAn4

Smitsman, A. (2021a). Economy of Life – The architecture of wholeness for an economy that is life sustaining and regenerative. In Klomp, K. & Shinta Oosterwaal, S. (Eds.), *Thrive: Fundamentals for a new economy*. Business Contact.

Smitsman, A. (2021b). Learning from living systems. Contribution to GTI forum: An Earth constitution: Has its time come? *The Great Transition Initiative*. https://greattransition.org/gti-forum/earth-constitution-smitsman

Smitsman, A. (2022). *EARTHwise Constitution for a Planetary Civilization*. EARTHwise Publishing. https://www.earthwisecentre.org/constitution

Smitsman, A., Baue, B., & Thurm, R. (2021). *Blueprint 9. Educational transformation–7 transformative learning perspectives for regeneration and thrivability*. r3.0. https://www.r3-0.org/blueprint-9-et/

Smitsman, A., & Currivan, J. (2019). Systemic transformation: Into the birth canal. *Systems Research and Behavioral Science*, 1–10. https://doi.org/10.1002/sres.2573

Smitsman, A., & Currivan, J. (2021). Healing our relationship with Gaia through a New Thrivability Paradigm. In J. Wright (Ed.), *Quantum thinking for agroecology: Theory and practice for the farming of tomorrow*. Taylor & Francis Group. https://bit.ly/3AvVG1K

Smitsman, A., & Houston, J. (2021). *The quest of rose: The cosmic keys of our future becoming*. Book 1 of The Future Humans Trilogy. Independently published via Oxygen Publishing.

Smitsman, A., & Houston, J. (2022). *Return of the Avatars: The Cosmic Architect Tools of Our Future Becoming. Book 2 of the Future Humans Trilogy*. Independently published via Oxygen Publishing.

Smitsman, A., & Laszlo, A. (Eds.). (2022). The New Paradigm in Politics. In *The new paradigm symposia series – Book 1*. SelectBooks.

Smitsman, A., Laszlo, A., & Luksha, P. (2020). Evolutionary learning ecosystems for thrivable futures – Crafting and curating the conditions for future-fit education. *World Futures: The Journal of New Paradigm Research*. https://doi.org/10.1080/02604027.2020.1740075

Smitsman, A., Murtha, T., Rau, T., & Kara Stonehouse, K. (2022). *The Hypha DAO and SEEDS case-study. As input for the r3.0 funding governance for systemic transformation blueprint*. https://www.r3-0.org/blueprint-8-fgst/

Smitsman, A., Patra, S. & Laszlo, A. (2023). Complexity and uncertainty in a world of emergence – Part 1. *International Journal of Complexity in Applied Science and Technology* [in review].

Steffen, W., Rockström, J., Richardson, K., Lenton, T. M., Folke, C., Liverman, D. Summerhayes, C. P., Barnosky, A. D., Cornell, S. E., Crucifix, M., Donges, J. F., Fetzer, I., Lade, S. J., Scheffer, M., Winkelmann, R., & Schellnhuber, H. J. (2018). Trajectories of the earth System in the Anthropocene. In *Proceedings of the National Academy of Sciences*. https://doi.org/10.1073/pnas.1810141115

Stockholm Resilience Centre. (2022). *Planetary Boundaries Framework*. https://bit.ly/3kHfVny

The Earth Charter. (2020). https://earthcharter.org/read-the-earth-charter/

The Guardian. (2022, August 5). *The Guardian view on accelerating global heating: Follow the science*. The Guardian Editorial. https://bit.ly/3ekDvWG

Treisman, S., & Guriev, D. (2022). *Spin dictators: The changing face of tyranny in the 21st century*. Princeton University Press.

Wang-Erlandsson, L., Tobian, A., van der Ent, R. J., Fetzer, I., te Wierik, S., Porkka, M., Staal, A., Jaramillo, F., Dahlmann, H., Singh, D., Greve, P., Cornell, S. E., Steffen, W., Bai, X., & Rockström, J. (2022). A planetary boundary for green water. *Nature Reviews Earth & Environment*, *3*, 380–392. https://doi.org/10.1038/s43017-022-00287-8

Chapter 6

Spiritual Leadership for Sustainable Development Policy

Naresh Singh

Abstract

Spirituality and leadership, both have an intrinsic goal where they incorporate clarity of understanding, vision and collective action and both have the potential to empower an individual or a team, with commitment and productivity. It is one of the rapidly growing areas of leadership. It takes responsible policymakers and leaders to build a nation that benefits multiple stakeholders and all citizens. The aim of the chapter is to explore the concept of spirituality and show how applied spirituality can provide moral and practical guidance for leaders of public policy to take bold and enlightened steps towards achieving sustainable development (SD) goals. We define spirituality as a way of understanding, inner awareness, personal integration, and a source of values that give ultimate meaning or purpose beyond the egoic self. As such the chapter will go beyond existing discussions of ethical, moral, or values-based leadership and raise issues of how a deeper spiritual understanding of human nature can guide leaders. Some helpful practices like mindfulness are also covered in this chapter. There are various relevant leadership styles including transformational leadership, servant leadership, moral leadership and participatory leadership. Although each of these has some positive characteristics, this chapter with the help of those characteristics would try to get a deeper insight and understanding of how spirituality can stimulate and add more value, and bring integrity, motivation and strong leadership qualities. This chapter covers the existing gap in the literature on applied spirituality and leadership and concludes that leadership when incorporated with spirituality plays a vital role in honing the skills of the leaders and changing their perspective towards the team. The chapter will conclude with ideas for discussion among faculty and students and suggestions for further research into the use of applied spirituality for leadership in sustainable development policy.

Applied Spirituality and Sustainable Development Policy, 117–131

Published under exclusive licence by Emerald Publishing Limited
doi:10.1108/978-1-83753-380-020231006

Keywords: Sustainable development goals; secular spirituality; Anthropocene; spiritual leadership; ethical leadership; policy leadership; egoic

Introduction

At all levels of society much is expected from leaders whether in civil society organizations, corporate sector or government from village panchayats through districts, states, national and international levels. Sustainable development challenges need astute, balanced and bold leadership in all these sectors and levels. Such leadership also requires a degree of enlightened self-interest and self-realization in order to lead others to rethink their values and become involved in the transformations needed to achieve the sustainable development goals. Secular spirituality based on the human experiential realization of what we truly are at the core of our being and at the same time so much bigger than ourselves as part of reality inspires a kind of leadership that I believe is the call of our times. Such leadership is however too rare at the moment and so this chapter seeks to begin defining what leadership anchored in applied spirituality might look like as well as to the make the case for and outline the ways in which such leadership might be expanded.

After the United Nations conference on sustainable development in Rio in June 1992, the Secretary General of the conference was asked how many leaders had attended. His response was telling. He said we had the largest ever number of heads of states and governments but I am not sure how many leaders were there. He had a clear understanding of the difficult political choices that would have to be made to lead the social, economic and ecological transformations that would be needed to steer our civilization towards sustainability. Many promises were made, an agenda for action laid out (Agenda 21) and then we moved to implementation. Now 30 years later, and after the 2015 agreement on the SDGs to be achieved by 2030, we are in a worse off situation on climate change impacts, species extinction, economic inequality and over all progress on the SDGs is unsatisfactory.

In this chapter we first consider the importance of leadership for sustainable development policy decisions, and implementation. This is followed by a consideration of what leadership based on applied spirituality might look like and finally we describe how such leadership might develop and implement an invigorated and transformative agenda to accelerate action towards the SDGs.

Leadership for Sustainable Development Policy

The Policy Context

In this section we focus on the public policy challenges the Anthropocene poses for finding solutions for a more sustainable human civilization. These challenges have been described in the earlier sections of this book and are reflected in each of the 17 SDGs. However, the specification of these challenges as wicked policy problems can help us better understand the complex nature of these challenges and the consequent challenges for leadership in sustainable development policy. Complex policy problems arise because of lack of social consensus as well as technical certainty of how to solve them. They frequently involve opposing interests and contrasting viewpoints among various stakeholder groups. Arguments over issues and regulations are triggered by a variety of things, such as vested financial interests, sociocultural ideologies and political trust. Rittel and Webber (1973) described wicked problems in public policy were defined as having numerous causes and sources, imprecise methods of acknowledging them, and being manageable but eventually unsolvable. Conventional approaches not only fail to address wicked problems, but they may also make matters worse by producing unfavourable outcomes. Every wicked problem is essentially unique so there is usually not much precedent or best practice to guide action. Both defining and solving wicked issues are incredibly challenging tasks. Technology, skill, reason and authority are common problem-solving techniques that fall short in this situation. The fact that individuals are both the problem and the solution for wicked issues makes them particularly evil (Hull et al., 2020).

Leaders in political, economic and social organizations debate whether topics should take precedence over others based on their assessments of risks, benefits and possibilities. To get widespread support for their preferred strategy, leaders frequently present issues and answers in clear, appealing narratives. Policy actors use evidence and knowledge in a selective manner to affect how credible their own preferred policy solutions are seen to be. Although policy discussions are shaped by the interaction of various types of information, values, emotions and interests, hard evidence is not prioritized in daily politics. Although expertise can help manage difficult issues, it never decides how things turn out.

It is necessary to remind ourselves that power, politics and the ensuing competition among vested interest groups; rather than evidence; usually determine the outcome of policies. Evidence is merely one input into policy formation. Bottom-up emergent behaviour by individuals and groups operating at the microlevel can unintentionally produce macro patterns that are larger or less than the sum of their parts in complex systems. Complexity theory offers options for making politics and power a positive sum game rather than the conventional zero sum that linear dynamics will lead to. Positive sum games enable important societal change that would otherwise be unachievable due to hierarchical, top-down control by the strong, such as the empowerment of the poor. It is unavoidable that different policy approaches and attitudes exist. Due to these discrepancies' intricate ties to ideologies, beliefs, interests and other factors, they are frequently ingrained or hard to alter.

Policy Leadership in the Context of the Anthropocene

Hull et al. (2020) suggest that solving wicked problems requires three sets of leadership skills and practices explained and illustrated in the chapter that follow – the abilities to connect, collaborate and adapt. In order to connect, leadership skills and practices are required to coordinate actions with others whom the leaders may never meet, don't have authority over, and may not even know exist: people located in different organizations, sectors, time zones, countries and supply chains. The collaboration skills and practices are required for widening differences of opinion, identity, expertise and culture – differences being fuelled by filter bubbles, echo chambers, network propaganda, confirmation bias and motivated reasoning. Finally, leaders need help people *adapt* to confounding uncertainty and accelerating change, avoid analysis-paralysis, fail forward and learn by doing. Importantly, Hull et al. (2020) claim that you can practice 'wicked leadership', regardless of your position, whether you are the person in charge, just a midlevel professional or a stakeholder engaging in a community planning effort where no one has authority over others. Moreover, wicked leadership skills and practices can be learnt.

Leadership, in the context of the Anthropocene might consist of *direction*, *alignment* and *commitment*. Hull et al. argue that these conditions exist pretty much any time and any place a group of people manages to get things done: people agree on the direction that defines what they want to achieve, align their efforts and resources to achieve that direction, and commit to helping each other and maintaining the work over time. The challenge in wicked policy situations, however, is precisely the lack of these conditions and the pressing need to get things done any way. This conception of leadership places responsibility for leadership on the shoulders of all stakeholders not just the few designated leaders or elected officials. In other words, leadership in the Anthropocene is something everyone can do, not just people in positions of formal authority. Everyone can and should lead from where they are. Indeed, it might very well be that the only way leadership can happen in wicked situations is if stakeholders co-construct direction, alignment and commitment. This conception of leadership is likely to be empowering.

These leadership elements seem quite attractive and can prove to be useful if the direction is towards sustainable, equitable and just development. It is quite common today that we collectively create results that nobody wants: environmental destruction, inequity, less happiness and well-being in spite of increasing GDP per capita. Most leaders, not only those at the top, but also grass root leaders feel incapable of changing this basic condition in which we create collectively that which we do not want. This fundamental leadership gap springs from two basic dimensions: one outer and the other inner. The outer missing dimension is the lack of appreciation and leadership at the complex adaptive systems level where wickedness arises. The inner dimension is the ability to draw from the ones' own spiritual core the recognition of your own true nature; the illusory notions of ego and separateness; the recognition of a shared consciousness; and the oneness of life. This implies leadership that is more connected to one's own consciousness including dimensions of mindfulness, presence and self-awareness. In practice of course, inner and outer dimensions do not exist as such and leaders make decisions from a seamless continuum of intent, bias, values, knowledge and experience. Nevertheless, in order to emphasize areas for leadership training and development we can employ these constructs with the recognition that they work together in practice.

Despite many promises that were made by the leaders at international and national fora for achieving the sustainable development goals (SDGs), there is increasing concern in most countries about lack of progress in implementing the SDGs. The performance of any country in achieving the SDGs, to a large extent, depends on its leadership at all levels. Effective leadership has the power to translate and implement sustainable development policies in meeting the needs of the citizens. To achieve this, we would need every single one of us to work towards creating a sustainable future. Leaders here could not only help bring us all together to work on a common goal with shared values but have the power to help us embrace the harsh realities, conflict and uncertainty on the path to achieve the goals. The world seeks effective leadership for sustainable development based on relational view of how the world works and who could work with others. In this world individual egoic drives are transcended to values based on interbeing, going beyond notions of separateness from each other and from nature. It seeks leadership that prizes being above having and hence seeks to make public policy with a balanced consideration of the political economy of having and of being. If spirituality could be recognized as a key element in leadership and in its delivery, would the leaders be more capable of handling their roles and giving out a better outcome in achieving the said goals?

Secular Spirituality

Elsewhere in this book the concept of secular spirituality has been alluded to. Consistent with those explanations we see secular spirituality as a common human experience not associated with any organized religion or dependent on any religious faith or belief system. Nevertheless, we recognize that spirituality has from time immemorial been associated with religion. We therefore reviewed the spiritual and mystical core ideas and teachings of the world's major religions and found that the tenets which we include under the rubric of secular spirituality are consistent with these teachings. Spirituality has been defined in many ways. Here we identify some attributes that have implications for leadership. For instance, Roof (1999, p. 35 Spiritual Market Place) contends that themes like a source of values and ultimate meaning or purpose beyond the self, a sense of mystery and self-transcendence, a way of understanding, an inner awareness, and personal integration are all part of what is meant by spirituality. Our spirituality is an integral aspect of all we are and do, not a distinct quality or nature that we possess. Some have come to the conclusion that spirituality possesses a strong, enigmatic aspect that cannot be reduced to a straightforward subject of study. 'We all see our lives, and/or the space wherein we live our lives, as having a certain moral/spiritual shape. Somewhere, in some activity, or condition, lies a fullness, a richness; that is, in that place (activity or condition), life is fuller, richer, deeper, more worthwhile, more admirable, more what it should be. This is perhaps a place of power: we often experience this as deeply moving or inspiring' (Charles Taylor, 2007. A Secular Age.)

Mysticism is in many ways akin to secular spirituality. Mysticism is not rooted in faith, principle, dogma or even belief. In Mysticism, direct knowledge of spiritual truth or ultimate reality can be attained through subjective experience. Nevertheless, at the core of all the major religions are mystical teachings around truth, love, transcendence, pure awareness or spirituality. Christian mystics such as Father Thomas Keating suggest that: Christianity is primarily about a transformation of consciousness. This takes spiritual practice and the cultivation of wisdom (Thomas Keating in Spirituality, Contemplation and Transformation (2007)). In *The Cloud of Unknowing*, a Christian mystic suggests that the work of contemplation is initially God's, ours is that of a responsive will, and this work of grace can be affected in a very brief time. In similar vein, the Bhagavad Gita suggests that only god can realize 'himself' and our task is that of surrendering which is not an act of the ego but the dawn of the light of self-realization. In Sufism, the focus is on eternal aspect within each of us, the eternal Self that is in harmony with all that exists and all that has ever existed. Sufism teaches that love is the annihilation of individual being in spiritual delight, and knowledge is the contemplation in bewilderment of the mystery of the divine Oneness.

Distilling out the principles of secular spirituality which are consistent with the core mystical teachings of all the world's major religions (Christianity, Islam, Hinduism especially Advaita Vedanta (but including other religions of India), Buddhism, Daoism, etc. can provide the framework for applied spirituality and leadership. Such principles are revealed to be an underlying ground of being, a cosmic consciousness which we all share, sometimes referred to as oneness or non-duality. The implication of this is that the false sense of the separateness from each other and from nature needs to be overcome in leadership for sustainable development policy. It is this egoic sense of the separate self that leads to feelings of isolation and insecurity and the need for more and more material acquisitions and external sources of comfort and security which we all know from experience is never satiated. The lack of feelings of security and the need to grab more and more can also be recognized as greed leading to overconsumption and even to conflict over resources and power and the desire to control others.

Most importantly spirituality is about recognizing our true nature and that of our fellow beings as being fundamentally from the same source. Yes, we have individual bodies and as our experiences are embodied, but a little reflection and self-will lead us to quickly see that we are not our bodies. During our evolutionary history we were conditioned to behave in ways that ensured our physical and biological survival. It is now becoming increasingly clear that those instinct which were once necessary are now being over done in the Anthropocene and are having disastrous feedback consequence. It is a time at which a new phase of human evolution, a spiritual awakening so to speak, is struggling to be born. The new era of leadership is about leading humanity through this transition with as little pain as we can manage.

Leadership: A Contextual Overview

The literature on leadership is huge and it is not the purpose of this chapter in any way to try and summarize that. However, we provide some context from which the points of departure for spiritual leadership might be better appreciated. One approach to define leadership is as a social influence process that maximizes the efforts of others in the pursuit of a goal (Kruse, 2013) or as the art of inspiring a group of individuals to behave in the direction of accomplishing a shared objective. Small business leadership is the capacity of an individual, group or organization to 'lead', influence or direct other individuals, teams or entire organizations. It is both a study field and a practical talent. The term 'leadership' is frequently seen as a contentious one. Expert literature disputes various points of view on the subject, occasionally drawing comparisons between Eastern and Western approaches to leadership as well as (within the West) North American vs European methods.

Leadership varies considerably depending on the dominant paradigm people use to make sense of the world. The positivist paradigm assumes that there are objective, universal, and unchanging facts that can be verified and predicted by methodical scientific observation, deduction, measurement and minimization of bias in research. This paradigm assumes there are fundamental facts about leadership. The aim of leadership theory and research in this area is to offer prescriptive solutions. Contrarily, constructivism holds that reality is a construction made from the viewpoints and experiences of each individual. Interaction and interpretation reveal reality, and bias in study is acknowledged. Here, leadership is viewed as being influenced by an individual's life experiences and hence having a wide range of cultural and contextual variations. Today, interactions and procedures with people are given a lot of consideration since leadership is increasingly viewed as relational. With the aim of identifying and changing socially unjust institutions, critical theory proposes multiple, created realities characterized by the interaction of power relations. Research is used as a tool to challenge beliefs and presumptions as well as co-create with participants. Here, leadership, which may be exploited as a tool to sustain social inequality, depends on an understanding of power. It is common for dominant groups' values and beliefs to define and reflect leadership. Postmodernism sees the world as fragmented, complicated, chaotic and ambiguous. Real life is in a state of flux and is influenced by how the social world is portrayed and how meaning is created. Due to the perception that objectivity and universality are unachievable, doubt everything presented as truth. Leadership and its relative value are seen as means to disrupt the status quo.

Traditional leadership approaches appear to have been based on: functionalism, positivism and designated hierarchical positions. Current viewpoints emphasize the social construction and relational aspect of leadership and are more interpretative, discursive and phenomenological. Such dynamics are particularly evident in dispersed and distributed leadership models where self-organizing systems and group activities are valued. These opposing viewpoints have created a theoretically informed study area that is now being used as the foundation for leadership studies that is considerably richer, more diverse and increasingly pluralistic (*Sage Handbook on Leadership Studies*).

Some common leadership misconceptions include that leadership is synonymous with seniority or that a domineering, take-charge charismatic individual is a leader. Neither of these common beliefs is true. Similarly, management and leadership do not have the same meaning. Among many other tasks, managers must plan, measure, monitor, coordinate, solve, hire and terminate. Managers often control things. People follow leaders.

Traditionally, spirituality is considered as a personal private matter and that continues to be true. But our world and public policy priorities badly need to reflect a novel set of values and what better than our own innermost values and realizations.

Spiritual Leadership and Complementary Leadership Categories

There is a wide range of leadership fields which are explored by scholars working in the field of leadership research. *The Sage Leadership Handbook* (2011) lists has 38 chapters each exploring a different area of leadership including Spiritual Leadership. Many of these have overlapping characteristics like participatory leadership and democratic leadership. Spiritual leadership is perhaps most closely related to and can draw from servant leadership, authentic leadership and ethical leadership. The application of spiritual leadership to sustainable development policy will require transformative leadership as distinct from transactional leadership. For our purposes in this chapter, we will weave the relevant threads from the various scholarly fields to present a coherent picture of the type of leadership based on applied spirituality which we believe is now of critical need for advancing sustainable development policy.

Spiritual leadership maybe conceptualized as derived from two basic premises: a spiritual understanding and a translation of that understanding into leadership practices. Firstly, it requires an understanding of the deep reality of human nature which results from contemplative or spiritual self-realization practices seeking, for example, the answer to the basic question: 'Who am I?'. Such investigations inevitably lead to an understanding of one's own spiritual nature as interconnected being, with a shared cosmic consciousness. One begins to recognize the imaginary egoic little self for what it is which would previously have been confused with one's true nature. The sense of separation from each other and from nature dissolves and is replaced by a non-dual oneness in which is the source of fundamental shifts in values and ethics. Values of compassion and love for all beings and for nature begin to replace the desire to have more and more control over others, over nature and to acquire more and more material things. Ethics shift from deontological priority concerns of following the rules, being morally upright based on the current temporal norms to an ontological basis of an ethics of being and of support for life in all diverse forms.

Secondly, spiritual leadership requires the capability to lead from this place of spiritual enlightenment. This implies a strong connection to this inner knowing and what one might call this elevated level of consciousness. Similarly, management and leadership do not have the same meaning. Among many other tasks, managers must plan, measure, monitor, coordinate, solve, hire and terminate. Managers often control things. People follow leaders. Many agree that it is 'the directing of self and others to achieve collective purpose from a sense of shared community' and 'as demonstrated through reflective practice, and the ethical, compassionate, and respectful treatment of others' (close single inverted commas?). In order to establish vision and value congruence at the level of the person, empowered team and organization, according to Fry, spiritual leadership entails the development of the leader's and the followers' spiritual well-being via calling and membership. The foundation of inspiration and insight for developing (1) hope/faith in a transcendent vision of service to important stakeholders and (2) the ideals of altruistic love is found in one's inner life or spiritual practice. This inner life or spiritual practice is the basis of spiritual leadership. Spiritual leadership, according to Fry, is 'more of an observable phenomena occurring when a person in a leadership position embraces spiritual principles such as integrity, honesty, and humility, producing the self as an example of someone who can be depended upon, respected, and appreciated'.

Authentic Leadership

As mentioned earlier, some related fields of leadership research contribute to this understanding of spiritual leadership. Authentic leadership has been described in terms of two components of authenticity: knowing one's true self and acting in accord with that true self (see for example Harter, 2002). At face value this seems like the same basis as for spiritual leadership. In other words, there is something continuous to be real about. This assumption underlies the authentic leadership paradigm, which is based on the modernist psychology view that each person has a 'true' self that is independent of circumstance and behavioural appearances. This remains controversial and the foundations are clearly different from those pertinent to spiritual leadership.

Servant-Leadership

While the concept of servant leadership is ancient, the hyphenated noun 'Servant-Leader' was coined by Robert Greenleaf in his 1970 essay: The Servant as Leader (Greenleaf, 1970). It is telling that the essay is entitled Servant as Leader and not the reverse. Increased service to others, a holistic approach to work, encouraging a feeling of community, and the sharing of authority in decision-making are all stressed by servant-leadership. Organizational success is an indirect, derived result of servant-leadership, whereas encouraging greatness in others is the primary motive and objective of a servant-leader. People are urged to be honest in both their professional and personal life through the adoption of a holistic approach to work. Servant-leadership challenges the institution's capacity to deliver human services and contends that only community, defined as associations of people who are jointly responsibility for one another both individually and collectively, is capable of fulfilling this role. Only the activities of certain servant leaders can foster this feeling of community (Greenleaf, 1970).

By fostering participative, empowering settings and supporting the abilities of followers, effective servant-leadership is visible in the development of servant-leadership in others. The motivation of a servant leader stems from a fundamental egalitarian idea that they are no better than the people they serve, and their values include honesty, integrity and generosity. Servant-leadership is not just another type of leadership; it is viewed as something more. It is a way of life that springs from the steadfast conviction that the core of your responsibility as a leader is to constantly push others, support them and provide them with opportunities to grow as people.

When faced with two options that seem to be in conflict with each other, the servant-leader chooses a solution where both opposing value sets are combined in such a way that they are actually strengthened, not weakened. Servant-leaders are not tempted into making a choice between two opposite values, and they also avoid choosing an unsatisfactory compromise. This is achieved through a dialectical process of thesis and antithesis, in which the servant-leader achieves a synthesis, which is always enriching. Insights from two authors make an operational link to spiritual leadership. Covey (1998) suggests that at the core of our being there is the thing we draw upon to rise above our current circumstances and our nature. When you do this, you can tap into an entirely new source of human motivation. Keith implies that servant leadership is nothing less than 'the creation of a better world': He concludes: 'I have no doubt that the world will be a better place when more leaders and organizations practice servant leadership. I also have no doubt that servant leadership is best for the leader. It is the most meaningful, satisfying way to lead. It is not about self-denial or self-sacrifice. It is about self-fulfilment'. We might add Self-realization, beyond the egoic self. In many ways it seems like servant leadership could be the practical expression of spiritual leadership which is more anchored in the leader's deeper philosophical and metaphysical understanding of her or his own true nature, emanating from the common ground of consciousness shared by servant and leader or follower and leader.

Ethical Leadership

The third area of leadership research which resonates with spiritual leadership but has several differences is Ethical Leadership. Power is a key component of the prevalent leadership model of today. It has to do with gaining, using and maintaining power. To make matter worse, power is seen as a zero-sum game in which the leader feels he or she will lose power if other become empowered. Ethics or morals do not commonly enter such leadership thinking. Ethical leadership, thankfully, currently is emerging as an important area of concern, research, teaching and some headway into practice is being made. Personal immorality coupled with power abuse is the moral flaw that people dread most in leaders.

According to others, the main objective of ethics is to analyse moral processes and describe them rather than judge their goodness, adequacy, or integrity. In contrast, morality is overtly normative since it aims to make it possible to tell the difference between right and wrong. Others have argued that ethics are sophisticated decision-making processes that reflect moral preferences, whereas morality is a more fundamental and individual assessment of an act's rightness or wrongness.

In this chapter and in the book as a whole, our focus is on applied spirituality for sustainable development policy much of which is public policy. A focus here on ethics for public policy is therefore relevant. Adequate guidance in this domain is available from Winston (2010) and Brommel (2019). Winston's six moral competencies for the practice of democratic governance are civility; fidelity to the public good; respect for citizens as responsible agents; proficiency in democratic architecture; prudence; and 'double reflection'. Brommel's six ethical competencies for public leadership, in the context with people who want and value different things are stated as personal resolutions of the leader committing to being: *civil, diplomatic, respectful, impartial, fair and prudent.* While some of these are rooted in personal values, much of these qualities are ultimately operationalized based on legal rules or behaviours expected by social norms and are duty based. Together they constitute a deontological ethical framework for guiding the public leader. Right or wrong behaviour is very often judged by the consequences or results of the action and are referred to as consequential or teleological ethics. While such ethical guidance of right and wrong behaviour or good and bad action actions are usually consistent with spiritual leadership, they fall short of an adequate ethical basis for spiritual leadership.

Leadership based on applied spirituality seeks an ontological ethical framework which explores an ethics of being rather than the ethics of doing. Questions such as why should one be deontologically or teleologically ethical arise? We could, of course, say that fear or pleasure or happiness is the reason we should act in an ethical manner, but is this an adequate explanation? At best, it seems like a partial or superficial truth. Advaita Vedanta in the teachings of Swami Vivekananda provide an ontological explanation which is that we do good because we are essentially good but we sometimes depart or forget our true nature which is the one *Brahman*. 'Purity, goodness, and fearlessness-all have their origin in the self which is identical with the absolute Self. The expression of this unity is called love and compassion and is the ontological foundation of our ethics. This is expressed in the dictum, 'You are That'. This high and lofty ontological ethics has no meaning if we do not practice it. And if we do not admit such an ontological basis of our actions, we cannot have any explanation for our good actions. In other words, only by doing good can we be good, and also as we are intrinsically good, we can overcome the superimposition of selfishness in our nature and realise our freedom 'Freedom is the realization of one's own nature'.

Fear and hatred have no place there. Our ego-imposed superimposition of our genuine nature leads us to believe that we are distinct from the ultimate truth. Additionally, it makes us selfish and distances us from our fundamental connection to others. The source of all our problems is our obsession with the idea of 'I and mine'. We become immoral because of our selfishness. Anything that is not selfish is moral, while anything that is selfishly motivated is immoral. This notion of ethics is based on the ontology of the human which is the identity of the individual self with the absolute Self. The ensuing philosophy of action is the elevation of the society and one's self. There is a close connection to the Buddhist universal care ethics but is nuanced in the sense that you achieve your good by doing good for others since in the other is you and vice versa. This action philosophy also implies that work is carried out in the spirit of service without hankering after selfish consequences. The root cause of selfishness, greed and the sense of separation from the other and nature is thus exposed and the possibility of course correction in human behaviour now has an ethical and action base. This we suggest is the basis for spiritual leadership for sustainable development policy.

Spiritual Leadership for Sustainable Development Policy

Sustainable development policy challenges require leadership at all levels of society and from people in all walks of life as individuals, in households, in communities and in the public, corporate and civil society organized sectors. This includes people who make their livelihoods in the informal and formal sectors. Traditional concepts of leadership as derived from formal authority in government, or as senior officials in corporate or civil society sectors have to be reconceptualized in terms we have discussed above under servant-leadership, authentic, ethical and spiritual leadership. For instance, senior officials are not the only ones in the public arena that conduct leadership that attempts to solve collective action difficulties as well as economic, social, or ecological challenges. Public leadership is also practiced by people, organizations and networks in the for-profit and non-profit sectors, the private sector, the academic community and the media. For achievement of the sustainable development goals a series of shifts are required in leadership as a function without over-reliance on individual leaders and their roles as is typical of much leadership scholarship. In this chapter we illustrate several of these shifts from public policy and public management perspectives. We draw from the 10 propositions for public leadership outlined by Hartley (2018).

The first significant proposition is a reconceptualization of public leadership and the definition proposed by Hartley (2018) as follows: 'mobilizing individuals, organizations and networks to formulate and/or enact purposes, values and actions which aim or claim to create valued outcomes for the public sphere'. Here, the focus is not only on individual actors but also on processes and practices which shape the attention and resources of others about publicly agreed or sought goals and actions. It is not solely about public-office holders but about those who shape public debate and action. This broad conception of public leadership is clearly consistent with the challenges of sustainable development policy which requires policy centric and multilevel governance, in order to deal with the complexity of sustainability at different scales. In addition, a multi-actor conception allows the leadership process to draw from the ontological ethical framework which is central to correcting many of the observed challenges to sustainable development. These arise from a fossil fuel-based civilization in which greed, selfishness and overconsumption of materials goods and services are central to economic growth defined as the hallmark of progress. At the same time the world is gripped by a profound set of interactive wicked policy problems. As acknowledged by Hartley, the impacts of globalization on societies have been both overwhelmingly favourable and profoundly bad, with rising economic and social disparity and a deepening feeling of grievance and unfairness. Technology advancements simultaneously present opportunity and threat to work, social interactions, democracy, public discourse, knowledge, wealth distribution, monitoring and crime, leaving many people uneasy and sceptical. Additional wicked issues like climate change, global commerce, immigration, population ageing and the growth of illiberal democracies, to name just a few, present a challenging combination for leadership to attempt to address.

Taking the VUCA (volatile, uncertain, complex and ambiguous) context into consideration for leadership is another proposition. Volatility concerns the nature, speed, volume and magnitude of change, which may change rapidly and suddenly. Uncertainty is of different types and needs to be unpacked to be understood for leaders to understand when they are dealing with uncertainty due to lack of knowledge or information or fake information (epistemological), or due to randomness which can usually be dealt with by probability treatments. Radical or ontological uncertainty is that which results from the very nature of the system in which leadership takes place and is connected to the interaction of the leader with the system. The very engagement of leadership changes the system in some predictable and other unpredictable ways. A deep understanding of one's own ontology then becomes central to engaging in meaningful leadership in these contexts. A system's overall interconnectedness, dynamics and processes – including both emergent and intended properties – are addressed by the concept of complexity. Ambiguity concerns the difficulties of coming to a clear understanding of the meaning of events in a situation of constant flux, coevolution in systems which are self-referential and do not have a fixed external reference frame. Spiritual leadership comes to the fore in such situations which also happen to be the dominant contest in which public policy for sustainable development takes place.

Leadership in sustainable development policy must deal with policy inconsistencies, various objectives, varied publics and a large range of stakeholders, each with specific interests. Leaders in the voluntary sector may support and campaign for currently controversial but important policy issues, whereas leaders in the commercial sector may be concerned about losing customers, markets, revenues or even their enterprises if required sustainable development policies are implemented. Leadership for SD policy must originate from and be anchored in a place of security and strength. Leadership in this context while appearing strenuous can be seen as a dance among stakeholders and among leaders and led. This kind of post heroic leadership is built upon the dynamics of distributed leadership which examines why, how and to what extent leadership roles are shared and shaped over time, and ın what circumstances they dynamically coevolve with the policy goals.

Public leadership representing the government will likely need to pay constant attention to a rapidly changing environment, to pluralist and occasionally highly divergent interests, to working in a context of polycentric governance, to mobilizing the workforce around purpose and to evaluating whether or not public value outcomes are being achieved in order to pursue the SDGs in a VUCA context. It is possible to feel exhausted or burned out due to the high physical, mental and emotional demands of leadership. The need for resilience as core characteristic of leadership must be recognized and built. While resilience depends on individuals' personal traits and conditioning, well known practices such as meditation and mindfulness can help to connect leaders to their ontological core, to their consciousness and self-awareness. This provides the well spring of resilience.

We conclude this section and the chapter by illustrating how spirituality might be applied to leadership for what is perhaps the most challenging and most urgent of the sustainable development emergencies: the climate change crisis. We are all aware of the long-standing Intergovernmental Panel on Climate Change (IPCC) consensus that the climate catastrophe we are experiencing is anthropogenic in origin and brought on by greenhouse gas emissions, including those of carbon dioxide and methane. Thus, the issue is rising temperatures, which have a number of negative social, economic and financial repercussions including an increase in the severity and frequency of extreme weather events, droughts and floods, as well as sea level rise and the erosion of shorelines. The accumulation of GHGs is the direct cause. Increased emissions, decreased sink absorption, and a variety of feedback loops that reinforce the changes are the main contributors to the accumulation. Reduced absorption results from the destruction of sinks like forests and unsustainable land use systems combined with the decreased absorptive capacity of existing sinks, such as acidification of the oceans due to CO_2 buildup, while increased emissions are caused by increased use of fossil fuels, which is the foundation of the global economic system. In a nutshell, our civilization is a form of capitalism based on fossil fuels, driven by the universally accepted public policy objectives of all nations, which are higher GDP per growth based on material consumption.

Conclusion

Growth at any cost is the high priest of progress. Overexploitation for excessive consumption driven by corporate and individual greed reinforces resistance to change. This problem is so essential to what we have come to consider as the ideal life that we focus all of our attention elsewhere, fiddling around with clever economic and technical advancements that amount to little more than rearranging the deck chairs. Since we have concluded (incorrectly in my view) that it is human nature to be greedy, we have come to believe that overconsumption will always exist and that capitalism is the most effective means of sating this drive. As the left hemisphere of the brain, with its grasping, individualistic, reductionist and deterministic qualities, grew prominent in western civilization and is now imitated by everyone, we lost this understanding, which is of course nothing new. The conclusion of this argument is that, simply put, a close examination of our own nature quickly reveals that we are fundamentally spiritual beings who share a common consciousness, that our perception of our separation from one another and from nature is erroneous, and that the sense of insecurity and inadequateness that drives us to constantly acquire material possessions is actually the result of an imaginary ego that we have mistaken for ourselves. Leadership which goes beyond mere intellectual understanding of these issues to a deep realization of the inherent and basic truth of this alternative reality and is practiced as such is the need of the hour.

References

Benington, J. (2000, April–June). The modernization and improvement of government and public services. *Public Money and Management*, 3–8.
Brommel, D. (2019). *Ethical competencies for public leadership*. Pluralist democratic politics in practice. Springer.
Bryman, A., Collinson, D., Grint, K., Jackson, B., & Uhl-Bien, M. (2011). *The Sage handbook of leadership*. SAGE Publications.
Covey, S. R. (1998). *The 7 habits of highly effective people*. Free Press.
Dunn, M. (2004). *Ibid: A life* (p. 556). MacAdam/Cage.
Greenleaf, R. K. (1970). *The servant as leader*. Center for Servant Leadership.
Harter, S. (2002). Authenticity. In C. R. Snyder & S. J. Lopez (Eds.), *Handbook of positive psychology* (pp. 382–394). Oxford University Press.
Hartley, J. (2018). Ten propositions about public leadership. *International Journal of Public Leadership*, *14*(4), 202–217.
Hull, R. B., Robertson, D. P., & Mortimer, M. (2020). *Leadership for sustainability: Strategies for tackling wicked problems*. Island Press.
Keating, T. (2007). *Spirituality, contemplation, and transformation*. Lantern Publishing & Media.
Keith, K. M. (2008). *The case for servant leadership*. Greenleaf Center for Servant Leadership.
Kruse, K. (2013). *What is leadership*. https://www.forbes.com/sites/kevinkruse/2013/04/09/what-is-leadership/?sh=5c879abc5b90
Mohanta, D. (2016). *Prabuddha Bharata* (Vol. 121, No. 7).
Ostrom, E. (2010). Beyond markets and states: Polycentric governance of complex economic systems. *The American Economic Review*, *100*(3), 641–672.
Rittel, H. W., & Webber, M. M. (1973). Dilemmas in a general theory of planning. *Policy Sciences*, *4*(2), 155–169.
Roof, W. C. (1999). *Spiritual marketplace*. Princeton University Press.
Taylor, C. (2007). *A secular age*. Harvard University Press.
Wikipedia. *Leadership*. https://en.wikipedia.org/wiki/Leadership
Winston, K. (2010). *Moral competence in public life*. SSA/ANZSOG Occasional Paper, 4. ANZSOG.

Chapter 7

Law and Applied Spirituality

K. Parameswaran

Abstract

Legal systems govern social behaviour. They attempt to regulate order, collective peace and harmonious developments in society. The external social behaviour that law deals with is also a part of internal human behaviour. This external and internal nature of human behaviour, needs to be consciously studied and interlinked when legal systems desire elements of justice, equality, liberty, fraternity, dignity, integrity and unity for social collectivity. These elements, that legal systems guarantee come from an integration of individual and collective life on matters of social, political, economic etc., of various levels. The individuality and collectivity on these matters and levels are deeply psychological and spirited in sense as human behaviour operates through stimulus from inside to leave external effects outside or vice-versa through a function of thought-emotion-sensation-body complex. Thus, we see, our behaviour gets shaped by a two-way process of inner motivation and outer circumstance, individual and collective dimensions on a given matter and level. At this juncture, a critical study on this two-way relation in human behaviour and a set of unifying values to be identified for progressive intersections seem to be the future of legal systems for achieving greater goals of humanity. Additionally, legal systems that deal with justice are now becoming more than social, economic and political justice as new knowledge is revealing interrelations of spirit-mind-body or thought-emotion-sensation-body complex leaving us to think of new dimensions in justice. Thus, spirituality, as an exercise of human experiment and experience, provides a new scope for legal systems to deal with human and social behaviour to achieve order, peace and development. At this juncture, one even finds another unknown dimension gaining grounds and sinking to integrate or bring holistic responses to human problems and social challenges of the collective is the actual linking of spirituality through or with psychology or vice versa. Law and legalities of the thoughts and norms are interspersed in between these two disciplines. This is indeed a welcome trend as the psychological human and the social collective have become the axis on which every wheel of knowledge is tested and allowed

Applied Spirituality and Sustainable Development Policy, 133–147

doi:10.1108/978-1-83753-380-020231007

to represent as spokes for inclusive, sustainable and harmonious inter-relational movement of things. One might see, know, feel or even ought to bear this interconnection that very often come in the actual spiritual practices where psychological dimensions emerge leading to wholesome experience of the state of our own individual and socio-collective nature. Among many kinds of spiritual experiences and experiments, two of them stand out for our legal consideration. One, an experience of timeless, space-less and boundless consciousness-awareness beyond life and world with which we witness, observe and understand the movement of things inside life and world, without our participation into them. Two, an experience of consciousness-awareness as power and force operating and animating through thought-emotion-sensation-body complex with our active participation in the movement of life and world. The former experience prepares the ground to remain free from all fetters of self-aggrandizing individualization before wider collectivity and, the latter experience prepares us to re-enter into wider collectivity to contribute with a freed sense of individualization, not imprisoned by its ego-aggrandizement that cuts the individual from the collective. These two spiritual experiences, one of the consciousness-awareness of freedom and, another of the consciousness-awareness with all potentials, when allowed to animate inside the human, it gives crucial understanding of the challenges of life and, pro-activation of solutions for those challenges that are extremely crucial for law and legal systems. A power of understanding the knowledge using spiritual experience of these two states of consciousness-awareness along with rationality, reason and logic, a strength operating through concentration of the energies in body aiding movement of knowledge, a harmony releasing itself through motivating-empathy and mutual-collaboration using knowledge and strength and, finally a near-perfect action operating through strategies, stages and steps in organizing daily life, human capital and all kinds of the systems of the world using knowledge, strength and harmony become our positive tools of empowerment. The combination of these two spiritual experiences of consciousness-awareness is useful to legal systems that look for solutions to human crises using interactive nature of individuality and collectivity on all issues of life, world and society. The chapter attempts to demonstrate that this kind of spirituality and its applied processes thus provide us the clue and strategy to achieve what the human nature and social existences of all kinds all over the world seek and aspire in the form of individual as well as collective peace, joy and compassion. It is also argued that this peace, joy and compassion that is spiritual in nature are in fact the origin and source of inspiration and stimulation for social, political and economic equality, liberty and fraternity in law, and the harmony and perfection of these elements seen as the justice that balances everything. The chapter demonstrates how applied spirituality can be used in law in the sense of law-making, judicial-interpretation, executive-governance, legal profession and finally a grand introduction of spirituality and its values into legal academics and research that are waiting to be liberated from the clutches of mere analytical knowledge of life and world moving towards new enriching powers of radiant collective life and wonderful harmonious world.

Keywords: Thought-emotion-sensation-body complex; applied spirituality; constitutional obligation; preamble; humanism; consciousness; awareness; life; time; space

Introduction: Law and Applied Spirituality: A Yet Unknown Meeting of the Two

The word spirituality has acquired enormous amount of meanings over centuries of disputations and scholarships of all kinds of what it means to be. They range from religious, occult and the mystical of the early period of the prehistoric mankind to that of the philosophical, sublime, augmentative, humanitarian, psychological, academic etc., of the mediaeval and modern human times. Some other common, popular and current forms of association with spirituality are its attributed meanings based on humanism, ethics, morals and ideals or even its transnational values like universalism, globalism, communitarianism, internationalism and so on, that contemporary social, political, economic, cultural, religious, legal systems, life, development, order etc., demand. There are also other specific thoughts on the meaning of spirituality that are seen as a matter of individual's search of one's self to discover the aim of life, purpose of world and nature of existence. Even a critical meaning of it as a figment of imagination of the human mind out of fear or fantasy, faith or hallucination intermingling it with human psychology and history of the development individual and collective in the society is also presented by the purely analytical and post-modern approaches to spirituality. Some even deny spirituality altogether and consider it as an irrational human pursuit of a domain of meanings devoid of logic, reason and sense. These and many more of these types of meanings make us keep one point in mind that there is no one single accepted universal meaning of the term spirituality. This is not because of the inability of the human mind to be intelligent enough to discover and attribute a meaning to spirituality. Rather, the orientation from the different types of meaning that spirituality can give to life, world and existence as a whole, whether complete and isolated, individual or collective is something unmanageably vast and immeasurably lengthy. This orientation can even go to an extent that a meaning of spirituality from one end can be diametrically opposite and completely cancelling to all that have been expressed on the other end. Thus, it seems, in order to finally discover and attribute a meaning to spirituality, we can arrive only at a meaning that comes from above all the meanings, which is of something that cannot be limited or defined in one particular way or, we need to project that all meanings are something purportedly given by those who accept and find value for such meanings.

Similarly, the meaning of law and its legal systems are seen from different angles. They all have come out as theories or schools or research approaches to study the meaning of the term law and the nature and function of the legal systems. Law that is understood as something natural is nothing but a phenomenon of that which is felt, universal, immanent and discoverable by reason. Or law that is understood as something positive is nothing but a tangible act and fact of that which is written, to be followed as a command and a punishment that will be imposed when that law is not adhered to. Law becomes real when it is understood as something to be applied or made applicable to a community interest or public policy by positions or a system of competent and capable authorities to the changing circumstances and requirements. Or law is critical when it is understood as something as a product of social forces and political influences emanating from the seats of structures intended specifically or have been made for that purpose. There are also other new branches in the discipline of law that are developing now as theories, schools and research approaches to law drawing strength from interdisciplinary and cross-fertilization of knowledge from many disciplines in order to fit into the requirements of the human and social issues. These new lines of thoughts also have brought various amendments in the form of departure from or inclusion of additional insights to the well-known schools, theories and research approaches to law and legal systems. All these meanings of law have their respective orientations when they come to the function of legal systems that accommodate the source, function and output of law. There are also other meanings to law purely from the domain of justice, which makes it much more complicated by bringing a cause and effect relationship between law and justice. In this venture, some accept law as a tool to serve justice. Some accept law as just one of the tools and not the only tool to serve justice and a corresponding strength and practice of knowledge from other disciplines is extrapolated to achieve this purpose of cause and effect between law and justice. One wonders at the end that it is not only for spirituality that the meanings given are complex, but also for the law and legal systems where the meanings become highly complex with social life and behaviour governed in any social situation to be regulated by law. Law and legal systems can then be seen as a product of human life and behaviour in an interdependent net of individuals creating yet another psychological chapter of legal knowledge to study leading the future spiritual school, theory, research and practice of law.

All these aforementioned positions with respect to meanings of spirituality and law seem to be valid and interesting for any amount of intellectual journey when they are studied independently without any correlation between them. However, where intricate interrelationships between an individual and the collective and the consequent output of such interrelationship is the core focus or a major study of cause and effect relationship between these two, a hitherto unknown meeting takes place between two; that of law and spirituality or it can also be called as correlations between legal systems and applied spirituality. However, such a correlative position has not yet been adequately taken in the form of a systematic and comprehensive study, though certain thoughts and ideas on this theme have been discussed in various forums under topics such as; (a) religion in law,

(b) religion as law, (c) law in religion and (d) law as religion.[1–4] It is important to bear in mind that religion is one of the foremost attempts of the mankind to study the inner meanings of the spirit of life, nature of the world, the universe, time, and space, a journey to the inner self, its discovery and experience. However, religion is only a tool, one of the mechanisms by which human aspirations experimented the higher or inner seeking to arrive at the core meaning of things. Thus, spirituality as a study and practice if it is not taken into consideration in its core essence to interrelate with law and legal systems, all research studies will remain incomplete though few points of intersection can be found or feeling satisfied with external aspects of religion dealt with under public order, tranquillity and taxes. And yet these points of intersection might not reach up to the integration that can show harmonious coexistence of unity and multiplicity that we are interested in. The spiritual and its experiential aspects are not contrary to any religious faith or feeling provided religions do not become dogmatic and sectarian. The difficulty comes only when religions or their practices bring a fixation in mind clinging to one particular meaning or ritual or formula or experience as an exclusive, sole or one single truth. All individual meanings, rituals or formulae or experiences are expressions of the truth that belonged to one particular time in evolution, for one particular necessity or group of people and with resources, techniques and materials available at that point of time. The supreme or the Spiritual truth is that it can always be expressed in many other ways. Religion like any other disciplines or methods must also come up to terms with the growth and development of the human consciousness. And, also the growth and development of the human consciousness shall not cancel any religious methods as long as they are self-contained without any disturbance to public peace and social tranquillity of the collective.

Law and Applied Spirituality: 3 Major Interactive Elements From Known Areas

When the aim and outcome or the vision and mission of law and spirituality are presumed to be inherently common in their source and end, or can be made to study and see the connecting threads in order to fulfil a greater objective for the meaning of life, world and existence, for the individual and collective life, one

---

[1]Almost all legal systems provide such a scope for legal systems to deal with religion to the extent that it only deals with place or institutions of worship and practice of faith, matters of tax and public order leaving consciousness-awareness experience as something private and personal.

[2]Personal laws dealing customs and family life etc.

[3]Extracting the modern legal principles from religious texts human rights and duties, governance by state, scriptural incidents revealing interpretations of justice etc.

[4]An approach to legal discipline to consider it as a standalone discipline of legal knowledge that can bring order, stability and development without any other aids of knowledge.

cannot afford to avoid studying this adventurous interrelationships.[5] Spirituality when it is connected with the law and legal systems acquires or ought to acquire a new meaning that can be highly useful to law and legal systems. Similarly, law and legal systems when they are connected with spirituality and its values acquire or ought to acquire a new meaning that can be intensely nourishing to the core spiritual life leading it to practical or applied spirituality in day to day living. Some of the interesting interactive elements are explained below to show how law and applied spirituality can be studied in legal discipline. This can develop new frontiers of legal knowledge leading to implementation of such new knowledge for interpretations of legal values. This can also bring transformative change in the meaning of legal values to aid ideals of justice as well as creation of support from the administration of the State in its governance to look at law and life, the individual and collective from a wholistic or spiritual angle without cancelling the social, economic, religious, political, scientific, technological etc.

Preamble of the Indian Constitution[i] and Scope for Applied Spirituality

> WE, THE PEOPLE OF INDIA, having solemnly resolved to constitute India into a [SOVEREIGN SOCIALIST SECULAR DEMOCRATIC REPUBLIC] and to secure to all its citizens: JUSTICE, social, economic and political; LIBERTY of thought, expression, belief, faith and worship; EQUALITY of status and of opportunity; and to promote among them all FRATERNITY assuring the dignity of the individual and the [unity and integrity of the Nation]; IN OUR CONSTITUENT ASSEMBLY this twenty-sixth day of November, 1949, do HEREBY ADOPT, ENACT AND GIVE TO OURSELVES THIS CONSTITUTION.

One can understand the importance that a Preamble has in the national charter of any country, State and Nation. Preamble guides the law making, executive governance, judicial interpretation and the policy drafts. No matter whether such wordings in the Preamble were created with or without the specific intentions of creating a spiritual value, we cannot avoid seeing the justice-values that are given in the Preamble such as liberty, equality, fraternity, dignity, unity and integrity that are inherently spiritual in substance and nature and

---

[5]The present author successfully introduced this adventurous interrelationships between law and applied spirituality since 2016 as a full academic course for one full semester titled under 'Law, Religion, Spirituality and Justice (LRSJ)' at Gujarat National Law University for undergraduate students along with numerous training programs that are aimed at capacity building of knowledge and skills on this subject for law students, teachers, PhD scholars, judicial officers and various other stakeholders of public policy, social and legal actions.

unfortunately not yet seen from that perspective. Also, when justice is defined as social, economic and political, one wonders whether justice can remain only social, economic and political alone while dealing with liberty, equality, fraternity, dignity, unity and integrity where individual meets the collective with fundamental characteristics of heterogeneity everywhere in place. If the answer is in the affirmative, it means, justice as a whole reduces the human only into the social, economic and political. Or one can even say, this idea of justice looks at the human only as an external movement of a body and behaviour in social setting and there is nothing internal, inner and deeper in the form of motivation, intention etc. In this age of advancements in cognitive behavioural psychology, neuro linguistic programing, integrated clinical hypnotherapy and other forms of transpersonal knowledge and therapeutic practices that have come as soothing and healing for the human sufferings of the psychological, and thus, to reduce a human into only a social, economic and political identity is a devaluation of the evolutionary spirit of the human-seeking that makes use of thought-emotion-sensation-body complex.[6] It will also be much more a form of degradation to the idea and ideal of justice itself, as justice cannot be quantified in units that sociologists, economists and political scientists assess the human from a reductionist and analytical point of view. Take for example, Article 14[ii] or Article 21[iii] of the Indian Constitution. The legal provisions of these two articles remain the same till today in the text of the Indian Constitution. However, the interpretations of these two articles have undergone radical changes since the advent of these two provisions through 100s of court judgements leading to new interpretation of dignity and human life. Does it not signify that the human is evolving? Does it not signify that the evolution of the human spirit is from the most tangible to the most intangible too by which the law of human dignity is becoming equally important to that of the law of human rights? Interpretations of both the Articles 14 and 21 respectively of the Indian Constitution show that in the process of evolution, a human integrates the social, economic, political with that of the psychological and other domains of inner seeking.

Thus, seeing the whole idea and ideal of justice in terms of social, economic and political and also the liberty, equality, fraternity, dignity, unity and integrity from the Preamble, there is yet another scope for the inclusion of the spiritual that comes into the scene. Various political experiments from the lessons of history show that when liberty is fully allowed, equality gets exploited. When equality is forced to follow, liberty gets suffocated. When liberty and equality go absent, fraternity is un-realized. When fraternity is lost, it is a tremendous loss to the very meaning of the idea of society where individuals have come together to live or

---

[6]The current author acquired certifications on cognitive behavioural psychology, neuro linguistic programing, integrated clinical hypnotherapy and other forms of transpersonal knowledge and therapeutic practices to understand the meaning and practice of these disciplines and consequently the interdisciplinary and cross fertilization of knowledge that can take place between law and deeper aspects of human life almost bordering towards the spiritual.

have to develop a spirit of cooperation to live. Thus, we see, spirituality when included in law and legal systems, it is the spiritual experience of the oneness, multiplicity and harmony that can come as equivalents to Constitutional equality, liberty and fraternity respectively. The spiritual experience proper as known to many realized masters speak of the essential oneness where one is in the state of spiritual consciousness-awareness that naturally ensures equality and the principle and practice of non-discrimination at the levels of thought, emotion, sensation, body, behaviour, decision-making, speech, interaction and so on. Similarly, yet another shade of experience of the spiritual consciousness-awareness is multiplicity. This experience of multiplicity comes when one is released from the helpless subjection to the sensory reactions. When sensory reactions are transcended, one feels the freedom not bound by fetters and thus, multiplicity automatically ensures freedom of one's own liberty. This can also lead to an understanding where liberty of the other starts and ends. Yet another case of the experience of spiritual consciousness-awareness is harmony that integrates this oneness and multiplicity. When one is capable of the experience of this integration, loving fraternity assuring the dignity of both the individual and the collective is manifest. In this way, the Constitutional obligation of the State to secure justice in the form of social, economic and political through liberty, equality, fraternity, dignity, unity and integrity can be achieved through experiences that takes care of the most crucial things such as the individual meeting and merging with the collective without cancelling the single individual and net of individuals in the collective liberty, equality and fraternity. This alone can give the dignity, unity and integrity that Constitution of India has promised through a national charter from which everything unfolds. In fact, it can also be said, it is spirituality and its experience, along with the necessary consciousness-experiments and spiritual exercises that can become a tool to realize this vast ideal that has been promised by the Constitution of India. Thus, spirituality and its spiritual experience is going to be the future tool and method to realize human unity through harmonious equality, liberty and fraternity. Spirituality in legal discipline in the coming future will exactly be what rationality of the analytic and positive theory of law was to the legal discipline few hundred years before when Darwinism and industrialization promoted the reductionist social, compensatory and quantitative economic, processing political and technological scientific.

Preamble, Article 1 and 2 of the Charter of the United Nations[iv] and Applied Spirituality

It is interesting to see some of the key words in the Preamble, and Articles 1 and 2 of the United Nations Charter where applied spirituality is aspired at the level of international relations, community and polity informing the Nation-States to think and act through their policies. The predominant themes behind those words in the Preamble are; saving the succeeding generations by establishing conditions for social progress and better standards of life through practice of tolerance by living together in peace with common interest in mind to promote advancement of everyone. This overarching socio-political and international vision in the Preamble is spiritual in one way or even distant in dream. Still, it can be or ought to be seen by a follow-up of a mission of detailed steps in Article 1 and 2 with values that are enchanting and universal to human and social seeking. Article 1(1) gives the sense of purpose by explaining the need to maintain peace indicating it to be our original state of nature. Article 1(2) explains the demand from international relations to accept equally the capacity of each and every country's polity to determine their state of nature without cancelling the diversity. Article 1(3) explains the modus operandi in the form of practical cooperation at all levels and finally Article 1(4) reminds every state to act as a centre of harmony in the realization of all these ideals. Article 2 gives an idea of a set of principles that ought to be followed to fulfil Article 1 and the Preamble. As we know, a principle is a fundamental truth or proposition aimed to serve a belief or behaviour with reasons that connect the vision and mission. The seven principles listed under Article 2 of the Charter are; equality among all, good-faith that binds, peace as process for dispute settlement, neither use nor threat to use force, support collective actions to prevent disturbances, ensure proactive steps for peace and its maintenance and finally not to interfere in domestic jurisdiction of any state based on the principle of innate diversity and pluralism. These values are spiritual because it is innate, intuitive and inspirational to our personal and collective life, national and international life. Though, these spiritual values cannot be seen as they are spirited in nature, internal and inner and thus, their outcome governs the individual and social human behaviour impacting from inside. Hence, these values are to be necessarily spirited from within and from one's own self first to bring out the desired effect outside.

The Preamble and the two Articles of the Charter of the United Nations are a telling example of something that has gone completely wrong in the history of the humans of the last century. What did the Nations-collectivity actually fail to do? How did it happen? There are researches that are still going on to show how and which Nations failed first triggering the disastrous Wars. However, when we see the aforementioned Preamble and two Articles of the Charter of the United Nations, we get the clear picture as to the real causes, not explaining the-who-how, rather explaining the-what. They all explain secretly the psychological propensities that went behind nations, communities, groups of people etc., through representations of leaders and crowds expressed on externalised issues such as territory, property, flags, dress, colour, activities, behaviour etc. All those are mental, emotional, sensory and psychosomatic causes that are internal, intentional, motivational and fear-driven. They stem from an attachment to power and control of others with a sense of self-aggrandisement and exclusivist mentality. One can explain all that can be explained on these psychological cores. However, when one goes little deeper unveiling the psychological layers and screens, one can clearly see a lack, a vacuity, an ignorance, a void, an emptiness, a darkness and an absence of a total spirit that could not see the whole or that could not feel the whole or that could not sense the whole. This something that which is missing could not connect the whole or could not unify the whole though territory, property, flags, dress, colour, activities, behaviour etc., as tangibles and movables remained where they were or wherever they were pushed and pulled, broken and torn apart by an invisible animation of a force, energy, power of disharmony and disorder that incomplete or half-full human gave shape to. This core lack and absence of unity is something substantial, fundamental, central, essential, and critical to the very breath and survival of the humanity itself. When we read these legal provisions that have come out in the call and cry through certain words, we can see the significance or even pain behind these words such as scourge of war, faith in life, dignity of the human, standards of life in larger freedom, tolerance, peace, equality, right to self-determination, good neighbours, the universal, harmony, common ends, security of everyone, common interests, advancement of all, the threat, breach, force etc. One can also see the elements and dimensions of time and space expressed. Time expressed in the form of prevention of such lacks and absences in the future and not to repeat that which happened in the past. Similarly, the element and dimension of space too got expressed in the form of expanding beyond boundaries of borders into a universal that are unfortunately trapped by vital energies of the mind of the human that are instinctively territorial, locked down and tied to ego and bordered pieces of lands. In one word, it is the lack and absence of the spiritual consciousness-awareness of the timeless, space-less and the boundless. Such lack and absence could be because of the slow and tardy development or trial and experimentation of the evolutionary sense that is growing gradually from ignorance to knowledge, from division to unity, from instability of energies to stability of consciousness that which can witness, collaborate and govern the sensory index of the human and the psychological from individual to collective, from national to universal, from one country to the other, from one side of the border to the other, from one to many. This experience can be created and can come in forms called as the spiritual consciousness-awareness where unity, multiplicity and harmony can coexist without dilution, where equality, liberty and fraternity can simultaneously manifest without diminution.

Indispensable Personality Dimensions: The Intra-Personality and the Inter-Personality

We see that the law and legal systems govern social behaviour. They attempt to regulate this social behaviour to manifest order, collective peace and harmonious developments in society as these three outcomes are part of the interaction between individual human behaviour and social behaviour. The external social behaviour that law deals with is nothing but a part of internal human behaviour. This external and internal nature of the human behaviour needs to be consciously interrelated when Constitution of India or any nation, country and State and its legal systems, executive governance and judicial interpretations desire goals of justice, equality, liberty, fraternity, dignity, integrity and unity for social collectivity. These goals we guarantee for ourselves in the form of 'we the people' come from an interaction and integration of individual and collective life on all matters and at all levels; social, political, economic etc. At this juncture we can understand that the relationship that an individual has with the collective is deeply psychological and spirited in sense as human behaviour operates through a stimulus from inside to leave an external effect outside or vice-versa through a function of thought-emotion-sensation-body complex acting from one side to influence the other side. Thus, human behaviour gets modelled by a two-way process of motivation that kindles the inner and, circumstance that forms part of the result in the outer. It is here that the spiritual experience of both kinds, the consciousness-awareness of freedom as well as consciousness-awareness of potential power to manifest solutions come to our rescue to pursue the goals of Constitution as enshrined in the Preamble, followed by law and legal systems. When one holds the experience of the consciousness-awareness of the timeless, space-less and boundless untouched by life and world in which we live, we tend to witness clearly, observe carefully and understand how a movement originates from inside and leads to a result of an action outside. Similarly, when one holds the experience of consciousness-awareness of the potential power of enthusiasm, force of inspiration and knowledge of outcome propelled by the need and stimuli to act for the purpose of the world, to solve an issue of life or understand things that have resulted in a particular way, it becomes easy for us to deploy and employ the needed course of correction and adjustment, generous compromise or rectification to manifest solution. Let us study one important example as that of the Sustainable Development with a well-stated meaning given to it.[v]

a. 'Sustainable development has been defined as development that meets the needs of the present without compromising the ability of future generations to meet their own needs'.
b. 'Sustainable development calls for concerted efforts towards building an inclusive, sustainable and resilient future for people and planet'.
c. 'For sustainable development to be achieved, it is crucial to harmonize three core elements: economic growth, social inclusion and environmental protection. These elements are interconnected and all are crucial for the well-being of individuals and societies'.

When one examines this simple dentition put before the humanity to practice and protect the life of our people as well as that of the protection of the planet, through legal provisions or judicial interpretations, we arrive at four core values; (a) need as against greed by bringing an element of self-restraint that belongs to one's own inner motivation and stimulus to think, feel, behave and act for oneself and for all others around in the way we meet only our requirements to sustain, (b) present generation not to compromise the ability of the future generation to meet their own needs where interrelationships between the individual and collective from one generation to the next is presented, (c) a concerted effort keeping in mind the ideal of inclusivity to connect everyone and everything, the inter-generational and intra-generational equity bringing the spiritual experience of the timeless consciousness-awareness, and finally (d) harmonization from balancing the economic growth in the form of demand and supply, scarcity and production, cost and inducement, risk and future keeping in mind social inclusion and protection of environment through transcending our experience of consciousness-awareness of the space-less and, thereby seeing earth just not limited to the human space because of an ignorant claim of anthropocentricism.

Challenges and the Way Forward: Some Strategies

It would be always better to give a focussed approach to the generation of ideas and insights first on spirituality and its values, followed by a spiritual experience of the consciousness-awareness of both the types. One, the freedom that come from a release of the subjection human energies trapped under the sensory reactions and their limitations and, allow the human to experience the state of a timeless, space-less and boundless points of attention, concentration, absorption, response to the all or call it a dynamic meditation. Two, the power to witness, to observe and then finally collaborate with the intentions to resolve, restructure and re-correct the course of things that have gone wrong as a result of the lack of the unity and unification, which are the underlying causes of disharmony and disorder in life and, the injustice of the legal systems. These two spiritual experiences give the human, a necessary connect with the issues that are present by which a gradual unification and unifying-ness progresses through inter-connecting the missing dots and drawing an outline to reveal completeness, order and harmony. It is known to all of us that this is the greatest challenge at present to introduce spirituality and its values as a discipline of study and experiential experiments in the current mainstream of education, academics and research in legal education or in the legal work of law-making, policies, governance and judicial interpretations in legal systems where analytical is more important than the experiential, tangible facts of verification is more than the felt-needs of the individual and the community beyond the tangibles and, finally a reduction of values through numbers and units to quantify has become indispensable before qualifying a set of values. Hence, the way forward is to introduce spiritual values as a course of study to gradually give way and scope for opportunities for young students, teachers, advocates, respective professionals etc., working on all fronts to experience these altered states of consciousness-awareness through appropriate trainings and capacity building without cancelling life and withdrawing from world done in the name of popular religion or spirituality. These two spiritual experiences are life-affirmative and world-embracing as against the popular life-denying and world-shunning ideas and ideals of spirituality and its values. An important caution that must be held at this stage would be to make learners understand that a temporary withdrawal or a short term focus of exclusive concentration by avoiding the life and world should not become the end goal. It is only a stepping-back for preparation and packing off to plunge into the unknown. This is only a transitory process to pass through in order to connect with the timeless, space-less and boundless outside the senses and to see how cognition, emotion, sensation can be kept still as well as vigilant unperturbed by the effervescence of the vital energies flickering through sensory networks. Once the stillness and vigilance are obtained through a concentrated focus, human nature gets trained and developed to see, to feel and to sense how energies in human being and body react, express and externalise. This leads to the formation of inspired cognition, empowered emotion and balanced sensation with fresh insights and perceptions and, thus it becomes relatively easier to insist and navigate, employ and deploy, guide and motivate those same energies of the senses to act in the way one wants, to expand in the way beyond narrow confines to a new set of terms agreeing to and creating unity, multiplicity and harmony leading to equality, liberty, fraternity and dignity.

Some of the spiritual values to be considered for study as well as for experiences are; sense of universalism transpiring through individual and collective consciousness, identifying the unique-ness of things by a recognition of inherent truth in all as evolving and constantly unfolding, recognizing the continuity of the time-frame of the past, present and future, active promotion of justice through prevention of injustice with a principle of no-harm, State-agencies and machineries to learn to operationalize these values through special research studies and work-forces, introduction of higher and inner wellbeing as ultimate justice in addition to social justice of inclusion, economics of distributive justice and political justice of fairness, a thorough familiarisation of various disciplines knowledge with that of the initial understanding of the psychological, course correcting the past errors to remove the causes of continuing conflict and friction as a method of restorative healing, holding non-sectarianism through observation of non-dogmatic approaches to thoughts and actions, inclusivism in terms of values, tradition, customs and cultures, sustaining the ecology through assimilation of the human needs with that of the flora and fauna and etc.[7] In this way, there is a new hope for the earth's future, planetary age, human unity, endless perfections and the resultant ever-unfolding richness of life. A new door opens to the knowledge of law, legal systems, justice, governance, research in legal education and legal discipline as a whole creating yet another set of multiple layers around its already existing extensiveness.

> The Unknown is not the Unknowable; it need not remain the unknown for us, unless we choose ignorance or persist in our first limitations. For to all things that are not unknowable, all things in the universe, there correspond in that universe faculties which can take cognisance of them, and in man, the microcosm, these faculties are always existant and at a certain stage capable of development. We may choose not to develop them; where they are partially developed, we may discourage and impose on them a kind of atrophy. But, fundamentally all possible knowledge is knowledge within the power of humanity. And since in man there is the inalienable

[7]The cognitive behavioural therapies, tools of neuro linguistic programing and hypnotherapeutic methods to deepen the perspective of knowledge merging the objective with the subjective.

impulse of Nature towards self-realisation, no struggle of the intellect to limit the action of our capacities within a determined area can for ever prevail.[vi]

The whole world yearns after freedom, yet each creature is in love with his chains; this is the first paradox and inextricable knot of our nature. Man is in love with the bonds of birth; therefore he is caught in the companion bonds of death. In these chains he aspires after freedom of his being and mastery of his self-fulfilment. Man is in love with power; therefore he is subjected to weakness. For the world is a sea of waves of force that meet and continually fling themselves on each other; he who would ride on the crest of one wave, must faint under the shock of hundreds. Man is in love with pleasure; therefore he must undergo the yoke of grief and pain. For unmixed delight is only for the free and passionless soul; but that which pursues after pleasure in man is a suffering and straining energy. Man hungers after calm, but he thirsts also for the experiences of a restless mind and a troubled heart. Enjoyment is to his mind a fever, calm an inertia and a monotony. Man is in love with the limitations of his physical being, yet he would have also the freedom of his infinite mind and his immortal soul. And in these contrasts something in him finds a curious attraction; they constitute for his mental being the artistry of life. It is not only the nectar but the poison also that attracts his taste and his curiosity.[vii]

For all problems of existence are essentially problems of harmony. They arise from the perception of an unsolved discord and the instinct of an undiscovered agreement or unity. To rest content with an unsolved discord is possible for the practical and more animal part of man, but impossible for his fully awakened mind, and usually even his practical parts only escape from the general necessity either by shutting out the problem or by accepting a rough, utilitarian and unillumined compromise. For essentially, all Nature seeks a harmony, life and matter in their own sphere as much as mind in the arrangement of its perceptions. The greater the apparent disorder of the materials offered or the apparent disparateness, even to irreconcilable opposition, of the elements that have to be utilised, the stronger is the spur, and it drives towards a more subtle and puissant order than can normally be the result of a less difficult endeavour.[viii]

Conclusion: The Emerging Bigger Picture: Linking Law and Spirituality With Sustainability

The sustainability that is popularly understood and yet waiting to be explained and expanded more than the usual economic, social and environmental is the crucial point of discovering an inter-link among these three pillars. One wonders what would inter-link those three pillars. How will the economics think through the social and environmental? Or how will the environmentalists help the society without cancelling the needed or permissible economic development through potential and positive harnessing of nature's energies and resources? Or finally how will a social person or group or political collective living in any planetary space internalise inclusive values through thoughts, emotions, sensations and behaviour to effect the spirit of balance in everyday life, individual and collective among those three pillars of sustainability? The answer seems to be not only in the personal and internal self-transformation but also through a carefully processed system of deliverable values where at every step and stage, one become conscious of the spirit that unifies all tangibles and seeming apparent inanimate that are there before us externally. There is no alternative to this spiritual exploration where social, economic and environmental needs to be threaded psychologically to first understand, feel, sense and practise leading the vision of underlying spirit embodying the collective. Law and legal systems seem to be genuinely attempting and struggling to find a harmonious way out for competing and conflicting ends of the economic, social and environmental that have gone linear in their slow marching of evolutionary pursuits. Spirituality has an answer for sustainability. Legal discipline cannot afford to ignore this. Academia and the policy think-tanks need to be bolder in taking this interlink to those who wield palpable action touching lives of every one, every system and every organism.

Notes

i. India Const. pmbl. https://cdnbbsr.s3waas.gov.in/s380537a945c7aaa788ccfcdf1b99b5d8f/uploads/2023/05/2023050195.pdf.

ii. India Const. art. 14. https://cdnbbsr.s3waas.gov.in/s380537a945c7aaa788ccfcdf1b99b5d8f/uploads/2023/05/2023050195.pdf.

iii. India Const. art. 21. https://cdnbbsr.s3waas.gov.in/s380537a945c7aaa788ccfcdf1b99b5d8f/uploads/2023/05/2023050195.pdf.

iv. Nations, U. (2016). Charter of the United Nations and Statute of the International Court of Justice. UN. https://www.un.org/en/about-us/un-charter/full-text.

v. Nations, U. (2022). The Sustainable Development Goals Report 2022. United Nations. Retrieved from https://www.un.org/sustainabledevelopment/development-agenda/.

vi. Aurobindo, S. (2006). The Life Divine (p. 15). https://www.sriaurobindoashram.org/sriaurobindo/downloadpdf.php?id=36.

vii. Aurobindo, S. (1998). The Complete Works of Sri Aurobindo: Essays in Philosophy and Yoga: Shorter Works; 1910–1950. https://www.sriaurobindoashram.org/sriaurobindo/downloadpdf.php?id=28.

viii. Aurobindo, S. (2006). The Life Divine (pp. 4–5). https://www.sriaurobindoashram.org/sriaurobindo/downloadpdf.php?id=36.

Chapter 8

A Holistic View to Approach Sustainable Development: Spiritual Roots and Evidence From Quantum Physics

Divya Bhatnagar and Sudip Patra

Abstract

An ecologically sustainable future calls for fruitful dialogues between spirituality, modern science and policymaking at large. What could be that connects them all? We found out that ideas about *holism* exist across time, space, culture and thinkers – ranging from mathematics, philosophy, sociology, medicine, education, religion and quantum physics to finding its roots in ancient Indian Vedic tradition and later usage in Greek and Roman cultures.

This chapter takes a look at the history and intricacies of two seemingly distinct but interconnected fields – spirituality and modern science, particularly quantum science – with an aim to uncover what these fields can teach us about the idea of holism. This chapter, therefore, highlights one of the most fundamental and profound spiritual principles of the unity and interconnectedness of the entire universe – encapsulated in the concept of holism – and its practical applications in approaching sustainable development. We hope to ignite further research on this topic.

Keywords: Holism; spirituality; science; unity; consciousness; quantum science; interconnectedness; sustainable development

Introduction

The notion of holism is deeply embedded in the philosophy of sustainable development (SD). Sustainability is understood as a dynamic equilibrium of interconnected and interdependent spheres of social, economic and environmental sustainability. The idea of holism, the view that the whole is greater and more complex than the sum of its parts, has profound resonance with the foundations

Applied Spirituality and Sustainable Development Policy, 149–166

doi:10.1108/978-1-83753-380-020231008

of sustainable development. This chapter describes how the concept of sustainable development is inherently interdisciplinary and holistic in nature and why treating it as such may fast-track our progress towards achieving sustainability.

To design effective policies for sustainable development and to have any real discussion on sustainability issues, we would need to put sustainable development in the context of social science, natural science and spirituality. To view it holistically we need to acknowledge and accept the external as well internal dimensions of what causes unsustainable development. Additionally, the progress in achieving the UN Sustainable Development Goals (SDGs) will expedite if we identify the inter-relatedness of all the 17 SDGs. In this chapter, we will explore the meanings of holism in the domains of social science, natural science and spirituality studies, which then will further contribute to the discourse on sustainable development.

We are aware of the fact that traditionally public policy literature has been deeply influenced by neoclassical and later by neoliberal schools of thoughts in economics. Which means that philosophically 'methodological individualism' has always been the guiding principle. More specifically, economic freedom/growth or economic utility optimization has been the cherished goal of such a policy paradigm. However, recurring crises of different forms and shapes have challenged severely the efficacy of such thinking. Particularly when it comes to sustainability.

Whether it is ecological view, or even Sen's 'capability' approach, we need to study complex interactions between several perspectives. Decision-making agents in a complex system affect and in turn get affected by the emergence in social sphere as well as natural sphere of life. Climate crisis is an example of this. Hence, to resolve problems in such areas we need integrative knowledge of different social and natural sciences. In this chapter, we provide a philosophical grounding to this idea.

From the scientific domain, we have chosen certain paradigms, for example quantum physics. We know that quantum physics has been a technological marvel, which is further supported by the 2022 Nobel Prize for Physics, where the entire prize is based on harnessing technological power from inherent features of quantum physics, which is entanglement or non-locality. Metaphorically, entanglement means 'holism'. Here however, our attempt is to bring out the underlying philosophical thoughts in the quantum science domain, which might have relevance for our framework.

Bohm's research in quantum physics and Einstein's search for a unified energy field and universal consciousness are often considered trailblazers in understanding holism. However, the concept is much older and may have roots in ancient Indian Vedic tradition and later usage in Greek and Roman cultures. The term *holism* was coined only in the 1920s by Jan Smuts when he noticed a 'tendency in nature for the ordered grouping of units to create a whole'. This penchant can be found to occur in microcosm – at the level of gluons, atoms, molecules – to the macrocosm of complex organisms and galaxies. However, the idea of holism doesn't restrict itself to just physics and science. It is seen to boundlessly flow and be found in varied disciplines of mathematics, philosophy, sociology, medicine and education. Quantum physicist, Brian Greene maintains that 'all things in the universe are interconnected by energy particles'. In mathematics, Quine's holism states that confirmation cannot be distinctively apportioned among the several mathematical sub-theories that make up whole theories. This is also called confirmational holism or epistemological holism. In theology, scholars maintain that man and God are interconnected and inseparable.

In health care, the holistic philosophy of caring for the sick in Vedic times is being utilized today to define well-being and the 'holistic health care' model is recognized by the National Institutes of Health, the United States primary agency for biomedical and public health research. The 'holistic health care' model deems the dependence of health problems on the balance of relationships among the person, the environment and the universe. In fact, by the 1970s, two schools of thoughts prevailed in the nursing field. One group considered human being to be *wholistic* in nature where the sum of parts equals the whole and the human body can be separated into independent parts and treated in isolation. The second group considered the body, mind and spirit to be inextricably unified and in a constant dynamic equilibrium. Therefore, to treat a body according to the holistic paradigm (Fig. 8.1) was to restore the lost balance of the person with himself or herself, other beings and the universe.

Science and Spirituality of Holism

Holism in Spiritual Traditions of the World

Centuries before science, gave us compelling insights into the concept of holism, the idea was being extensively discussed in various wisdom traditions around the world. The spiritual roots of its philosophy are deep and are mentioned in Buddhism, Hinduism (such as in Advaita Vedanta and Kashmir Shaivism), Islam, Christian mysticism, Taoism and the Baha'i faith among others.

In the various schools of Hindu philosophy, *Advaita* refers to the idea that there is only one reality, sometimes called as *Brahman* or the singular ultimate reality in the universe. All the other aspects and characteristics of the universe are but the expression of that universal existence, transient and analogous to how bubbles come into being and disappear in a pool of water. *Ātman* is a Sanskrit word that denotes 'the Self, the inmost Self or, the life principle' or the witness-consciousness. It is important to note that in Vedic traditions the concept of *Ātman* is distinct from ego (*Ahamkara*), mind (*Citta*) and embodied existence (*Prakṛti*). The spiritual discipline of *Advaita Vedanta* offers key insights into the concept of holism or *non-dualism* as it states that the *Brahman* and the *Ātman* are identical in nature.

Another Sanskrit word '*sarvah*' is used in ancient Vedantic tradition to signify wholeness, intactness, or being uninjured. It is used to describe the essence of the human being as an integral part of the universe.

> The implication is that holism is the natural state of the human being; there should be interconnections within the human, between humans,

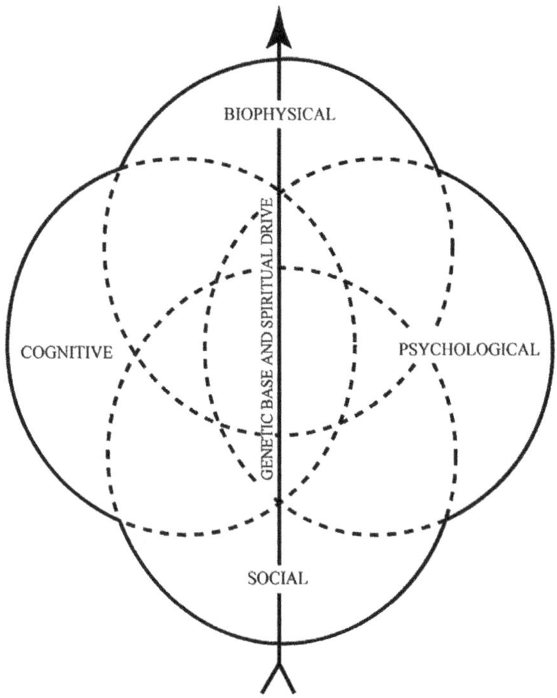

Fig. 8.1. Holistic Model. *Source:* Erickson (2007). Philosophy and Theory of Holism.

> and between humans and the universe. In the unnatural form, there is division among the components, the spirit is disconnected from the physical form, and the human is disconnected from the universe. This would cause 'injury to the whole'.
>
> (Erickson, 2007)

Under the Mahayana Buddhism, the *Śūnyavāda* school of thought hits the core of reality's interdependent nature. *Śūnyatā* describes the emptiness of inherent existence. In his popular work *Mūlamadhyamakakārikā*, Nāgārjuna writes: 'Since nothing has arisen without depending on something, there is nothing that is not empty (24.19)'. He claims that because of causality and certain conditions, all things are transient and originating in dependencies. Nāgārjuna calls this *prajñaptimatra*.

It is interesting to note here the different conceptions of the Holism described by the Mahayana Buddhism, Advaita Vedanta and Kashmir Shaivism. In comparison, the Mahayana Buddhism assumes a process ontology wherein there is nothing eternal and everything is relational and the existence of *Ātman* and a personal agency is questioned. In *Advaita Vedanta*, the nonplural nature of the world is designated to Brahman and witnessed by the *Ātman,* whereas the phenomenal world is false and is called *maya*. In Kashmir Shaivism, everything is a derivation or a manifestation of the *Brahman* and phenomenal world is very much real and rooted in Consciousness.

Islamic writings goes in great details to address and mend the disconnect of human beings with their own selves, other human beings, animals, plants and the planet. It is interesting to observe that the values mentioned in *Quran* and *Hadeeth* regarding oneness resonate with the principles outlined in the 'Earth Charter' and the theory of sustainable development. '*Tawhid*', a founding principle in Islam, means holism or oneness of *Allah*. It requires humans not only to see singular divinity but also to abandon worldly desires such as money, social status, recognition, or egoism. The *Quran* traces back all of creation to a single source: Allah says that He has 'made from water every living thing' (21: 0 Quran). In line with the notion of holism, it is no surprise that the *Quran* instructs humankind to inflict no harm to not just living beings but also non-living things. This can be observed in an English-translated verse 'and seek not mischief in the land' (28:77 *Quran*) directing humans to not become *Mufsidun* – one who oppresses and commits sins. Another reference from *Hadeeth* emphasizes the holistic perspective of *all life*: Allah's Apostle told that a sinful woman was forgiven by *Allah*, because, passing by a panting dog near a well and seeing that the dog was about to die of thirst, she took off her shoe and tying it with her head-cover she drew out some water for it. Hence, *Allah* forgave her of her past sinful life (Book 54, *Hadeeth* 538).

Among several ancient Chinese traditions, third century BCE saw the birth of another holistic school of philosophy called Taoism. It exemplified holism by educating to live in harmony with the intuitive knowledge of life or 'the way' or 'tao'. One of the tenets of Taosim is the concept of yin and yang. The dark swirl is 'yin' and the light swirl is 'yang' and both have seeds (the dots in the figure) to transform into one another. They are relative to each other and interdependent and are necessary to come together for something to exist. Yin and Yang together is called *tao*. It is fascinating to note that scholars have drawn parallels of these principles with systems thinking as noted below:

> Taoism in any case coincides with systems thinking in that it regards the conception of the universe as an interconnected web of relations and the cosmic web is intrinsically dynamic. Furthermore, it contributes to systems thinking the concept of Yin and Yang. Taoism stresses the wholeness instead of parts, combinations of Yin and Yang instead of Yin or Yang, and also the dynamic cyclical pattern within Yin and Yang. It provides, in some sense, an excellent philosophical background to important new theories of contemporary science, that is, an interdisciplinary science with a body of comprehensive knowledge, attempting for universal applications, to be used in collaborative research

> projects. It is in the nature of systems thinking and Taoism that other areas can penetrate its realm and use its methods.
>
> (Lan & Zhang, 1999)

It would be appropriate now to mention the Baha'i faith as it acknowledges and takes into account all spiritual teachings of the world and provides a holistic background. The Baha'i faith is sometimes considered as a New Age Movement (NAM), possibly because of possessing some common features such as holism, pantheism and consciousness. The Baha'i faith claims that in order to view one reality, we have to see Divine truth as one and that it comes from one Source. This truth reveals itself gradually and unravels in cycles. It maintains that all the major religions are nothing but successive series of spiritual chapters. The Guardian of the Baha'i Faith offers us a much needed holistic base to understand all the schools of philosophical thoughts and observe their differences in relativity:

> Religious truth is not absolute but relative . . . Divine Revelation is progressive, not final. Unequivocally and without the least reservation [the Baha'i Faith] proclaims all established religions to be divine in origin, identical in their aims, complementary in their functions, continuous in their purpose, indispensable in their value to mankind.

Scientific Holism

Abraham Maslow, in his later thinking, discussed a state of consciousness that we think is closely linked with the holistic view to approach sustainable development we propose in this chapter: *self-transcendence*. This is quite different from his popular theory, Maslow's hierarchy of needs, in the sense that self-transcendence focuses on transcending the self or the individual ego altogether to a place where one's sense of identity has expanded to experience 'the transpersonal or the underlying unity of all reality' (Messerly, 2019). In this state of consciousness, an individual's own needs are dissolved (or rather minimized) in favour of service to others. More importantly, Maslow considered that *everyone* has the capacity to achieve this level of consciousness (unlike the 'hierarchy of needs' in which an individual can achieve self-actualization only after all his other needs are met).

'Transcendence refers to the very highest and most inclusive or holistic levels of human consciousness, behaving and relating, as ends rather than means, to oneself, to significant others, to human beings in general, to other species, to nature, and to the cosmos.' (Maslow, 1971)

These ideas bring Maslow's transpersonal psychology in direct contact with how holism is approached in various spiritual traditions of the world. Therefore, in this subsection, we focus, as we mentioned above, on how modern science characterizes consciousness and 'the underlying unity of all reality'. We raise the interdisciplinary question: Can foundational movements in natural science, with their deep philosophical implications, provide us with some lessons on sustainable development thinking? The reason why we ask this question is that modern science, particularly quantum science, has challenged deeply the objective utilitarian perspective of looking at ecology, which has remained as the dominant view in SDG or public policy literature. Three main principles, have radically shifted our world views, namely, contextual decision making or in other words Contextuality creates realities, rather than a pre-existing objective reality, two, of ontological uncertainty at the heart of existence, and three that holism or non-locality is the very fabric of nature. We can no longer return to the Newtonian or even Platonic world view fully. Recently with the rise of quantum-like framework in cognitive science there has been a surge in the interest in applying mathematic-philosophical concepts used in quantum science to decision making in different domains, including economic thinking. We mention here quantum science, rather than quantum mechanics, since by no means we suggest any reductionism entailing reducing policy decision making to any underlying physical processes. Rather the term quantum science is more comprehensive, including information theory and computational models. We are also aware of the proposal by Sir Roger Penrose that consciousness fundamentally might be a non-algorithmic and non-computational process. Hence in this subsection we provide a brief de-tour of philosophical implications of quantum science since its birth in 1920s, and more particularly in Solvay conference debates throughout that decade, involving giants like Einstein and Bohr.

The Copenhagen interpretation is one of the most mind-bending attempts of quantum mechanics (QM) to describe the behaviour of our microcosm. Copenhagen school of quantum mechanics, since 1920 explains that a quantum particle does not exist in one state or another, but in all of its possible states at the same time. Observation is needed to collapse the wave function and see the reality of the state.

However, before we provide the particular arguments based on the Copenhagen ideas, it is also worthwhile to keep in mind the broader scientific realism philosophy, which has motivated major frameworks in science since Newtonian Physics, for example in the 20th century, namely the Special and General Theories of Relativity which are also very much based on the realism view. We may further distinguish between two types of realism, overall scientific realism and particularly physical realism. According to the first school of thought, the real non contextual objective world is 'out there' independent of our thoughts, which also includes mathematical truths, for example pure number theory. Whereas, physical realism includes the mind independent physical processes. Certainly the emergentist view would then hold that mind itself is emerging from physical processes, which is a typical physical closure argument in a way to resolve the vexing mind-body dichotomy since the days of Descartes. Quantum mechanics in general has challenged realism view, such that as of now we have two broad strategies for interpreting quantum mechanics, one realist and another anti-realist/ instrumentalist/non-representational (a term coined by David Wallace (2020) to address interpretations like Qbism). However, QM may also be argued to fall in the pragmatist school, again argued by Healey, which relaxes the stringent need for QM to describe the objective world in perfection, rather it might relate to it up to a certain degree. However, in all of these frameworks the thorny problem of consciousness remains, since fundamental awareness cannot be successfully included in any of them.

It was evident even in the Classical Physics era that reductionism is limited and that it cannot be effectively used as a method in all circumstances. The classic example of this is thermodynamics, where in practice it is impossible for even supercomputers to compute every individual trajectory that molecules of a system – like boiling water – would take for all age of the universe! Let alone any more complex system. Hence development of statistical mechanics, or recasting thermodynamics in statistical theory terms began, certainly James C Maxwell and Ludwig Boltzman were the biggest pioneers in that journey.

The scientific idea of 'emergence' was also one of the important fruits of thermodynamics, there might be many possible microstates (or configurations) corresponding to the same emergent macro state or configuration. The formidable second law of thermodynamics is also best understood in terms of statistical theory of emergence. Is emergence less fundamental than its micro constituents are? The surprising answer is no. Laws corresponding to the emergent levels are as fundamental as the lower level laws (for example Newton's equations of motion or Shrodinger's equation in Quantum mechanics). David Deutsch (1998), the noted physicist and philosopher, provides detailed reasoning of fundamental importance of emergent phenomenon.

Generally, we think of two forms of emergence: epistemological and ontological. While the former is based on the argument that all the underlying processes can be fully specified in a reductionist way, in practice we may work with high level description of natural or social phenomenon. What profoundly interests us, however, is that the latter argues that even in theory one cannot derive in a reductionist way the high level from the low level (hard emergence). We also note that since the beginning days of Quantum Mechanics, founders (see for example Rovelli, Helgoland) were deeply intrigued by the complex relationship between parts and the whole, rather Heisenberg wrote a classic text on the same topic (1958). Here we would raise the question were the founders of QM inspired in some ways by the ancient spiritual wisdom traditions. The reason being that concepts of emergence, or relational aspects (in modern day terms relational ontology) have been debated very intensely in ancient spiritual philosophies, particularly, in Eastern philosophies, Advaita Vedanta, Kashmiri Shaivism and Sunnyavada Buddhism being some well-known examples. We would also then explore the current motivations which some noted scientists have drawn from such traditions. Hence we would conclude with some future thoughts on how confluence between modern science (particularly QM and complexity science or complex adaptive systems views) and spiritual traditions might be fruitful, in providing us right acumen to survive in this radically uncertain times.

Exchanges Between Modern Science and Spiritual Philosophies

Our arguments are based on philosophical principles of modern science and what we can learn from them for sustainable development. Where again particular mathematical or qualitative frameworks might be built (as we refer to in the conclusion). Hence it is important to see what connections modern science might have with Eastern philosophies in particular, since latter is in many cases devoted to the concept of fundamental consciousness and or holism. Particularly relational ontological foundations of Buddhist philosophies and its exchanges with quantum science is of good help here.

There is a complex history of exchanges between modern science and Eastern spiritual philosophies. Even recent publications (Peters, 2022 for example) explore such nearly forgotten transactions. During 1930s when quantum physics was on rise as a new paradigm, it was not simply a continuation of earlier scientific worldviews, or so called Newtonian worldview, but a foundational shift, particularly in the view that observer needs to be at the centre of any observation (whether the observer needs to be conscious or not is another matter of intense debate. Generally standard view would be anything which is capable of recording and interacting with other systems, or capable of generating memories or traces of the 'past'), or the relational aspect needs to be a foundational feature of universe. Spiritual traditions like Buddhism, particularly, Śūnyavāda tradition pioneered by Nagarjuna (Garfield, 1995 for example), had since long emphasized on relational ontology. Very recently, 'relational quantum mechanics' framework, first proposed by Carlo Rovelli (1996), and now a promising interpretation of quantum mechanics, draws some motivation from Śūnyavāda. Consciousness fundamentalism, which is the central aspect of Advaita philosophy, is also referred to in modern scientific thinking (Duquette, 2011 for example), here though consciousness is not any species' specific 'emergent' property of brain or nervous system, but the very existence of universe is in 'universal' consciousness. Recent thinking of Biocentrism has some analogy to the Advaitic philosophy. However, *'sat-chit-ananda'* concept of Advaita should never be confused with anthropocentric view.

It is well known that many pioneers of QM, for example Heisenberg or Schrodinger, and later to some extent Pauli were deeply motivated by Eastern philosophical traditions. Heisenberg has written in multiple places that his readings of Buddhist philosophies had helped in realizing the seemingly mysterious features of QM better. One reason behind this might be the non-binary logic nature of many spiritual philosophies. Rather some physicists got surprised when it was found that in countries like Japan, wave-particle duality of QM was not taken as that much of a surprise as in west, since many such features become less esoteric if Aristotle's law of excluded middle is relaxed.

Hence, in a more secular vein, we can observe that different logical frameworks of Eastern philosophies can also enrich modern science. Recently authors (Patra & Ghose, 2022 for example) have demonstrated that non-binary logic frameworks, for example as in Syadbad or Anekantabad in Jain school of philosophy might be quite appropriate to describe features like wave-particle duality in quantum physics. More directly the wave-particle duality in quantum science bring forth a feature in reality which is not fully captured by age old mind-body dualism, or substance dualism. Later when David Bohm and his collaborators extended the duality perspective and formulated their own theory (not typically Copenhagen version), a double ontology of both particle and wave was adapted with a non-local quantum potential. Certainly here we are not proposing any one-one correspondence between such theories and holism in sustainable development, but it has been showed in many mathematical models that Bohm's approach might be mathematically adapted for a better understanding of behaviours of complex adaptive systems like financial markets. Such complex adaptive systems are also important for sustainability policy making. Hence these examples bring forth different dual or multiple aspects of social systems, which might be effectively modelled based on scientific tools.

Eastern philosophies might provide newer insights. For example 'contextuality' is ingrained in Syadbada non-binary logic system, propositions there take a truth value (which are not simply true, or false, but also 'excluded' middle is allowed, which is abyaktam or unmanifest) only in a specific context. It is well known that in quantum physics experimental observations are defined only in a context, which is again a shift from earlier 'non-contextual' concept of truth in classical physics.

Various Perspectives on Consciousness and Cognition From the Copenhagen School and Their Modern Counterparts

Here we are concerned with the perspectives of the founders of the Copenhagen Interpretation camp in formulating the possible relation between consciousness/cognition and QM. Consciousness is for sure a bigger and harder problem. Philosopher David Chalmers coined the now expressed phrase 'hard problem of consciousness', whereas cognition can be viewed as a simpler, yet related problem of human cognitive processes or decision making in general (AI included).

Neils Bohr in particular was curious since the early phases of the Copenhagen discussions about analogies between human thought processes and QM. Contextuality and complementarity as dual concepts seemed to be central to both domains of human activities. However, Bohr's conception of contexts, in his words 'experimental conditions', was very different from the other founders, particularly Heisenberg's. Also, Schrödinger's views one may observe were different, as he held the view that even though our bodies are in the external world, subject to space-time approaches, our mental existence is outside, which is a different picture from Bohr's contextuality (see recent literature for example pioneered by Andrei Khrennikov, example in 2021). While Heisenberg famously introduced the concept of 'CUT', meaning a transition 'above' a certain scale (somewhat arbitrarily chosen) wherein the world would be governed by the laws of classical physical (which includes the observer and experimental/laboratory apparatus) while 'below' that scale the world would only be truly quantum mechanical (consisting of the 'measured' or observed system), Bohr used to hold the view that whenever there is a 'measurement', by default it would imply the formation of an undivided wholeness between the observed system and the larger experimental conditions. Hence, no detectable as such CUT would exist.

Over time the technical literature on contextuality, whether in QM or cognition, has evolved in different directions than Bohr's original ideas. The celebrated frameworks of 'non-contextual' inequalities developed by John S. Bell (Khrennikov, 2022 for example) and later by CHSH which is a more simplified version of the original Bell inequalities, have taken the centre stage, where the observability of a joint probability distribution of random variables is the main issue. Very recently (Khrennikov as cited earlier), some mathematical frameworks for describing Bohr's contextuality have begun to appear based on the technical literature of quantum instruments. However, a framework describing holism is still warranted in mathematically precise terms, going beyond, the exception being, the David Bohm-Basil Hiley framework.

Soon after Bohr, the founders, particularly von Neumann, provided a consistent mathematical framework to what now is termed the 'Orthodox view' as formulated by Henry P. Stapp, extending Copenhagen and favoured by one of the current authors (Menas C. Kafatos, Debashish Banerji and Daniele Struppa, who edited a recent 2022 volume, to be published). One should note that the Copenhagen school's view of the 'ad hoc' postulate of non-unitary or truly random 'collapse' of the wave function, is still being debated as not compatible with the unitary and deterministic evolution of the linear Schrödinger equation for the wave function. Such seeming discrepancy is termed the measurement problem in QM based on the Hilbert space formulation. It was proposed that to resolve the problem of how and when the wave function collapses, where one has to evoke non-material consciousness.

Such frameworks have been intensely debated, with a main concern, that consciousness should be outside the realm of quantum mechanics or physics altogether, hence violating the causal closure principle of physicalism, causal closure principle would hold that all phenomena in this fundamentally physical universe can be explained only based on physical principles. Certainly, emergence is fully accepted in this view, but physical principles lie underneath all possible phenomena. This view seems to be the cornerstone of mainstream science. Yet, we argue here that this mainstream view may indeed be limiting, if not altogether erroneous.

QBism and Relational QM (RQM) in the Current Context of Different Approaches

QBism has evolved as a subjective and personalist view of QM, where the main suggestion has been that the 'quantum state' or the 'wave function' may not have any true ontological status but rather represents more the *knowledge of the experimenter or observer, which would mean that the existence of an absolute objective reality independent of experience might be hard to sustain.* (even not restricted to human observers) about the observed system, and updating of such knowledge, following a general formulation of Born's rule akin to the Bayesian probability updating. *Measurements* here would mean personal experiences, which observers acquire about the external world, which are up to a certain degree malleable by the observers' actions. QBism has over the years moved closer to phenomenology (see for example Christopher Fuchs' extensive writings on the same, for example in 2017), where objectivity would mean a shared and invariance of some experiences between different observers, whereas variance of experiences would mean subjectivity, also referred to as qualia.

RQM on the other hand is grounded on physicalism. Here only physically experienced or observed systems have an ontological status, therefore the wave function is just a mathematical tool to compute probabilities of some future events. Physical systems are in relations between each other, correlations to be specific. Hence facts are always relative to some systems, termed relative facts. However, there may be a subset of facts, known as stable facts which need not to be labelled against any other system. One needs to invoke the 'de-coherence' process to involve stable facts. Philosophers have observed that in RQM one cannot have a description of the universe as a whole, since based on only relational aspects such a question is meaningless. Consciousness or at least the entire qualia issues need to still be better formulated in the RQM framework.

A more recent attempt to account for consciousness and QM linkage is IIT (integrated information theory). The authors (Chalmers & McQueen, 2021 for example) have provided different versions of the 'consciousness led wave function collapse', which is different from the von Neumann/Wigner substance dualism view. Here consciousness is taken as an emergent property of a complex system, associated with an overall measure of integrated information, which the proponents term as φ. Consciousness thus typically does not allow macroscopic superposition states to exist. Attempts are proposed of a 'collapse operator' in the non-linear Schrödinger equation of a spontaneous collapse theory, which is associated with φ. Such a theory has not been found as Steven Weinberg has pointed time and again.

Recent Frameworks

Recently some novel frameworks have been suggested, for example quantum-like framework or quantum social science by another name, or complex adaptive systems framework, which are proving to be fruitful in the areas of decision science, social sciences and policy thinking.

These frameworks have been directly influenced by mathematical concepts widely used in natural sciences, Physics in particular, but also evolutionary Biology. Such frameworks have been able to make better contributions as compared to mainstream 'neoclassical' or 'neoliberal' frameworks in the very areas. Here we argue that, though mathematical concepts are central to those frameworks, by no means they can fully be considered as formalist's approaches, since there are deep philosophical underpinnings also. Such philosophical underpinnings might be traced back to some eastern philosophical traditions also.

One specific framework is quantum-like framework, which we refer to in this chapter elsewhere too. Such a framework is not based on the real quantum brain hypothesis, or not based on reductionism, rather would be based on philosophical principles which are common in different domains of knowledge. Such principles are namely: Contextuality creating its own reality, deep Uncertainty in the world and Non-locality (without violating theory of relativity). Such frameworks have now been used for better understanding of international relations in a complex adaptive world.

More particularly we have two frameworks, or interpretations of quantum mechanics, namely, relational quantum mechanics and QBism which are deeply ingrained in philosophical backgrounds. In relational quantum mechanics we are dealing only with observables, so no need for a wave function ontology other than calculation purpose. However, the observables are always defined in relation to each other, relation is the context in which quantum mechanics assumes meaning. However it is also true in that framework that observation need not be anthropocentric or based on any consciousness, an observer can be any one between the related systems (a principle of relativism one may say), which have the ability to interact and record traces of past interactions. Memory in this framework is thus a thermodynamic view. However, the relational ontology view is compatible with Mūlamadhyamakakārikā pioneered by Nagarjuna. QBism is also very much based on the phenomenology approach, where direct subjective experiences can never be ignored in the quantum physical framework also. Certainly observers would agree with some facts, but then qualias cannot be shared fully.

In cognition literature, recently authors (Patra and Ghose op cit) have argued that non-binary logical frameworks which were crucial to many Eastern philosophical thinking (for example, many valued logic of Syadbada Jainism school) can be harnessed to describe certain features like wave-particle duality in quantum mechanics. Rather it can be argued that many 'spooky' features in modern quantum mechanics including entanglement might not look spooky according to non-binary logic theories, some of which might be found in Eastern philosophies.

Hence based on the deep philosophical interconnections between spiritual heritage and modern science, authors (Kafatos & Patra, 2023, forthcoming) have suggested a new world view, which they have called as 'quantum-like reality'. This world view is based on the concept that there are certain universal principles which are true in different spheres of reality, for example in classical physics world, or in quantum physics world, or in cognitive world. Such principles are that of contextuality, deep uncertainty and non-locality.

View on consciousness from the Copenhagen camp particularly has been that quantum formalism itself can't define what consciousness is (though as we have observed there can be striking parallels between cognitive processes and QM, which is further extended in the quantum-like paradigm), the logic being more general, wherein a specific formalism cannot define its own user. For example, QBism, in many sense a modern heir of the Copenhagen school, would hold that QM is a rule book for navigating in a world where events happen, but remains silent on what is that describes a decision maker who uses that rule book. Certainly, the Wigner's friend problem and several of its new versions have been a challenge to the consistency of overall QM framework.

As far as we understand, RQM might not have any special view on consciousness at all, interestingly RQM is motivated by Buddhist philosophy of sunnya vada which promotes the idea of non-self.

Other versions which are still physicalisms, for example ORCHOR, would hold that consciousness is neither fully quantum, nor fully classical, but emergent, the very precise unitary evolution at the quantum level gets interrupted at larger mass displacement scales, which might generate proto-consciousness. Roger Penrose used a beautiful metaphor of a mermaid which is half in the water (the quantum world) and half outside in the air (the classical world), which symbolizes the emergent consciousness.

Holism and Sustainable Development

Einstein, in early 20th century, conceptualized a unified field theory that could explain the emergence of all energy from a single fundamental field. Quantum physicists scrambled to attempt to prove it and the pursuit is ongoing in the formulation of the Superstring theory. There are certain evidences of the existence of such a subtle energy or a fundamental field, though there is no conclusive proof. Yet, similar idea has been seen to exist in different cultures and traditions. The concept of 'spiritual energy' or 'universal energy' has existed since time immemorial. This non-physical entity is called by different names across spatial and temporal differences. It is called 'qi' or the 'vital force' in the East Asian culture, 'Ātman' in ancient Indian culture, 'pneuma' in the Greek culture, 'logos' as used by Aristotle and the Stoics, and as the 'breath' or 'soul' in popular culture. 'It is what people tap into when they draw from universal energy or life force energy'.

The idea that same energy runs through all of us and connects us to a single source is key to discuss the true meaning of sustainability. This idea string us together in a holistic framework that makes everything and everyone thrive on the principles of interdependence and interconnection. Such a holistic ecosystem will achieve sustainability when humans are cognizant of their true self, connect with their own and other beings' (including non-human animals and plants) spiritual energy, perceive planetary energy as the manifestation of the same universal energy and work in an active equilibrium to sustain and nourish all. As we discussed in the sections above, several cultures recognize this oneness in one form or the other, however, there is no single unifying framework for humanity to understand our common roots and thus sustain ourselves and each other. Through this chapter, our aim is to start the discussion and possibly sow the seeds to comprehend the common non-physical spiritual energy that is already mentioned across various wisdom traditions and investigated by science, especially quantum physics. We discussed the variations and differences in the conception of holism in different schools of philosophical thought and our goal is to appreciate them as expressions of same underlying knowledge of oneness. This perception gives us an approach to tap into our collective energy and evolve in resonance and harmony.

The challenges we are facing today – such as climate change, rising air pollution, decreasing forest cover, challenges of migration and displacement, poverty and inequality, gender inequality and overall poor health and wellbeing – and the challenges we will face in the coming time will be easier to address with common understanding and common solutions. These problems have been exacerbated with the onset of the COVID-19 pandemic and have revealed disconnection and severe fault lines in the current public policies and in the economic and social systems we have in place. For the last two centuries, our development models are screeching incoherence and equating happiness with material prosperity and economic 'growth'. It measures development in terms of Gross Domestic Product (GDP). The public policies are designed, implemented and evaluated based on these models in all sectors including health, education, economics and sustainability. However, this development paradigm blatantly misses the spiritual aspect of social and environmental dimensions we discussed above. Recognizing our common universal energy can bring about miraculous changes and heal us and our planet from our self-inflicted wounds. Self-awareness will make us more collaborative and conscious on our journey together to a better future – a healthy planet, better health and wellbeing, decent standard of living, equality, a paradigm of politics based on our conscious self, social justice and better conflict resolution. By appreciating and developing our inner self we can expect to leave our future generations with a better world to live in as well.

The spiritual and quantum principles of Holism we discussed should be directly applicable to:

- Decision-making process in politics and policymaking:

By looking at the similarities and differences in our cultures as transient expressions of a common source of energy, we will naturally develop empathy that is crucial in policy making and politics. This will bring a revolutionary shift in what we observe in politics today.

- Understanding our cognition as global citizens and leaders to adopt sustainable practices:

The recognition of interdependence in our holistic framework will move us, irrespective of our social positions, to be responsible and accountable for moving towards sustainable development.

- A move from a multi-disciplinary approach to an inter-disciplinary approach to sustainable development.
- Our discussion of a common understanding of holism has expounded the details of the inability to solve sustainable challenges in isolation. Pain in one part of the body brings hurt to the whole being.
- International collaboration for Sustainable Development Goals:

International disagreement have deterred us from collective action for sustainable development for a long time now. Agreeing on the core principles of holism and recognition and respect of mutual spiritual energy can solve this long standing challenge. A holistic approach will drop our egos, greed and fear, freeing us to act in unison.

The holistic view we propose does not evaluate each policy separately, rather it provides us with a policy *environment* as one complex, emerging, and evolving system. It will be intuitive and preventive in nature to predict and avoid unsustainable energy and events. Therefore, through this approach, we address not just the need for change in current policies but also deliver tools to adapt policies in the future according to our progress towards sustainable development.

Limitations

Often, dualism and anthropocentrism is attributed to the western and modern world and it is presumed that to reverse the effects of climate change, unsustainable consumption and production, and poverty, the concept of holism mentioned in various spiritual traditions of the world will come to rescue and facilitate sustainable development. This philosophy, however, should be put in context. For example, there is a case study from Japan where authors positively correlate the environmental degradation and aspects of Buddhism and Shinto. It is, therefore, crucial to define and recognize the nuances of the teachings of wisdom traditions and put them in context. It is key to avoid selective reading and cherry picking phrases from texts that support sustainable development.

Conclusion

Sustainable development requires acknowledgment of interconnectedness and interdependence of all its dimensions, be it social, economic, environmental or any other, and that it can only be achieved holistically. To this end, this chapter explored the idea and meaning of holism across spiritual traditions of the world and its characterization in physics. This is done with the hope of providing a new perspective and its usefulness to approach and achieve sustainable development.

This chapter also aspires to open up possibilities for the exchange of fruitful ideas between natural and social sciences to explore ways to address sustainable development. With this in mind, we investigated ideas from Eastern philosophical traditions and determined how such concepts can be compatible with existing modern science concepts (Bartley, 2011; Bohm, 2005; Bohm & Hiley, 1995; Bronkhorst, 2009; Craig & Firm, 1998; Peressini, 2008; Rojek, 2012; Rovelli, 2021), and sustainable development (Singh, 2014; Smuts, 2021; Sullivan, 1972).

Acknowledgements

Authors were significantly helped by deep suggestions from Professor Menas C. Kafatos.

References

Bartley, C. (2011). An introduction to Indian philosophy *(Annotated)*. Continuum.

Bohm, D. (2005). *Wholeness and the implicate order*. Taylor & Francis.

Bohm, D., & Hiley, B. J. (1995). *The undivided universe: An ontological interpretation of quantum theory* (1st ed.). Routledge.

Bronkhorst, J. (2009). *Buddhist teaching in India (studies in Indian and Tibetan Buddhism)* (1st ed.). Wisdom Publications.

Chalmers, D. J., & McQueen, K. J. (2021). Consciousness and the collapse of the wave function. arXiv preprint arXiv:2105.02314.

Craig, E., & Routledge (Firm). (1998). *Routledge encyclopedia of philosophy*. Routledge.

Deutsch, D. (1998). *The fabric of reality: The science of parallel universes – And its implications*. Penguin.

Duquette, J. (2011). "Quantum physics and Vedanta": A perspective from Bernard D'Espagnat's scientific realism. *Zygon®*, *46*(3), 620–638.

Erickson, H. L. (2007). Philosophy and theory of holism. *Nursing Clinics of North America*, *42*(2), 139–163. https://doi.org/10.1016/j.cnur.2007.03.001

Fuchs, C. A. (2017). Notwithstanding Bohr, the reasons for QBism. *Mind and Matter*, *15*(2), 245–300.

Garfield, J. L. (1995). *The fundamental wisdom of the middle way: Nagarjuna's Mulamadhyamakakarika*. Oxford University Press.

Heisenberg, W. (1958). The representation of nature in contemporary physics. *Dædalus*, *87*(3), 95–108.

Kafatos, M., & Patra, S. (2023, forth coming). Quantum-like reality. In M. C. Kafatos, D. Banerji, & D. Struppa (Eds.), *Quantum and consciousness revisited*. D. K Publishers.

Khrennikov, A. (2021). Can there be given any meaning to contextuality without incompatibility? *International Journal of Theoretical Physics*, *60*, 106–114.

Khrennikov, A. (2022). Contextuality, complementarity, signaling, and Bell tests. *Entropy*, *24*(10), 1380.

Lan, K. R., & Zhang, J. L. (1999). A Taoist foundation of systems modeling and thinking. *International System Dynamics Conferences*.

Maslow, A. H. (1971). *The farther reaches of human nature*. New York, NY: Viking Press.

Messerly, J. (2019, November 8). Summary of Maslow on self-transcendence. *Reason and Meaning*. https://reasonandmeaning.com/2017/01/18/summary-of-maslow-on-self-transcendence/

Patra, S., & Ghose, P. (2022). Classical optical modelling of social sciences in a Bohr–Kantian framework. In S. Sriboonchitta, V. Kreinovich, & W. Yamaka (Eds.), *Credible asset allocation, optimal transport methods, and related topics. TES 2022*. Studies in systems, decision and control (Vol. 429). Springer. https://doi.org/10.1007/978-3-030-97273-8_16

Peressini, A. (2008). Confirmational holism and its mathematical (w)holes. *Studies In History and Philosophy of Science Part A*, *39*(1), 102–111. https://doi.org/10.1016/j.shpsa.2007.11.008

Peters, M. A. (2022). Wittgenstein, Nāgārjuna and relational quantum mechanics. *Educational Philosophy and Theory*, *54*(12), 1942–1951.

Rojek, C. (2012). *Fame attack: The inflation of celebrity and its consequences.* Bloomsbury Academic.

Rovelli, C. (1996). Relational quantum mechanics. *International Journal of Theoretical Physics*, *35*, 1637–1678.

Rovelli, C. (2021). *Helgoland. How quantum theory is changing our world.* Penguin.

Singh, J. (2014). Spanda-Karikas: The divine creative pulsation. In *Motilal Banarsidass* (2012th ed.).

Sullivan, W. (1972, March 29). The Einstein papers. A man of many parts. *The New York Times.* https://www.nytimes.com/1972/03/29/archives/the-einstein-papers-a-man-of-many-parts-the-einstein-papers-man-of.html

UNDP. (2022). *Human development report 2021/2022: Uncertain times, unsettled lives: Shaping our future in a transforming world.* United Nations.

Wallace, D. (2020). On the plurality of quantum theories: Quantum theory as a framework, and its implications for the quantum measurement problem. In S. French & J. Saatsi (Eds.), *Scientific realism and the quantum* (p. 78). Oxford University Press.

Chapter 9

Spirituality, Wisdom and Quantum Theory: Wisdom Has a Measurement Problem Too

David Rooney

Abstract

Wisdom is a very difficult construct to work with in research and practice. One reason for this is that wise people can deal with metaphysical questions and experience spiritual phenomena, both of which are hard to measure meaningfully. Although metaphysical and spiritual matters are not imponderable, they have significant measurement problems that are also part of the shortcomings of standard social science statistical frameworks. A second reason is that for many wisdom theorists, wisdom is context-dependent because wisdom is defined by and responds to what its context presents to it. We can therefore argue that wisdom is essentially context, which in quantum physics is theorised as a superposition of random variables that interact. This chapter, therefore, ponders the 'immeasurable' from the perspective of quantum-like social science and quantum theory to render wisdom, including its spirituality component, in formal mathematical models. The mathematical formalism of quantum physics allows for the presence of metaphysical phenomena in its ontological foundations and its mathematical models. This chapter, therefore, also presents an argument for understanding wisdom from the superposition perspective and, in particular, the internal interactions between random variables contained within it. If the challenge of measuring wisdom as a nondeterministic system is met, we may finally have an opportunity to measure wisdom in ways that embrace wisdom's complex ontology. A third reason is that wisdom depends on people making first-person subjective judgements. Subjectivity is central to many interpretations of quantum theory, and we can borrow the analytical formalism used in quantum physics for wisdom research. Finally, the chapter discusses future approaches to empirical wisdom research that adopt quantum-like social science methods.

Applied Spirituality and Sustainable Development Policy, 167–180

doi:10.1108/978-1-83753-380-020231009

Keywords: Quantum theory; self-transcendence; empathy; transcendence; QBism

Introduction

Wisdom is a very difficult construct to work within research and practice because it has so many elements to it (Rooney, 2013). In this chapter, I want to discuss the links that wisdom (as a quantitative social science construct) has to quantum theory and spirituality including spirituality's underlying metaphysics as well as its reliance on subjectivity.

Wisdom is an exemplary, virtuous social practice that is situated in time and space that creates a flourishing and sustainable world (Rooney et al., 2010). To explore wisdom and spirituality, I will discuss ontological, epistemological and especially metaphysical problems that have hindered the progress of contemporary wisdom research. In short, I will argue that wisdom, like quantum mechanics, is fundamentally about context and includes metaphysical (including subjective) elements. In this chapter, metaphysics refers to asking questions about what is fundamental to reality and how those fundamental things, including consciousness, purpose and subjectivity, work. The metaphysics that I will focus on deals with spirituality and its fundamental questions (Desmond, 1995) about meaningful lives, the greater good and a higher purpose. This will then be linked to sustainable development policy as a critical public policy challenge because sustainable development has a higher purpose (by definition) and, as I will show, requires wisdom to implement. The term metaphysics can also be understood to mean 'in-the-midst'. This, though, is a much less appreciated meaning attached to the word, but it applies to wisdom concerning sustainable development because we must implement policy in-the-midst-of a difficult and messy world. Thus, it is worth invoking this sense of metaphysics because wisdom, as a situated or contextual phenomenon, occurs in-the-midst-of many interacting variables in-the-midst-of trying to live a good life. One must make sense of reality in-the-midst-of much clutter and noise. This observation notwithstanding, the chapter is more concerned with the fundamental questions aspect of metaphysics because much of this is profoundly linked to the fundamental human connections that bind humanity together as a collectively conscious (across time and space) species, and that this scenario is very much the scenario that sustainable development needs to be understood to exist in. After all, it is very likely that we are the only species that has a sense of belonging to a particular species that includes understanding that all people in all locations on earth, even those we can never meet, and also those who have existed in the past and those who will exist in the future are fellow member, with us, of our species. Sustainability must rest on a strong sense of belonging being part of the context.

I have set my task to focus on the nature of context and how it relates to wisdom to make clear what a significant ontological and epistemic challenge we face in conducting quantitative research about wisdom is. In doing this, I hope to open new doors for quantum-like social science to investigate. But, first, we must consider what is wisdom's ontology.

What Is Wisdom?

One way to think about what is wisdom is to see it as a person's ability to integrate human mental capacities, including emotion, insight, creativity, spirituality, empathy and self-transcendence, to name just a few of the elements needed to achieve wisdom's exceptionality that is aimed towards the greater good (Ardelt, 2008; Rooney et al., 2010). Of course, we should not neglect cognitive capabilities like logic, reason, intelligence and memory either, but I emphasize the transcendent capacities because they relate strongly to the greater good or greater purpose aspects of wisdom's metaphysics that underpin spirituality. The greater purpose efforts of individuals are motivated by their spirituality, that is, their sense of belonging to and having obligations to something greater than themselves and a sense of our shared humanity, indeed, collective consciousness. This is where our sense of knowing what a greater purpose is comes from. Sustainability is a greater purpose.

The discussion will come back shortly to these empirically difficult parts of wisdom, particularly those that relate to metaphysical capacities like metaphysical and ontological acuity, spirituality and self-transcendence (cf. Webster, 2007). However, before coming back to these matters, it is important to take a high-level look at wisdom's larger ontological shape.

Theorizing Wisdom

A good place to begin discussing ways of theorizing wisdom is with Aristotle (1984) who distinguished between conceptual (or theoretical) wisdom (*sophia*) and practical wisdom (*phronesis*) (Eikeland, 2008; Trowbridge & Ferrari, 2011). Conceptual wisdom leads to wise thinking and wise judgement, but practical wisdom leads to wise action in the 'real' world but is predicated on wise thinking, or, rather, wise reasoning. Practical wisdom is generally regarded as the ultimate kind of wisdom in the Aristotelian view (Flyvbjerg & Sampson, 2001). The main reason for placing practical wisdom at the pinnacle is that Aristotle saw it as the executive virtue that integrates the moral and intellectual virtues in such a way the people who possess practical wisdom have a positive impact on civic life to make the world a better place. And this is a central purpose of public policy. Love was important for Aristotle as well (Kristjánsson, 2021). Love for humanity and life was central to Aristotle's system of social philosophy and therefore to his notion of wisdom, and love of life is what underpins sustainable development ambitions.

If we probe Aristotle's idea of virtue (MacIntyre, 1984), it reveals a lot about what practical wisdom is. The first step is to understand that everyone has a set of values and that values are simply the things that we think are important to do in our life. We can think of four classes of values:

(1) Espoused values are the values that we say we hold (Jonsen et al., 2015).
(2) Values in action; are the values that others could infer you hold based on their observations of how you behave in the community, and these are often quite different from your espoused values (Ruch et al., 2010).
(3) Self-oriented, sometimes negative, values are values that do not have the purpose of making the world a better place for everyone. You might place a high value on developing a collection of magnificent diamonds for your own enjoyment, and although that is not an intrinsically bad thing, it is self-oriented. Another but different example of these values might be that you drive a poorly maintained car that produces excessive carbon emissions. This is a negative value because not only is it self-oriented (at the least because you have not taken personal responsibility for limiting those emissions), but it is unethical and probably illegal and has very negative environmental impacts (Schwartz, 2012).
(4) Eudemonic values are values, i.e., virtues, that you hold that make the world a better place. If you value doing volunteer work in the community that is a eudemonic value. Because these values are both other-oriented and because such actions make a positive difference to others, we can say that you embody those values/virtues (Nussbaum, 1992). Embodied eudaimonic values are values in action and action defines what positive values count as virtues. In Aristotle's framework, a person who is excellent at being virtuous in their life is a person of good character and virtue ethics is often called character ethics.

If virtue and eudemonic outcomes are the endpoints of practical wisdom, the engine room of it is found in the executive (Eikeland, 2008) aspect of the process. At the core of the executive process are ethical reasoning (Taylor, 2016) and empathy, including compassion and love. How you weigh and balance competing factors, discern what is important to consider and what is not, how good your judgement, insight, creativity and perspicacity are, and how and when you decide exactly what ought to be done are critical factors in this formulation of the ethics of wisdom. For example, taking responsibility for our own carbon footprint requires practical wisdom's virtue. It takes love, effort and resolve to reduce your own carbon footprint and so having wisdom is clearly a benefit.

There is a formula of sorts for determining what is virtuous. The virtuous person will

(1) Do the right thing,
(2) For the right reason,
(3) In the right way,
(4) At the right time (that is, with the right timing), and
(5) With the right outcome.

The ethical standard is very high here and interestingly the word virtue shares its linguistic roots with the word virtuoso. A virtuoso is someone who performs at the very highest level to produce the very best of outcomes, consistently. We need people working in the sustainable development space to be virtuosic.

Let's pause for a moment to consider the five 'right' imperatives. The question here is how do you decide what is right? The answer is that, in a way, you don't. that is, you don't until you assess the situation or context in which you must be wise. It's never going to be easy because there is no formula or rule of thumb to follow, and so wise reasoning may require post-conventional ethical reasoning. In particular, how do we decide what the five rights look like in sustainable development? A good starting point to decide this is with a contemporary update of practical wisdom.

An updated version of practical wisdom is the Social Practice Wisdom (SPW) framework (Rooney, 2015; Zhu et al., 2016). This framework also has five elements, and they are:

(1) *Qualities of mind and consciousness (metaphysics)*: An aware, equanimous, compassionate, humble and actively open mind with an integrated habitus of dispositions that drive insightful and virtuous action. This involves mindfulness, empathy, non-attachment (distancing), acceptance and self-awareness to understand uncertainty and the relativities of life, including conflicting values, identities, cultures and politics, as well as imperfect knowledge.

(2) *Agile, transcendent and reflexive reasoning (cognition)*: Reflexively integrating knowledge, including aesthetic knowledge (direct, embodied, sensory, non-rational knowing and conceptual knowing), transcendence (e.g. creativity, foresight, intuition, trans-conceptuality [non-linguistic knowing]), different perspectives and clear insight to adroitly deliberate and judge to assist transformative understandings of a situation despite uncertainty and ambiguity.

(3) *Ethical purpose and virtuosity (compassion)*: This includes virtues, ethical competence and the ability to understand and act positively in response to people's emotional (emotional maturity), social and material needs. Furthermore, it entails ego transcendence and virtuous alignment of values with social behaviour; and insight into the human condition and its shifting social relations to find the right and virtuous thing to do at the right time.

These first three process qualities and abilities recursively interact with each other as a habitus (or system of dispositions) to create the conative impulse for an embodied wise praxis that leads to excellent outcomes that improve the conditions of life. The final two elements are at the practice and outcome levels are:

(4) *Embodiment and Praxis (mastering wise action)*: Drawing from one's habitus of dispositions to creatively, responsively and decisively embody and enact wise performative skills in a situation. Wise performance draws on experience and understanding and is based on judgements that are executed and communicated in a timely and aesthetic way. This involves sensing and

knowing why, how and when to adapt to the surroundings and why, how and when to change them, and how to astutely make necessary trade-offs.

(5) *Outcomes that improve the conditions of life*: This involves galvanizing, purposeful leadership and artful communication to effect virtuous change with exceptional outcomes. Creating positive cultures and sustainable communities are central to this.

The embodied experience of being wise (or even trying to be wise) and the outcomes of such practice are also used by wise people, reflexively, to feedback on principles 1, 2 and 3. Finally, despite understanding others and life so well, a wise social practitioner is not selfish or manipulative.

Strictly speaking, the five principles are not a formal model or theory of wisdom, but they are useful in creating models or analytical frameworks for wisdom according to different situations, needs and purposes. Developed primarily for qualitative research, the SPW approach respects the situatedness of wisdom, i.e., it respects the great extent to which wisdom is determined by the situation that requires it. Moreover, the SPW approach, based on serious ontological grounds, spurns a thoughtless adherence to parsimony. This has much to do with SPW's original grounding in Aristotelian philosophy and ethics, including Aristotle's social and civic philosophy, but also with Platonic metaphysics and then Buddhism's ethics, metaphysics and psychology of freedom or liberation (soteriology).

The central dynamic in SPW is a complex multidimensional integration that creates clarity and decisiveness through equanimity and corresponding dispositions that generate the insight, composure and motivation to embody and deploy the precise and unique package of resources needed to act excellently and successfully in the best interests of oneself, others and the planet in a specific situation.

From a sustainable development perspective, multidimensional integration is a very large challenge. The SPW framework gives us a reasoned scaffold with which to design processes that lead to multidimensional integration. We can name all the most important dimensions, including those that are not normally included in the policy context like equanimity, love and transcendence. There is an opportunity here to change the sustainable development policy discourse for the better.

An important question that remains, though, is can we adequately quantify many of the core components of wisdom using a standard social science approach to statistics. The short answer is no, probably not to a sufficiently reasonable degree of accuracy, explanatory power and ability to predict.

Wisdom and Context

It is useful to dig deeper into the idea that wisdom is context-dependent. In other words, sustainable development exists in a context and what wise sustainable development is is defined by that context? So let us explore this in general terms. If we focus on practical wisdom, that is wisdom as a way of being that shapes how you conduct yourself in daily life, we can say that wisdom is situated. Wisdom as a situated social practice/activity says that the basic components of wisdom like qualities of mind, knowledge, ethics, praxis and what results from the activities of a practically wise person is context-dependent. By way of restating wisdom as context in a different way, we can say that a person may have a set of attributes that predispose them to be wise, but because they need to be wise in the range of situations that could unfold as they go about their life, and because each new situation can therefore potentially be radically different from previous situations calling for very different assemblages of the components set out in the SPW framework, it is the particular nature of the new situation that determines what is wise (or not) at that time and place. Wisdom is in some ways like a chameleon, always changing colour to fit its changing circumstances.

A situation is a context and the total of all potential situations a wise person might face is a very large number. Moreover, it would be very difficult to predict exactly how a wise person will adjust to act in any new situation. An important reason for this unpredictability is that there is a near-infinite number of variables in the contextual superposition. The wise person must employ certain abilities (cognitive and affective (including the subjective and inter-subjective), and motor skills), and not others, and has to integrate the abilities that are needed for the situation in a particular way and in particular ratios to each other as the situation demands. But how can we predict what is needed? There is a breathtaking level of skill in getting this complex mix right, but it is the context that determines what is the right mix because the wise person merely responds to what the situation presents them with. Uncertainty reigns because there is randomness in this system, making it non-deterministic and this is where quantum formalism shines.

Let's say that a big part of wisdom's context is culture (Rooney et al., 2010). Culture is, among other things, a shared set of values, beliefs and assumptions. Culture is like a collective mind or consciousness, and it is inter-subjective. Even if you only implicitly understand the rules and conventions of your culture, you are still a product of that culture and how you live is very much shaped by it. You are part of a collective consciousness already. A discursive shared consciousness impacts everyone and its impact on thought and action are central interests of, for example, discourse analysis (Rooney et al., 2010). We cannot escape from the inter-subjective fact that what I think you think about a shared concern and what you think I think about it, shapes how we both act. This shared or collective consciousness must also impact the capacity of all people to be wise (Rooney et al., 2021). Yet, we know almost nothing about how consciousness plays a role in wisdom. Given that a core function of wisdom is ethics, including love for humanity and life, then, part of that collective consciousness in wisdom is, as already discussed, concerned with something greater than the self, the greater good. This observation leads us to spirituality (where spirituality is not confined to religion). It also seems likely that wise people often think at very fundamental levels, for example, considering questions like what is the value of a life, or what is the good, or how does one lead a meaningful life? As I have argued, asking fundamental questions is to engage in metaphysical inquiry, and should also be important in sustainable development policy development and implementation.

Spirituality and Metaphysics in Wisdom

The mix of abilities and the content of the context are further complicated by the fact that there is an inevitable metaphysical element within a context and the makeup of the wise person. Ultimate questions about the universe are of the order of why is there something rather than nothing, or what is the most fundamental thing from which the universe arises. In the context of life being able to continue on our planet, we might ask why should there be something rather than nothing. At the level of humanity, we could ask additional fundamental questions such as what is the most fundamental component of the human condition, what is a person or self, what makes humans different from animals, or what is the purpose of a human life? Each of these is a difficult question to answer, and, in fact, each of them may be unanswerable. What is clear is that we do not have universally agreed-on answers to many metaphysical questions. How we answer such questions depends significantly on our (inter)subjectivity or subject positions (Fairclough, 2003; Küpers, 2007, 2014; Taylor, 2016). Concomitantly, we face a great deal of uncertainty around dealing with such slippery questions, because of the levels of subjectivity that necessarily influence our decisions about such elusive phenomena. From a wisdom perspective, what is most important here is to ask such questions about sustainability and to find good answers even if we cannot know if they are correct answers.

One thing that we can be sure about is that the unique nature of human consciousness is that we inevitably ask metaphysical questions because we crave answers to them. Human psychology may have evolved along a path that made wisdom possible by building on a prior disposition for metaphysical concern. Equally, that we all experience a sense of kindred spirit (Küpers, 2014, 2017), that is, that there is a feeling that we are all connected and that there is a greater community of humanity that spans space and time may also be a necessary prior condition in the evolution of our capacity for wisdom.

Spirituality is part and parcel of the human condition and metaphysical pursuits are connected to spirituality (Desmond, 1990; Tahora et al., 2019). Spirituality is not to be taken to only mean religiosity; spirituality is broader than that. Religiosity is an epiphenomenon of spirituality and our metaphysical needs. Spirituality signifies our inner need to find meaning in life through commitments to something larger than ourselves, and larger than our immediate experience of the world. The quest for meaning overwhelms so many of us (Vervaeke & Ferraro, 2013), but less so those who have wisdom. So, one general agreement among contemporary wisdom scholars is that ethics/morality is essential to wisdom and must be part of any theory or other construct representing wisdom (Grossmann et al., 2020). To be genuinely ethical, by which I mean, to practice what Aristotle called virtue (or character) ethics, you must be able to do ethical reasoning and have some level of commitment to the greater good and the common ground that all humanity shares. As the early parts of this chapter have made clear, virtue must be part of sustainable development processes. To be truly ethical, you are well served by having a strong affection for humanity and for life and to feel meaningfully connected to greater humanity and life. This is a metaphysical conflagration staring in the face of empirical wisdom (and ethics/morality) research. But are the self-report questionnaires so often used in social science research a valid method for researching such phenomena, particularly if we take wisdom's ontology seriously?

If context contains vastly many variables with very large degrees of freedom, then there is overwhelming uncertainty produced by this superposition, but if we add in the unmeasurable and indefinable metaphysical aspects of context with the kaleidoscopic intersubjectivity of a shared collective consciousness added to it, the challenge is incalculably greater. There is a non-deterministic and inter-subjectivity that we all participate in, yet wisdom requires excellence in bringing metaphysical answers together in-the-midst-of intersecting subjectivities.

If I am being brutally honest, I would have to say that contemporary wisdom research has made very little unique contribution to our knowledge of wisdom. And at a time of global sustainability crisis, when we need wisdom more than ever, we really must do better than this. One sensible response is to question our methods and the assumptions that underpin them. Quantum-like social science is a plausible way forward for wisdom and sustainability research.

Wisdom's Measurement Problem

Given this view of wisdom, it is fitting to admit that we, too, just as in quantum physics, have a measurement problem (Bangen et al., 2013; Brocato et al., 2020). Wisdom is (1) a product of context with vast numbers of variables, including (2) vast numbers of hard to measure variables, (3) all of this means analysis must deal with enormous degrees of freedom and (4) wisdom is a non-deterministic complex adaptive system. Standard social science statistical analysis pales in the face of such a challenge. The idea that if you can't measure it, it is not important, or if you can't measure it, redefine the phenomena so that it fits within the limits of analytical tools with ontologically unrealistic horizons is not anywhere near good enough, both ontologically and epistemically.

Quantum Measurement

I will leave presenting the formalism of modelling wisdom as I describe it for others who are more qualified in mathematical modelling than I am, but I will summarise several of the most promising mathematical interpretations of quantum theory that could help us model wisdom. To do this I will summarise Rooney and Patra's (2022) discussion of QBism, VAXJO and Context By Default theories concerning measuring context in ways that include wisdom's subjective, metaphysical and spiritual components.

QBism

QBism's origins rest in Quantum Bayesianism (Fuchs et al., 2014). More specifically, QBism applies Bayesian probability in the context of quantum physics.

QBism is an important interpretation of quantum mechanics and is an interpretation of the quantum state that adopts a purely epistemic, or subjective and phenomenological ontology. This understanding of the wave function accounts for an observer's subjective belief state about reality. Seen from the perspective of wisdom research and social science more generally, QBism explicitly allows for psychological phenomena or ideas or perhaps the broader notions like inter-subjectivity and consciousness to be part of a quantum-like system, for example in human cognition modelling. What is, arguably, more important is that QBism also implies that the entanglement of psychological phenomena (thoughts) has a role in creating the reality that we experience (Maudlin, 2005). Crucially, QBism measures the expectations and beliefs about reality that observers have and also the processes through which those expectations and beliefs are formed as a result of an observer's accumulated activities and experiences. As experience teaches us, we update our beliefs, and so QBism accounts for learning.

For understanding wisdom, it is very important to acknowledge that QBism can include inter-subjectivity, memory, information and learning over time, each of which is important for sustainable development.

In QBism, measuring a series of updates of an observer's belief states depends on Born's rule, which is required to calculate the distinctive probability density of a wave function collapsing in a particular way to create a unique result. In social scientific terms, Born's rule is understandable in that it computes the probability of a particular context will lead to a person deciding on one thing rather than another. As Khrennikov et al. (2018) have argued, QBism is excellent for developing general decision-making theory and this is highly relevant to wisdom.

VAXJO

VAXJO (Khrennikov & Haven, 2009) probability analysis is also applicable in social science. VAXJO, as an interpretation of quantum mechanics, is a statistical method that can compute contextual relativity as probabilities. Although VAXJO calculates probability, it does so by adopting a realist or deterministic stance instead of the subjectivist approach offered by QBism. This approach may be useful in understanding, for example, how logical thinking contributes to wisdom. This leads to an important question about how to incorporate analytical approaches with different underlying ontological assumptions into a suite of tools for studying wisdom.

Understood in mathematical terms, VAXJO's important difference, when compared to QBism, is its adoption of generalized mathematical objects, called positive-operator valued measures (POVM), in analysis. Positive operators are useful in decision-making research to handle cognitive observables so that perturbations can be measured in relation to cognition, particularly in understanding cognitive or belief state updates in systems that contain 'noise', and where decision-making errors occur. In other words, VAXJO has an important facility that can work with the messy and imprecise social interaction and inconsistent individual cognitions that are so common. Such perturbations could, for example, be a function of high levels of emotionality, feelings of uncertainty, political behaviour, or deliberate deception. It is clear that these kinds of contextual factors relate to the realities of sustainable development processes and are also discussed in the most recent Human Development Report (Sachs et al., 2022).

Contextuality by Default

Contextuality by Default (CBD) is an approach that can deal with maximally coupled variables and it assumes that all variables in a superposition are contextual. If we say, for example, that wisdom is only context and is comprised of many interacting variables, then CBD is very useful. In analysis, CBD applies a very general probabilistic method to quantum mechanics when compared to VAXJO and QBism (Dzhafarov & Kujala, 2016).

In short, we can say that CBD measures context by measuring random variables along with other random variables, including somehow connected or joint variables. This includes treating any joint measures as contexts in their own right.

Furthermore, and importantly for social research, a critical capacity of CBD is that it can determine if the meaning of a random variable significantly varies because it is currently being measured with another random variable. Thus, if I have a belief about how important writing a paper is and a belief about deforestation is bad for climate change and I connect the two beliefs, my attitude to writing a paper could change, but will it? Or if someone is a lifelong believer in social democracy but they receive copious amounts of disinformation painting a populist demagogue in a positive light on their most trusted social media platform, will they change their lifelong commitment to social democracy in favour of the demagogue? Context by default theory might help us answer these and similar kinds of questions.

If we think about the mathematics used in CBD, what we see is that it takes binary measures of a very large number of random variables that are maximally interconnected. This can be done with CBD because it measures if the probability distribution of a particular random variable is changed when in the presence of another. In this light, it is easy to see that CBD understands context as dense patterns of connection. The value to wisdom research of measuring specific patterns of connected variables, like beliefs, values, information and feelings in different situations is potentially very powerful. Among other things, CBD analysis has implications for sustainable development for public policy in terms of governance, spirituality and freedom (soteriology). By using the CBD approach, it is also possible to analyse order effects and response replicability effects in decision-making.

To summarise, Quantum measurement methods have great potential in social science and in wisdom research in particular. Quantifying context is not something that quantitative social science is historically very effective at. However, with the judicious use of the methods like those outlined above, research can elegantly handle some very human social systems phenomena such as noise, intersubjectivity, memory, choice making and temporal evolution, all of which are relevant to understanding wisdom and spirituality and applying them in sustainable development and to how wisdom works such that subjectivities and metaphysical issues, including spirituality, can be better understood.

Conclusion

The very nature of wisdom lends itself to adopting a quantum-like social science approach. If we take a view that (1) foregrounds context in defining what wisdom is in each situation in which it is required, (2) includes first-person subjectivity and (3) the influence of metaphysical phenomena, and in particular spirituality, then, quantum-like social science has a strong capacity to fulsomely deal with each of these in quantitative research. Moreover, I argue that not only can quantum-like social science deal with these phenomena fulsomely but that it can do so in ways that are more accurate in ontological terms than do the research studies of wisdom that use standard social science statistical analyses.

If it is true that we inhabit a world facing a growing crisis and that the world needs more wisdom if we are to overcome our major challenges, then, it makes sense that we make research progress in better understanding what wisdom is and how to develop it. Given the contextual nature of wisdom, the importance of spirituality (and its metaphysics), and that subjectivity (including inter-subjectivity) is necessarily part of being wise, then it makes sense to become better at dealing with these difficult to measure components.

Although metaphysical and spiritual matters are not imponderable, they have historically been challenging to measure while being adequately faithful to their ontologies. To put it glibly, this chapter ponders the (im)measurable from the perspective of quantum-like social science and quantum theory. Fortunately, the mathematical formalism of quantum physics allows for the presence of spirituo-metaphysical phenomena and potentially does so in open recognition of wisdom's complex ontological foundations.

This chapter, therefore, has presented an argument for understanding wisdom from the perspective of context and its internal interactions between random variables, many of which are challenging for measurement.

If the challenge of measuring the immeasurable is met, we may finally have an opportunity to measure wisdom in ways that acknowledge wisdom's complex ontology rather than ignore it. Moreover, if we can model wisdom in this way and can do so in the context of sustainable development, we create new opportunities for a better future. This, I suggest, is something that we urgently need for a sustainable planet.

References

Ardelt, M. (2008). Wisdom, religiosity, purpose in life, and death attitudes of aging adults. *Existential and Spiritual Issues in Death Attitudes*, 139–158.

Aristotle. (1984). *Nicomachean ethics* [H. G. Apostle, Trans.]. The Peripatetic Press.

Bangen, K. J., Meeks, T. W., & Jeste, D. V. (2013). Defining and assessing wisdom: A review of the literature. *American Journal of Geriatric Psychiatry*, *21*(12), 1254–1266.

Brocato, N., Hix, L., & Jayawickreme, E. (2020). Challenges in measuring wisdom-relevant constructs in young adult undergraduate students. *Journal of Moral Education*, *49*(1), 46–70. https://doi.org/10.1080/03057240.2019.1576124

Desmond, W. (1990). *Philosophy and its others: Ways of being and mind*. Suny Press.

Desmond, W. (1995). *Being and the between: Political theory in the American Academy*. SUNY Press.

Dzhafarov, E. N., & Kujala, J. V. (2016). *Contextuality-by-Default 2.0: Systems with binary random variables*. Paper presented at the International Symposium on Quantum Interaction.

Eikeland, O. (2008). *The ways of Aristotle: Aristotelian phronesis, Aristotelian philosophy of dialogue, and action research* (Vol. 5). Peter Lang.

Fairclough, N. (2003). *Analysing discourse: Textual analysis for social research*. Routledge.

Flyvbjerg, B., & Sampson, S. (2001). *Making social science matter: Why social inquiry fails and how it can succeed again* [S. Sampson, Trans.]. Cambridge University Press.

Fuchs, C. A., Mermin, N. D., & Schack, R. (2014). An introduction to QBism with an application to the locality of quantum mechanics. *American Journal of Physics*, *82*(8), 749–754.

Grossmann, I., Weststrate, N. M., Ardelt, M., Brienza, J., Dong, M., Ferrari, M., ... Vervaeke, J. (2020). The science of wisdom in a polarized world: Knowns and unknowns. *Psychological Inquiry*, *31*(2), 103–133. https://doi.org/10.1080/1047840X.2020.1750917

Jonsen, K., Galunic, C., Weeks, J., & Braga, T. (2015). Evaluating espoused values: Does articulating values pay off? *European Management Journal*, *33*(5), 332–340.

Khrennikov, A., Basieva, I., Pothos, E. M., & Yamato, I. (2018). Quantum probability in decision making from quantum information representation of neuronal states. *Scientific Reports*, *8*(1), 1–8.

Khrennikov, A., & Haven, E. (2009). Quantum mechanics and violations of the sure-thing principle: The use of probability interference and other concepts. *Journal of Mathematical Psychology*, *53*(5), 378–388.

Kristjánsson, K. (2021). Collective Phronesis in business ethics education and managerial practice: A Neo-Aristotelian analysis. *Journal of Business Ethics*. https://doi.org/10.1007/s10551-021-04912-2

Küpers, W. (2007). Phenomenology and integral pheno-practice of wisdom in leadership and organization. *Social Epistemology*, *21*(2), 169–193.

Küpers, W. (2014). Embodied inter-affection in and beyond organizational lifeworlds. *Critical Horizons*, *15*(2), 150–178.

Küpers, W. (2017). Inter-play (ing)–embodied and relational possibilities of "serious play" at work. *Journal of Organizational Change Management*, *30*(7), 993–1014.

MacIntyre, A. (1984). *After virtue*. University of Notre Dame Press.

Maudlin, T. (2005). 461 Distilling Metaphysics from Quantum Physics. In M. J. Loux & D. W. Zimmerman (Eds.), *The Oxford Handbook of Metaphysics* (pp. 461–488). Oxford University Press.

Nussbaum, M. C. (1992). Human functioning and social justice: In defense of Aristotelian essentialism. *Political Theory*, *20*(2), 202–246.

Rooney, D. (2013). Grounding organizational wisdom theory: Ontology, epistemology, and methodology. In W. Küpers & D. Pauleen (Eds.), *A handbook of practical wisdom: Leadership, organization and integral business practice*. Gower.

Rooney, D. (2015, May 2). The knowledge economy, knowledge policy, & wisdom site. https://sites.google.com/site/davidrooneyknowledge/

Rooney, D., Küpers, W., Pauleen, D., & Zhuravleva, E. (2021). A developmental model for educating wise leaders: The role of mindfulness and habitus in creating time for embodying wisdom. *Journal of Business Ethics*, *170*(1), 181–194. https://doi.org/10.1007/s10551-019-04335-0

Rooney, D., McKenna, B., & Liesch, P. (2010). *Wisdom and management in the knowledge economy*. Routledge.

Rooney, D., & Patra, S. (2022). Embracing weird: Quantum context and quantum social sciences. *Mind and Matter*, *20*(2), 249–279.

Ruch, W., Proyer, R. T., Harzer, C., Park, N., Peterson, C., & Seligman, M. E. (2010). Values in action inventory of strengths (VIA-IS). *Journal of Iindividual Differences*, *31*(3), 138–149. https://doi.org/10.1027/1614-0001/a000022

Sachs, J., Kroll, C., Lafortune, G., Fuller, G., & Woelm, F. (2022). *Sustainable development report 2022*. Cambridge University Press.

Schwartz, S. H. (2012). An overview of the Schwartz theory of basic values. *Online readings in Psychology and Culture*, *2*(1), 11.

Tahora, S., Shah, S., & Rooney, D. (2019). Vedanta philosophy's contribution to wisdom development for leadership: Grounding Indian practical wisdom in higher knowledge and purpose. In *Applying wisdom to contemporary world problems* (pp. 309–336). Springer.

Taylor, C. (2016). *The language animal: The full shape of the human linguistic capacity*. Harvard University Press.

Trowbridge, R. H., & Ferrari, M. (2011). Sophia and phronesis in psychology, philosophy, and traditional wisdom. *Research in Human Development*, *8*(2), 89–94.

Vervaeke, J., & Ferraro, L. (2013). Relevance, meaning and the cognitive science of wisdom. In M. Ferrari & N. M. Weststrate (Eds.), *The scientific study of personal wisdom: From contemplative traditions to neuroscience*. Springer.

Webster, J. D. (2007). Measuring the character strength of wisdom. *The International Journal of Aging and Human Development*, *65*(2), 163–183.

Zhu, Y., Rooney, D., & Phillips, N. (2016). A practice-based wisdom perspective for social entrepreneurship learning and education. *The Academy of Management Learning and Education*, *15*(3), 607–625. https://amle.aom.org/content/15/3/399

Chapter 10

Public Policy for Sustainable Development: A Gandhian Paradigm

Pooja Sharma

Abstract

The present world is captivated by the global challenges of climate change, environmental and ecological degradation, challenges related to migration, inequality, conflict and unrest. The development process failed to appreciate and signify the role of non-value, non-materialistic and altruistic value of both living and non-living natural entities. Thus, a significant disconnect or gap between public policy and human well-being has been observed. The departure of human beings from their true self has also distanced humans from the rest of the species and ecosystem. The essence of altruistic value and its recognition is plausible only through the upliftment and evolution of the inner self. The interconnectivity of the inner and outer world can be perceived through self-evolution. A public policy that is driven by the force of self-enhancement and realization, connecting and synthesizing human and non-human interactions selflessly, is required for revolutionizing the development paradigm. Against this backdrop, Gandhian philosophy that values the individual and his relationship with his true self becomes instrumental in ethical transformation. The self-transformation, manifestation and realization of truth and love are deeply embedded in Gandhian Revolution. Gandhian philosophy is a phenomenal illustration of self-transformation based on self–realization and soul force (Satyagraha) that acts as a driving force for a paradigm shift. Gandhian thoughts recognize the otherness of others (either human beings or nature), embedded in the notion of 'Sarvodaya'. Based on spiritual inquiry and ethical value judgement, and cosmic interdependence, the Gandhian notion constitutes a building block for a non-violent socioeconomic system guided by empathy and the law of non-possession. The twin models, 'The trusteeship model' and 'Economy of Permanence', advocate a spiritual inquiry and ethical value judgement in economics and governance. Addressing the economic problem of scarcity and choice, the attributes of decentralization, self-sufficiency and self-reliance envisage that individuals are satisfied with

Applied Spirituality and Sustainable Development Policy, 181–200

Published under exclusive licence by Emerald Publishing Limited
doi:10.1108/978-1-83753-380-020231010

minimum consumption. In addition, non-violence, truth and love create a subsequent balance in ecology and the environment. Ethical responsibility is not just limited to socio-economic and political systems but also integrates environmental and ecological sustainability.

Keywords: Public policy; Gandhian philosophy; sustainable development; Sarvodaya; trusteeship model; economy of permanence; decentralization

Introduction

The present world is threatened by the global challenges of climate change, environmental and ecological degradation, challenges related to migration, inequality, conflict and unrest. Critically examining the socio-economic and political dimensions, the development paradigm adopted has failed tremendously. On the economic front, excessive consumerism and economic growth have ignored the fundamental aspects of welfare, non-materialistic well-being and environmental sustainability. Similarly, on the socio-political dimension, the development discourse of human civilization has resulted in poverty, unequal distribution, socio-economic exclusion, social and political unrest, and conflict. Consequently, human ethics, equity and inclusivity have been compromised and discarded. The absence of fundamentals of ethics and values in our socio-economic and political interactions has departed the human race from its true consciousness and awareness. Therefore, eventually, a tremendous disconnect or gap between public policy and human well-being has developed. The departure of human beings from their true self has also distanced humans from the rest of the species and ecosystem.

United Nations emphasized the importance of public service in achieving sustainable development goals (SDGs), United Nations.[1] Public institutions can be mobilized to implement the SDGs. The effective and equitable delivery of quality services for achieving all SDGs is plausible with a robust public policy mechanism. Such an effective public policy framework will not only ensure sustainable development goals and sustainable development pathways but also provide a peaceful environment for growth and development.

It is the result of limitations of the scope of the development process to appreciate and signify the non-value and altruistic value of both living and non-living natural entities. The essence of altruistic value and its recognition is plausible only through the upliftment and evolution of the inner self. The interconnectivity of the inner and outer world can be perceived through self-evolution. Thus, a framework that comprehends and values the missing discourse on consciousness and a non-material, altruistic value system is the need of the hour. Much needed appreciation of self-consciousness that connects humans with both

[1]United Nations. Department of Economics and Social Affairs, https://www.un.org/en/desa/un-highlights-importance-public-service-achieving-sdgs.

living and non-living entities of the ecosystem is the demand for public policy design.

Against this backdrop, it is imperative to synthesize the missing link of self -consciousness in the development discourse and visualize a shift in the development paradigm for overall sustainable development. The plausible interlinkages between spirituality with public policy and how applied spirituality can address the complexities of public policy have been explored in this chapter. The hypothesis is that the Gandhian philosophy based on spirituality significantly correlates with public policy, spirituality and sustainable development.

Thus, Gandhian philosophy that values the individual and his relationship with his true self becomes instrumental in ethical transformation. The evolved consciousness becomes the driving force of the perceived paradigm shift. Moreover, the self-transformation, manifestation and realization of truth and love are deeply embedded in Gandhian Revolution. Gandhian philosophy is a phenomenal illustration of self-transformation based on self–realization and soul force (*Satyagraha*). Gandhian thoughts negate the otherness of others (either human beings or nature), embedded in the notion of 'Sarvodaya'. The notion of the otherness of other identifies the difference between various entities, the differences among human beings based on caste, religion, gender, etc., or the difference between human beings, species, or nature. The concept of *Sarvodaya* rejects the notion of the otherness of others in the sense that the creation of othering or otherness tends to classify individuals or species in hierarchical groups. In other words, otherness and identity are two sides of the same coin (Staszak, 2009).

Based on spiritual inquiry, ethical value judgement and cosmic interdependence, the Gandhian notion constitutes a building block for a non-violent socioeconomic system guided by empathy and the law of non-possession. In addition, these attributes of empathy and non-possession develop a profound inseparable balance between ecology and environment. Ethical responsibility is not just limited to socio-economic and political systems but also environmental and ecological sustainability. Gandhian ideology advocates that self-governance is the key to self-transformation; political governance is driven by service for humanity guarding and protecting the dignity and respect of every individual.

The present development process has immensely failed to appreciate and signify the non-use value, and altruistic value of both living and non-living natural entities, leading to a socio-economic framework that is not sustainable. Spirituality, non-violence, Truth and cooperation are some of the elementary aspects of the Gandhian model of Trusteeship, Economy of Permanence, *Sarvodaya*, and Satyagraha. The fact that a spiritually evolved self acknowledges the Truth of mankind becomes the driving source of service to humanity and also recognizes the essence of altruistic value and its recognition is plausible only through the upliftment and evolution of the inner self.

The twin models 'The trusteeship model' and 'Economy of Permanence' originating from Gandhian thoughts advocate a spiritual inquiry and ethical value judgement in the functioning of economics and governance. Addressing the economic problem of scarcity and choice, the attributes of decentralization, self-sufficiency and self-reliance envisage that individuals are satisfied with minimum consumption. In addition, the profound interconnectivity of aspects of non-violence which conceives an act of love, a subsequent balance in ecology and environment is created. Ethical responsibility is not just limited to socio-economic and political systems but also endeavours related to environmental and ecological sustainability.

Moreover, the indivisibility of super consciousness is realized and manifested in the policies. The only vision and purpose of the policy is selfless service for not only humans but the ecosystem. Such a public policy will revolutionize the development paradigm. The underlying notion of Gandhian models unfolds the complexities of public policy, conflict resolution, social justice and law, and environmental and ecological sustainability. The chapter will present the foundations of Gandhian philosophy that can play a critical role in visualizing the role of public policy in the shift in the development paradigm.

Spirituality and Sustainable Development

The role of public policy lies at the heart of the developmental process. The developmental regime of a state is instrumental in setting up the road map for the socio-economic, environmental and ecological framework. Appropriate policies are needed for resolving socio-economic and environmental challenges. The notion of super consciousness is the proposed state of mind that is able to acquire knowledge through meditation and other related practices that enable them to access superconscious mind. Such practices are placed under the scope or prism of spirituality. Thus, spirituality is the state of mind when the indivisibility of super consciousness entails that human consciousness is connected naturally to one another.

If our consciousness is connected deeply, then the associated challenges of human life are also connected to one super consciousness and they are indivisible. It is evident that all the present global challenges are interrelated to each other, therefore a framework that provides an explanation, considering all challenges together is the need of the hour. Moreover, spirituality is devoid of time and space. Therefore, the complexities related to sustainable development must be addressed in a context that is free from time and space. What it means is that all the dimensions of sustainable development should be in sync with each other irrespective of time and space. The present development models are devoid of well-meant. Therefore, there is a need to transform such a development framework that has resulted in de-wellmeant to 'well-meant', which implies safety, ingenious and hurtless. Well-meant is that stage of progress based on the decisions and actions intended to be kind or helpful. In other words, those decisions or systems that are directed towards the well-being of all.

Moreover, spirituality could be viewed as the journey from the outer world to the inner world. This journey of the inner self towards self-upliftment could be synchronized with the socio-economic development of society or humankind as a whole. Spiritual endeavour is a journey towards the evolution of human beings while sustainable development is the pathway to achieve the overall development of a socio-economic system that sustains human life. Spirituality is an exploration of the state of bliss or Euphoria, while sustainable development is a journey towards sustainable growth or a state of general equilibrium. Therefore, there exists a massive potential for synchronizing both the pathways of growth and upliftment. In other words, a significantly high correlation is expected between the two processes. Finally, spirituality is the underlying phenomenon of a development process that aspires to achieve the overall upliftment of mankind.

Public Policy, Spirituality and Gandhian Perspective

Spirituality is the fundamental base or foundation of Gandhian thoughts. Based on the basic attributes of Truth and non-violence, the Gandhian thoughts represent a remarkable model for a public policy framework for sustainable development. Gandhian philosophy values the individual and his relationship with his true self. Thus, the individual self becomes instrumental in ethical transformation. Gandhian philosophy is a phenomenal illustration of self-transformation based on self–realization and soul force (Satyagraha). The elementary strategy of the path of Satyagraha is to protest against injustice through peaceful means consistently. A persistent effort and consistent pursual are expected to bring about what is attributed to a 'change of heart'. The concept of Satyagraha pertains to the transformation of the inner self. *Satya* means 'Truth', which is soul or spirit, and *Agraha* means 'insistence', a synonym for force. *Satyagraha*, therefore, means love and firmness for truth, and represents a synonym for force or soul force. It is a form of non-violent resistance. The firmness on holding on to the Truth or soul manifests a change of heart. The ethics of interconnectedness is primarily to look within oneself. Change oneself and then change the world. Satyagraha signifies appealing to the opponent's heart and changing it by suffering of self as a method of passive resistance.

Based on spiritual inquiry and ethical value judgement, and cosmic interdependence, the Gandhian notion constitutes a building block for a non-violent socio-economic system guided by empathy and the law of non-possession. The notion of *Sarvodaya* originates from self-realization and consciousness that brings forth the perspective of our universal existence, which connects human life to the whole universe and signifies our universal existence and implications. Therefore, the underlying notion of Gandhian thoughts is sufficient to unfold all the present challenges and failures of the present social, economic (deprivation, inequality and discrimination) and political systems, such as conflicts, unrest and disorder. The appeal for Truth or soul force, as described above, will transform the opponent's heart and, thus, achieve a win-win situation under all conflicts and discontent.

The twin models, 'The trusteeship model' and 'Economy of Permanence' originating from Gandhian thoughts, advocate a spiritual inquiry and ethical value judgement in economics and governance. In addition, the profound interconnectivity of aspects of non-violence, which conceives an act of love, creates a subsequent balance in ecology and the environment. Ethical responsibility is not just limited to socio-economic and political systems but also environmental and ecological sustainability endeavours.

Gandhian thoughts advocated a consensus-based decision-making system, more conducive to a decentralized system. Decentralization is a consensus-based, most efficient democratic system that provides a policy framework or regime that is inclusive and empowers every individual. Such a system is self-sufficient and self-reliant, with lesser production, and lesser use of resources based on indigenous resources and skills, and is sustainable. It is the most inclusive method of policy implementation.

In the context of education policy, the Gandhian notion of *Nayi Taleem* is a remarkable breakthrough in the education system. *Nayi Taleem* is based on the principle that knowledge and work are not separate. The lifelong character of education, social character, and the holistic process are the foundation of Gandhi's notion of 'Nayi Taleem'. The core of this pedagogy is to impart education of body, mind, and soul through handicrafts taught to the children. Any work based on skill or handicrafts teaches a spiritual journey by enhancing focus and concentration. This learning at an early age will provide a unique skill for earning in life and spiritual progress for a healthy mind, body, and soul. An education system that revolutionizes the individual self towards a successful and sustainable life.

Spirituality, non-violence, Truth, and cooperation are some of the elementary aspects of the Gandhian model of Trusteeship, Economy of Permanence, *Sarvodaya*, and Satyagraha. A spiritually evolved self acknowledges the Truth of mankind, becomes the driving source of service to humanity and recognizes the essence of altruistic value. Its recognition is plausible only through the upliftment and evolution of the inner self. The only vision and purpose of public policy remain selfless service for humans and the ecosystem. The underlying notion of Gandhian models unfolds the complexities of public policy, conflict resolution, social justice and law, and environmental and ecological sustainability. In other words, a model that generates sustainable development.

Gandhian thought is primarily guided by self-upliftment or transformation. The philosophical inquiry of Truth and ethical value judgement underlying these models distinguishes them from other development paradigms. Originating from ethical inquiry and value judgement, the Gandhian models are comprehensive, spanning the huge spectrum of human civilization. The role of the state is motivated by the service of mankind, ethics and justice. The Gandhian models have socio-economic, geopolitical, environmental and ecological implications for mankind and human civilization. It is indeed a Gandhian paradigm of human civilization. The following sections present clear evidence of public policy and sustainable development being advocated extraordinarily through Gandhian thoughts.

Sarvodaya: A Concept of Spiritual Inquiry

Essentially, the notion of *Sarvodaya* may be viewed as an egalitarian concept that originates from the self-transformation of individuals. The concept of *Sarvodaya* can be considered the most democratic and decentralized system of functioning. 'In his Gita commentaries, one can observe the strong influence of Gandhi's understanding of Ruskin's Unto This Last in the egalitarian inclusivity focus...' (Allen, 2019, p. 84).

When the individual experiences self-transformation, the notion of the welfare of all that pertains to not only the welfare of the human race but the whole of ecology manifests. Gandhi embarked on the *Sarvodaya* movement in addition to his ongoing movement of non-violence. The word *Sarvodaya* mainly reflected 'progress of all' or 'Universal uplift'.[2] The underlying principle of *Sarvodaya* is that the good of the individual is contained in the good of all. *Sarvodaya* stands for the progress of all. Individuals should follow the law of non-possession.

> I have made it a profession to serve Daridranarayana. Hence, whatever other occupations I may take up my own profession will always be the focal point. But, if you cannot pay me more, help me in my work of communal unity. Let there be no distinctions of caste or community among the students and, if you cannot help the suffering poor at least sympathize with them by being good to them. (CWMG 87:470) Collected Works of Mahatma Gandhi.
>
> (Gandhi, 1958)

Thus, the desire for the greatest good for all, serving the plight of the poorest of the poor is, originating from the fundamental principles of *Sarvodaya*. The main purpose of the *Sarvodaya* movement is to visualize a society based on cooperation and inclusivity, leading to economic and political freedom. Some of the critical elements of the notion of *Sarvodaya* were economic equality, moral and ethical values, village economy, or *Gramrajya*, the *Bhoodan movement*. The Gandhian notion of development model was the village-centric development model, also known as *Gramrajya*. A development model that is democratic and that involves all the stakeholders in the decision-making process is underlying principle of *Gramraj*.

Sarvodaya rejected private ownership as it was considered an instrument of exploitation and the source of social and economic discrimination. Thus, the concept of *Sarvodaya* addresses the SDG 1 of no poverty, SDG 10 of reduced inequalities, and SDG 3 of good health and well-being.[3]

The concept of *Sarvodaya* was promoted by Vinobha Bhave, Dada Dharnadhikari, Dhirendra Mazumdaar, Shanarrao Deo, K.G. Mashruwala during 1950s and 1960s. One of the most remarkable *Sarvodaya* movements is *Bhoodan* and *Gramdan* movements. It was considered a land gift movement, initiated by Gandhian Vinoba Bhave in Pochampally village, Pochampally.[4] The *Bhoodan Movement* or Land Gift Movement was engineered and mobilized by Acharya

[2]Rathi, D. S. Gandhian philosophy of Sarvodaya and its Principles. *Article On and By Gandhi*. https://www.mkgandhi.org/articles/gandhi_sarvodaya.html.

[3]Sustainable Development Goals, United Nations Foundation, SDGs, 2030. https://www.globalgoals.org/goals/.

[4]Social Science Contemporary India II: Textbook in Geography for Class X. New Delhi: NCERT. 2019. p. 43. ISBN 978-81-7450-644-3. OCLC 1152150287. https://www.worldcat.org/title/1152150287.

Vinoba Bhave in 1951, Pochampally village now in Telangana. The movement is also addressed as Bhoodan Pochampally. It emerged as a remarkably successful movement by adopting a peaceful methodology of *Satyagraha.* The movement synthesized a cohesive technique to embark on the notion of 'commons' and 'common ownership' related to natural resources and, specifically, land. The movement achieved remarkable success in empowering landless labourers, emphasizing the significance of limited resources such as land and the role of ownership in attaining inclusivity and socio-economic welfare. The wealthy landowners were persuaded to voluntarily give a proportion of their land to landless people. This movement not only ensured economic freedom for all and inclusivity but also embodies the attribute of non-possession among the individuals in the society.

The inherent character of non-procession inspires individuals to adopt the trusteeship model. The egalitarian aspect of *Sarvodaya* advocates a democratic system of governance and decentralization, which profoundly ensures peace, inclusivity, and non-violence and empowers each individual in the society. In addition to the ownership and decentralized system, education is a crucial sector for any development process. Originating from the notion of *Sarvodaya*, the education model of *Nayi Talim* is advocated, involving austerity, body labour, and self-supporting schools with training in crafts that have not been taken well in post-independent India.

Consequently, based on spiritual inquiry, the notion of Gandhian thoughts constitutes a comprehensive socio-economic framework for society. The framework incorporates the elementary dimensions of human development covering all the essential spectrum of social infrastructure such as education, healthcare, drinking water and sanitation, creation of sustainable livelihoods, women's empowerment, care of the vulnerable and marginalized sections of society, animal care, etc. Implementing this framework as a road map for public policy would not only provide a robust public policy regime but also ensure the attainment of sustainable goals for the nation.

Spirituality and Gandhian Economic Models for Sustainable Public Policy

The mainstream discipline of Economics advocates a maximizing level of satisfaction for consumers and maximizing profits for the producers. Accumulation of more and more wealth is the objective for economic optimum. The inherent desire to acquire more and more has been detrimental to the limited resources and ultimately administered an unprecedented possession of resources. The outcome of greed has been 'the unchecked capitalism' that breeds more and more economic growth. Thus, the uncontrolled and unlimited human wants have resulted in a concentration of wealth in the hands of a few. Later, political economy plays a critical role in disrupting equity in the distribution and the existence of the welfare state.

The forces of demand and supply or the 'invisible hands' of profits, were responsible for capitalism to grow uncontrolled and detrimental to the extent that it destroyed human values and ethics (Smith, 1987). Further, the Keynesian notion of increasing demand that claimed the role of the multiplier in distributing growth to the poorest of the poor has subsequently failed. In addition, the political economy guided by vested interests inhibits the flow of well-being to every section of society.

However, we observe rising levels of poverty and inequality along with economic growth. The log-run viability and prospects of economic growth are delimited by ecological imbalance and growing inequalities associated with it.[5] The two well-known economists Lucas Chancel and Thomas Piketty, also contended that the gap between the rich and poor got exacerbated from 1980 to 2014 in India (Chancel & Piketty, 2019). The purpose of the development process must be to converge and reduce the inequality levels prevailing in the economies. The extensive literature on growth theories confirms that the rich are becoming more affluent, and the poor are becoming poorer, which is increasing inequalities (Chandrasekhar & Ghosh, 2007; Sengupta, 2009). In all the development debates 'regional inequality' has been ignored. The existence of high-income inequality challenges the basic argument of Solow's growth theory, which advocates those competitive forces and inter-regional migration will allow regional inequality to disappear through gradual factor price equalization (Solow, 2000). The famous Kuznets curve in 1955 advocated an inverted U – curve postulating that inequality first increases and then decreases over time (Kuznets, 1955). An inverted U-shaped curve has been suggested between inequality and development. It suggests that with more and more development, inequality reduces. Baumol (1986) and Barro (1991) determined convergence in developed countries while divergence in less developed nations. Convergence primarily refers to the 'catch-up effect'. When technology is introduced at the early stages of industrialization, the developing nations gradually 'catch up' with more advanced nations.

The underlying motivation behind economics is not to attain a higher standard of living but to achieve the minimal possible respect for human and social values. It is mainly the basic objective of decent work and economic growth SDG 8 that is addressed by Gandhian economics. Gandhian economics is guided by an evolved consciousness that realizes the Truth of existence and therefore seeks ultimate satisfaction. Therefore, an evolved and enlightened soul seeks to dwell in a world comprising non-violent and peaceful socio-economic settings. Uncontrolled and unprecedented consumerism is in no way a method to achieve individual satisfaction.

The basic economic problem, 'the problem of scarcity', finds its fundamental solution in Gandhian Economics. The underlying phenomenon that 'Human wants are unlimited, but resources are limited' is resolved by the distinction

---

[5]Economic & Political Weekly, Present Crises of Capitalism and its Reforms. https://www.epw.in/journal/2020/17/special-articles/present-crises-capitalism-and-its-reforms.html.

between 'wants' and 'desires'. This distinction provides a necessary rationale for ethical wants. Thus, the elementary purpose of the economy is to attain the welfare of the community. Therefore, the state's ethical responsibility is to ensure human dignity and eliminate inequalities of ownership and income. Finally, all economic systems must intend to attain inclusivity and economic equality by narrowing the class gap in society. As a result, Gandhian economics ensures human dignity and inclusivity in the community.

There is enough for everybody's needs and not for everybody's greed; therefore, the concept of trusteeship originates from non-possession, emphasizing that possessing material things that we do not need is similar to stealing. The best alternative is to own resources as custodians of nature. In this context, the Trusteeship model is a remarkable breakthrough in economic thought, unfolding the dilemma of the economic problem of unlimited wants and limited means. The trusteeship philosophy is based on the notion that 'One must care about the world one will not see'. This philosophy of trusteeship is essentially aligned with SDG 13, the Climate Action (Sustainable Development Goals, United Nations Foundation, SDGs, 2030). SDG 13 mainly focuses on strengthening resilience and adaptive capacity to climate-related hazards and natural disasters and integrating climate change measures into national policies, strategies, and planning.

Before the climate change debate began, Mahatma Gandhi had said that we should act as 'trustees' and use natural resources wisely as it is our moral responsibility to ensure that we bequeath to future generations a healthy planet (INDC, India, 2015).[6] The thought advocates that the world's bounties are primarily for the entire human race and not for any particular individual. When an individual possesses more than is rationally needed, he has the ethical responsibility to distribute (Harijan, 23 February 1947).

> Supposing I have come by a fair amount of wealth – either by way of legacy or by means of trade and industry – I must know that all that wealth does not belong to me; what belongs to me is the right to an honourable livelihood, no better than that enjoyed by millions of others. The rest of my wealth belongs to the community and must be used for the welfare of the community.
> -Mahatma Gandhi

Thus SDG 1 (No poverty) and SDG 2 (Zero hunger) are significantly addressed by the Gandhian notion of trusteeship. The belief that when an individual possesses more than what is rationally needed, he has an ethical responsibility to distribute will ensure both SDG goals 1 and 2.

Suppose we want to visualize sustainability and the lost harmony with nature. In that case, the definition of economics has to get evolved from the individual self, then to society, and finally to the state. All three entities, individuals, firms,

[6]Government of India. (2015). India's intended nationally determined contribution: Working towards climate justice. *Vikaspedia*.

and the state, have to function in the same direction with the same objective. It is then a socioeconomic transformation that will originate, referred to as Gandhian Economic Revolution. It is only then that we can visualize a Climate-resilient society or world is created that ensures a better place to live for our future generations.

The interconnectedness of human beings and, later, with the ecosystem is an underlying phenomenon for transforming an individual self at three levels. First occurs at the individual level of self-upliftment. In contrast, the second occurs at the level of connection between the transformation of fellow beings, changing the relationship with other beings in terms of love, respect, and tolerance. Finally, the third form of transformation is where human interaction with non-human forms or ecology gets revolutionized. This is mainly because the ethical and moral responsibility of human existence encourages humans to preserve nature consisting of both transient and permanent elements. Thus, the relationship of humans with nature or non-human forms is completely transformed.

Later, based on Gandhian philosophy, J.C. Kumarappa formulated an 'economy of permanence'. The concept is comparable to the lines of 'the cradle-to-cradle philosophy, generating lesser wastage and using renewable sources in production processes. The concept of Permanent is absolute, beyond Time and Space. Such a concept of Permanent could be attributed to God, Truth, and Love that is unchangeable. Within the gambit of Time and Space, nothing is permanent. For Gandhi Nature was analogous to God. However, when Nature is not considered God and is understood as limited by Time and Space, then nature could strikethrough in the future. In this context, human life is said to be Transient compared to that of Nature which is Permanent.[7] The economy of permanence mainly signifies and addresses the global goal SDG 11 of sustainable cities and communities and SDG 12 of responsible consumption and production.[8] SDG 11 and SDG 12 invoke the notion of sustainability by maintaining the cycle of life as described by the concept of 'The economy of permanence' or 'the cradle to cradle' philosophy of generating lesser wastage and using renewable sources in production processes. Thus, promoting responsible consumption and production.

However, it is important to comprehend that nature consists of some materials fixed in quantities, such as coal, petroleum, iron, copper, etc., considered transient (Kumarappa, 1948).[9] While the water in the river and constantly growing timber in forests may be considered 'permanent' as their stock is inexhaustible and permanent. The underlying phenomenon of nature's permanency is based on close cooperation that exists to maintain the continuity of life. Nature has the inherent capacity to support the continuity of life. This aspect of continuity is referred to as Cradle to Cradle as a sustainability concept (McDonough & Braungart, 2010). The notion of recycling is reinforced in this philosophy. Therefore, maintaining the continuity of life provides the most suitable strategy to address the issues

---

[7]See footnote 6, p. 9.

[8]Sustainable Development Goals, United Nations Foundation, SDGs, 2030. https://www.globalgoals.org/goals/.

[9]See footnote 8, p. 9.

related to Climate Action. This phenomenon is the best strategy to address the challenge of resilience and adaptive capacity to mitigate Climate change disasters highlighted in SDG 13.[10]

The Gandhian philosophy of non-violence and absolute love inspires the notion of continuity of life. The moment there is a break in continuity, it results in violence leading to unrest or conflict, dismantling the continuity process. Any violence breaks the chain and harmony and is detrimental to continuity. Nature is faithful and submissive to those who respect her. When the life cycle breaks, violence manifests. Further, violence leads to destruction and waste. Finally, humans must cooperate with nature and maintain harmony or equilibrium with the environment. The Gandhian economic model of trusteeship and J.C Kumarrapa's Economy of Permanence based on Gandhian thoughts mainly indicate responsible consumption and production Goal 12 and Goal 13 of Climate Change of SDGs.[11]

In the context of industry, innovation and scientific research which is critical to human evolution, the Gandhian perspective entails the attributes of ethics, responsibility and fairness. In the era of energy transition and technological innovation, the choice of consumer related to energy source must be crucial. It should be at the centre of policy formation or regime. Assigning freedom to individuals and the objective of inclusivity must be accomplished. All individuals, irrespective of income category, class, caste, religion, or any section in society, have the right to express their energy choice. This will ensure the inclusivity of all sections of society irrespective of income, class, caste, etc. In other words, the aim behind lobbying or symbiosis of various stakeholders must be to achieve inclusivity and affordability. Thus, the Gandhian ideology signifies SDG 7, affordable and clean energy.[12]

Decentralization: A Consensus-Based Public Policy

A socio-economic system based on Gandhian thoughts aspires an enriched life that values human dignity and achieves the minimal possible respect for human and social values is the fundamental aim of the Gandhian framework for society. Such a system can be achieved with a system of governance or regime that adopts a consensus-based policy mechanism, taking into account the interest and voice of every individual.

Each individual requires freedom and the right to voice their opinion since the upliftment of every individual is at the heart of the overall upliftment. Therefore, while designing the socio-political system, a consensus-based democratic regime that guarantees the freedom and right of individuals provides the preliminary foundation for a peaceful, self-sufficient and self-reliant socio-economic system.

---

[10]Sustainable Development Goals, United Nations Foundation, SDGs, 2030. https://www.globalgoals.org/goals/.

[11]See footnote 10.

[12]See footnote 11.

In other words, a decentralized system that caters to the needs of every individual in society, and empowers everyone.

When there is a situation of scarcity of capital, a decentralized system of governance is the only plausible option. Further, in the case of excess labour, the case of unemployment and underemployment, centralization tends to aggravate the problems. The decentralization method would be the best way of producing goods when raw materials and markets are in the proximity of production centres (Jahanbegloo & Sharma, 2022). This system would lead to a far more equal distribution of wealth and also make people tolerant. This process of production includes the distribution of wealth in a more equitable manner. It is a consensus-based system where every individual matters in making any socio-economic policy or decision. A decentralized setting empowers each producer and makes him an entrepreneur, improving his standard of living, and further uplifting the average intelligence of the nation as a whole (Jahanbegloo & Sharma, 2022).[13]

In a decentralized framework, there will be no disturbance of peace at the nationwide level. Moreover, where small producers are working in a decentralized setting, the raw material required for production would be exploited only locally. The system will not entail exercising its power over the raw materials. Therefore, such an economy would lead to a non-violent economy where supply meets its demand without any violence involved. Such an economy does not provide any opportunity for a wealthy person at the cost of another. This would further inculcate human values among the people living in society. Effectively speaking, a sense of human values will direct economic activity, and various negativities in the global environment, such as international rivalry, jealousy and competition, would be minimized, leading to human progress, peace and prosperity.

Such nations are peaceful and non-violent with equitable distribution of wealth. Decentralized self-sufficient communities will ensure peace, and justice and are backed up by strong institutions. Given such an economic setup or regime, the resources of the economy must be produced and consumed sustainably. Thus, the self-sufficient and self-reliant communities would not only comply with SDG11 (Sustainable Cities and Communities) of Global Goals but also guarantee the SDG 12 of responsible consumption and production.[14]

There can be numerous examples of self-sufficient, self-reliant societies, symbolizing the success stories of anti-globalization and protectionism. The survival of economies after the segregation from the globalized, interconnected economies in the case of Cuba decently performed after the US embargo in 1960. Village *Mendha,* a small village of Gonda tribals in central India, in the *Dhanora tehsil* of *Gadchiroli* district in the State of Maharashtra, has maintained its unique characteristics like the non-existence of disputes and differences of opinion in the village. There is no problem of poverty, hunger, or unemployment, and no

[13]See footnote 12, p. 14.
[14]Sustainable Development Goals, United Nations Foundation, SDGs, 2030. https://www.globalgoals.org/goals/.

economic disparities. The village functions effectively based on the unanimous decision of the village community to taking critical decisions of the village community under a village assembly called *gaon-samaj-sabha* comprising all the adult villagers as its members. In the meeting of the village assembly, it was decided to impose Rs.150 on the practice of cutting trees in the forest for fruits, leaves, and branches or even honey. The villagers depend on forests for food and fuel and use biogas as a source of energy. Finally, this village serves as a remarkable example of people's power.[15]

A decentralized community set up based on a consensus-based decision-making system provides a social capital for economic growth and development that is defined by an ethical and moral value system.[16] It is self-rule in a true sense that shapes decentralized governance. Having visualized a socio-economic framework conducive to Gandhian thoughts, it is crucial to examine a sustainable education system. Based on Gandhian ideology that signifies the role of the individual in framing and shaping the development process, individual growth or self-upliftment is central to the overall development of the nation. In this context, education plays an instrumental role in determining the development pathways.

Nayi Talim: An Education Policy from Gandhian Perspective

Gandhi's notion of *Nayi Talim* is a remarkable illustration of manifesting the traditional knowledge of spirituality, academics and life skill in a child. This was a unique method designed by Gandhi to train every individual right from his childhood on the true meaning of connection with ecology where the student is trained in sustainable skills for life. These skills originate from the philosophy of reducing, reusing, and recycling and provide a source of livelihood for their lifetime.[17] Gandhi was equally aware and mindful of inculcating good sanitary habits among the people of the community and was the biggest advocate for use of bio-gas and manure for cooking and other activities. The model community biogas plants are actively functioning in all the Gandhi Ashrams. Gandhi Ashrams were the repositories that transform human waste into organic fertilizers.[18] Moreover, several experiments continue to date related to toilets involving scarce water resources.[19] *Nayi Talim* is a breakthrough in the education system that is based on the principle that knowledge and work are not separate. Such an education system provides a foundation for holistic development providing life skills.

Gandhi's reverence for life and respect for animals was not confined by intolerance, which he considered another name for violence (Lal, 2000). He was actively tolerant of all humans having diversified food habits even though he was

---

[15]Devaji Tofa, M. H. *Mendha (Lekha)*. Wardha: Mohan Hirabai Hiralal.

[16]https://www.ipcc.ch/site/assets/uploads/2018/02/ipcc_wg3_ar5_chapter3.pdf.

[17]RE, O. C. (2014). REDUCE, REUSE AND RECYCLE: SEN GANDHI GLO.

[18]See footnote 17, p. 23.

[19]See footnote 18, p. 23.

a strict vegetarian.[20] Lal phrases the expression of the life of Gandhi in the most appropriate manner 'Gandhi's entire life functioned much like an ecosystem'.[21] Gandhi's everyday life from the prism of every minute act, emotion, and thought was well-placed and appropriate and was never without ethics and morality.

In the light of the global development agenda reflected in Goal 4 of SDG 4 of 2030, the agenda for Sustainable Development adopted by India in 2015 is to ensure the inclusive and equitable quality of education and promote lifelong learning opportunities for all (National Education Policy, 2020).[22] This goal calls for a substantial transformation of pedagogy of education policy in India. The pedagogy needs to evolve to make education more experimental and fun. It should focus on character building manifesting the attributes of empathy, compassion, rationality etc. Thus, the National Education Policy adopted by India consists of a substantial component of *Nayi Talim.*

The scope and spectrum of the Gandhian ideology are not only proposing robust policy regimes but also empowering humanity with the technique of dissent in cases of oppression and injustice. The policies advocated are resilient to oppression, injustice, political economy, and self-interest, and the method of dissent referred to as 'Satyagraha' is the most popular, non-violent technique for embarking on social revolution guided by the soul force for Truth and justice. Gandhian method of Satyagraha as a tool that will not only enable and empower individuals to raise their voices against injustice but also inspire the social systems to attain the ultimate Truth or Reality.

Satyagraha: A Voice Against Injustice

Ever since the evolution of humankind, humans have found themselves trapped in a socio-political order that needs a revolution or merely raising a voice that rejects the injustice to the human race. Several ways to deny oppression have evolved, among which Satyagraha formulated by Mahatma Gandhi emerged as a remarkable breakthrough in the class of all methods of protest against discrimination. This method was adopted by Mahatma Gandhi to reject British rule and the injustice done by the Britishers in Africa and India. The Britishers were powerful and loaded with arms and weapons. The most rational and strategic method that was developed and eventually propagated by Mahatma Gandhi was the method of 'Satyagraha'.

'Satyagraha' is a method of resistance that does not call for physical force. It is one of the most remarkable methods of conflict resolution. The method is embedded in the inherent meaning of the term 'Satyagraha', mainly defining Truth as 'soul.' In this aspect, Satyagraha is simply an inner urge to seek the

[20]See footnote 19, p. 23.
[21]See footnote 20, p. 24.
[22]National Education Policy 2020. https://ruralindiaonline.org/en/library/resource/national-education-policy-2020/?gclid=Cj0KCQjwqc6aBhC4ARIsAN06NmOzWwDnc32XPtbdc5tky3H1_LroUsP1KnA6PvFPA-QKmMAIMQzR0okaAjqkEALw_wcB.

Truth or soul. The firmness on holding on to the Truth or soul manifests a change of heart. This method to seek the Truth is defined as *Satyagraha,* Vol 1 of Anasakti Darshan (Lindley, 2006).[23] The soul is informed with knowledge; the absolute form of knowledge is Love. The genesis or the origin of *Satyagraha* is the supreme concept of Truth. The Truth, in this context, refers to the ultimate form of reality and the ultimate reality is 'love and compassion'. This continuum of force generated by adhering to the Truth of Love and compassion is referred to as 'Satyagraha' (The fundamental requirement of Satyagraha is the clarity of means and end.[24] While signifying means and ends, there should be an absolute clarity of one's goals. The sole aim or the purpose of the *Satyagrahi* must be to seek the ultimate Truth. When there is absolute clarity in one's goal, the means adopted to attain that goal must be pure. The purity of ways simply indicates the 'Truth' is the very substance. Thus, a satyagraha is effectively a campaign based on 'clarity of ends', the purity of means and the unity of means and ends (Galtung, 1990).

Satyagraha is not a physical force, and a person who practices *Satyagraha* does not inflict pain on the adversary and does not seek destruction. While adopting the method of *Satyagraha*, there is no ill will involved. The power of an oppressor is a person who denies exercising his fundamental elementary rights. The tyrant can win power entirely because people are willing to obey. Such people who refuse to revolt and accept oppression by following unjustified rules and commands and succumbing to power can be threatened in various ways. They can be thrown to prison under the threat of imprisonment and guns and even if they are not threatened the mere act of obedience of injudicious commands is against the path of 'Truth'.

The elementary strategy of the path of Satyagraha is to protest against injustice through peaceful means consistently. The concept of *Satyagraha* pertains to the transformation of the inner sense. The preliminary reason for the success of Satyagraha is conditioned upon three elementary conditions. The one who adopts this form of protest should never have hatred in his heart against the opponent. Secondly, the agenda or the issue for which the protestor stands for is true and substantial, and finally, the *Satyagrahi* must be prepared to suffer till the end of the cause.

It is crucial to recognize the fact that the path of *Satyagraha* is the process of educating public opinion, directing it towards peaceful protest and gradually inculcating the revolution of the whole social structure. It is the path towards not only the individual transformation but also the entire social transformation.

Forms of Satyagraha and Its Applications

Satyagraha as a tool for dissent against injustice can adapt various forms and variations. One of the most influential forms is *Negotiation and Arbitration*, dialogue, building up the necessary understanding and trust. Most of the conflicts

---

[23]Lindley, M. (2006). Gandhi on Corresponding Duties/Rights. *Anasati Darshan, 2.*

[24]India, Y. (1920). Edited by MK Gandhi.

originate through misunderstandings and miscommunications. The negotiations initiated must be exercised within the constitutional rights, non-threatening, and should not result in crises. The second form of Satyagraha is *Agitation*, a situation when the volunteers mobilize and propagate their viewpoint to people by deploying various mediums of communication. Conscious-provoking activities acquaint people with noble and just causes. Communication through speeches, letter-writings, articles in the newspaper, organizing volunteers for group communication skills, mass media technology, and use of non-verbal communication etc.

The third unique form of *Satyagraha* is through 'Demonstrations and the Ultimatum', meetings, manifestations marches, and processions etc. are another form of exhibiting *Satyagraha.* The non-violent representation of masses, posters and slogans specifying the list of demands is another way of expressing discontent. The fourth way proposed in *Satyagraha* is 'Self-purification', resorting to fasting and public prayers. Gatherings like this will inculcate morale amongst people and unity of purpose. The fifth version of *Satyagraha* is resorting to 'Strikes', a tool to raise their voice against authorities/government, industry, or commerce. The sixth method is 'Picketing' is considered a direct result of the strike. the public is requested to withdraw the support, and it mainly symbolizes refusal to support the just cause.

The 'Dharna', the *seventh form of* 'Satyagraha' is a simple sit-down and can prove to be highly effective since it is based on the principle that no industry that itself is dependent on the public for its market can belittle the just cause of public or alienate public opinion.[25] The eighth version of 'Satyagraha' prescribed the 'Economic Boycott', a most widely adopted means of protest, withdrawing from the businesses and business relations with the opponent by boycotting their products. Here, 'Non-payment of taxes and hazrat', is where people refuse to pay taxes with the aim of cutting financial resources of the government and demonstrating a way of rejecting any policy or unjust act. People encounter beatings, shootings, confiscation of property etc. Patience is the key component that is paid the most.

The 10th version of Satyagraha is '*Non-Cooperation and Ostracism*'. This is again a prevalent method of demonstrating Satyagraha. It is a combination of exhibiting rejection of oppression in the form of non-cooperation and ostracism, where the section of the population that fails to join the movement of 'non-cooperation' owing to the fear of losing jobs are ostracized non-violently on account of their unsocial and unethical attitude. Another effective method of Satyagraha is 'Civil Disobedience', which is the 11th method. In this case, the state is considered a mere formal structure, the participants of the protest begin to disobey the unjust laws. Finally, 'The Constructive Programme', is the foundation of *Satyagraha* on which the entire success of the movement rested, is the 12th

[25]Shridharani, pp. 19–23. Dhurna (also spelled Dharna) was organized in 1922. The Non-cooperators sat down in the gates of Calcutta University and blocked the passage of their fellow students.

version of *Satyagraha*. Gandhian Satyagraha approach led several campaigns, such as *Bardoli Satyagraha* in 1928 in Gujarat, eventually led by Vallabhbhai.[26]

Several illustrations exemplify the relevance of Gandhian *Satyagraha* as a tool or technique for a successful revolution that not only enlightens the inner consciousness of *satyagrahi* but directs the whole society towards the ultimate Truth or reality. The *Bardoli* movement victory enabled and facilitated the nationwide freedom struggle (Arnold, 2014). Another Satyagraha named *Champaran Satyagraha* was the farmer's uprising took place in *Champaran* district of Bihar against farming of indigo without any payment (Gandhi, 1927). The Kheda Satyagraha in the Kheda district of Gujarat was organized to support the Indian independence movement.[27] Mahatma Gandhi adopted a non-violent protest of the *Dharasana* Salt March to Dandi (Johnson, 2005). While Flag *Satyagraha* was a peaceful campaign or civil disobedience during the Indian Independence Movement in the city of Nagpur in 1923 and later spread across all states. The *Guruvayur* Satyagraha in Thrissur district, in Kerala, was an effort to allow entry of untouchables into *Guruvayur* Temple.[28]

The Non-cooperation movement on 4 September in 1920 initiated by Mahatma Gandhi was based on self-governance, seeking to withdraw its support for British reforms as quoted by Shashi Tharoor in 2003.[29] The Quit India Movement, launched in Mumbai, was the historical 'Leave India Movement', demanding an end to British Rule of India.[30] The *Dandi* Satyagraha was an act of non-violent civil disobedience, a campaign against taxes, a non-violent protest against the British salt monopoly.[31] The *Vaikom* Satyagraha was against caste discrimination in Hindu society of Kerala.[32]

---

[26]Global Non-violent Action Database, 2017. 'Bardoli peasants campaign against the Government of Bombay, 1928 | Global Nonviolent Action Database'. *nvdatabase.swarthmore.edu*. Retrieved 2017-12-21.

[27]'100 years of Kheda Satyagrahaaa and Gandhi's journey from Mohandas to Mahatma | India News'. Retrieved 2018-10-30. https://www.timesnownews.com/india/article/kheda-satyagraha-how-gandhi-made-the-journey-from-mohandas-to-mahatma/210282.

[28]'Welcome to Guruvayur. The Bhooloka vaikunda'. Archived from the original on 23 November 2009. Retrieved 22 January 2000. https://en.bharatpedia.org/wiki/Guruvayur_Satyagraha.

[29]https://www.hindustantimes.com/columns/shashi-tharoor-s-word-of-the-week-satyagraha/story-eBeTCOI0Ne8FNYZonCsHAI.html.

[30]'1942 Quit India Movement – Making Britain'. www.open.ac.uk. Archived from the original on 23 June 2018. Retrieved 1 May 2018.

[31]'National Salt Satyagrahaaa Memorial | List of names' (PDF). www.dandimemorial.in. Retrieved 11 August 2019. https://nssm.in/.

[32]Gandhi, Mohandas Karamchand. Non-violent resistance. p. 180 Courier Corporation, 2012. https://books.google.com/books?id=CfPBAgAAQBAJ&printsec=frontcover#v=onepage&q&f=false.

Conclusion

In the present era, the world is full of hatred, racism, and conflict. Global oppression is defined in the form of soft power if not hard power, the war of technology and markets in the name of Climate change, if not arms and weapons, and sacrifice of human value system in the name of politics and subjugation. Such a world order once again needs a revolution to render humanity a path towards, the Truth. Against this backdrop, this chapter enlightens the readers with the plausible interlinkages between spirituality with public policy and how applied spirituality can address the complexities of public policy. The Gandhian philosophy which originates from spirituality is adopted by the study to examine the hypothesis of a plausible relationship between spirituality, public policy, and sustainable development.

Gandhian philosophy that values the individual and his relationship with his true self becomes instrumental in ethical transformation. The evolved consciousness becomes the driving force of the perceived paradigm shift. Moreover, the self-transformation, manifestation, and realization of truth and love are deeply embedded in the Gandhian notion of Satyagraha and *Sarvodaya*. The education model of *Nayi Talim* is advocated, involving austerity, body labour, and self-supporting schools with training in crafts that have not been taken well in post-independent India. Finally, the twin models, 'The trusteeship model' and 'Economy of Permanence', originating from Gandhian thoughts, resolve the economic problem of scarcity and choice and address several. Sustainable Development Goals, SDGs, United Nations Foundation.

References

Allen, M. (2019). Techno-Satyagraha: Integrating economics and life goals through Gandhi's 'Back and Forth' method between capitalists and socialism. *The Acorn*, *19*(2), 149–169.

Arnold, D. (2014). *Gandhi*. Routledge.

Barro, R. J. (1991). Economic growth in a cross section of countries. *Quarterly Journal of Economics*, *106*(2), 407–443.

Baumol, W. J. (1986). *Productivity growth, convergence, and welfare: What the long-run data show* (pp. 1072–1085). The american economic review.

Chancel, L., & Piketty, T. (2019). Indian income inequality, 1922–2015: From British Raj to Billionaire Raj? *Review of Income and Wealth*, *65*, S33–S62.

Chandrasekhar, C. P., & Ghosh, J. (2007). Recent employment trends in India and China: An unfortunate convergence? *Social Scientist*, *35*(3/4), 19–46.

Galtung, J. (1990). *International development in human perspective* (pp. 301–335). Human needs theory.

Gandhi, M. K. (1927). *Autobiography of my experiments with truth*. Navajivan Publishing House.

Gandhi, M. (1958). The collected works of Mahatma Gandhi. *(No Title)*. https://www.gandhiashramsevagram.org/gandhi-literature/collected-works-of-mahatma-gandhi-volume-1-to-98.php

INDC, India. (2015). https://pib.gov.in/newsite/printrelease.aspx?relid=128403

Jahanbegloo, R., & Sharma, P. (2022). *Living in truth: A Gandhian paradigm*. Rupa Publications. 978-93-5520-782-1.

Johnson, R. L. (2005). *Gandhi's experiments with truth: Essential writings by and about Mahatma Gandhi*. Lexington Books. 978-0-7391-1143-7.

Kumarappa, J. C. (1948). *The economy of permanence: A quest for a social order based on non-violence*. Maganvadi.

Kuznets, S. (1955). Economic growth and income inequality. *The American Economic Review*, *45*(March), 1–28.

Lal, V. (2000). Gandhi and the ecological vision of life. *Environmental Ethics*, *22*(2), 149–168.

Lindley, M. (2006). *Gandhi on corresponding duties/rights* (Vol. 2). Anasati Darshan.

McDonough, W., & Braungart, M. (2010). *Cradle to cradle: Remaking the way we make things*. North Point Press.

National Education Policy. (2020). *National Education Policy 2020*. https://www.education.gov.in/sites/upload_files/mhrd/files/NEP_Final_English_0.pdf

Sengupta, M. (2009). Unemployment duration and the measurement of unemployment. *The Journal of Economic Inequality*, *7*(3), 273.

Smith, A. (1987). *The essential Adam Smith*. WW Norton & Company.

Solow, R. (2000). *Growth theory*. Oxford University Press.

Staszak, J. F. (2009). *Other/otherness*. https://www.unige.ch/sciences-societe/geo/files/3214/4464/7634/OtherOtherness.pdf

Sustainable Development Goals, United Nations Foundation, SDGs. (2030). *What are the Sustainable Development Goals?* United Nations. https://www.undp.org/sustainable-development-goals/no-poverty?gclid=Cj0KCQjwi7GnBhDXARIsAFLvH4kmil5aM5a3FQwPVJHflJtDB0NP7rKc-5J8crLe2DJ3StfXtRZaaBoaAhPzEALw_wcB

Chapter 11

An Exploration of the Nonmaterial Dimension as the *Sine Qua Non* of 'Sustainable Development'

Vern Neufeld Redekop

Abstract

The nonmaterial dimension of reality is contrasted with the material, observable and empirically verifiable dimension that rose to dominance with the Enlightenment. The nonmaterial dimension includes orientation, memes, tacit knowledge and spirituality. The orientation of an individual, group, or institution can be towards violence – getting ahead at the expense of the other – or blessing – working in such a way that there is mutual benefit. Orientations can be expressed through memes, cultural or behavioural patterns that are mimetically transmitted broadly within a society and diachronically through generations. If they catch on within a group, they can determine the institutional or group culture. Spirituality can be a source of change of orientation from violence to blessing and of growth in creativity, resilience and empowerment. David Peat and David Bohm posit an implicate order in the universe, thought as a system (in the context of dialogue), and gentle action. Neil Douglas-Klotz points out that the Aramaic words *malkuta d'bwashmaya* (kingdom of heaven) used by Jesus constituted a nonmaterial reality containing vision, norms and empowerment that exists within and among us – like the implicate order – and is accessed by those who truly wish to 'see' it. The emerging spirituality coming out of this engagement has a capacity to replace memes like those of empire, self-interest and grandiose leaders with memes that channel passions and energy towards bio-interest, transnational interest, transpersonal interest, empathy and widespread empowerment. And this could make all the difference in effecting truly sustainable development.

Keywords: Anthropocene; mimetic theory; consciousness; malkuta; tacit knowledge; integrative thinking

Applied Spirituality and Sustainable Development Policy, 201–221

Published under exclusive licence by Emerald Publishing Limited
doi:10.1108/978-1-83753-380-020231011

Introduction

'Sustainable Development' points broadly to the evolution or emergence of that which will promote the flourishing of humankind and the biosphere over the long term. The locus of 'development' is ubiquitous and includes both regions of the world that have well established education, economic, health and political systems and those parts of the world that have had ancient systems decimated through colonialism and have since been deemed first 'under-developed' and later 'developing'. At present the global community has given definition to its aspirations through the sustainable development goals (SDGs) as discussed in Chapter 2 and listed in Annex 1.

My goal is to explore nonmaterial aspects of the development process in the hope that awareness of these aspects will lead to attention to them and, with that, the cultivation of that which will enhance the process. To begin, I will position the 'nonmaterial dimension' of a phenomenon within a quadratic model (Friesen et al., n.d., provide ample evidence of a variety of such models). Ken Wilber's Integral Theory (IT) framework (2000, 2001; McGuigan & Popp, 2016) is one example of how the nonmaterial dimension relates to the material dimensions of a phenomenon in a quadrant framework. Wilber posits four quadrants with the left two quadrants (L) representing a phenomenon's nonmaterial interior aspects i.e., its individual (U) and collective (L) dimensions. The righthand quadrants (R), representing a phenomenon's material external realities, are material and observable. The nonmaterial dimension includes interconnected aspects such as intrapersonal consciousness and interpersonal relations, personal and shared values, spirituality, cultural memes, language and customs, personal and agreed-upon ethics, individual and collective meaning-making processes and community processes, along with personal and cultural growth and development. These are entangled with how development action is taken and hence its sustainability. Taken together they provide for a holistic or integrated approach to 'sustainable development' (there is a debate about whether 'sustainable' is the best word to describe optimum development at this time; since that is not the focus of this paper, I have simply chosen to put quotation marks around it).

Since the Enlightenment, Western thought has focused on the material quadrants in the spirit of empirical evidence-based validation of truth claims (Kauffman, 2020; Wilber, 2000). The external side of things is manifest in the material/energy side of existence and, as such, is relatively easy to document and measure. What is easy to measure becomes the basis of truth; hence, methodologies then demand 'empirical evidence', and this, tautologically then, reinforces the primacy of the material side of reality. Coupled with this has been the pervasiveness of 'self-interest' which is appropriated as a meme based on observations – cf. Charles Darwin, Adam Smith, Hans Morgenthau – of how the world is morphing into how it should be in the domains of evolution, economics and international relations respectively, with further empirically driven evidence to reinforce this (Kauffman, 2016). Furthermore, the narcissistic attention to the individual self (immortalized by Descartes) has detracted from an emphasis on relationships and connections for our own ontology, intentional focus and ethical vision (Ricoeur, 1992).

While continuing to affirm the benefits (scientific and technological advances) and importance of empirically driven aspects of inquiry, I wish to concentrate on the left side, the interior side constituting the nonmaterial dimension, to show what may have been forgotten in 'sustainable development'.

The diagram below (Fig. 11.1), my own adaptation of the quadrant model,

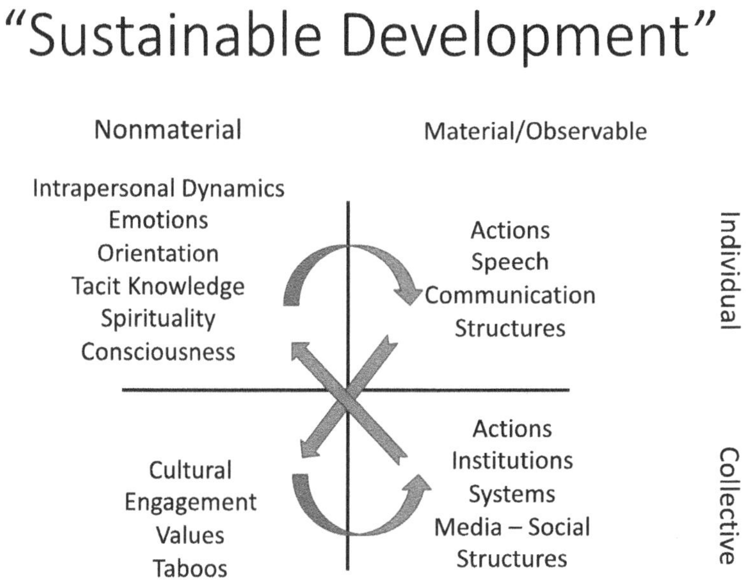

Fig. 11.1. Author's Adaptation of the Quadrant Model.

suggests that out of the various elements of the nonmaterial dimension, Intrapersonal Dynamics (UL), will come action that contribute to what is 'sustainable' – understood as that which contributes to the long-term well-being of the biosphere and humanity. This new action will have a cultural impact as it contributes to new memes and paradigms that shift values and imaginations in the Cultural Engagement (LL) quadrant. This then can lead to broad-based system change (LR) which will further stimulate new thinking and perceiving in the Nonmaterial Dimension of individuals (UL). This is but one possible sequence of dynamic changes, which could start in any of the quadrants.

The title is ambiguous: the first, and most obvious, meaning of the title is that this is an exploration of how vitally important it is to *attend to the nonmaterial dimension of realit*y for mutually healthy and beneficial development to occur. The second way of reading the title is that it is the *exploration* of the nonmaterial dimension that is essential for 'Sustainable Development'. The subtle difference is that what is important is that the nonmaterial dimension needs to be explored –

acknowledged, studied and reflected upon – and that resources, energy and resolve be put into 'An Exploration of the Nonmaterial Dimension as the *Sine Qua Non* of Sustainable Development'.

In his examination of the Self, Ricoeur (1992) identified several dialectics – that is, there are two parts, which cannot be dissolved into each other, that form a whole in which both are essential – in human identity and two of these dialectics come into play in what follows. The first dialectic is that between *idem* and *ipse* where *idem* refers to well established characteristics that are synchronic and *ipse* is the temporal dimension, expressed as narrative of the past and future intentions. The second dialectic involves Self and Other – we are essentially relational, and one cannot think of a Self apart from the Other – in contrast to the Cartesian individualistic *Cogito ergo sum*. Hence, we will first look at characteristic categories of the Interior nonmaterial dimension (*idem*) at the individual and collective level. Then we will turn our attention to the *dynamics* of the nonmaterial dimension (*ipse*). Running through all this will be an underlying sensitivity to the relational reality of human existence. After this exploration of interiority, we will look at the implications for sustainable development as the interior is embodied and lived out in the external, empirically accessible dimension.

The Nonmaterial Dimension: Individual Qualities

In order to map out nonmaterial realities at the individual level, I will introduce ground-breaking work in a number of categories. First, we will look at emotions as the drivers of thought, judgement and action using the research of Katherine Peil Kauffman. Second will be the importance of spirituality, understood broadly and inclusively. Third, we will look at the significance of orientation towards the Other, whether it is characterized by violence or blessing. We will then show, fourth, how one's tacit knowledge impacts judgements, prognoses and actions. Fifth, we will touch briefly on mindfulness and conclude, sixth, by looking at consciousness.

Emotion-Based Interpretation

Katherine Peil Kauffman (K. P. Kauffman, 2020, 2021; Peil, 2014) argues that the emotional part of our brain evolved from the elementary consciousness that developed from the earliest single-celled organisms on. This consciousness evolved out of a basic sense of 'what is bad for me' and 'what is good for me'. Factors corresponding to the first put in motion negative feedback loops – behaviours that move us away from what is harmful. Likewise factors that feed into what is 'good for me' trigger feedback loops meant to encourage more of this.

In the case of humans, the emotions of anger, fear, sadness, shame, insecurity/depression and disgust are associated with what is harmful to us and invoke behaviours like fight, flight, freeze, or fawning to help reduce what we feel hurts us. Likewise, emotions of joy, self-actualization and satisfaction encourage behaviours that allow these to increase.

With our enhanced brains involving a thinking cortex integrated with the limbic system, our *interpretations* of events and messages become the data that prompt emotional reactions. Associated with our judgements is a sense of justice which is clearly linked to our emotional frameworks: we become angry when we perceive something unjust has happened and satisfied when 'justice is done' – something that frequently takes the form of vengeance but can happen through reconciliation processes.

Our sense of justice is based on deeply engrained values that have been picked up through family, culture, media and experience. Moral psychologists (e.g. Haidt, 2013) argue that our emotional brains are coded with three key programs: what is forbidden what is obligatory, and what is permitted. They go on to posit that when confronted with a new situation we make immediate, emotion-based, judgements based on our own codes. As soon as a judgement is made, we invoke our formidable cerebral cortexes to find a rationale for our judgements to prove them right.

As Peil Kauffman argues, our thoughts are guided by this highly developed emotional system, which has embedded in it considerable tacit wisdom, if we are able to discern it.

Development challenges raise many questions that have a variety of emotional responses. Global warming, for instance, raises *fear* of dire consequences; prevention raises an awareness of who are the greatest polluters inciting *shame*, and for those who see themselves as victims there is a sense of injustice, invoking *anger*. However, some of those polluters *fear* a loss of income and even failure of their enterprises if they are forced to eliminate pollution. They too will get *angry* about what is required of them. Those that feel *impotent* to change the juggernaut trajectory of global warming become *depressed*. Cleavages that result from different understandings of the problem or from those at different levels of vulnerability – for example those in coastal cities that could be flooded by rising ocean levels – create *alienation* and *enmity*. Individuals who happen to have any of these emotional reactions find 'research' to prove something that they already believe to be true based on an emotion-based interpretation of events.

These emotion-based dynamics function as hidden codes for everyone, playing a significant role in what they think, say and act.

Spirituality

Katherine Peil Kauffman also makes a case for there being an interface between the powerful internal emotional framework and what she calls natural spirituality:

> Our natural spirituality is the source of the most sacred experiences of human being, and the context of any enduring existence beyond the earthly life. It moves us to build and maintain a connection with something "greater than the self." It creates and expresses the personal capacities that make us unique individuals. It gives particular definition to soul, understood here as the core of who

> we are. It is the seat of our moral conscience – our impulses to be and do the best we can and concerns building some strategy and daily practice to guide and manifest these impulses. (K. P. Kauffman, 2020, p. 65)

She adds:

> Our natural spirituality also concerns what seem to be the most serendipitous aspects of life – the portentous coincidences, sacred friendships, and lucky events that befall us. These point to the source of providence, and our blessed good fortune. Natural spirituality is also the source of our deepest challenges, our cursed calamities, and the most devastating dark nights of the soul. (K. P. Kauffman, 2020)

In her view, we are all *contributing co-creators* to what happens in our world.

Cultures around the world hold within them evidence of attentiveness to this natural spirituality. In formalized religions, attention is paid to elements of spirituality even though they might be shrouded in myths and 'laws'. Although there is presently a movement of people who claim to be spiritual but not religious, the root metaphors of spirituality derive from religious traditions. In Hebrew, Aramaic, Greek and Latin, for example, the word for 'spirit' is the same as the word for 'breath' or 'wind'. This word becomes a metaphor for something that is real, yet nonmaterial and flowing. As such it is invisible when it comes to physical 'seeing' and hence, not subject to empirical methods. However, within various traditions the word for 'seeing' becomes a metaphor for seeing a deeper level, noticing things that are real yet physically not perceptible. Hence prophets speak of people seeing, yet not seeing – not getting the meta-reality that impinges on our lives. In Greek, there is a separate word for seeing as perceiving: *theoreo* from which we get the English word 'theory', which has the connotation of being able to 'see' things in a new way.

Spirituality can be perceived through how it is applied. It produces certain effects – Jesus and the Apostle Paul talked about fruit as a metaphor for these effects. We notice that certain people, through their presence and actions, have positive impacts on their environments. Many of these engage in 'spiritual practices' that are rooted in historical religious/spiritual traditions. Secular spirituality is an emergent reality; it leaves open the possibility of people who do not identify with a religious tradition and who might be more comfortable with a humanistic or scientific identity to still reflect a spiritual sensitivity, outstanding responsiveness to other people, and a concern for a transcendent good that includes not only humanity but the entire biosphere (S. Kauffman, 2008).

Spirituality is sometimes understood as a journey through time. It is not static but always responsive to new developments. It also develops as people are exposed to insights and processes and mimetically appropriate the ways of being and action of spiritual exemplars (Duyndam, 2014).

Orientation

The orientation of an individual, group, or institution can be towards violence – getting ahead at the expense of the other – or blessing – working in such a way that there is mutual benefit, including a sense that the enhancement of the Other is an enhancement to the Self (Redekop, 2002). An orientation of violence can morph into entrenchment and rigidity, limiting options. Similarly blessing can manifest as transcendence, inclusivity, mutual understanding, creativity and reconciliation (Redekop, 2014a). The same action, as viewed through a camera lens, can take on completely different meaning depending on the orientation of the people involved. As the Apostle Paul put it in I Corinthians 13, an action performed without deep caring for others can be completely empty; with 'blessing-based love' it becomes meaningful and produces good results (Redekop, 2014b). An orientation within a relational system translates into a mimetic structure or pattern of imitation that marks the actions of participants over a period of time (Redekop, 2002).

Spirituality can be a source of change of orientation from violence to blessing and of growth in creativity, resilience and empowerment. It leans in the direction of positive, inclusive, relationships. It transcends the boundaries of specific religious, ideological and ethnocultural identity groups.

Tacit Knowledge

Philosopher/scientist Michael Polanyi (1964) argues that most of what we know we cannot put into words – this is the 'tacit dimension.' This knowledge includes skills, a sense of 'how things work', aesthetic knowledge (what looks good, tastes good, etc.), and judgement knowledge. This knowledge is acquired through experience, through observation (first of parents and then of mentors), and engagement with a field. Scientists, for instance, interiorize 'rules of rightness' within their research fields (Polanyi, 1964); these go beyond the formal statements of methodology. A seasoned mechanic intuitively finds the source of a mechanical problem in short order – noticing subtle deviations from a well-functioning machine. Effective politicians know how to 'read a crowd' and experienced professors can easily spot plagiarism, just as humanitarian workers know what needs to be done first in a disaster situation.

The skills of knowing that Polanyi ascribes to the tacit domain form the basis for judgements. They also form a platform for the emergence of what can be made explicit. Out of our tacit knowledge we can start explaining what we know – and these explanations can contribute to another level of tacit knowledge. For example, one of Polanyi's examples is that when we see a face we can tell if the person is happy, sad, depressed, etc. but we cannot say exactly what it is that forms the basis for that knowledge. Well past the time of his writing, scientists identified 5000 different facial expressions, nuancing and making explicit many different moods and feelings (The Dalai Lama & Goleman, 2004).

When it comes to 'development' the tacit domain of one's interiority becomes a significant resource, contributing to emergent ways forward in the face of a challenge. Indwelling a field (Csikszentmihalyi, 1996; Polanyi, 1964), including pondering a profound problem over a long period of time, can provide the tacit knowledge base needed for emergent creativity in the mind (Redekop, 2021).

Mindfulness

Mindfulness can be thought of as self-conscious attentiveness to what is happening at the present time, paying particular attention to inner thoughts, attitudes, feelings and perceptions. It includes an awareness of what is happening in relation to other people whose lives impinge on oneself. Buddhists have cultivated the discipline of mindfulness; it opens up the possibility of releasing one from ego-driven impulses and self-destructive behaviours. The skill of being mindful makes a qualitative difference in how one interacts with others as well as how one responds to challenges. It also allows one to tap into the tacit domain of knowledge and the subconscious repository of emotional memories that help constitute intuitive sources of insight.

Consciousness

Consciousness combines values, intuition and worldview with intellectual, affective and spiritual skills of reflection on self, others and the world (Price, 2023), making connections, and balancing each whole with the parts. Scholars such as Kegan, Wilber and McGuigan document an evolutionary growth in consciousness, pointing out the emergence of what Wilber calls vision-logic. McIntosh (2008) synthesizes this as 'an integration of intellectual capacity with intuition in a way that brings together the body and the mind so as to produce this new ability to recognize relationships and approach problems with enhanced creativity' (p. 82). He goes on to describe its volitional character as follows:

> The process of integrally informed dialectical evaluation recognizes how conflicting values and worldviews actually work together within a larger evolutionary system, mutually supporting each other in opposition, in a manner that can be compared to the function of a tension strut in an architectural structure.... However, it is only by appropriately *valuing* each element of the system that we can actually correctly perceive its crucial function within the system as a whole. (p. 83)

For those who see consciousness as primarily evolutionary/developmental stages, the vision-logic stage of consciousness is immediately preceded by post-modern (progressive), modern and traditional stages. In an earlier narcissistic stage people are concerned only with themselves and have little or no capacity for self-critical reflection nor for understanding others. This then evolves to a kinship stage in which there is concern only for 'one's own people or group' – tribalism.

The development of competence in dealing with complexity becomes critical in supporting sustainable development, since the challenges that impede sustainability involve many constantly changing and mutually dependent factors (Redekop & Redekop, 2020).

Nonmaterial Dimension: Collective Aspects

While the individual aspects discussed above could be applied to the collective as well, in this section we will focus on particular aspects of our collective lives together. These categories could be used to deconstruct key internal realities of groups which might see one another as the 'Other'. They will be seen to be key factors affecting development that function beneath the empirical radar. First, we will look at the power of memes and paradigms that play a determining role in how people interpret reality. Second will be a deconstruction of language as it pertains to identity, connection and relationships between collectives.

Memes and Paradigms

Orientations can be determined or expressed through memes – 'elements of a culture or system of behaviour passed from one individual to another by imitation or other non-genetic means' (Oxford Dictionary). Memes have a tacit dimension in that they work at an unconscious level influencing values, decisions and behaviours. If they catch on within a group, they can determine institutional or group culture. For example, the meme of self-interest through a particular interpretation of Adam Smith, influenced the nature of economic systems for centuries, providing a freedom, or even imperative, for entrepreneurs to maximize profits (out of self-interest) even to the point of oppressing others in the process. Through Darwin's 'survival of the fittest' meme, the self-interest meme, permeated societies undergirding an orientation of violence in many relational systems.

Paradigms are like lenses through which we 'see' reality. They determine how we interpret data. They include assumptions, organizational clues, categories and judgements. People with different paradigms can view the same data and see completely different things.

Paradigms can infuse a field or a discipline such that for a time everyone in the field works out of the same paradigm. However, when there are discrepant events that cannot be understood within that paradigm, questions are raised. When enough questions are raised, the search begins for a whole new approach. Eventually a new paradigm emerges resulting in a paradigm shift. Paradigms are like complex adaptive systems; a new paradigm emerges when the old way of looking at things no longer works. The new paradigm not only deals with what didn't work in the old way – discrepant events – but provides new meaning, new relative value and new interconnections to all the elements within the purview of the paradigm.

At any point in time, a group has particular memes and paradigms and these form the basis for judgements about what is going on and what should be done.

For example, a new paradigm regarding human relations to the environment is known as the Anthropocene, which carries within it a sense that human activities have a significant effect on the environment, especially when it comes to global warming. Over the last few decades there have been politicians and business-people who have resisted this paradigm, clinging to a much older paradigm based on a mistranslation of a Hebrew text that suggests it is up to humans to 'subdue the earth and have dominion over it' (Genesis 1:28 KJV), thus undergirding a self-interest meme on the part of humans. The recent exponential growth of extreme weather events makes it ever more untenable for those denying the negative impact of human activity on the biosphere to hold onto the old paradigm.

Whether one sees the world as an interconnected whole with humans taking responsibility for how their actions affect the biosphere (Anthropocene paradigm) or as offering resources for exploitation, ownership and self-gratifying profit (Self-Interest paradigm) has huge implications for how data is evaluated, laws that are passed, and actions are regulated.

Language

Language plays a huge role in the nonmaterial reality. We can think of language in terms of ancient and living languages that have evolved, the language of experience, and discursive hegemonic structures. There is an exterior aspect of language – it can be observed and studied. Besides the overt aspect of language there is the inner organization of meaning, intention and understanding.

Each language that has evolved has words with unique meanings and connotations that cannot be translated exactly into other languages. Each has its own 'take' on the world and is, in that sense, a gift to all of humanity. An in-depth knowledge of a language provides mental models of reality, including a significant amount of tacit knowledge about words, phrases and poetic forms that provide a World of meaning (Lakoff & Johnson, 1980; Nudler, 1990).

People using the same language also develop unique worlds of word-usage whereby people who have had similar experiences understand language in a special way. People with the same experiences can tell in a matter of seconds that they are talking with someone who has gone through the same things and understands them in a particular way. This may pertain to someone from a similar ethnic background, vocation (NGO, military), or human experience; for example, in a Muslim Christian dialogue on the theme of mysticism there was immediate mutual recognition of what was talked about by people from both religious traditions who had had similar experiences.

Language can also be used to reinforce power differentials of domination and being subjected to domination through discursive hegemonic structures (Cummings, 2013; Gramsci, 1968; Redekop, 2002). Accent, words of identification, and the spirit or emotion behind the words can express entitlement and domination, on the one hand, or deference, inferiority and subservience on the other. When there is an indwelling of structures of domination, these nonmaterial, invisible aspects of language can be present without there being a conscious awareness of them. The technical term for language-based domination is 'discursive hegemonic structure'.

Respect for the rich resources of different languages and various specific languages of experience can enhance one's overall understanding of reality. Below I will present an example through an exploration of the Aramaic word *malkuta*.

Dynamic Elements of the Nonmaterial Dimension

Having explored synchronic aspects, we will now attend to diachronic dynamics that affect individuals and groups. First, we will examine mimetic dynamics that tend to dominate relational systems. Second will be a sensitivity to the Implicate Order and with that an integrative approach to viewing the world and taking effective action within a complex web of complex systems. These will lead to an examination of dialogue as a context for 'thinking together' – itself a collective Interior dynamic – and Gentle Action. These will prepare the ground for another level of understanding of the *malkuta*, a term Jesus used to describe nonmaterial reality.

Mimetic Dynamics

'Mimetic' is derived from the Greek word *mimesis* from which we get the words 'mime' and 'imitation'. It refers to a capacity to replicate that which can be perceived in others. As an external phenomenon it can be observed to be an imitation of behaviour, writing, style, or language. As an inner phenomenon it manifests as empathy – an imitation of feelings – and as mimetic desire – the imitation of what another desires. This latter concept was developed in depth for over five decades by French-American theorist, René Girard (1976, 1977, 1986, 1987, 2010).

Girard showed how mimetic desire is a primary motivator of human behaviour. As people observe others desiring, and enjoying, material objects as well nonmaterial goals such as recognition and prestige, they want the same for themselves. This becomes a two-way street as two parties mutually desire what the other has or wants – mimetic rivalry. Through feedback loops this can intensify to the point where it leads to violence. It also works at the collective level.

This internal process carries with it, according to Girard, an ontological overtone: we not only mimetically want particular objects, but we also desire the apparent joy and satisfaction that ostensibly accompany their acquisition. This then amounts to an ontological mimetic desire: we wish to *be* the other.

There is another side to mimetic desire that is inspired by the breakthrough discovery of Rebecca Adams into loving mimesis (2000, 2002). If there is a desire for the well-being, or full subjectivity, of a wounded subject, and if this is mimetically appropriated, the wounded subject desires their own wellness, this contributes to a sense of dignity and eventually to the development of a capacity to take healthy and health-giving action (Redekop & Ryba, 2013).[1]

With mimetic consciousness (Azubuike, 2016) comes a capacity to de-construct and disempower the acquisitive mimetic desire that fuels destructive rivalries and replace it with a life-giving form of mimetic empowerment manifest in mimetic structures of blessing – patterns of mutual enhancing orientation, attitudes and actions (Redekop, 2002; Redekop & Ryba, 2014).

Implicate Order and Integrative Thinking

Physicists David Bohm and David Peat turned from a siloed study of physics to an examination of connections they saw between dynamics at the quantum level and broader patterns in the natural world and human interactions (2010). Similarly, cell and systems biologist Stuart Kauffman looked for patterns of emergent creativity from the emergence of initial cells to the emergence of economic and other systems of human endeavour (2008).

Bohm and Peat show a tendency for humans in the Modern era to adopt a fragmentary approach to dealing with challenges to understanding, action and survival. This is manifest in the academic tendency to develop new disciplines and sub-disciplines with the foci of research becoming increasingly specialized and narrow. In contrast, they call for integrative approaches that link insights from many disciplines in a broad approach that looks for inter-connected insights and broad multi-faceted ways of taking action.

Bohm and Peat perceived within the universe an implicate order. That is, there is a nonmaterial order that connects all phenomena – from quantum dynamics to complex systems (Bohm & Peat, 2010).

Stuart Kauffman (2020), along with medical scientist Neil Theise (2020, 2021, 2023), emphasize common patterns in complex adaptive systems from the micro to the macro. They show how an understanding of the principles of emergent creativity can help to create conditions where the potential for creativity can be enhanced. These conditions can be understood through Kauffman's concept of criticality. In brief, when there are too many elements interacting and too many ways of making combinations there will be chaos with little chance of emergent creativity. Similarly, when there are too few elements and too few possible connections, a system will be static with little possibility of something new emerging

[1] Adams' initial term was 'Proto Subject', which works philosophically; in real life it is hard to find a precise term that captures the sense of someone's subjectivity being in particular need either through deep hurt or blocked development. 'Wounded subject' becomes a placeholder for someone in this position. Insofar as anyone's capacity to take independent action, grow or flourish is thwarted, they could benefit from Loving Mimesis.

(cf. 'group think' or 'old boys club'; Sunstein, 2003). Criticality is that 'sweet spot' in which there is an optimum number of elements and ways of combining them. When anything significant does creatively emerge, it generates what Kauffman calls 'Adjacent Possibles'. These new possibilities could take the form of substitutions, complements, or new creative developments. For example, one Adjacent Possible of personal computers was the internet, which then made possible social media. Kauffman (2016) also allows for the Universe to have consciousness and posits that we become co-creators with this consciousness.

Stuart Kauffman (2008), along with Mario Beauregard (2021; Beauregard & O'Leary, 2007), argue against reductionism. Every new case of emergent creativity results in something with its on ontology that cannot be predicted by nor reduced to what was before. For example, the emergence of life cannot be explained by the 'laws of physics', nor can it be reduced to material reality.

Building on these understandings, I have made a case for emergent creativity within the mind (2021, 22–25), enabled by a deep indwelling of a field combined with relentless pursuit of new understandings.

All this has led to such things as Integrative Peacebuilding (Redekop, 2019), integrative thinking and integrative action. These depend on people from diverse fields, action areas, disciplines and experiences coming together in a spirit of deep collaboration and a passion for mutual understanding.

Dialogue

David Bohm developed a practice of dialogue that has been a model and inspiration for a whole field of dialogue studies. His approach to dialogue as the free flowing of meaning includes several features that are important in the exploration of interior dynamics (Bohm, 1997). First, he emphasized proprioception on the part of dialogue participants. He adapted this word from its physiological meaning of understanding intuitively where one's body is in space to describe an awareness of all that is going on inside oneself during a dialogue. This would include consciousness of emotions, physical changes and ideas stimulated by the discourse. Any of these interior changes could then be shared with the dialogue group.

Second, Bohm gives thought itself its own nonmaterial ontology when he develops the idea of thought as a system (1994). He encourages dialogue group members to think together in such a way that thought itself becomes a collective dynamic.

Gentle Action

With an awareness of complexity and how at certain bifurcation points a small change can have a huge impact, David Peat (2008) developed the concept and practice of Gentle Action. One way in which he described this was through a thought experiment that contrasted the action of dropping a big stone into the centre of a pond, creating a big wave, with many pebbles dropped into the periphery of a pond with their ripples combining at the centre to produce a big wave. Gentle Action starts with an inner realization that it is possible to look at things differently and by doing so change the nature of one's activity.

Naresh Singh, for example, has framed his assets-based approach to poverty as 'gentle action'. Instead of viewing people in poverty as poorly off and needing help from the outside, he framed them as having assets already and that the work of any outsiders was to cultivate those assets and work with those in poverty at developing their own capacities.

The Malkuta

Let's look at the teachings of Jesus as an illustration of nonmaterial reality. The emergence of a new paradigm of Jesus, captured in the Aramaic version of his name – Yeshua – provides an understanding of his self-understanding, spirituality and teachings that can reshape one's inner core. Central to Yeshua's teaching was the *malkuta d'bwashmaya* (the Aramaic words he used) which came to be translated 'kingdom of heaven'. Aramaic scholar and mystic, Neal Douglas-Klotz (2022) has identified the meaning of this phrase as being a nonmaterial reality containing vision, norms and empowerment – the 'I Can' – that exists within and among us and is accessed by those who truly wish to 'see' it.

Juxtaposing the concept of *malkuta d'bwashmaya* with the work of mystic physicists (my designation) David Peat and David Bohm we see that it resonates with the concepts of implicate order, thought as a system (in the context of dialogue), and gentle action. When Yeshua prays, in the famous prayer attributed to him, that the desire of the Creative Consciousness of the Universe be embodied/lived out on earth in the same way as it is in the nonmaterial reality of the *malkuta*, he is praying, in the language of Peat and Bohm, that the implicate order of the universe be understood, acted upon and materialized in our contemporary context through gentle action that coaxes out of all of us a capacity to use our gifts and resources in a life-giving, mutually empowering manner.

Implications for 'Sustainable Development'

Embodying the Nonmaterial

The emerging spirituality coming out of an engagement with the nonmaterial reality has a capacity to replace memes like that of self-interest with memes that channel passions and energy towards bio-interest, transnational interest, transpersonal interest, empathy and widespread empowerment. And this could make all the difference in effecting truly 'sustainable' development. If we take Douglas-Klotz's deconstruction of the *malkuta d'bwashmaya* as a heuristic starting point, we can see that the nonmaterial dimension contributes vision, norms and empowerment that can guide development.

The vision is developed through 'thinking together' in the process of generative dialogue processes. The vision includes both the ends and the processes and actions needed to make these ends come alive. In other words, the nonmaterial vision needs to embodied, and, as such it becomes concrete and visible – applied spirituality.

From the point of view of emergent creativity, the development of norms and values as real nonmaterial entities cannot be reduced to material realities. It may be true that, as Katherine Peil Kauffman argues, they are an extension of the consciousness of primitive life that moves towards 'what is good for' and away from 'what is bad for you', but there is a categorical difference between complex normative systems and these primitive impulses. In her studies of 'Peaceland' for instance, Séverine Autesserre has identified normative challenges for development work that come from how development has been carried out by ex-patriates living in isolation from the societies they are trying to help and basing their actions on sources of knowledge that are limited to that coming from elites and technical experts. In other words, they are cut off from the rich nonmaterial dimensions – tacit knowledge, linguistic fecundity, spirituality, values, teachings and perceptions – of the populations they are trying to serve.

To be effectively creative in relation to development challenges there is a need for individual and collective empowerment, especially in the fostering of criticality for emergent creativity. This can happen within an individual mind as well in the context of generative dialogs. Sometimes it is a combination of the two.

In our exploration of the nonmaterial dimension of reality we have identified spirituality as one aspect of that dimension. We can now show that spirituality is linked to the other aspects of the nonmaterial dimension.

- Spirituality draws on and expresses aspects of our deep emotional system; in its fullness it is marked by joy and satisfaction.
- Our spirituality enables a shift in orientation from violence to blessing.
- Our tacit knowledge base includes things we know as spirituality that we cannot put into words as well as extensive knowledge of significant events that we perceive as linked together in a transcendent way that may be inexplicable, such as David Bohm's sensing an Implicate Order that cannot be fully explained.
- Our spiritual sensitivity allows us to 'see' how certain memes are 'bad for humanity' and identify memes that would be good for both humanity and the biosphere. Likewise, the very inclusion of spirituality and attentiveness to the nonmaterial dimensions of humanity would lead to the emergence of a new paradigm of development.
- Paying attention to language, including the substantial tacit knowledge associated with words for aspects of spirituality would uncover similarities in understandings of experiences, values and sources of empowerment that transcend differences in culture. There would also be value-added insights when looking at the root-metaphors for these concepts in different languages (see the insights gained from a study of different words for reconciliation in Redekop, 2002, pp. 285–87).

- Mindfulness can be both an expression of spirituality and spiritual discipline and the means of tapping into deeper meaning and dynamics of what is happening.
- Dialogue as the free flow of meaning, including an articulation of inner dynamics can be the context for deep transpersonal connection and as 'thinking together' occurs it can take on the qualities of spiritual experiences.
- Spirituality includes a creative capacity.

Administrative Blessing

Every task and responsibility associated with development has within in a certain measure of discretion. If that discretion is used to maximize for the well-being of the Other, the collective good, and the flourishing of the biosphere it can be thought of as administrative blessing. At times, the discretion is minimal – tasks are precisely defined, and roles are spelled out with a high level of specificity. In other instances discretion is broad as mandates are provided in general terms. Whatever the degree of discretion, how that discretion is used is subject to the orientation, values, perceptions and judgements of those taking action. Hence, the range of actions at every turn can do harm to certain people, limiting them or quashing their dreams and capacity for action, or they can empower people. That is the difference between administrative violence and administrative blessing. What goes into how discretion is exercised is a matter of the nonmaterial dimension.

Heart

Picking up on concepts embedded in Ancient Hebrew and Aramaic, we note that the words used for 'heart' go beyond the material hearts as organs that pump blood. Heart is understood as the core of where thinking, feeling, judging, desiring and taking initiative occur. It is out of the heart that behaviour occurs. This metaphorical sense of heart is a good way of describing the nonmaterial dimension of what is happening. Paying attention to heart orientation is key to having true 'sustainable development'. Indeed, it is the passion that impels a creative search for the best way forward that will motivate collaboration, resourcefulness and compassionate responses to human hurt and needs.

On-Going Reconciliation

Within relational systems, ranging from interpersonal to international, there is always the potential for mutual misunderstanding and hurtful actions resulting in distrust at a minimum and vengeful attitudes, actions and orientation at an extreme. There is a need for on-going reconciliation, including forgiveness (Duffy, 2009; Redekop, 2011). Otherwise, conflicts can deflect energies from 'sustainable development' and may even move situations in a contrary way, destroying what may have already been developed. Dealing with conflict creatively and in a healing manner, involves dealing with the intangible realities that include emotions, trauma and 'spirit'.

Taking Responsibility for the Nonmaterial Reality

If it is truly the case that attentiveness to the nonmaterial dimension of humans at the individual and collective levels is necessary, how can there be a transformation of policies, programmes and initiatives such that all the things identified with this dimension do not 'ooze between the cracks?' On the one hand, we can say it is the responsibility of all parties to attend to this for themselves. We could also suggest that it be a matter of policy, planning processes and review that there be times to reflect individually and collectively on how nonmaterial values and dynamics are being manifest in what is happening. I would suggest that in addition to these general observations, there should be at least two actual positions be established in organizations to enhance the potential of using the nonmaterial/spiritual resources of people involved to the full: namely, something akin to a chaplain and developmental evaluators.

Over the past five decades I have had the privilege of being deeply involved with both penitentiary and military chaplains. This involvement has enabled me to see first-hand the powerful contribution of people who have a position with a spiritual mandate attached to it, combined with a relational mandate that transcends the polarities and power positions of those in the respective systems. In each case, chaplains have had direct access to those in charge, be they wardens of penitentiaries or commanding officers of military units.

Prison chaplains have a concern for the personal well-being and spiritual lives of prisoners, first and foremost. But their concerns also extend to guards, prison staff and administration. Not only that, prison chaplains have a concern for victims of crime and communities affected by crime. They are invested in all the parties. At one time the Commissioner of the Penitentiary Service told me that in his younger years, when he was a warden of a prison, he witnessed the extraordinary changes wrought by sensitive chaplains who played this role of looking out for everyone and attending to the system as a whole.

One of the most striking examples of this transcendent role for chaplaincy has been a team of prison chaplains in Rwandan prisons designated for perpetrators of genocide. With Pierre Allard, former Chaplain General of the Canadian Penitentiary Service and his lifelong spouse Judy, as mentors, they have developed a reconciliation process that involves prisoners writing letters of apology to victims (Just.Equipping (justequipping.org)). The letters are hand-delivered to the victims who are told that the letter is there, but they do not have to read it. They usually do read the letters and when they do, they are given an opportunity to meet with the perpetrator to have their unanswered questions about the last experiences of their loved ones answered. The reconciliation processes engendered through this process are astounding. The changes in the 'hearts' of those involved are impressive.

Military chaplains are engaged to deal with the spiritual needs of soldiers first and foremost. However, they also do have a role as confidants of commanding officers in private sessions in which they can offer moral perspectives that transcend questions of strategy and operations. They can also give leadership to Religious Leader Engagement (RLE). As Moore points out (2013), Canadian chaplains serving with peacekeeping units in Bosnia and Herzegovina in the 1990s, when inter-ethnic violent conflict was still going on, were approached by local religious leaders who talked with these chaplains as religious leaders, in their own right. These Serbian Orthodox priests, Croatian Catholic priests and Bosniak Muslim Imams all had a passion for peace within the country. With the chaplains leading the process they came together to collaborate on humanitarian relief and joint prayers for peace. In Iraq, when the US Army was involved in the country, Mike Hoyt, a military chaplain, and Canon Andrew White, a Special Envoy from the Archbishop of Canterbury, convened a gathering of about 60 religious leaders from the different parts of Iraq representing both Sunnis and Shiites (Moore, 2013). This group, the Iraq Inter-religious Council, adopted a joint declaration calling for peace and about 10 of them formed an on-going council to advise political leaders. This group was able to resolve a number of violent situations behind the scenes. These impulses led Padre Dr Steve Moore (2013) to develop a framework for Religious Leader Engagement.

All of this suggests that development initiatives should consider appointing some people, akin to chaplains, who are charged with attending to the nonmaterial aspects of life. These people should have spiritual resources available that can empower people to adopt the orientation, ethical vision and empowering spirit so that official policies enhance values of mutual blessing and that the myriad of decisions involved in implementing those policies be shaped by administrative blessing.

A second type of position that should be part of development initiatives should be that of 'developmental evaluators' (Singh, 2021). The rationale for this type of position comes out of applied complexity thinking that recognizes that in a complex situation, some of the most significant developments are those that could not be planned or predicted. The Developmental Evaluator's job would be to identify these new developments so that adjacent possibilities can then be acted upon. In the light of what has been said about the nonmaterial dimension of development we can see that developmental evaluators could also be attentive to these intangible dynamics and work with the 'chaplains' to address problems in the nonmaterial domain, affirming the positive and surprising manifestation of 'Spirit'.

Conclusion

The development of human beings and their subsequent actions on the environment, relational systems and structures is a complex undertaking that involves what is material and observable and what is nonmaterial, but equally real. If development is 'sustainable' it will continue with some sense of continuity. If it is not, by definition, it will come to an end in its present form. How, or to what degree, it will come to an end is an open question. However, whether it continues or comes to the point of radical change, it should be clear that how we as humans act as co-creators of future possibilities that will be actualized will depend on the many aspects of the nonmaterial dimension of reality as outlined above.

At the 'heart' of action are the vision, values and orientation of the actor. These in turn are largely influence by memes, paradigms and experiences that fill the tacit knowledge categories of what is permitted, forbidden and obligatory. Those with positions of responsibility often have considerable latitude in how exactly they fulfil their responsibilities – administrative discretion – along with a capacity to shape policies and initiatives. Action is the final step in a string of mental actions that end with judgement (M. Price, 2020). Judgement is based on this nonmaterial indwelling of values, along with emotions attached to them. For actions – including on-going practices – to be oriented to optimize what is required for development to be as 'sustainable' as possible – that is to meet the Sustainable Development Goals – it is imperative that all actors, from leaders to bureaucrats, government agents to local workers, be passionately committed to work for the good of humanity and the biosphere, otherwise they will direct their actions towards self-serving short-term goals. For that reason, we cannot leave the nonmaterial dimension to chance and for that reason attending to it is really the *sine qua non* of sustainable development.

References

Azubuike, N. (2016). *Dimensions to ethnic conflict in a pluralistic democratic state: A critical analysis of mimesis using the Nigerian case study of Ife-Modakeke crisis.* Unpublished masters research project. Saint Paul University.

Beauregard, M. (2021). *Expanding reality: The emergence of postmaterialist science.* IFF Books.

Beauregard, M., & O'Leary, D. (2007). *The spiritual brain: A neuroscientist's case for the existence of the soul.* Harper One.

Bohm, D. (1994). *Thought as a system.* Routledge.

Bohm, D. (1997). *On dialogue.* Routledge.

Bohm, D., & Peat, D. (2010). *Science, order, and creativity.* Routledge.

Csikszentmihalyi, M. (1996). *Creativity: Flow and the psychology of discovery and invention.* HarperPerennial.

Cummings, G. (2013). Black theology and Latin American theology. In D. Batstone (Ed.), *New visions for the Americas: Religious engagement and social transformation* (pp. 215–229). Fortress.

Douglas-Klotz, N. (2022). *Revelations of the Aramaic Jesus: The hidden teachings on life and death.*

Duffy, M. (2009). *Paul Ricoeur's pedagogy of pardon: A narrative theory of memory and forgetting.* Continuum.

Duyndam, J. (2014). Hermeneutical mimesis. In V. N. Redekop & T. Ryba (Eds.), *René Girard and creative mimesis* (pp. 249–258).

Friesen, E., Tenney, E., Waters, L. J., & Edwards, M. (n.d.). *Integral metatheory: Practicing the science of inclusion*. Unpublished manuscript.
Girard, R. ([1961] 1976). *Deceit, desire and the novel: Self and other in literary structure [original: Mensonge ronamantique et vérité romanesque]* [Trans. by Yvonne Freccero]. The Johns Hopkins University Press.
Girard, R. ([1972] 1977). *Violence and the sacred [original: La Violence et le sacré]* [Trans. by Patrick Gregory]. The Johns Hopkins University Press.
Girard, R. ([1978] 1987). *Things hidden since the foundation of the world [original: Des choses cachées depuis la fonadation du monde]* [Trans. by Stephen Bann and Michael Metteer]. Stanford University Press.
Girard, R. ([1982] 1986). *The scapegoat [original: Le bouc émissaire]* [Trans. by Yvonne Freccero]. The Johns Hopkins University Press.
Girard, R. ([2007] 2010). *Battling to the end: Conversations with Benoit Chantre [original: Achever Clauswitz]* [Trans. by Mary Baker] Michigan State University Press.
Gramsci, A. (1968). *The modern prince and other writings*. International.
Haidt, J. (2013). *The righteous mind: Why good people are divided on religion and politics*. Vintage Books.
Kauffman, K. P. (2020). Natural spirituality and the biology of emotion. In V. N. Redekop & G. N. Redekop (Eds.), *Awakening: Exploring spirituality, emergent creativity, and reconciliation* (pp. 65–88).
Kauffman, K. P. (2021). The biology of emotion: Implications for self-development, spirituality and justice. In V. N. Redekop & G. N. Redekop (Eds.), *Transforming: Applying spirituality, emergent creativity, and reconciliation* (pp. 41–68).
Kauffman, S. (2008). *Reinventing the sacred: A new view of science, reason, and religion*. Basic Books.
Kauffman, S. (2016). *Humanity in a creative universe*. Oxford University Press.
Kauffman, S. (2020). The re-enchantment of humanity: The implications of 'no entailing laws. In V. N. Redekop & G. N. Redekop (Eds.), *Awakening: Exploring spirituality, emergent creativity, and reconciliation* (pp. 19–48).
Lakoff, G., & Johnson, M. (1980). *Metaphors we live by*. University of Chicago Press.
McGuigan, R., & Popp, N. (2016). *Integral conflict: The new science of conflict*. SUNY Press.
McIntosh, S. (2008). *Integral consciousness and the future of evolution: How the integral worldview is transforming politics, culture and spirituality*. Paragon House.
Moore, S. K. (2013). *Military chaplains as agents of peace: Religious Leader Engagement in conflict and post-conflict environments*. Lexington.
Nudler, O. (1990). On conflict and metaphors: Toward an extended rationality. In J. W. Burton (Ed.), *Conflict: Human needs theory* (pp. 177–204). St. Martin's Press.
Peat, D. (2008). *Gentle action: Bringing creative change to a turbulent world*. Pari Publishing.
Peil, K. (2014). Emotion: The self-regulatory sense. *Global Advances in Health and Medicine*. https://www.ncbi.nlm.nih.gov/pubmed/24808986
Polanyi, M. (1964). *Personal knowledge: Towards a post-critical philosophy*. Harper Torchbooks.
Price, J. (2023). *The call: The spiritual realism of Sargent Shriver*. SSPI Press.
Price, M. (2020). Intentional peace: The role of human consciousness in the emergence of peace and conflict. In V. N. Redekop & G. N. Redekop (Eds.), *Awakening:*

Exploring spirituality, emergent creativity, and reconciliation (pp. 267–282). Lexington.
Redekop, V. N. (2002). *From violence to blessing: How an understanding of deep-rooted conflict can open paths to reconciliation.* Novalis.
Redekop, V. N. (2011). Spirituality, emergent creativity, reconciliation and peacemaking. In S. A. Nan, A. Bartoli, & Z. Mampilly (Eds.), *Peacemaking: From practice to theory* (Vol. 2, pp. 285–600). ABC-CLIO (Praeger).
Redekop, V. N. (2014a). Blessing-based reconciliation in the face of violence. In V. Redekop & T. Ryba (Eds.), *René Girard and creative reconciliation* (pp. 67–94). Lexington.
Redekop, V. N. (2014b). Blessing-based love (Agape) as a heuristic to understanding effective reconciliation practices: A reading of I Corinthians 13 in a peacebuilding context. In T. Matyok, M. Flaherty, H. Tuso, J. Senehi, & S. Byrne (Eds.), *Peace on earth: The role of religion in peace and conflict studies* (pp. 47–66). Lexington.
Redekop, V. N. (2019). The emergence of integrative peacebuilding: A complexity-based approach to leadership development. *Journal of Peacebuilding and Development*, *14*(3), 14–23.
Redekop, V. N., & Redekop, G. N. (Eds.). (2020). *Awakening: Exploring spirituality, emergent creativity, and reconciliation.*
Redekop, V. N., & Redekop, G. N. (Eds.). (2021). *Transforming: Applying spirituality, emergent creativity and reconciliation.* Lexington.
Redekop, V. N., & Ryba, T. (Eds.). (2013). *René Girard and creative mimesis.* Lexington.
Redekop, V. N., & Ryba, T. (Eds.). (2014). *René Girard and creative reconciliation.* Lexington.
Ricoeur, P. (1992). *Oneself as another* [Trans. by K. Blamey] University of Chicago Press.
Singh, N. (2021). Development as emergent creativity. In V. N. Redekop & G. N. Redekop (Eds.), *Transfroming: Applying spirituality, emergent creativity, and reconciliation.* Lexington.
Sunstein, C. R. (2003). *Why societies need dissent.* Harvard University Press.
The Dalai Lama, & Goleman, D. (2004). *Destructive emotions: How can we overcome them?* Bantam Books.
Theise, N. (2020). Microbes and mystics: A response to Stuart Kauffman's call to 'reenchangment. In V. N. Redekop & G. N. Redekop (Eds.), *Awakening: Exploring spirituality, emergent creativity, and reconciliation* (pp. 49–64).
Theise, N. (2021). Harnessing principles of complex systems for understanding and modulating social structures. In V. N. Redekop & G. N. Redekop (Eds.), *Transforming: Applying spirituality, emergent creativity, and reconciliation* (pp. 377–394). Lexington.
Theise, N. (2023). *Notes on complexity: A scientific theory of connection, consciousness, and being.* Spiegel and Grau.
Wilber, K. (2000). *A brief history of everything.* Shambhala.
Wilber, K. (2001). *A theory of everything.* Shambhala.

Chapter 12

Applied Spirituality and Mediation: Overcoming Challenges of Sustainability Using Inter-Relational Settlement Model

K. Parameswaran

Abstract

Mediation is defined as a process, whether referred and agreed to by the expression mediation, pre-litigation mediation, online mediation, community mediation, conciliation or any other expression of such similar import, whereby party or parties, request an independent third person referred to as mediator or mediation service provider to assist them in their attempt to reach a peaceful settlement of a dispute. The peaceful settlement of any dispute to be initiated, processed, guided and moderated in the process of successful mediation before parties, needs mediator to have four major new skills such as witness-awareness, stillness-concentration, empathy-motivation and a pragmatic-sensibility for fulfilling the aims and outcomes of mediation. These four skills are deeply inward and psychological, which can be accessed and empowered by an exercise of deepening experience called spiritual in content and application. However, a crucial interchange of meaning and value that very often come into this situation between spirituality and psychology is an important one to be mentioned here. The two seemingly distant disciplines of experience, one of psychology and another of spirituality lies in the orientation that an individual and a collective give to life and world as a whole. When life and world are accepted in totality, spirituality can be life-affirmative and world-embracing giving us a direction to the individual psychological states of though-emotion-sensation-behaviour complex to embrace and enhance values of inclusion, harmony and development at the collective and universal level. These psychological states, both individual and collective, gradually open the vision and mission of values to live within and outside, to be and to become, and finally manifest a future world of stability, order, richness and growing perfection by solving challenges that come to our existence. It makes life both spiritual and earthly. This chapter

Applied Spirituality and Sustainable Development Policy, 223–239

doi:10.1108/978-1-83753-380-020231012

demonstrates that this kind of spiritual meaning, value and experience entering into and operating through psychological capacities give mediator four major new skills for easing the process and purpose of mediation exercise. One, an objective awareness to witness the proceedings of the mediation calmly within the conscious cognition and without having any bias and fixed beliefs towards any issues of the parties. Two, a stillness with sensory concentration to avoid unnecessary reactions or agitations that human nature is prone to in taking sides on issues or become lop-sided in approach and consequently affecting mediation's outcome of peaceful settlement. Three, an empathy that animates and motivates parties to look for win-win situation for both as against the adversarial method currently present in the legal system where one party loses and another party gains grounds, which results in bitterness in parties' relationships, rights and obligations. Four, a pragmatic sensibility or practical responsibility by which costs or damages or injuries of all kinds such as social, economic, profit-loss ratio, psychological or organizational stress etc., can be pre-calculated, meaningfully distributed and harmonized between parties by the mediator. With millions of pending legal cases in the existing system of the courts of law that are supposedly designed to provide access to justice and, unfortunately have become fragile as a result of severe shortage of resources of all kinds to deal with sheer quantity and intricate complexity of issues in the disputes, applied spirituality in mediation can pave way for easy, flexible, quick, cost-effective and satisfactory justice to both sides of the parties when these four major new skills are developed through application of spiritual experience and experiments in the whole process of mediation. The author explains in this article the method of acquiring these four major new skills in experiential form in any mediation scenario and the rationale for infusing applied spirituality in mediation. Author also discusses the Indian situation of mediation in the light of new developments sought for enhancing the alternative dispute resolution. At the end, this chapter demonstrates the bigger picture that represent the need of spirituality using these four major new skills while mediating challenges of sustainable development. It will be shown in the end how spirituality, sustainability and mediation for settlements of disputes of sustainable development have something common, core and collective. This is the premise based on which the relationship between applied spirituality and mediation in overcoming the challenges of sustainability are expressed with the help of intuitive, inspirational, integrative and intelligent actions for a sustaining our future age, new humanity and harmonious space.

Keywords: Mediation; interrelationships; Alternative Dispute Resolution (ADR); applied spirituality; sustainability; witnessawareness; stillness-concentration; empathy-motivation; pragmatic-sensibility

Introduction: Introducing the Seemingly Irreconcilable Relationships

One often wonders about the existence of the nature of interrelationships between applied spirituality on one side and mediation on the other side. One would even doubt whether there is any typographical error as to the word mediation in place of meditation. We might as well come to the conclusion at the end of this written analysis that there is no error in the typography between these two words while introducing and explaining the existence of the nature of interrelationships, rather, there is a conscious attempt to announce the advent of a new interrelationships between the seemingly irreconcilable elements such as applied spirituality and mediation, which the author believes it to be the future of justice in the administration of conflict resolution and settlement system in our living spaces. A deeper look into the meanings of these two themes would be the first emerging point to open the gateways towards the light of understanding the exploration of applied spirituality in mediation. It is important to keep in mind while reading the author's demonstration that the meaning of word spirituality is taken in a universal context or one can say spirituality in its pure and applied sense of inner experience that results in the outer action of peace, progress and harmony in all aspects of our daily life that legal systems are attempting to regulate. This meaning and application might or might not be specific to only one method or approach of philosophy or religion or culture or belief or faith or practice or moral or ethic generally associated with the term spirituality, which are often intellectual excursions of expressions in mental and analytical terms the experiences of the deeper dimensions of the spirit of life or the spiritual awareness of life. Also, the meaning of the word mediation and its application is taken in the Indian context in order to make it specific to a national and domestic legal jurisdiction and to justify the relevance of the theory and practice as aimed in this study of 'applied spirituality and mediation'. It goes without saying the title that is given as 'applied spirituality and mediation' also implies 'applied spirituality in mediation' because of the mutual and complementary nature of the interaction between them that is profoundly intricate allowing it to take shape in both forms without any contradictory meanings.

Scattered Scenario of Mediation: Multiple Legal Provisional Instances

Mediation generally understood is one of the modes under Alternative Dispute Resolution (ADR) where legal conflicts are settled outside the traditional court system that are established by a legal system under the Constitution of India. It is a voluntary process where parties attempt to settle their legal conflicts with a flexible assistance and collaborative intervention of an independent third person called the mediator. The whole platform and process of mediation is undertaken by a reference to it through a formal agreement whereby expressions such as mediation, pre-litigation mediation, online mediation, community mediation, conciliation or any other expression of such similar import are agreed to, in which parties in a legal conflict request an independent third person referred to as mediator or a mediation service provider to assist them in their attempt to reach a peaceful settlement of their conflict. Thus, mediation becomes purely a choice of the parties with no strict or binding rules of procedure leaving the whole legal relationship voluntary and non-adversarial to move towards a harmonious re-continuation or ending of relationships of the parties under a legal spectrum. Consequently, the flexibility and autonomy that parties have and, the tempo and effectiveness that mediation process have in initiating and concluding the mediation, parties' interests and non-adversarial nature not only adds swiftness and efficiency but also gets legal finality to the consensus in settling the legal battles. In sum, mediation leads to a deeper peace in the legal relationships and happiness of inner satisfaction of the parties for themselves as individuals who are litigants before a legal system in addition to being conscious citizens socially helpful to reduce the overburdening of the systems of the courts where legal cases are docketed and waiting for their painful pendency to be ended.

A Mediation Bill is currently pending before the Indian Parliament[i] and there are two important reports submitted by the members of the Parliament revealing wealth of information on the whole scattered scenario of mediation that is emerging in India. However, before, we analyse the nature of interrelationships between applied spirituality and mediation, we must study certain features of mediation from various scattered legal sources including these two reports as they are legally relevant and socially important in order to appreciate the future role of applied spirituality in mediation as conceived in various legal statutes, judicial pronouncements and in the voices coming out from legal and judicial family. A brief overview of the legal situation dealing with mediation in India becomes indispensable to understand the various attempts to keep mediation as a point of conflict settlement and resolution. They are listed as follows.

(1) Pendency of the cases in the Indian Legal System:

The total number of pending cases in the Indian Court systems are 4,25,85,652 (both civil and criminal cases).[ii] There are also staggering and scary predictive assessments by various analysts to show the sheer number of years ranging to even few 100s of years that courts of law in India might take to complete all the legal proceedings of these pending cases. It goes without saying as to number of higher appeals that one of the parties might prefer from the concluded cases that gets added up to the list of pending cases while at the same time new cases might get registered by the litigants arising out of the ever growing developmental nature of the society and complexities of the individual and collective socio-economic vicissitudes of life. Any amount of prediction on this situation though can give an overview of the alarming situation but the legal details that are locked inside in the multi-tiered court-system and its processes might even make one less hopeful of the legal system to show confidence before the common public.

(2) Absence of a Standalone Statutory Law on Mediation:

Considering the situation that there is no standalone Statutory law on Mediation at present in India except with a Bill on Mediation still pending before the Parliament for passing, one cannot avoid to consider the numerous legal provisions related to Mediation from various existing laws as shown in the Report 117 Volume 1,[iii] submitted to the Parliament. Those numerous provisions from various legal systems when read carefully, we find they deal with mediation either directly or indirectly indicating the significance of the emergence of mediation in legal disputes and the future era of litigation and settlement models. It would not be redundant or preposterous to also show how the current legal issues under various statutory laws and provisions when they become mediation-enabled for peaceful settlement of disputes post mediational provisions enacted in respective statutory laws and provisions under various Acts, they would inevitably attract or even force challenges of sustainability and issues of sustainable development to come under the purview of mediation. The future legal days are not far especially when sustainability issues are rather complex that cannot be solved strictly under the existing reductionist, formalist and substantive position. An innovation, a creativity, a novel thought process and a holistic system comprising mutual positions of complementary values etc., are long pending in our jurisprudence for our healthier tomorrow.

The statistics as per the data published by the National Legal Services Authority for the year 2021–22 has the following facts that explain the mediation scenario in India.[iv] Currently, the Alternative Dispute Resolution (ADR) centres in India are 464 of which 397 are functional, a total 570 mediation centres, 16,565 mediators, and close to 53,000 cases were settled through mediation. All the aforementioned facts shown brings us more close and intense to feel the need for the study of interrelationships between applied spirituality and mediation. With sustainability challenges looming large threatening the future of humanity and society, world and planetary space that we all collectively share, a mediation with four major new skills of spirituality seems to be the key to provide peaceful solutions.

Advent of the Role of Applied Spirituality and Mediation

The current and modern times that we live in are ripe for many fertile thoughts with many advancements in knowledge taking place that can show new promises only when they are interrelated. Future is for those who integrate knowledge and its practices. The outright rejection of the spirituality as a discipline as well as its spiritual language expressing spiritual values and experiences as something intellectually contradictory, scientifically non-empirical and hence unverifiable for explanation of its truth etc., leading to a conclusion of its worthlessness as marshalled by all kinds of logical positivists or rational scholars of the last century is no more valid at present. The very fact of the lop sidedness that we see, feel, sense, bear and live through the conflicts that arise from the linearity every now and then leading to friction, exclusivity and disharmony is a significant pointer to something deeper that which is behind or pushing or leading our mind, emotion, sensation and life as a whole to move towards individually and collectively, inclusively and exhaustively. The evolutionary spirit seems to be endless in its search for peace, progress and perfection since the journey from mineral to plant to animal to man to human unity to universal humanity and its crowing harmony with flora, fauna and deep ecology. And, thus, the consequent failures we see from many fronts of lop sidedness such as scientific methods of rationalism based on mere reductionism, socio-economic materialism based on pleasure as the only ultimate value of life and resourceful capitalism as the best method of guarantee to enhance equality and affordability through a balance in supply and demand to one and all etc., have not yet yielded the unity we look up to and the meaning and satisfaction of a life we crave for. And, hence, the conflicts are getting added one over the other leading to a hopelessness too in life, devoid of direction and purpose. This seems to be a clear proof of the thirst of human quest and its spirit that is not yet fully satisfied with the half and incomplete nature of the experience of life in all these social, economic, political and the scientific areas. Thus, human spirit seeks for something beyond and yet within the life and world, within the time and space. It is like a play of hide and seek, that human nature does half-knowingly or helplessly in this game of life as chance without conscious choice. In some spheres, this human quest has led to a resurgence of religious fevers and fears through reactions with a hope that a return to the earlier path can save and secure humanity without conflict and strife. And, for some others, a claim for a path of secular humanism with a uniform set of solutions and principles as answers on all issues seem to be a way forward. It is at this juncture that the knowledge of spirituality acquires enormous meaning as it deals with the spirit of life that which governs our human mind, living, and body as well as everything that is present in the universe. Especially for the legal discipline, as it deals with regulation of social-human behaviour implying an understanding of the psychological-human behaviour. However, the psychology of the last century has moved from Freudian complexity of the id-ego-super ego and sexuality of the sub-conscious to that of the self or soul or mindfulness or awareness of super-conscious-something that permeates human thought-emotion-sensation-body-behaviour complex. One glaring example of this movement is the attempt though not yet fully complete in its understanding and scope is the realm of new age philosophy and practices like positive psychology, well-being psychotherapies of numerous kinds, neuro linguistic programing and biological circuits and mapping, integrated clinical hypnotherapy etc., where subjective experiences are accepted as inner evidences, as deeper meanings to life and living are based on what one experiences in his or her inner awareness no matter it is verifiable and accepted necessarily in the form of units and quantities that post-modern reductionist era and other formalist and substantive schools viewed everything in totals, numbers and labels. In legal and justice discipline too, the word dignity is acquiring enormous proportions of meanings in the current age of mere socio-economic-political human rights as these determinations of outward security and material compensations for justice is not considered as a full or complete measure of what justice is all about or ought to be, which the Constitutional Law has guaranteed under its Preamble.[v] Victims or litigants look for predictability and stability in their security and safety keeping their state of innocence and purity in the nature of things, and not just mere compensation-seeking in monetary terms post-injury where human-beings are reduced to human-litigants in the prism of law. This is seen as a problem of a State that ought to look into to prevent it and not just only remedying it post-factum economically or socially. It is here when legal relationships go frustrated, they look up to a legal system of courts and judicial administration of justice and it is all the more painful when existing legalisms of the system of courts have little scope for peaceful interaction between parties to ease disharmonies when accusation, doubt, proof and evidence of the adversarial system has little meaning to the suffering of the seeking-self craving for dignity and sense of worth that is present in the deep and psychological human, nature and being. Probably, this is what has led to conflicts making the society litigious and leading the court-systems with a pendency of the cases numbering more than 400 lakhs of cases in India with parties busy fighting their litigations to come out of their pain without knowing where the exit routes are. Here, we have three major issues to be dealt with if human and legal scenes have to come out of this sorry situation trapped in the mind and man-made self-prisons. One, the reduction in the pendency of the litigating cases, two, the process of settlement between the litigating parties needed to be peaceful, amicable and reconciliatory, and three, the procedure to be adopted be simple to meet not only the legal analytical eyes and ideas of external costs but also, allow the expressions of emotions, feelings and sensations without fear and doubt, rather with trust, hope and an ever ready acceptance to move forward by spirit of collaboration between parties. Certainly not a situation in which one party wins and another loses. All these need a person or a system to possess or knowledge to give certain core skills when the litigation proceedings are taking place with litigants in the stressful situation unsure of the next step towards their own future. It is here that mediation as a peaceful mechanism of solution to conflicts can play a crucial role as shown in the aforementioned understandings through various but scattered legal provisions with a Mediation Bill waiting to come out successfully through the gates of the Parliament of India. Mediation has become almost indispensable in areas of civil and commercial conflicts, family and property issues, labour and community issues or even on issues when there is no involvement of State as a party in the sense of collective identity and public policy for the common benefit of all. It might not be an exaggeration to say that mediation and mediators are going to be the future messengers of justice in terms of real settlement and resolution of conflicts. It is interesting to study two important documents namely the Mediation Training Manual of India prepared by the Mediation and Conciliation Project Committee of the Supreme Court of India[vi] and Designing the Future of Dispute Resolution – The ODR Policy Plan For India[vii] prepared by The NITI Aayog Expert Committee on ODR. Reading these two documents takes legal profession from traditional court of law to modern method of mediation.

Four Core Skills of Mediator

There are four core skills needed for a mediator that must be first learnt and practiced. This can be done by a person of law or even by a person who is moved by the spirit of reconciliation, harmony and progressive realization of human life in the individual and collective, in the social, economic, political, scientific etc. It goes without saying that the mediator in general possesses the skills of holistic capacity for thinking, feeling, sensing, acting, listening and creating spontaneously according to the parties' requirements in relation to amicable solution. Once these are developed, mediator is now ready for four more core skills of mediation.

(1) An objective awareness to witness the proceedings of the mediation calmly within the conscious cognition and without having any bias and fixed beliefs towards any issues of the parties.
(2) A stillness with sensory concentration to avoid unnecessary reactions or agitations that human nature is prone to in taking sides on issues or become lop-sided in approach and consequently affecting mediation's outcome of peaceful settlement.
(3) An empathy that animates and motivates parties to look for win-win situation for both as against the adversarial method currently present in the legal system where one party loses and another party gains grounds, which results in bitterness in parties' relationships, rights and obligations.
(4) A pragmatic sensibility or practical responsibility by which costs or damages or injuries of all kinds such as social, economic, profit-loss ratio, psychological or organizational stress etc., can be pre-calculated, meaningfully distributed and harmonized between parties by the mediator.

If the existing legal system can bring these four core skills, through legal education, legal research and legal training to ultimately result in legal and judicial system, it would not be a difficult case to argue for applied spirituality and mediation. However, the current legal education, legal research and legal training alongside the legal and judicial system are still in the mode of the analytical-legal with reason and logic as the prime mover of the proceedings of the justice. With reason and logic, it is only the tangible and verifiable data that can hold the way. However, a conflict in a legal situation and settlement of the same is tangible and verifiable only in its outcome, not in its origin and spirit, where psychological feelings about solutions of the conflict are more important than mentally calculated thoughts about solutions or psychological feelings about solutions of the conflict are equally important with all of its counterpart. This is one of the reasons in the development of the law of human dignities to move deeper from the law of human rights. Current paradigms of law have not yet fully grasped that the human conflict is a product of friction between an individual's personal response and the community's response back to the individual. Conflict originates in the inner psychological leading to the outer social and economic. When this conflict seeks a legal solution or advice which when not addressed or healed properly either at the procedural or at the outcome level to impact the origin of the inner psychological, it can lead to a bigger problem in the society, to its community or the collective public leading to a furtherance of conflicting situation in the nature of life creating a network of tensions, frictions and consequent conflicts. Sociologists and economists of the quantitative reductionism that legal scholars often borrow have forgotten to see the inner shades and, thus their research is complacent with the finding and treatment of the outer symptoms. Human mind and society as a collection of interdependent individuals will not be satisfied if conflict is resolved by law only at the external level leaving the internal to wither worrying about another assault of the unpredictability of situation where human movement becomes unstable and insecure gearing up for another litigation-probability or remaining fearful of situations. In case a litigation is lost, human energies feel the worse. It is here that a spiritual understanding of life, the human and society gives the knowledge of the true nature of awareness of interdependence of all existing things through oneness and unity, and the dimension of a conflict as product of ego's fear of losing its touch with things and objects leading to divisions, crises of survival and acceptance of identities and meanings. It is for this reason, the popular notion of spirituality is to talk about renunciation of the world and its relations as the ego is strong and inflexible, unwilling to give up attachments that are stuck to senses and its sufferings. The spirit of oneness is alarming to the senses of the body as they have to lose their individuality in the collective. However, this does not answer the fundamental question of why life and how world came to be in this way that is important to understand the conflict, its origin and method to resolve it. Ideal question would be to know what the ways to master human life are and free it from sensory clutches and yet live in the world with all relations without attachments. The standard example of the lotus leaf left untouched by the water in which it lives or the blossom of beautiful lotus unknown to the dirt in which it grows seems to be an intuitive suggestion to deeper art of living[viii] and an insightful science of living.[ix] Spirituality and its experience in awareness of oneness and unity, freedom from fear of division, true liberty from interdependent harmony etc., can give hope to mankind. Legal discipline must take this into account if justice is true and ought to be complete. Legal knowledge must take the spiritual insight to cut through legal reason and logic to move around integrating the threads of social, economic, political, scientific etc., aspects of life from both movements of inside-out and outside-in. Inside-out as inner consciousness guiding and shaping the outer action and outside-in as an external stimuli to prepare and explore the inner discovery of things. This two-way integration brings the nature and scope of the meaning of applied spirituality through four core skills needed for mediation to deal with a conflicting situation. In short, mediator or mediation will move parties both inside-out and outside-in and connect the threads of social, economic, political, scientific etc., to bring win-win situation for both parties as well as win-win situation for all shades of life and finally a win-win situation to the amicably accepted identities and meanings. Among the many definitions of spirituality, the definition given by Sri Aurobindo[x] seems to be the most effective and useful definition for law, justice and mediation process and outcome as it is highly exhaustive as well as inclusive, world embracing and life oriented. This definition seems to have the clue for what is sustainability, and what are the challenges of sustainable development from a practical base with an experiential awareness in daily life while dealing with objects and resources that mediators or problem solvers and conflicting parties have to be first introduced, then internalized and finally institutionalized.

'Spirituality is not a high intellectuality, not idealism, not an ethical turn of mind or moral purity and austerity, not religiosity or an ardent and exalted emotional fervour, not even a compound of all these excellent things; a mental belief, creed or faith, an emotional aspiration, a regulation of conduct according to a religious or ethical formula are not spiritual achievement and experience. These things are of considerable value to mind and life; they are of value to the spiritual evolution itself as preparatory movements disciplining, purifying or giving a suitable form to the nature; but they still belong to the mental evolution, – the beginning of a spiritual realisation, experience, change is not yet there. Spirituality is in its essence an awakening to the inner reality of our being, to a spirit, self, soul which is other than our mind, life and body, an inner aspiration to know, to feel, to be that, to enter into contact with the greater Reality beyond and pervading the universe which inhabits also our own being, to be in communion with It and union with It, and a turning, a conversion, a transformation of our whole being as a result of the aspiration, the contact, the union, a growth or waking into a new becoming or new being, a new self, a new nature'.

Interrelationships Between Applied Spirituality and Mediation: Practical Strategies to Develop

Based on the aforementioned definition of spirituality taken from Sri Aurobindo to integrate with law, justice and mediation, let us examine the four core skills of mediator useful for mediation and the practical strategies to develop those skills. When the mediator practises and develops these core skills,[1] it leads the mediation from all fronts. Mediation procedures become party-friendly, process-oriented in terms of structure without being adversarial, response-reflective at every level as per the convenience and acceptance of parties and finally amicable and agreeable to parties giving the sense of worth to value the identities and meanings they look for. This method of integration of applied spirituality and mediation can usher a liberation from the existing traditional system of adversarial nature as well as ease the release from pendency of cases that the system of the legal past crippling the present and the future of human tomorrow.

---

[1]Immersive workshops of cognitive behavioural psychotherapy, Neuro linguistic programing, solution focussed brief theory and integrated clinical hypnotherapy are some of the modalities available from the domain of modern human psychology that can possibly develop these experiential skills. These skills ought to be progressively integrated between the spiritual experiences of unity, multiplicity and harmony and legal ideals of equality, liberty, fraternity and dignity.

i. Core Skill: An objective awareness to witness

Meaning: An objective awareness to witness the proceedings of the mediation calmly within the conscious cognition and without having any bias and fixed beliefs towards any issues of the parties.

Strategies to Develop: Objective awareness to witness is developed when one practices the impersonality through constant disengagement of one's own ego by being conscious of any imposition and assertion of one views and meanings for the parties. This practice becomes easy when at every stage of the mediation, the mediator becomes mindful of things spoken, feelings shared and outcomes motivated for parties as per their choice. Control of the mediation as a balanced process ought to be left to the pace of parties and not to be regulated by the mediator in the conventional sense. A two-way method is to list down all the things that parties are identified with their problems that led to this litigation as well the expectation of the parties that range from all the tangibles to intangibles. Mediator moves around objectively witnessing the state of things that are gradually developing in the mediation process. Mediator paces and leads the parties.

ii. Core Skill: A stillness with sensory concentration

Meaning: A stillness with sensory concentration to avoid unnecessary reactions or agitations that human nature is prone to in taking sides on issues or become lop-sided in approach and consequently affecting mediation's outcome of peaceful settlement.

Strategies to Develop: A stillness with sensory concentration is developed when one practices the identification of detached observations of all reactions that take place in one's body, nervous systems, sensory reactions and perceptive judgements that the mind of cognition develops as coping-up mechanisms to express. Litigants know this very well as every stage of litigation is troubled by anxious expectations that builds pressure in both the central and physical nervous systems influencing the cognition, emotion, feeling, sensation and consequently the behaviour that demands a particular direction of solution. Mediator must be free first from his or her own reaction to things in mediation. Mediator must be like a mirror to reflect the face of the parties to make them understand the position they have taken and the position they prefer to through the use of positive suggestions. Mediator becomes a catalyst to move parties from problem-state to the solution-state or present-condition to preferred condition. By the presence of mediator, parties can experience the altered state of mind free from the pain of the problems confronting them.

iii. Core Skill: An empathy that animates and motivates

Meaning: An empathy that animates and motivates parties to look for win-win situation for both as against the adversarial method currently present in the legal system where one party loses and another party gains grounds, which results in bitterness in parties' relationships, rights and obligations.

Strategies to Develop: An empathy that animates and motivates parties to look for win-win situation for both sides is developed when mediator senses two things to lead the parties in mediation to observe, understand and collaborate. One, the sense of oneness that pervades as the unity of life at the background and two, sense of seeing and understanding the conflicts as evolution from divisiveness to progressive unity and the wanting of the need of harmony in interrelationships. Mediator must be capable of reflecting this inner reality of unity by which parties can experience the inner reality of the unity they need to live for. This art of reflecting or transposing the inner reality through kinaesthetic association of energies between parties and mediator makes it possible when mediator has the empathy to accept first the divisiveness in the nature of things without characterization of the same as right or wrong, judgement as good or bad leading to progressive exhaustive inclusion of things from both the sides. This gives a concrete example for the parties when they are in front of the mediator possessing this quality. Conflict is because of the multiplicity that is not yet tied down to the unity of the apparent divisive dots at the external level. Conflict and mediation is in fact a greater opportunity to grow and reinvigorate new terms in relationships.

iv. Core Skill: A pragmatic sensibility or practical responsibility

Meaning: A pragmatic sensibility or practical responsibility by which costs or damages or injuries of all kinds such as social, economic, profit-loss ratio, psychological or organizational stress etc., can be pre-calculated, meaningfully distributed and harmonized between parties by the mediator.

Strategies to Develop: A pragmatic sensibility or practical responsibility is developed only when parties accept the state of situation not as a point of tension rather a point of cohesion to develop. This practicality is crucial only when we accept spirituality as life-oriented and world-embracing through the knowledge of both oneness as unity without cancelling the multiplicity or diversity in which everything is integrated in the tripartite net of dependence, independence and interdependence. Thus, it can even be said that the mediator needs to be an applied spiritualist accepting life, challenges and a readiness to solve issues progressively and consultatively. To put the same in spiritual language, this kind of a mediation done by a mediator is truly a form of a dynamic meditation. And, to achieve success in this dynamic meditation, which we may now call as spiritual mediation, the mediator may need to actually sit in a quiet place inside within himself or herself, close eyes to sensory reactions and meditate upon how mediation ought to be in thinking, feeling, acting and behaving before parties. The various psycho-mental-sensory techniques and facilities of visual, auditory and kinaesthetic imagination and preparation can be helpful preliminarily tools towards a new pathway for mediation and settlement of conflicts.

The Bigger Picture: Infusing Four Major Spiritual Skills and Practical Strategies for Mediating Challenges of Sustainability

Sustainability and spirituality in one way mean the same thing or connect to certain common awareness when it comes to solutions. If sustainability in general means the one that which sustains, it can only be that, which is at its core whose phenomenon handles everything around from within and without. And, what is present at the core of anything is the spirit that underlies its inner composition holding from inside and the external organization of it in its movement outside. It is like the axis which holds all the spokes allowing the movement for an even and stable rotation. What is this axis that can connect the inner and outer phenomenon? It cannot be only social or economic or environmental or even a composition of all these three or even some of the two. This axis can only be the spirit or essence, universal, cosmic and eternal that can hold and move without disintegration of what it is made of which is getting expressed outwardly through the social, economic and environmental development of things in the march of human energies and socio-economic civilization. In this understanding of the core essence present at the axis of all, we arrive at a significant inter-related meanings common for both sustainability and spirituality. This axis connects the individual with the collective without cancelling the individual. It also connects the social, economic and environmental without any disintegration or destabilization or even cancelation of the life and world. It meets the world of resources with highest respect given to by connecting with the essential spirit of the resources. The discovery of this axis can be called the spiritual exploration that gives rise to integration outside from within which is what the struggle of the world of polarities are all about to find out the true source. This true source is the essence or consciousness or spirit from where an individual or a mediator or the parties of conflict experience all the four major new skills namely; an objective awareness to witness, a stillness with sensory concentration, an empathy that animates and motivates and a pragmatic sensibility or practical responsibility.

Unfortunately, we often hear about the sustainability only from the point of view of social, economic and environmental. There is nothing to show where the source-contact is or spirit-connect is. This external struggle to arrive at a cumulative point to feed our comfort and convenience created by the age of industrialization, self-aggrandisement, consumerist-commercialism etc., are just a shade that has caught the attention of the well-meaning people who dream to resolve this conflict outside without connecting it to the anchoring harmony from inside. This conflict can be harmonized only when we catch hold of the spirit that is glowing inside whose tentacles are developed outside as per the requirements of the society that human societies extrapolate outside seeing the supply and demand mode of the social, economic and environmental urgencies. The final call is that the human must plunge within to see what is there in store for all of us inside all the resources of the earth that we often touch without sense of its spirit. The method of learning to touch and sense the spiritual in every object, resource and thing is the future way of world and life. In short, it can be explained in this practical way. When the mediator holds the four major new skills as outlined above, they in turn leads him or her to the following co-equivalent skills or powers or values needed to resolve the challenges of sustainability through conflict settlement. They are outlined in the chart below (Fig. 12.1).

This is an experiential exercise that mediator needs to get trained through proper methods and techniques that are spiritual in core and follow through the path of the psychological elements of thought-emotion-sensation-body behaviour complex and taking inputs additionally from the social, economic and environmental. Four co-equivalent skills that get developed when connected with the inner and outer reflecting from both sides are; an intuitive sense that comes when witness position takes place from a state of peace and conscious awareness, an inspirational power that comes when senses are concentrated in the stillness of energies, an integrative assessment that comes from empathy which animates the motivation to identify the senses that cause the conflict to loosen, and, finally an intelligent action that aims at party reconciliation using pragmatic sensibility and practical responsibility common to both clients and meaningful to sustainability challenges. All these elements such as intuition, inspiration, integration and intelligence are outward dimension of the spirit that emanates from the inward dimension of the spiritual essence of the core from elements of witness, concentration, empathy and sensibility respectively. The actual challenges of the sustainability in conflict resolution that parties fight are on one side, whereas the conflicts between the social, economic and environmental are another set of challenges on the other side. The challenges of the mediator is to bring these two

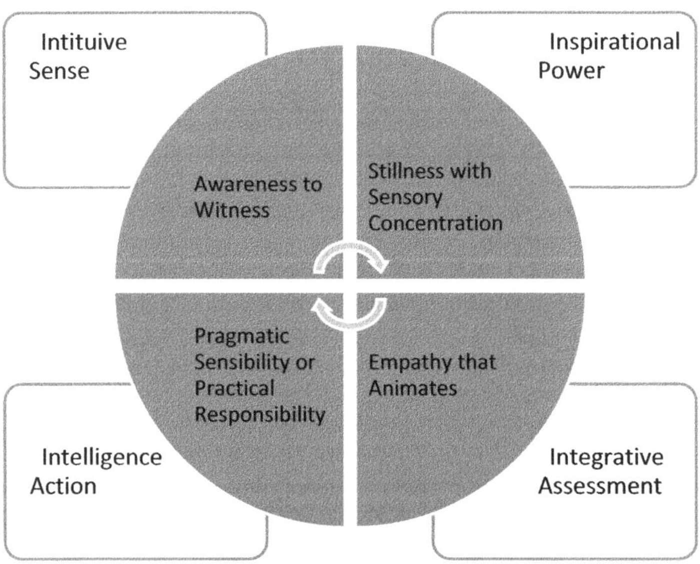

Fig. 12.1. Values Needed to Resolve the Challenges of Sustainability Through Conflict Settlement.

conflicting sides together harmoniously in the settlement of disputes using intuition, inspiration, integration and intelligence alongside four major new skills. The need to connect the inner and outer is from the side of issues as well as from the side of the parties who stick to their respective conflicts. Mediator becomes a catalyst in bringing the experience of all these dimensions of the issues and the parties in conflict when he or she remains in the position of the spirit using these four major new skills and co-equivalent skills and applying the same in the social, economic and environmental. This ought to be aided by training on the understanding of integral knowledge. At this juncture, Sri Aurobindo's explanation of integral knowledge becomes crucial to study here in the context of spirituality, sustainability and mediation.

An integral knowledge then must be a knowledge of the truth of all sides of existence both separately and in the relation of each to all and the relation of all to the truth of the Spirit. Our present state is an Ignorance and a many-sided seeking; it seeks for the truth of all things but, – as is evident from the insistence and the variety of the human mind's speculations as to the fundamental Truth which explains all others, the Reality at the basis of all things, – the fundamental truth of things, their basic reality must be found in some at once fundamental and universal Real; it is that which, once discovered, must embrace and explain all, – for 'That being known all will be known': the fundamental Real must necessarily be and contain the truth of all existence, the truth of the individual, the truth of the universe, the truth of all that is beyond the universe. The Mind, in seeking for such a Reality and testing each thing from Matter upwards to see if that might not be It, has not proceeded on a wrong intuition. All that is necessary is to carry the inquiry to its end and test the highest and ultimate levels of experience.[xi]

An integral knowledge demands an exploration, an unveiling of all the possible domains of consciousness and experience. For there are subjective domains of our being which lie behind the obvious surface; these have to be fathomed and whatever is ascertained must be admitted within the scope of the total reality. An inner range of spiritual experience is one very great domain of human consciousness; it has to be entered into up to its deepest depths and its vastest reaches.[xii]

The integral knowledge, then, can only come by an evolution of our being and our nature, and that would seem to signify a slow process in Time such as has accompanied the other evolutionary transformations. But as against that inference there is the fact that the evolution has now become conscious and its method and steps need not be altogether of the same character as when it was subconscious in its process. The integral knowledge, since it must result from a change of consciousness, can be gained by a process in which our will and endeavour have a part, in which they can discover and apply their own steps and method: its growth in us can proceed by a conscious self-transformation.[xiii]

This is an interesting phase in the history of dispute settlement hitherto unknown as the legal system has not yet seen such kind of trans-disciplinary interventions while dealing with conflicts of the human fighting against the resources of the Mother Nature. Though, this might sound new or novel or even awkward for those who are legal reductionists, this spiritual intervention cannot be avoided in any case as the issue of conflict cannot be resolved in the existing system of interventions using the social, distributive and political processes or to put it simply, using the mind that has a limitation to pierce through the veils to see the truth of the matter by experience.

Conclusion: Challenges Ahead

It must be remembered that all the four core skills along with co-equivalent skills are to be integrated with each and every other skills to form the perfect interrelationships to create a nexus between applied spirituality and mediation. These four core skills when developed in gradations, one sees each and every skill developed adds the development of the rest of the other skills. Essential challenge would be in the practice of the experience of the sense of awakening to that inner reality of our being, to that spirit or self or soul which is other than our mind, life and body where unity, oneness, harmony and acceptance are natural and automatic. This must be first borne by the mediator himself or herself either by self-training or institutional training. It is altogether a serious challenge when legal education and justice mechanisms have to become more aware of this experience of spiritual consciousness and its values useful for the discipline of law, justice and settlement by mediation. If mediator develops the inner calling and aspiration to know, to feel, to enter into contact with the greater Reality beyond that which is pervading the universe of all things in the society and that which inhabits also our own being, individual and collective, parties in the mediation, it becomes easy to be in communion with it, flow with it and finally pass on to those parties who are expecting a peaceful and agreeable solution through mediation and mediator. Rest of the developments come after this initial awakening and consequent turning to, a conversion to, and a progressive transformation of our whole being for successful mediation. A constant aspiration to get the connect with that harmony, a union with that unity using all the five sensory acuities and strategically observing the four core skills and co-equivalent skills can usher a new way towards a self and nature that is just, peaceful, harmonious and yet progressive to oneself and to all others around. This kind of applied spirituality and mediation can be a new way forward for sustainability.

Notes

i. The Mediation Bill, 2021, Volume I & II – Reports, presented to Hon'ble Chairperson, Rajya Sabha on 13th July, 2022, forwarded to Hon'ble Speaker, Lok Sabha on 13 July 2022, Report No. 117 before the Parliament of India, Rajya Sabha, Department-related Parliamentary Standing Committee on Personnel, Public Grievances, Law and Justice, Rajya Sabha Secretariat, New Delhi, July 2022/Ashadha, 1944 (Saka). For more details: https://prsindia.org/files/bills_acts/bills_parliament/2021/SC%20Report_Mediation%20bill.pdf for Volume I, https://prsindia.org/files/bills_acts/bills_parliament/2021/SC%20Report_Mediation%20bill_II.pdf for Volume II.

ii. Welcome to NJDG – National Judicial Data Grid. (n.d.). https://njdg.ecourts.gov.in/njdgnew/index.php.
iii. n.d. (i).
iv. Settlement through Mediation Report April 2021 to March 2022. (2022, April 25). National Legal Services Authority! https://nalsa.gov.in/statistics/settlement-through-mediation-report-april-2021-to-march-2022.
v. India Const. art. 19, cl. 1 (a). India Const. art. 269. Retrieved from https://cdnbbsr.s3waas.gov.in/s380537a945c7aaa788ccfcdf1b99b5d8f/uploads/2023/05/2023050195.pdf.
vi. MT Manual OF India – Contents Mediation Training Manual of India CHAPTER-XII 65- Role of Referral – India Supreme Court committee (n.d.). https://main.sci.gov.in/pdf/mediation/MT%20MANUAL%20OF%20INDIA.pdf.
vii. THE ODR POLICY PLAN FOR INDIA DESIGNING THE FUTURE OF DISPUTE RESOLUTION. (n.d.). https://www.niti.gov.in/sites/default/files/2021-11/odr-report-29-11-2021.pdf.
viii. Art of Living, M.P Pandit, Dipti Publications (1969), Sri Aurobindo Ashram, Pondicherry.
ix. Aurobindo, S. (1995). The Mother. Lotus Press. http://saccs.org.in/texts/mother/-ma-scienceofliving.php.
x. Page 889–890, The Life Divine, Sri Aurobindo, Volume 21–22, Sri Aurobindo Ashram Publications, 2005, Pondicherry.
xi. Page 680, The Life Divine, Sri Aurobindo, Volume 21–22, Complete Works of Sri Aurobindo, Sri Aurobindo Ashram Publications Department, 2005, Pondicherry.
xii. Page 677–678, The Life Divine, Sri Aurobindo, Volume 21–22, Complete Works of Sri Aurobindo, Sri Aurobindo Ashram Publications Department, 2005, Pondicherry.
xiii. Page 682, The Life Divine, Sri Aurobindo, Volume 21–22, Complete Works of Sri Aurobindo, Sri Aurobindo Ashram Publications Department, 2005, Pondicherry.

Chapter 13

Compassionate Policies to Relieve Systemic Suffering: *Visions, Obstacles, Strategies, Actions**

Robertson Work

Abstract

In this critical decade and century of climate chaos, ecocide and interconnected crises, a public policy approach is needed based on the primacy of compassionate action and ecological regeneration. Ecological regeneration focuses on the health of the Earth's planetary systems of water, soil, air, minerals, microbes, plants, insects and animals. Compassionate action is concerned with relieving the suffering and enhancing the happiness of the entire human population, present and future. An integral process is needed that brings these two priority concerns into the creation of new individual mindsets and behaviours and collective cultures and policies. The innovative leadership methods needed to realize these changes include mindfulness taught by Thich Nhat Hanh, group facilitation as formulated by the Institute of Cultural Affairs in its Technology of Participation (ToP), social artistry as developed by Jean Houston and four-quadrant thinking, planning and acting as expounded by Ken Wilber in his Integral Quadrants.

In this chapter, we will first identify some of the dimensions of humanity's systemic suffering. Next, we will review how the principles and practices of engaged Buddhism and compassionate action might help relieve that suffering. Then, we will explore some of the visions, obstacles, strategies and actions of compassionate policies that can help relieve systemic suffering.

Keywords: Public policy approach; technology of participation (ToP); patriarchy; misogyny; oligarchy; plutocracy; corporatocracy

*The chapter is based primarily on the first two chapters of the author's book A Compassionate Civilization: The Urgency of Sustainable Development and Mindful Activism – Reflections and Recommendations (2017).

Applied Spirituality and Sustainable Development Policy, 241–264

doi:10.1108/978-1-83753-380-020231013

Breathing in peace for myself, breathing out peace for people and planet.

Breathing in happiness for myself, breathing out happiness for people and planet.

Breathing in understanding for myself, breathing out understanding for people and planet.

Breathing in compassion for myself, breathing out compassion for people and planet.

Introduction

We are living in the most critical time in human history, a time to do what is needful or face the direst of consequences. Never in the past 5000 years have humans faced such colossal dangers and such exhilarating possibilities. The very future of life on Earth is at stake. We face multiple, interlocking crises, any one of which could be decisive – climate chaos, misogyny, systemic poverty, oligarchy, prejudice and a culture of violence. A whole system transformation is underway, and we are at the brink of either mass extinction or a whole new way of being human on planet Earth. The outcome depends on what you and I do with our lives.

Humanity's Systemic Suffering

Climate Chaos and Degradation of Ecosystems

The natural systems of Earth that have supported human civilization for the past 12,000 years are changing drastically, and human societies must change quickly, as well as adapt to an already-different Earth over the long term. The effects of global climate change and degradation of ecosystems are upon us. We had thought that fossil fuels were a brilliant solution for our energy needs. It turns out that they have been destroying our life support systems of air, water, ice, soil, plants and animals by releasing carbon dioxide from the extraction and burning of coal, oil and gas, creating 'death energy' – energy derived from dead life forms that is killing living beings now. Carbon dioxide, methane gas and other greenhouse gases released into the atmosphere are rapidly warming the planet. The Greenland ice cap is melting. Antarctica, which boasts 90% of Earth's ice, is melting. Mountain glaciers in the Andes and Himalayas and the Siberian permafrost are melting. We are at over 400 parts per million (ppm) of carbon dioxide in the atmosphere, already above 350 ppm, which has been calculated as the highest concentration possible without dangerously heating up Earth.

If the rise of carbon dioxide and the warmth of Earth's atmosphere go unabated, the oceans will rise up to six feet, flood coastal cities and submerge many island nations and other inhabited landmasses. We already see acidification of the oceans, extensive deforestation, massive desertification, droughts, wildfires and food collapse.

Mega-storms will become the norm. There is already a massive dieback of species, indicating the sixth mass extinction (the first five: Ordovician-Silurian, Late Devonian, Permian, Triassic-Jurassic and Cretaceous-Tertiary). There will be social, political and economic volatility with mass migrations and resource wars. Drinking water will become scarce, and wars will be fought over this life-essential resource. The next several years will tell the story of our future – misery or happiness. We must and can change our ways now.

Patriarchy and Misogyny

For thousands of years, it has been often understood that men are dominant and should control and lead women and society as a whole. This view – *patriarchy* – has been strengthened by the world's religions with their predominately male gods, male saviours and male priests. Some men fear and even hate women. Women have often been kept silent, subservient, abused, trapped at home and pregnant and have not been allowed to exercise their human rights of speech, choice, career and leadership. This is *misogyny*.

The problem with these views is that in addition to harming women themselves, they have kept women from exercising their rightful leadership in society at all levels. Without honouring women's views, knowledge and wisdom, societies have become overly masculinized and promote and celebrate violence and warfare, destruction of the natural world, harmful competition and technology without heart.

Systemic Poverty and Social Deprivation

648 million people live on less than two dollars per day (December 2022, World Bank), and 4.2 billion lack access to sanitation (June 2019, World Health Organization). Some 2.2 billion have no access to safe water. Around 5 million preventable child deaths occur each year. In the past 30 years, income inequality has skyrocketed. One percent of the world's population owns 50% of the world's wealth. And in the United States, the top 1% owns as much wealth as the bottom 90%. We humans are still plagued by illiteracy, illness and ignorance. Our educational systems are not adequate for all the people. Likewise, our health systems are tragically unable to provide even basic care to all people everywhere, and people suffer senseless illnesses.

Our modern economies are based on capital, profit, debt, interest and the global gambling casino of investing. Money accumulation for a few has become more important than the well-being of all people and nature. Economic enterprises based on fossil fuel energy pollute the air, water and soil, and abuse human labour. Our economies are often killing us, other life-forms and our planetary ecosystems. Fiscal policy is made by global elites that control the formation and movement of capital through central banks and investment firms. The 1% has become consumed by greed and power. Austerity for the masses and opulence for the few is not the human way.

The number of poor people has expanded, and the middle class has been significantly weakened. Many people don't have adequate income or access to quality education and health services. The global COVID-19 pandemic has taken a much larger toll on the poor. The economic system based on accumulation and greed is designed to favour the wealthy. If you have money, you can make money with money. If you don't have money, you must work for wages that are often inadequate to support you and your family. One of the many problems with this situation is that most people are suffering and do not see how they can sustain their lives.

Oligarchy, Plutocracy and Corporatocracy

The democratic experiment of more than 300 years is faltering badly around the world. Oligarchy, plutocracy and corporatocracy are masquerading as democratic regimes. Elites are manipulating democratic institutions to maintain control of political, economic and military power. We are experiencing a deep crisis of governance. Democratic elections and representation around the world have been greatly weakened by a few powerful people. For example, only 158 families provided half of the money supporting presidential candidates for the 2016 US elections. When a few families control a country, it is an *oligarchy*. When a few wealthy people control a country, it is a *plutocracy*. In the United States and other nations, corporations are controlling elections, legislation and the mass media to control society. This is *corporatocracy*. One of the problems with this trend is that the needs, voices and wisdom of middle-class and poor people are being ignored, and they are suffering.

Bigotry and Prejudice

People who are different or in the minority are often looked down on and frequently harmed. This includes people of different races, ethnic groups, religions, economic classes and sexual orientations. People often fear and hate others who exhibit different beliefs, cultural norms and personal behaviours. We face a crisis of the 'sunset effect' – that is, when an era is ending, there is often the appearance of its strengthening, as in the last burst of a sunset's rays. We see this effect in fear-based religious fundamentalisms that are at war with an empirical, scientific worldview and the principles of inclusiveness and respect for differences of opinion. This is *bigotry* or *prejudice.*

These confused views are based on ignorance and misunderstanding of the basic rights of every person and group to be who and what they decide. Many people are not aware that there are not many races but rather only one human race. The problem with these views is that they cause many people to suffer.

Continuous Warfare and a Culture of Violence

There are enough nuclear weapons on Earth to destroy human civilization several times over. Some countries shoot missiles into other countries without being attacked or provoked and without UN authorization. Some conflicts rage on for decades, destroying infrastructure and human communities and creating huge numbers of refugees seeking safety and new homes. People in other countries are often feared and attacked with massive use of armaments. This is *militarism*. People think that their country is always right and is the only one that is important. This is *nationalism*. The wars in Ukraine, Yemen, Myanmar and Syria are some of the latest tragedies of this sort.

Many people assume that a pervasive culture of violence is natural and inevitable. Entertainment, media and video games extend violence into the everyday life of adults and children. The value and meaning of human life are demeaned or denied in all of this.

These six crises are interwoven and mutually causative. There is, however, a doorway and a pathway forward. The crises themselves can be opportunities that can wake us up to our delusions and self-inflicted suffering and motivate us to reinvent our societies.

Engaged Buddhism and Compassionate Action

Compassion is not to pity but to suffer with, to understand, to empathize, to feel, to be with and for. I am on your side. I am like you, and you are like me. We are one. We both suffer. We both desire happiness and the relief of suffering. I vow to help relieve your suffering. Compassion.

Civilization is civil, civility, about the citizen, the one who belongs. It has many dimensions – cultural, social, political, economic and environmental. What if everyone were to belong to this emerging civilization, all people and all life-forms – an Earth community, the biosphere, the noosphere (the layer of consciousness enveloping our planet), human society as part of great nature?

Even now, a compassionate civilization is emerging. We have come thus far over these billions, millions, thousands, hundreds of years. Will we yet go further, further than ever before? Will we, you and I, embrace all, everyone, as a sister and fellow citizen of Earth society? Will we suffer together? Relieve our suffering together? Laugh together? Be happy together? Realize our full potential together? It is possible. And it has become an utter necessity. Will we make it together or not make it at all?

The choice is ours. Would we not rather angle towards a compassionate civilization? Let's go together.

How would we design such a civilization? How would we construct it? How would we embody it in our minds, behaviours, cultures and policies?

Let's explore together. In fact, many are already at work on this great and noble task. Many individuals of goodwill and their organizations, networks and movements are hard at work around the planet. Let's recognize each other, thank each other, encourage each other and move forward together. Some are at work on climate chaos mitigation and adaptation, renewable energy and sustainable environment. Others are promoting gender equality and human rights. And still others are working for social and economic justice, cultural and religious tolerance, participatory and transparent governance, peace and nuclear disarmament, and spiritual practice and enlightenment.

Yes, of course there is resistance. There are powerful forces saying that it is impossible to construct a compassionate civilization. They will resist, block and fight. They will say that human beings are weak and selfish and must be controlled and punished. The powerful will say that they deserve their power and will try to maintain a civilization of inequality, injustice, unsustainability, nonparticipation, intolerance and violence. They will use force to get their way. But the eight billion of us humans and countless billions of other life-forms can move forward like an unstoppable tidal wave, droplet by gentle droplet. The stakes are too high not to press on.

I was very pleased when Jeremy Rifkin published in 2009 his groundbreaking book, *The Empathic Civilization*. Contrary to the belief that human beings are basically selfish, he clearly shows that human beings are fundamentally empathic. We are programmed to feel what others feel.

When I imagined a world of sustainable human development catalysed by a movement of movements, I began to use the term *empathic civilization*. Over the past few years, I wrote and spoke about this vision in UN global conferences and in my graduate classes at NYU Wagner: 'Ours is a critical decade and century of crisis and opportunity. We *can* create a new, empathic civilization. We can and must mitigate climate chaos, protect the environment, achieve gender equality, promote social and economic justice, institutionalize participatory governance, realize cultural tolerance, and foster peace'.

After working with this for some time, I came to understand that we must move beyond empathy to build a *compassionate* civilization. What is the difference? With empathy, we feel what others are feeling and identify with them. Compassion goes further by sharing in the suffering of others and vowing to relieve their suffering. We suffer together, and we will relieve our suffering together. My own experience confirms what all the world's wisdom traditions have articulated – that compassion and understanding are the deep structures of being human.

For me, combining compassion and civilization provides an inspiring vision of a macro-historical-societal system infused with a powerful ethical stance based in human nature itself. My hope is that this concept may empower those of us working to create a better world, a world that works for everyone and protects the environment, one that is both pro-people and pro-planet.

May we relieve the suffering of all beings everywhere.

It has been said that compassion and wisdom are the two inseparable wings of the bird of awakening, allowing movement through life's often-volatile currents. Compassion is 'suffering with' and vowing to relieve another's suffering as one's own. Wisdom is the understanding of the fundamental nature of reality, its utter interdependence and continuous transformation.

As we negotiate the early years of this make-or-break century, we need to cultivate and manifest these two skilful means in mind, body, heart, speech and action. Fortunately, there are many practices to help us do this, including meditation, ethical studies, yoga, journaling, movement, art, reading, spending time in nature, volunteering, prayer, contemplation, liturgy and being part of a practice community. The most important practice, however, is to bring mindfulness and kindness into our daily lives, moment by moment.

How does compassion manifest itself, and from where does it arise? It seems to me that its basis is a gift of our mammalian heritage.

All mammals have awareness of and empathy with others of their kind. This is true especially of our close relative, the chimpanzee, but it is also true of elephants and dolphins. Neurologically, we know that the mammalian brain's mirror neurons allow one organism to literally experience what it sees happening to another. We warm-blooded mammals have evolved to care about each other and to express affection for each other.

With human beings, this capacity is both deepened and broadened. We feel each other's suffering and desire to help another relieve her or his suffering. We know what our own suffering is like, and we want to relieve it. In like manner, we want to help others relieve their suffering because we know what it is like when it is our own.

But with us, our compassion extends far beyond our own species. We also can experience compassion for other animal species and for Earth's plants, water, air, soil and minerals. This I believe is because we are essentially Earthlings and children of the evolving cosmos. Someone has said that we are a star's way of looking at a star. I would add that we are a star's way of loving a star.

Compassion arises from our basic nature of empathy, care and love – our basic goodness. This is one reason why we are shocked when someone harms another person. It is not expected; it is shocking and is not our usual way of being. We are communal beings. We love to be with others of our kind and to care for each other. The source of compassion is neither more nor less than our very being. Compassion, then, is ontological, as well as biological and sociological. We are the heart, eyes and hands of compassion itself.

But why then, you ask, do you and I harm others if our basic nature is compassion? Why are there violence, warfare, poverty and injustice in human society? One answer is that our basic goodness becomes obscured and distorted by negative emotions of fear, anger, hatred, greed, ignorance, jealousy and pride. Our attachment to what we mistakenly see as our separate self or ego poisons our mind and heart and creates confusion and harmful behaviour.

Therefore, we must continually *practice* letting go of self-attachment and *practice* cherishing others. We must wake up again and again from the nightmare of our confused mind to our true nature of interdependence. We must train our minds to follow our deepest impulses – that is, compassion – and not be overtaken by negative emotions.

How do we know compassion? We can read about it. We can ask others about it. We can experience receiving it. We can experience giving it to others. But what is it, and how do we know that it is it?

Compassion is to be with suffering, either someone else's or one's own, and to help relieve that suffering. There are of course many forms of suffering, including pain, anxiety, worry, fear, angst, disorientation, boredom, ignorance, sickness, abuse, dissatisfaction, anguish, loss, grief, humiliation and on and on. What is involved in being with and relieving our own suffering?

Sometimes, we can relieve our suffering by doing something tangible. If we are hungry, we can eat. But what if there is no food available? If we have a headache, we can take a pain killer. But what if it doesn't help? What if there is nothing tangible to be done to relieve our suffering? Then, we can work with our suffering in the following ways.

First, we can *acknowledge* our form or experience of suffering. Then, we can *accept* this suffering. Next, we can be utterly *present* to it. We can *comfort* it and be *kind* to our suffering. We can then *recognize* its true nature of impermanence and interdependence – that is, it will not be forever. It will change when causes and conditions change. It will dissipate and become something else. Finally, we can *let go* of our suffering.

Once we have learnt how to relieve our own suffering, we can help others relieve theirs. If someone is hungry, we can give him food. If someone is sick, we can take her to a doctor. At the societal level, we can relieve suffering by creating compassionate policies and programs, such as food stamps, universal health care, affordable housing, job training, a living wage, affirmative action and environmental protection.

The epistemology of compassion involves shining the light of awareness on the experience of suffering and letting that pure awareness begin to transform that experience and our relationship to it. May our compassion release and guide us to be there for others, as well as for us.

Next, we explore the visions, obstacles, strategies and actions that can carry us towards our greatest potentials as humans.

Visions, Obstacles, Strategies and Actions of How to Relieve Systemic Suffering with Compassionate Policies[1]

A Vision of Compassionate Policies

Today, we celebrate the victory before the victory. We celebrate the emergence of a new civilization of compassion. It is even now in our midst. It is often hard to see, given the chaos and suffering surrounding us and filling our minds. Yet we see it again and again in the many simple acts of kindness between and among people.

Earlier, I shared a few thoughts about a compassionate civilization. Before sharing a few concrete images of a vision of a new civilization of compassion, I should first say something about the nature of visioning.

[1]This section is based on the four parts of the strategic planning process of the Technology of Participation (ToP) created by the Institute of Cultural Affairs (ICA.) The four parts are vision, obstacles, strategies and actions.

I agree with the statement 'Where there is no vision, the people perish' (Proverbs 29). Having a sense of where you are going – or, more importantly, where you want to go – is very important to human motivation and happiness. If we are cut off from a sense of a meaningful future, it is often hard to live in this moment. However, the good news is that this moment is full and perfect and contains memories, anticipations and the gift of the 'eternal now'.

The more visceral and experiential our vision is of a hoped-for future, the more motivation we have to move towards it. It is what Dr. Jean Houston calls the 'lure of becoming'. We are literally pulled towards an attractive image and vision of a future that we desire. When we begin to envision a new civilization of kindness and happiness, we must do so on many levels and dimensions. We will experience this vision in four dimensions as Dr. Houston teaches in her work on social artistry, with our five senses (physical), with our mind's eye (psychological), through stories and symbols (mythic), and with a profound sense of embodiment (unitive). We will also envision a hoped-for future in terms of the Ken Wilber: mindsets, behaviors, cultures and systems that comprise it as in Ken Wilber's integral quadrant model.

We need to be clear on the crises, problems and challenges, but we also need to dream of a new world that is so attractive that it beckons us and motivates us to create it. What are your greatest hopes for the future? What is indeed possible? What is necessary? What would a new civilization of compassion look like? Remember, compassion is not only feeling the pain of others but also vowing to relieve others' suffering.

Compassion in the first instance is not religious or even spiritual. It is a natural response of living beings who have empathy for each other and want to help each other. Parents are one of the best examples of compassion. Most of them will do anything to help relieve the suffering of their children and to help them be happy. A compassionate civilization is the universalization of this quality of compassion directed towards all beings everywhere. Or it can be called love, or care, or being neighbourly, or helpful.

What might a new civilization of compassion look like? It will be based on six principles: sustainability, equality, justice, participation, tolerance and nonviolence.

Environmental Sustainability

The new civilization of compassion will embody environmental sustainability at its very core. As Naomi Klein writes, 'Climate change isn't just a crisis. It's a chance to build a better world'. We will protect the natural environment. People will realize that there can be no human life without healthy ecosystems of air, water, soil, plants and animals. We will keep the remaining fossil fuels – death energy – in the ground. All energy will be from renewable sources, such as the sun, wind, water, geothermal sources and algae – or 'life energy'. The new economy can be 100% environmentally friendly. The green energy revolution can sustain life on Earth for millions of years.

Gender Equality

A compassionate civilization will embody gender equality in every facet of human society. Women will be leaders at every level of society. They will be paid the same as men for the same work. The voices, views and wisdom of women will be honoured and celebrated. Men will respect and protect the sovereignty of women's bodies and minds. Gender and sexual orientation will be understood and accepted as taking a multiplicity of forms. Women, who 'hold up half the sky', will be free to be who and what they are.

Socioeconomic Justice

A compassionate civilization will embody socioeconomic justice. Everyone will have meaningful engagement, adequate income and access to high-quality education and health services as a human right. We will reinvent money as a means of caring for all life on Earth and stop the endless drive for profit, extraction, consumption, production and wealth accumulation. We will learn 'sacred economics' from Charles Eisenstein, with capital not being based on debt and interest. Bartering will increase. Local currencies will be developed. We will create local, national and global economies that are pro-people and pro-planet. We will make the shift from an economy based on greed to an economy of generosity.

Participatory Governance

A compassionate civilization will embody participatory governance to achieve the UN's 17 Sustainable Development Goals (SDGs). The needs, voices, views and wisdom of all people will set the policy agendas for society through new processes and institutions of direct democracy. This will include face-to-face and online policy dialogue. Accountability, transparency and responsiveness will be present at all levels of governance. E-governance will bring policy-making closer to the people.

Cultural Tolerance

A compassionate civilization will embody cultural tolerance. It will be understood and accepted that all people of every race, ethnic background, religion, culture, economic class, lifestyle orientation and nationality will be respected and free to exercise their rights as human beings. People will enjoy learning from others who have different backgrounds and orientations to life. Empathic consciousness will be the new common sense. An evolutionary Earth story will be understood by all.

Peace and Nonviolence

A compassionate civilization will embody peace and nonviolence. Nuclear weapons will be outlawed. War itself will be seen as illegitimate. A culture of peace will prevail as everyone comes to understand empathy and compassion as the underlying foundations of being human.

At this point, you may be saying to yourself, 'But all this sounds utopian. Is it possible to achieve?' If we do not head for utopia, we will be left in endless dystopia of environmental degradation and social misery.

Using Ken Wilber's Four Integral Systems Quadrants to Envision at Hoped-For Future

Using the framework of Ken Wilber's four integral systems quadrants (interior/exterior and individual/collective), what will be the new mindsets, behaviours, cultures and policies of the emerging civilization of compassion? (Table 13.1)

Individual Mindsets

Individuals will exhibit a common sense of mutuality and interdependence. An awareness of our planet's fragile ecosystem will be widespread. Individuals will understand whole systems and think in integral patterns and processes. Intuition will be as important as rationality. Individuals will value integrity and kindness above all else. Education will have expanded people's understanding to include vast stretches of time and space. Individuals will grasp that they are each unique and unrepeatable and have special capacities to be developed and shared with others. People will think of themselves as citizens of the universe, the Milky Way galaxy, our solar system and planet Earth.

Individual Behaviours

People will tend to act responsibly towards each other and the natural world. Leadership will have become servant leadership – facilitative, interactive, dialogical, participatory, profound, inspirational and authentic. Teamwork and

Table 13.1. Based on the Four-Quadrant Integral Framework of Ken Wilber from his book *The Integral Vision*, 2007.

Four-Quadrant Integral Framework (Based on Ken Wilber's Writing)		
	Interior	***Exterior***
Individual	Mindsets	Behaviours
	Consciousness	Interpersonal
	Awareness	Group Skills
	Values	Relationships
	Attitudes	Partnerships
Collective	Cultures	Systems
	Myth/Stories	Policies
	Rituals	Institutions
	Symbols	Organizations
	Norms	Communities

collaboration will be common practice. Individuals will be genuinely interested in other people of different mind-sets, lifestyles, cultures and religions and desire to learn from them. People will gather in beautiful, green public spaces for social and political discourse and to share their insights, creativity, knowledge and questions. Almost everyone will be engaged in spiritual practices such as meditation, contemplation, prayer, yoga, visualization, journal writing, or community celebrations.

Collective Cultures

Cultures will have evolved to assume sexual and gender equality and human rights as the natural order of things. Equality and justice will be held as universal values. Care for natural systems of water, air, soil, plants and animals will be deeply ingrained in the collective psyche. New stories and myths will have been fashioned from empirical observation and analysis of the evolution of the universe and life on Earth. There will be many powerful symbols of unity, compassion and understanding. The historical religions will have evolved to honour each other's profound insights of reality, human nature, love and truth. Many heroines and heroes who helped humanity realize a civilization of compassion will be celebrated widely. Happiness and well-being will be understood as the birthright of every living creature. Great celebrations of life on Earth will take place frequently.

Collective Policies

Renewable energy will be the law of the land, and climate change will have been dealt with through mitigation and adaptation. Governance institutions, policies and systems will be highly responsive, accountable and transparent to citizen participation and opinion by virtue of respectful face-to-face dialogue and consensus-building and through the internet and social media. Education, health care, housing, water, food and income will be universal rights, as will other necessities of life. Economies will be designed to provide needed goods and services for the well-being of all people and nature. Money will have been reinvented as an instrument for universal well-being rather than for individual power and control. The family will have evolved to embrace different possibilities for localized commitment, care and nurture. The justice system would have shifted its orientation from judgement and punishment to accountability, reconciliation and rehabilitation.

Imagining a New World of Sustainable Human Development

Imagination is very powerful. Architects imagine their creations before putting pen to paper. Drafters of constitutions imagine how their nations will function effectively. Athletes imagine achieving perfect form before competing. Visualizing, dreaming and envisioning are practical tools for inventing the new. Each one of us imagines what we hope the future will bring. How might we imagine a new world of sustainable human development?

I dream a world of.

- an abundance of safe water, food and other life sustenance and a sharing of that abundance with all people and all life-forms
- societies devoted to creating conditions that foster the discovery and realization of each person's full creativity, potential and spiritual awakening
- women in leadership roles at every level of society in equal partnership and mutual respect with men
- ubiquitous music, art, poetry, dance and theatre performed and enjoyed by everyone who wishes
- a universal love for learning about, reading about and exploring mental landscapes
- peace, harmony and tranquility balanced with passion, challenge and a zest for living fully
- natural beauty of land, water, air, plants and animals
- architectural elegance of dwellings and the commons for all
- 100% renewable energy from the sun, wind, water and geothermal
- sustainable local communities of significant, trusting and happy relationships
- planetary virtual conversations involving 10 billion human minds and voices
- meaningful celebrations of every individual birth, life milestone and death and every societal, cultural, religious and planetary milestone
- physical, emotional and mental health enjoyed by all
- participatory decision-making in governance at local, national, regional and planetary levels
- lifelong education for all children and adults in the physical and social sciences and the arts and humanities
- fiscal, monetary and economic systems that promote the well-being of all people and all of nature
- a rich diversity of lifestyles with mutual respect, understanding and sharing of insights about being human
- families devoted to the development of children and the care and happiness of each member
- continuous innovation of safe technologies that will enhance the experience of being alive
- a vast number of optional and changing roles for living, working, serving, creating and learning

May we each awaken and live our dream. May our dreams indeed come true. May our dreams lead us, pull us and push us ever onward with hope and passion. May the words *I have a dream* always resound in our hearts. May 'dream time' be our time. May you have a good dream this day and this night, so that many others may wake up one fine day in a new reality.

Most change agents are focused on a single issue. If we have a civilizational vision, we can feel ourselves being part of a massive movement of movements, moving relentlessly towards our most cherished hopes and dreams. By identifying an emerging civilization based on principles of compassion, sustainability, equality, justice, participation, tolerance and peace, we can sense our individual contributions as part of something larger and more profound. We are not only mitigating climate change, but we are also catalysing a whole system shift resulting in a compassionate civilization.

I am reminded of the old story of the stonecutters in the Middle Ages of Europe. Someone asked one stonecutter what he was doing. He said, 'I am cutting stones'. The person asked another stonecutter the same question. He replied, 'I am supporting my family'. Then, the person asked yet another stonecutter, who said with dignity and passion, 'I am building a cathedral!' Was each stonecutter doing the same thing? What difference does your vision make in your day-to-day life?

We know that there is only change. We look back at history and evolution and should be astounded by the radical transformations that have brought us to this moment – from clans of hunter-gatherers, to farming settlements, to cities, and empires, to a single planetary ecology. And we are all visionaries. Our visions are hopeful, despairing, or boring. How we use our imaginations, not just our intellects, is a powerful force in creating the future. If we are indeed able to avoid dystopia, what are our best hopes and dreams for the future of life on Earth?

What Might a Compassionate Civilization Look, Sound, Feel, Taste and Smell Like?

When I walk around in a hoped-for future, I see smiles, hear laughter, feel warmth, taste gratitude and smell possibility. I see art everywhere and groups of people sharing ideas and stories. I hear someone acknowledging a challenging experience a stranger is having in a way that honours that stranger. People stop to tell me that they feel happy to be alive. People are enjoying the fascinating tastes of healthy foods from different cultures. I smell fresh air.

I see the headline 'CEOs Agree Tenfold Is Fair' marking a new policy that a company's highest salary will be no more than 10 times that of the lowest. I hear people talking with each other about their observations, art practices, crafts, gardens, reflections, poetry, inventions, commitments and spiritual practices. People feel at ease with others from very different backgrounds and lifestyles. People taste oneness and smell compassion.

What about you? When you close your eyes and visualize a hoped-for future, what pops up? What is going on in your new compassionate culture, family structure, economy, political process, health system, educational structure and ecosystem? Enjoy the image, and then let the warmth of your vision flow into your life and work.

In a compassionate civilization, empathy, altruism and kindness will be pre-eminent values and expressions. Whole societies will greatly admire these qualities and the individuals and groups that manifest them. Greed will be seen as a base desire. Selfishness and harming others will be understood as tragic character flaws. Humility, sharing, cooperation and collaboration will be celebrated as highly evolved traits.

It will be commonly understood that happiness is a way of being instead of a goal to be sought. Happiness will not be experienced in the acquisition of things but through helping others and being alive to daily relationships, observations, reflections, learning, creativity and communication.

Entire societies of a compassionate civilization will exalt the common good and will ensure that both the natural and the built commons are sustained and sustainable while celebrating the unique contributions of individuals, communities, organizations, cultures and bioregions. Societies will continually refine themselves to ensure that optimal conditions are in place for developing and sharing the full potential of each living being.

In a compassionate civilization, humanity has awakened from the trance of ever-increasing consumption-production and has evolved to never-ending learning-caring. One resource that illustrates this vision beautifully is the profound Charter for Compassion movement launched by Karen Armstrong.

May we each realize happiness, peace, understanding and compassion!

The future is both a continuation of and a departure from the past. On the one hand, there is nothing new under the sun. On the other, nothing is ever the same. There is only change. And what we do in the present moment can bend history or spark evolution in entirely new directions.

The flow of cause and effect, including DNA and cultural assumptions, maintains the repetition of old habits. Yet a new idea, word, deed, or technology can create a surprising new possibility. How can this be? How can these two forces inform those who would catalyse a compassionate civilization?

Earlier, we did a bit of dreaming of a new future of deep structural compassion and understanding. From today's perspective, it may seem utterly impossible to realize. However, when we look at transformations in evolution and history that have brought us to this moment, we are shocked by discontinuity after discontinuity.

For example, our species has journeyed from the advent of speech, to writing by hand, to movable type, to the printing press, telegraphy, radio, telephone, television, faxes, the Internet, and now social media, virtual reality, and artificial intelligence. Five thousand or even 100 years ago, who would have believed that we could be blogging with anyone on planet Earth in real time?

Or think of the ideas and social inventions that have changed human history. A short list could include the advent of tribal customs, ethics and law, the polis, conscience, universal love, common law, freedom, equality, democracy, the scientific method, human rights, evolution and ecology.

Our dreams can become reality if we invest in them with clarity and passion and commit ourselves to speak, write, invent and embody them regardless of doubts, setbacks and disappointments.

Yes, we *can and will* catalyse a compassionate civilization of climate change mitigation and adaptation...renewable energy...sovereignty and leadership of women at all levels of society...participatory and transparent governance...universal education and health care...economic opportunity and justice...cultural and religious tolerance...individual creativity and expression...and spiritual practice and development. The movement of movements is alive and well.

Continuing with the strategic planning process of the technology of participation (ToP) developed by the Institute of Cultural Affairs (ICA), next we will begin to analyse the obstacles that could block the realization of a policy vision of a compassionate civilization (of which there are many). Next, we will identify the strategies that will deal with those blocks and move us towards our policy vision. Then, we will create actions and implementation plans for the policies.

Obstacles That Could Block the Creation of Compassionate Policies

What do you think are the biggest obstacles facing us? What is holding us back from realizing a compassionate civilization? What blocks, gaps and inhibiting factors do we presently experience? They are legion, of course and powerful and threatening. But after we identify them and their underlying root system, we may discover that they are the doorways to the future. Let us look with unflinching honesty at some of our current obstacles.

Using Wilber's quadrants of mindsets, behaviours, cultures and systems again, here are some of our current roadblocks.

Mistaken Individual Mindsets

'I'm all that matters. Climate change is a hoax. Women are men's property. Nature is an endless resource for humans. Guns keep us safe. War is the natural way to resolve disputes. Animals don't have intelligence or feelings. Water is just a commodity. Austerity will strengthen the economy. The bottom line is money. If people can't make it on their own, they should not live. My race is superior. Poor people are lazy. Only my religion is true. If someone does something wrong, that person should be locked away. We don't need government. Government is the problem. The UN is trying to take over the world. Evolution is not true. Science and learning are dangerous. Unlimited profit keeps the economy going. My language is superior. Greed is good. I am filled with hate. Narcissism is natural'.

Harmful Individual Behaviours

'I must pack a gun. Rape is the woman's fault. Child abuse just happens. I have many addictions (TV, sex, drugs, overeating, etc.). Sometimes, my wife makes me hit her. Human beings are naturally violent. Sometimes, you must be disrespectful and put people in their place. Bullying is part of being a kid. Lying is the way to get your way. If I get angry or am afraid, I will probably have to shoot someone'.

Misguided Collective Cultures

'We believe in male dominance in government, business, family, etc. We champion the profit motive. The suit is our uniform. We value greed, wealth, and conspicuous consumption. We must consume more and produce more. We humans are destined to dominate nature. We believe that we will always have poor people. We believe that might makes right'.

Harmful Collective Policies and Systems

'We must extract, process, and burn fossil fuels. We remove mountaintops. We pollute the air and water. We frack. We are increasing ocean acidification. We are causing mega-storms, droughts, fires, deforestation, food-production collapse, glacial melting, sea rise, and the loss of coastal areas and islands. We promote GMOs and unhealthy food. We have costly or unavailable health care. We have systemic poverty. We have nuclear power plants with radioactive waste. We must have dividends and interest to make money from money. We should have low taxation for the rich for "trickle down." We encourage unlimited incomes. We have crumbling infrastructure. We abuse and neglect the commons and public goods. We must govern ourselves through fascism, plutocracy, oligarchy, corporatocracy, systemic corruption, biased media, or cronyism'.

What Is Blocking the Emergence of a Compassionate Civilization?

What are the deep roots supporting and holding the realities that are blocking the emergence of a compassionate civilization? Greed, pride, fear, anger, hatred and ignorance are some of the deepest roots of confusion and harm.

Greed: the belief that one cannot have too much, even if others have little or nothing; the behaviour of amassing more and more wealth and power and being unwilling to share with others; the culture of narcissism, conspicuous consumption and materialism; the systems that allow a few individuals to make money with money without appropriate taxation for the maintenance of the commons, public goods and assistance for those who are less fortunate.

Pride: the belief that my race, class, gender, sexual orientation, culture, religion, nation and political ideology are superior to all others; the behaviour of caring only for oneself and one's small circle; the culture of egoism, patriarchy, racism, sexism, ethnocentricity, xenophobia, theocracy, homophobia and ideological rigidity; the systems that allow a few people to oppress others and force their views on them.

Fear: the belief that the self is in danger and that people who are different are dangerous; the behaviour of armouring and arming oneself; the culture of insecurity, defensiveness and self-protection; the systems that protect the wealthy and the powerful at all costs.

Anger: the belief that one's negative emotions towards others should be expressed; the behaviour of doing harm to others with words and actions; the culture of violence; the systems of weapons and warfare as inevitable.

Hatred: the belief that the other deserves to be despised; the behaviour of harming others; the culture of violence; the systems that allow the other to be controlled and punished.

Ignorance: the belief that other people and nature are separate from and not as important as oneself; the behaviour of doing harm to other people and ecosystems; the culture of total self-absorption; the systems that allow a few wealthy and powerful people to distort society towards their own gain without concern for others.

We must find and create many ways to awaken ourselves and others to authentic understanding and compassion. Remember: 'The task before us now, if we would not perish, is to shake off our ancient prejudices, and to build the Earth' (Teilhard de Chardin, *Building the Earth*, page vii).

Strategies to Move towards Compassionate Policies

What is the responsible thing to do when you sense imminent danger? Should you make other people aware of it, even if you don't know what they should do? I think so. If you see a tornado forming, you should send out the alarm, even though you can't tell each person and family exactly what they should do.

Well, I sense that a perfect storm is brewing, involving not only climate chaos but political, economic, cultural and social chaos as well. I wish it were not true. I hope that it doesn't happen. But I think that I have sighted a hurricane heading our way. Look out. Prepare. Act. Care for self and others.

Climate chaos is headed our way and is already here with mega-storms, floods, droughts and fires. The oceans are dying of rapid acidification. Ice caps and glaciers are melting and will flood coastlines and islands. Food production will be reduced. And so on. What to do? How to prepare? How to stop further environmental degradation and suffering? We know that we must stop burning fossil fuels. But will we? Just say yes.

Political chaos is headed our way with government shutdowns, unlimited campaign contributions, gerrymandering and more filibusters. And so on. What to do? How to prepare? How to stop further degeneration of democratic institutions? We know that we must have government by, for and of the people. But will we? Just say yes.

Economic chaos is headed our way with possible defaulting on the debt, possible currency devaluation, increased joblessness and more toxic investments and bubbles. And so on. What to do? How to prepare? How to stop further collapse of the economic system? We know that we must have an economy that is fair and provides a living wage for all the people. But will we? Just say yes.

Cultural chaos is headed our way with increased fear, hysteria, the belief in 'post truth', and hatred of women and people of different races, religions, or sexual orientations. And so on. What to do? How to prepare? How to stop further deterioration of the fabric of trust and respect? We know that we must have a vibrant culture of dialogue and diversity. But will we? Just say yes.

Social chaos is headed our way with attacks on health care reform and quality and affordable education for all our children and youth. And so on. What to do? How to prepare? How to stop further unravelling of our social fabric of care for all the people? We know that we must strengthen our social contract and ensure a decent and happy life for all the people. But will we? Just say yes.

What does *yes* look like? How do we speak, live and do it?

There is a big difference between this perfect storm and a hurricane. In this case, we the people can affect many of the outcomes, whether for good or ill, whether short lived or long term. Yes, let us do that.

As I write and speak about our time of whole systems transformation, it is dawning on me afresh that this entails a messy, challenging period of collapse; a time of gooeyness, redesign and struggle; and then an energetic rebuilding phase. It's sort of like becoming a butterfly after caterpillar deconstruction and interim gooeyness and reorganization. We are in the first phase of collapse but need to be working on the design of a new societal order.

Are we headed towards a degraded planet ruled by the superrich and religious fundamentalists? Or are we going to create a new civilization based on compassion, sustainability, equality, justice, participation, tolerance and peace? What strategies for compassionate policies are needed now and over the next two decades that will deal with what is blocking movement towards our noble vision? Let's brainstorm a few strategies to get started, again using Wilber's integral quadrants.

Transforming Mindsets and Values

- Universal education from preschool to university in the arts, humanities, social sciences, evolution and other physical sciences
- Training in mindfulness practices, such as meditation, yoga, journaling and community celebrations
- Training in compassion for and understanding of all people, air, water, land, animals and plants
- Training in creative thinking regarding time, space, energy, patterns, models, relationships, societal systems and Earth ecosystems

Changing Individual Behaviours

- Training and modelling of group facilitation, integral development and social artistry
- Training and modelling of team building, dialogue, collaboration and cooperation
- Training and modelling of responsible behaviour in relation to people and planet
- Training and modelling of nonviolence and peacemaking

Catalysing Cultural Evolution

- Assuming a new common sense of sexual and gender equality and human rights
- Promoting a culture of compassion, understanding, happiness and peace
- Manifesting a culture that celebrates learning and the realization of each person's full potential

- Creating science-based myths and stories of the evolution of the universe, the earth, life and consciousness

Redesigning Whole Systems and Policies

- Designing policies and institutions that ensure sustainable ecosystems that protect the atmosphere, oceans, land, animals, plants and humans
- Designing social policies and institutions of health care, education, protection and justice for all
- Designing economic and fiscal policies and institutions that ensure access to capital and necessities of life for all
- Designing participatory and accountable governance systems by, for and of the people

Will those turn us into butterflies? *How* will we execute these strategies? When? Where? And most importantly, who will execute them? Which of them are you working on, or to which do you want to dedicate your life?

Actions to Realize the Strategies Towards Compassionate Policies

What a time to be alive! This is it! Everything is up for grabs. The world is challenged by climate chaos, oppression of women, plutocratic political regimes, grossly inadequate health and educational systems, elite capture of fiscal policy, massive unemployment and tensions among religions and lifestyles.

We are in a whole systems transformation with no guaranteed outcomes. Will we be a species managed by the superrich and the ideologues or empowered through a self-governing system of learning, creativity and compassion? Will our societies be focused on surveillance, control and punishment or on the development of the full potential of every living being? Will we live on a planet of catastrophic suffering? Or will we choose to create a new possibility for life on Earth – a compassionate civilization?

These are the questions. The answers reside in what the eight billion of us decide and do in this decade and century. Where do you and I stand? What are we each going to do?

This is the time to manifest our care for life on Earth by being engaged in relieving suffering and catalysing a new civilization. For me, I am putting my energy into calling forth a future based on six principles – environmental sustainability, gender equality, participatory governance, economic and social justice, cultural tolerance, and peace and nonviolence.

After many years of community and organizational development work with the Institute of Cultural Affairs, local governance policy advice with UNDP, and teaching innovative leadership at NYU Wagner, my own efforts now include being an ecosystem/justice activist and nonfiction author. I am helping promote innovative leadership for sustainable human development locally in the Swannanoa watershed in the mountains of western North Carolina based on Kate Raworth's *Doughnut Economics* models and processes, and around the world. The Swannanoa Watershed Action Network (SWAN) is helping create a just and safe space for all the people and all of nature in the watershed. My fellow and sister volunteers are individuals and organizations of civil society, government, business and local communities committed to social justice and ecological regeneration in this local area of planet Earth. What about you? What do you want to be doing?

Work of every sort is needed in all fields and at all levels. We need effective projects, programs and policies in every sector. We need transformative work within families, communities, municipalities, states, nations and bioregions and at the planetary level.

We need a movement of movements bringing together all those of goodwill who are driven by a transformative wind. 'Not I, not I, but the wind that blows through me! A fine wind is blowing the new direction of time. If only I let it bear me, carry me, if only it carry me!' (D. H. Lawrence, 1959, p. 194).

Amid our work, we need to have compassion for those trapped in fear and anger over threats to their identity, worldview and moral sense and for those stuck in greed and pride for the increase of their wealth and power. Compassion, yes, but not capitulation. What is at stake is the very future of the human experiment – of consciousness of consciousness of consciousness.

We humans know the difference between right and wrong. It is time to stop doing what is wrong and start doing what is right. Sound simple? It is, and this is what we need to stop, now:

- Stop extracting, processing, selling and burning fossil fuels that damage our planetary ecosystem and cause harm to billions of people and other forms of life.
- Stop all activities that damage Earth's water, air, soil, plants and animals.
- Stop passing laws that take away a woman's sovereignty over her own body.
- Stop paying a woman less than a man for the same work.
- Stop paying workers a wage that they and their families cannot live on.
- Stop allowing our fellow human beings to live in poverty.
- Stop the fiscal, monetary and economic systems that allow 1% of the population to own 43% of all assets, and for the bottom 80% to own only 6%.
- Stop financial institutions from creating and marketing toxic investments.
- Stop allowing our children to grow up without an education.
- Stop denying health care to every person.
- Stop the filibuster from being used to block legislation.
- Stop gerrymandering voting districts that ensure a permanent majority for one party.
- Stop passing laws that make it difficult or impossible for women, youth, the elderly and the poor to vote.
- Stop the government and corporations from spying on citizens.
- Stop people of one religious belief system from controlling and harming people of another tradition.

- Stop people of one sexual persuasion from harming people of another orientation.
- Stop people of one race from harming someone of another race.
- Stop maintaining a prison system that must generate inmates to make a profit.
- Stop allowing the manufacturing and selling of arms.
- Stop attacking and killing people around the world with drones or other means without due process, a UN resolution, or a declaration of war. (In fact, stop harming anyone for any reason by any means.)

We can do what is right by changing our individual minds and behaviours and by transforming our collective cultures and systems. We need a moral awakening that expresses itself in new values, citizen action, policies and institutions. We can do this, now. But first, we must *STOP*.

Conclusion

Faced with interconnected, systemic suffering, concerned citizens and leaders in government, business and civil society can and must design and implement compassionate public policies of sustainable development based on a powerful vision of a possible future, identification of underlying obstacles, creation of effective strategies and carrying out transformative actions. May it be so.

> *Breathing in gratitude as this Earthling, breathing out gratitude for the Earth community.*
>
> *Breathing in commitment as this Earthling, breathing out commitment for the Earth community.*
>
> *Breathing in courage as this Earthling, breathing out courage for the Earth community.*
>
> *Breathing in acceptance as this Earthling, breathing out acceptance for the Earth community.*

References and Recommended Reading

350.org

ACLU. www.aclu.org

A Compassionate Civilization (blog). http://compassionatecivilization.blogspot.com/

Berry, T., & Brian, S. (1994). *The universe story*. Harper One.

Big History Project. www.bighistoryproject.com/home

Bregman, R. (2016). *Utopia for realists*. The Correspondent.

Charter for Compassion. www.charterforcompassion.org

Cheema, G. S. (Ed.). (2003). *Reinventing government for the twenty-first century*. Kumarian.

Cheema, G. S., & Popovski, V. (Eds.). (2010). *Engaging civil society*. UN University Press.

Democracy Now. www.democracynow.org/

Democracy Spring. www.democracyspring.org

Disruption. watchdisruption.com

Eisenstein, C. (2011). *Sacred economics*. Evolver Editions.

Emberling, Dennis. 2005. *Stages of [leadership] development*. www.developmentalconsulting.com/pdfs/Stages_of_Development_vA.pdf

Emmott, S. (2013). *Ten billion*. Vintage.

Greenpeace. www.greenpeace.org/international/en

Gross National Happiness. http://www.gnhcentrebhutan.org/what-is-gnh/

Hanh, N., & Thich (1998). *The heart of the Buddha's teachings*. Parallax.

Harman, W. (1990). *Global mind change*. Grand Central.

Hock, D. (2000). *Birth of the Chaordic Age*. Berrett-Koehler.

Houston, J. (1982). *The possible human*. J. P. Tarcher.

Human Rights Watch. www.hrw.org

IndivisibleGuide.com. www.indivisibleguide.com

Institute of Cultural Affairs (ICA) International. www.ica-international.org

Integral Institute. in.integralinstitute.org/integral.aspx

International Association of Facilitators (IAF). www.iaf-world.org/site

King, M. L., Jr. (2010). *Strength to love*. Fortress.

Klein, N. (2014). *This changes everything: Capitalism vs. the climate*. Simon & Schuster Paperbacks.

Klein, N. (2017). *No is not enough*. Haymarket Books.

Kolbert, E. (2014). *The sixth extinction: An unnatural history*. Henry Holt.

Korten, D. C. (1995). *When corporations rule the world*. Kumarian and Berrett-Koehler.

Kosmos. www.kosmosjournal.org

Lama, D. (2001, 14). *Ethics for the new millennium*. Riverhead Books.

Lawrence, D. H. (1959). *Selected poems*. Viking Compass.

McKibben, B. (2011). *Eaarth: Making a life on a tough new planet*. St. Martin's Griffin.

New York University (NYU) Wagner Graduate School of Public Service. wagner.nyu.edu

One World House. oneworldhouse.net

Our Revolution. ourrevolution.com

Pale Blue Dot. www.youtube.com/watch?v=p86BPM1GV8M

Peoples Climate. peoplesclimate.org

People's Summit. www.thepeoplessummit.org

Reich, R. B. (2016). *Saving capitalism*. Vintage.

Rifkin, J. (2009). *The empathic civilization*. J. P. Tarcher/Penguin.

Sanders, B. (2016). *Our revolution*. Thomas Dunne Books.

Social Artistry. www.jeanhouston.org/Social-Artistry/social-artistry.html

Stanfield, R. B. (2000). *The art of focused conversation*. The Canadian Institute of Cultural Affairs.

Stanfield, R. B. (2002). *The workshop book*. The Canadian Institute of Cultural Affairs.

Staples, B. (2012). *Transformational strategy*. Canadian Institute of Cultural Affairs.

Technology of Participation (ToP) Network. icausa.memberclicks.net
Teilhard de Chardin, P. (1959). *The phenomenon of man*. Harper Colophon Books.
The Story of Solutions. www.youtube.com/watch?v=cpkRvc-sOKk
Timsina, T. (2012). *Changing lives, changing societies*. ICA Nepal.
Transition Towns. www.transitionus.org/transition-towns
Trusted Sharing. www.trustedsharing.com
UN Department of Economic and Social Affairs (UNDESA). www.un.org/development/desa/en
UN-Habitat. unhabitat.org
United Nations Development Programme. (2012). *Human Development Report 2011*: Palgrave Macmillan/United Nations.
United Nations Development Programme. www.undp.org
United Nations Sustainable Development Goals. www.un.org/sustainabledevelopment/sustainable-development-goals
Universal Declaration of Human Rights. www.un.org/en/universal-declaration-human-rights/
Warren, E. (2014). *A fighting chance*. Metropolitan Books.
Wilber, K. (2007). *The integral vision*. Shambhala.
Williams, R. B. (2006). *More than 50 ways to build team consensus*. Corwin.
Work, R. (2007). *Strengthening governance and public administration capacities for development: A UN background paper*. United Nations.
Yousafzai, M. (2015). *I am Malala*. Back Bay Books.

Index

Actualization process, 46, 98–99
Agenda for action, 58, 62, 118
AI-based Community Learning, 97
AI Data-input for Ecosystemic Governance, 97
Alternative Dispute Resolution (ADR), 225–227
Ambedkar, B. R., 12, 35–36
Anava mala, 17
Ancient science of spirituality, 6
  condition for freedom, restraint as, 23
  constituent elements, 20–23
  dialogue, criticality of, 28
  divine, omnipresence of, 20–21
  existence, inter-connectedness of, 22–23
  farm policy, agro-ecological direction for, 32–34
  fundamentalism, rejection of, 28
  fusion of horizons, 29–30
  illustrations, 26–30
  implications, action and goals, 24–25
  inside-outside, 29
  nimble-footedness, valorisation of, 28
  policymaking process, 26–27
  structure of reality, 20–23
  theory of change, 16–18
  transformative politics, 34–37
  transformed state of being, 18–20
  water policy, India, 31–32
Anthropocene, 7, 12, 32–33, 43–44, 74–75, 81, 87, 119, 121, 209–210
Anthropocentrism, 7, 42, 143–144, 164
Anthropogenic challenges, 76–81
Applied spirituality, 138, 140, 225–227, 229, 232, 234
Authentic leadership, 125, 128

Baha'i Faith, 62, 151, 154
Bigotry, 244
Buddhism, 4, 22, 45, 71, 74–75, 77, 122, 151–152, 172, 245, 248
Buddhist
  approach, 71, 74–77, 79, 81, 87
  Taoist systems, 71, 75, 77, 81–82, 87

Catechism of the Catholic Church, 57–58
CBD. *See* Contextuality by Default (CBD)
Civilizational transformation, 91–92
Climate change, 91
Climate chaos, 242–243
Cognition, 82, 144–145, 158–159, 171, 176–177, 230, 233
Cognitive behavioural therapies, 138–139, 145–146
Collective cultures, 252
Collective policies, 252, 257
  systems, 257
Communitarianism, 135
Compassionate action, 245–248
Compassionate civilization, 246, 249–250, 254, 256–258
Compassionate policies
  collective cultures, 252
  collective policies, 252
  compassionate civilization, 257–258
  cultural evolution, 259–260
  cultural tolerance, 250
  environmental sustainability, 249
  gender equality, 250

harmful collective policies and systems, 257
harmful individual behaviours, 256
individual behaviours, 251–252, 259
individual mindsets, 251
Ken Wilber's four integral systems quadrants, 251
mindsets and values, transforming, 259
misguided collective cultures, 256
mistaken individual mindsets, 256
nonviolence, 250–251
participatory governance, 250
peace, 250–251
redesigning whole systems, 260
socioeconomic justice, 250
strategies, 258, 260, 262
sustainable human development, 252–254
vision of, 248–256
Compassion Cultivation Training (CCT), 56
Complementary leadership, 124–128
Complexity awareness, 75–76
Complexity theory, 3–4, 54, 119
Consciousness, 71, 76, 107, 110, 158–159, 171, 208–209
path, 75–76
Consensus-based public policy, 192–194
Constitutional
equality, 139–140
obligation, 139–140
Constitution of India, 139–140
Context, 7–8, 28, 72, 108, 122, 124, 150, 158–159, 168–169, 172–173, 190, 192, 205–206, 214, 225
Contextuality, 154, 158–159
Contextuality by Default (CBD), 177–178
Continuous warfare, 244–245
Cooperative learning, 58–59
Copenhagen School, 158–159, 161
Corporate governance, 61
Corporatocracy, 244
COVID-19 pandemic, 1–2, 42, 163, 244
Cross-cutting knowledge, 5–6
Cross-fertilization, 135–136
Cultural/collective inner transition, 44–45
Cultural evolution, 42, 46, 259–260
Cultural tolerance, 250, 260
Culture of peace, 56–57, 250
Culture of violence, 244–245, 257

Daoism, 122
Decentralization, 8–9, 183–184, 192–194
Decentralized Autonomous Organizations (DAOs), 93, 96
Degradation of ecosystems, 242–243
Democracy, 62, 90, 92, 128–129, 177, 250
Designated hierarchical positions, 123–124
Disputations, 135
Dualization of politics, 105–107

Earliest systems thinkers, 74–75
Earth Charter, 48–49, 153
EARThwise Constitution, 93–95
EARTHwise Futures DAO, 95–97
East-West Knowledge Gap, 71, 73–74, 76
Economic globalization, 61
Education policy, 194–195
Embodiment, 9, 83, 171
Emotion-based interpretation, 204–205
Empathy, 169–171
Emptiness, 78–79, 141–142
Environmental sustainability, 249
Espoused values, 169–170
Ethical purpose and virtuosity, 171
Eudemonic values, 170
Evolutionary coherence, 107–110

Finish educational systems, 58–59
Food and agriculture, 60
Foundations, spiritual values as, 54–58

Functionalism, 123–124
Future Creative, 98–99

Gandhian paradigm
  consensus-based public policy, 192–194
  decentralization, 192–194
  education policy, 194–195
  Nayi Talim, 194–195
  philosophy, 183
  public policy, 185–186
  Sarvodaya, 186–188
  Satyagraha, 195–196, 198
  spirituality, 184–186
  sustainable development, 184–185
  sustainable development goals (SDGs), 182
  sustainable public policy, economic models for, 188–192
  The trusteeship model, 183–184
Gender equality, 250
Globalism, 135
Governance, 62, 90, 99
  mechanistic growth, 102–103

Happiness, 55–56
Harmonization, 8, 143–144
Health, 1–2, 59–60, 91, 190, 243, 250
Hinduism, 3–4, 45, 122
Holism
  cognition, 158–159
  consciousness, 158–159
  frameworks, 160–162
  limitations, 164
  modern science, 156–158
  QBism, 159–162
  relational QM (RQM), 159–162
  science, 151–162
  scientific holism, 154–159
  spirituality of, 151–162
  spiritual philosophies, 156–158
  spiritual traditions, 151–154
  sustainable development, 162–164
Humanism, 1–2, 42, 135, 227, 229
Humanity's systemic suffering
  bigotry, 244
  Buddhism, 245–248
  climate chaos, 242–243
  compassionate action, 245–248
  continuous warfare, 244–245
  corporatocracy, 244
  culture of violence, 244–245
  degradation of ecosystems, 242–243
  misogyny, 243
  oligarchy, 244
  patriarchy, 243
  plutocracy, 244
  prejudice, 244
  social deprivation, 243–244
  systemic poverty, 243–244
Humankind, 45–46

Impermanence, 79–80
Indian Constitution, 138–139
  preamble of, 138–140
Indian legal system, 226
Indispensable personality dimensions, 142–144
Individual behaviours, 251–252, 259
Individualism, 42, 51
  mindsets, 251
  qualities, 204–209
Industrial Revolution, 72
Integral knowledge, 237
Integrative thinking, 212–213
Intellectual Property Rights, 61
Interactive elements, 137–138
Interconnectedness, 54–55
Inter-connectedness, 18, 22–24, 31
Interdependence, 77–78
Interdisciplinary, 135–136
Intergovernmental Panel on Climate Change (IPCC), 2, 130
Internationalism, 135
Inter-personality, 142–144
Interrelationship, 136–137
Intra-personality, 142–144
Investments, 61, 258

IPCC. *See* Intergovernmental Panel on Climate Change (IPCC)

Jainism, 18–19, 45
Justice, 36, 60–61, 184, 195, 205, 232–233, 250

Karma mala, 17
Ken Wilber's four integral systems quadrants, 251

Language, 9, 210–211, 227, 229, 256
Law and applied spirituality, 135–137
  challenges, 144–146
  Indian constitution, preamble of, 138–140
  indispensable personality dimensions, 142–144
  interactive elements, 137–138
  inter-personality, 142–144
  intra-personality, 142–144
  strategies, 144–146
  sustainability, 146–147
  United Nations, 140–144
Law, Religion, Spirituality and Justice (LRSJ), 137–138
Leadership
  anthropocene, 119–121
  authentic leadership, 125
  categories, 124–128
  contextual overview, 122–124
  ethical leadership, 126–128
  policy context, 118–119
  secular spirituality, 121–124
  servant-leadership, 125–126
  sustainable development policy, 118–121
Liberal democracy, 62
Liberated companies, 59
Life, 55
Living systems protocols, 95
Love, 56
Lucas, Chris, 4–5

Malkuta d'bwashmaya, 214
Materialism, 42, 52–53, 92, 227, 229, 257
Mayiya mala, 17
Measurement problem, 175
Mechanistic systems, 101–102
Mediation
  applied spirituality, 227, 229, 232, 234
  core skills of, 230–232
  Indian legal system, 226
  irreconcilable relationships, 224–225
  multiple legal provisional instances, 225–227
  scattered scenario of, 225–227
  spiritual skills, 235–238
  Standalone Statutory Law on, 226–227
  sustainability, 235–238
Mediation Bill, 226
Mental health, 59–60
Metaphysics, 174–175
Middle Way, 80
Mimetic dynamics, 211–212
Mindfulness, 57, 208
Mindfulness All-Party Parliamentary Group (MAPPG), 57
Mindsets and values, transforming, 259
Misguided collective cultures, 256
Misogyny, 243
Mistaken individual mindsets, 256
Modern science, 12–13, 54, 57, 156, 158
Monetary systems, 61
Mystery, 16, 57, 121
Mysticism, 122, 151, 210

NAM. *See* New Age Movement (NAM)
Nayi Talim, 194–195
Negative peace, 56
New Age Movement (NAM), 154
New Paradigm Storyteller, 99

Nonmaterial dimension
collective aspects, 209–211
consciousness, 208–209
dialogue, 213
dynamic elements of, 211–214
emotion-based interpretation, 204–205
gentle action, 213–214
implicate order, 212–213
individual qualities, 204–209
integrative thinking, 212–213
language, 210–211
malkuta d'bwashmaya, 214
memes and paradigms, 209–210
mimetic dynamics, 211–212
mindfulness, 208
orientation, 207
spirituality, 205–206
tacit knowledge, 207–208
Nonviolence, 183–186, 188, 192, 250–251

Oligarchy, 244
Omnipresent, 20–21
Organization-as-a-machine, 73

Paris Agreement on Climate Change, 2
Participatory governance, 250
Patriarchy, 243
Pattern Weaver, 99
Peace, 56–57, 250–251
Planetary civilization
acknowledging global interdependence, 110
actualization process, 99
consciousness, 107–110
dualization of politics, 105–107
EARThwise Constitution, 93–95
EARTHwise Futures DAO for, 95–97
evolutionary coherence, 107–110
governance, 90–99
living systems protocols, 95
maturation and autonomy, 108–110
mechanistic growth, governance of, 102–103
mechanistic systems, 101–102
new paradigm future archetypes, 98–99
new paradigm politics, 90–99
new paradigm tools, 92–93
political agency, new paradigm forms of, 97–98
politics, new paradigm in, 110–112
politics of dualism, 105–107
systemic boundaries, 108–110
systemic thrivability barriers, 103–105
systems and technologies, 92–93
tipping point times, politics and governance for, 99–105
universal responsibilities, 110
worldviews, 101–102
Planetary health diet, 60
Planetary stewardship, 91
Plutocracy, 244
Political agency, 97
new paradigm forms of, 97–98
Politics
agenda for action, 58–62
cultural/collective inner transition, 44–45
cultural evolution, 42–46
dualism, 105–107
early childhood and family, 58
economic development, life satisfaction by, 47
economy, 61
education, 58–59
evolutionary civilizational crisis, 42–43
food and agriculture, 60
foundations, spiritual values as, 54–58
good society, vision of, 57–58
governance, 62
happiness, 55–56
health, 59–60
institutions and individuals, 51
interconnectedness, 54–55
justice, 60–61
life, 55

love, 56
mindfulness, 57
mystery, 57
nature, 60
new development paradigm, 47–48
new paradigm in, 110–112
ongoing transformation, 45–46
peace, 56–57
theory of change, 52–54
work and organizations, 59
Positivism, 123–124
Practical responsibility, 234
Pragmatic sensibility, 234
Praxis, 171
Preamble, 138–140
Prejudice, 244
Prototype for Ecosystemic Governance, 96–97
Public policy, 185–186

QBism, 159, 162, 175–176
Qualities of mind, 171
Quantum measurement, 175
Quantum mechanics, 154–156, 159, 161, 176
Quantum theory, 168, 175, 178

Redesigning whole systems, 260
Reductionism, 42
Reductionist thinking, 72–73
Regenerative growth models, 90–91
Relational QM (RQM), 159–162

Sakina, 19
Sarvodaya, 186–188
Satyagraha, 195–196, 198
Scholarships, 135
Science, 151–162
Scientific holism, 154–159
Scientism, 42
Secular spirituality, 3–4
Self-aggrandisement, 141–142
Self-determination, 141–142
Self-transcendence, 168–169
Sensory concentration, 233
Set of simplex methods, 81–87
Social credit system, 49–50
Social deprivation, 243–244
Social Practice Wisdom (SPW) framework, 171–172
Socioeconomic justice, 250
Sowing Ecological, Equitable and Decentralising Societies (SEEDS), 97
Spiritual consciousness-awareness, 139–140
Spirituality, 174–175, 184–185
development, 4–5
philosophies, 156–158
roots, 151
traditions, 151–154
Spiritual leadership, 124–128
sustainable development policy, 128–130
Standalone Statutory Law on Mediation, 226–227
Story of separation, 42
Sustainability, 146–147, 235, 238
Sustainable development, 162, 164, 184–185
administrative blessing, 216
heart, 216
implications for, 214–218
nonmaterial dimension, 204–209
nonmaterial embodying, 214–216
nonmaterial reality, responsibility for, 217–218
on-going reconciliation, 216–217
Sustainable development goals (SDGs), 2, 121, 182
Sustainable human development, 252–254
Sustainable public policy, economic models for, 188–192
Systemic boundaries, 108–110
Systemic challenges, 81–87
Systemic poverty, 243–244
Systemic thrivability barriers, 103–105

Tacit knowledge, 204, 207–208, 215
Taoist approach, 74–79
Teal organizations, 59

Theory of change, 52–54
Thought-emotion-sensation-body complex, 138–139, 142–143
Tipping point times, politics and governance for, 99–105
T-Qualia, 82–83
Transcendence, 171–172
Transformation, 45–46
The trusteeship model, 183–184
Truth, 183, 185–186, 195–196

United Nations, 140–144
United Nations Development Program (UNDP), 43–44
United Nations Framework on Climate Change, 2
Universalism, 135, 145–146
Universal principles-based systems approach, 76–81
Universal responsibilities, 110
Upliftment, 182–186, 192–193

Values-driven organizations, 59
VAXJO, 176–177
Vedantic tradition, 151–152
Vision, 248–256
Volatile, uncertain, complex and ambiguous (VUCA), 7–8, 129

Wholeness Coder, 98
Wisdom
 context, 172–173
 Contextuality by Default (CBD), 177–178
 definition, 169
 measurement problem, 175
 metaphysics, 174–175
 QBism, 175–176
 qualities and abilities, 171–172
 quantum measurement, 175
 Social Practice Wisdom (SPW) framework, 171–172
 spirituality, 174–175
 theorizing, 169–172
 VAXJO, 176–177
Work and organizations, 59
Worldviews, 101–102
Wuwei/natural doing, 80–81

Yin-Yang Creative Tensions (YYCT), 83–84

Zen Business Model (ZBM), 84–87

Printed and bound by CPI Group (UK) Ltd, Croydon, CR0 4YY

15/09/2026

14962486-0004